RUSSIA
TRANSFORMED

RUSSIA TRANSFORMED

Dmitry Mikheyev

Hudson Institute
Indianapolis, Indiana

Hudson Institute
Indianapolis, Indiana

Printed in the United States of America

This book may be ordered from:
Hudson Institute
Herman Kahn Center
P.O. Box 26-919
Indianapolis, Indiana 46226
(317) 545-1000

CONTENTS

Chapter 3:
Yeltsin

Prologue
and
Acknowledgments

Work on this book began in the winter of '91-'92, on the heels of my previous book, *The Rise and Fall of Gorbachev*. The study originated from my fascination with the Russian Young Turks Yegor Gaidar and his team who had taken on the task of transforming Russia's economic system. Two years later, the Young Turks left the government and were replaced by experienced industrial managers. It soon became clear that reform of the economy triggered reforms in all aspects of society. What began as economic reform evolved into a revolution transforming Russia. In the fall of 1994, with the help of Neil Pickett and Pavel Waisburd, we decided to broaden the scope of the study and include the transformations occurring in Russian institutions and culture.

I am extremely grateful to many people, and foremost among them is R. Daniel McMichael, the Secretary of the Sarah Scaife Foundation and a true statesman. His lifelong interest in the security of the United States and concern for its competitiveness made all three of my books possible. He helped secure funding for the project despite the fact that it was still evolving and behind schedule. I also deeply appreciate the moral and financial support I received from Oliver Bernier, President of The Ann & Erlo Van Waveren Foundation. I also wish to thank the Woodrow Wilson Center and Blair A. Ruble for the opportunity to work in the Kennan Institute and the Library of Congress. My longtime friend and editor, Todd Leventhal, deserves special thanks. He corrected my English and endorsed my methodology.

I thank Professors Aleksandr Shtromas, Sheila Puffer, Adam Ulam, Richard Pipes, Roger Hamburg, Roger Kanet, Dick Braugart, Herbert Ellison, Paul Viliere, Mary Dakin, and Rolf Theen and fellow "think-tankers" Anders Aslund, Gary Geipel, and John Clark for reading drafts and making useful comments and suggestions. With their help, I was able to eliminate mistakes and clarify points. Although we did not always agree on assessments and interpretations of events in Russia, their input was very valuable.

I am deeply grateful to Rebecca Arrick for secretarial assistance, and to Gwen Rosen, our extremely capable librarian, who along with Linda McDonald provided inspiration and technical and moral support throughout my work on this book.

Finally, I would like to credit George Tsukanov, who took the picture of the resurrected cathedral of Christ the Savior in Moscow that graces the cover of this book. It was taken in February 1996, a year after construction began. The reconstruction of this national monument is widely regarded as symbolic of Russia's transformation, and I take no credit for originating this idea.

I dedicate this book to the young reformers of Russia.

PREFACE

Since the fall of the Soviet Union and its replacement by several successor republics, the news has been decidedly mixed. Free from communist domination, the Warsaw Pact nations have begun the long journey from totalitarian governments and planned economies to democratic institutions and the market economy. The successor republics to the Soviet Union seem so far to have been less successful in this transition. Indeed, recent news from Russia has been almost invariably worrisome. Tanks bombard the Parliament, soldiers crush Chechnya, Zhirinovsky rises to frightening prominence, and General Lebed and the communist Gennadi Zhuganov threaten to capture the parliament.

Nonetheless, Russia has made great efforts to dismantle the institutions of totalitarianism and replace them with an entirely new economy and political system. This is certainly a monumental task, and one that has never been attempted before. Since the years of *perestroika* and *glasnost,* Russia has changed radically in every respect—economically, politically, culturally, and in its international status and aspirations. The transition has been extremely arduous for the Russian people. They have suffered wrenching changes in social conditions, and vexing problems such as persistent monetary inflation, confusion regarding the nation's international posture, and social pathologies such as crime, alcoholism, political corruption, and poverty.

Despite its travails, Russia remains one of the world's most important nations, with its large land mass, economy, and population. Its future will profoundly affect the rest of the world. A new Russia stands in the place of the Soviet empire, but this Russia is somewhat inchoate and mercurial— and therefore just as much a "riddle wrapped in a mystery inside an enigma" as ever. In response, the Western attitude has careened from cold war to euphoria to a "cold peace."

It is in this context of confusion mixed with hope and a sizable helping of anxiety that Hudson Senior Fellow Dmitry Mikheyev presents *Russia Transformed*. In the best Hudson tradition, this isn't merely another look at the political and economic landscape of the "new Russia," but an interdisciplinary study, using cognitive psychology to unwrap the complex personality of Boris Yeltsin and the new Russian elite about which we read so much but understand so little. Mikheyev's examination takes us to the next step—helping us to forecast the future of this powerful and complex nation.

This book was made possible by the generous support of the Sarah Scaife Foundation. Although it bears no responsibility for the conclusions of this work, Hudson Institute gratefully acknowledges their assistance.

Leslie Lenkowsky
President
Hudson Institute

Introduction

Russia and the United States Shaped the 20th Century

A century and a half ago, Alexis de Tocqueville argued that America and Russia had such extraordinary potential for growth and expansion that they seemed "to hold in their hands the destinies of half the world."[1] This proved to be prophetic. These two nations have, indeed, been largely responsible for shaping the technological, economic, and political configuration of the twentieth century. Their contributions, however, were strikingly different, both in size and nature.

The technological contribution made by the United States is immense. It includes new means of transportation—cars and airplanes, a new form of energy, television, information-processing technology, and the exploration of space. The United States also developed the concept of mass production and contributed greatly to the defeat of several totalitarian and imperial powers, thus securing beyond any serious challenge the existence of the liberal economic and democratic system. America also has the dubious distinction of creating the culture of consumerism and popular entertainment.

Russia's cultural, scientific, and technological contributions during the twentieth century are relatively modest, although she did launch the space age and was one of the two nuclear superpowers.

However, Russia was a principal political actor during the century. She played decisive roles in both world wars and was the principal contributor to the demolition of the Nazi military machine. In 1917 Russia launched a major social experiment, imposing on its society a revolutionary social theory and attempting to construct a "civilization based on an entirely new pattern."[2] The social experiment soon assumed global dimensions and largely defined the political climate of the century. In contrast the West relegated itself to the containment of communism and self-defense. Only the inherent tendency of communism to stifle life, not any pro-active policy on the part of the West, enabled the liberal democracies eventually to triumph in the struggle of two ideologies and systems.[3] Nevertheless, the United States deserves almost the entire credit for winning the Cold War, because it took on itself both the leadership and the brunt of the effort.

Russia's Destiny for the Eurasian Continent and the World

As the century concludes, American civilization with its technocratic mentality and culture of professionalism, mass consumption, and popular entertainment increasingly defines the evolution of society.

However, Russia remains a major factor on the largest, most populous, most economically powerful, and currently most dynamic continent, Eurasia, where four major cultures—European, Muslim, Indian, and Chinese—meet, interact, and often clash. Eurasia is currently experiencing "one of the greatest dramas of modern history, the results of which will have an enduring impact not only on the peoples of Eurasia but on those of the entire world."[4]

Whether Russia explodes in a civil war of enormous scope and disintegrates, rebounds and attempts to recapture its lost territories, or evolves into a civilized member of the world community, a peacekeeper and an economic powerhouse, the fate of Russia will have profound ramifications for both Eurasia and the world at large. Some analysts even believe that Russia "will condition economic and political development, everywhere in the world."[5]

One can regard Russia as naturally positioned to act as a conduit for the spread of European culture throughout Eurasia and therefore as an entity that should be welcomed by the Western community. However, to the Western mind, Russia remains, as Winston Churchill put it, a "riddle wrapped in a mystery inside an enigma," despite the current openness of the country and all the information-processing technology available to researchers. In this century, the West has been gravely misled twice about Russia's intentions and these miscalculations have cost it dearly, once when Russia proclaimed that it was building a society of equality, brotherhood, and harmony, but instead erected the most ruthless totalitarian dictatorship in modern history; a second time, when the Soviet Union allied itself with the Western democracies and helped them defeat Nazism, fascism, and Japanese imperialism, only to then subject a number of "liberated" countries to an even more insidious dictatorship.

For years, since "the strange death of the Soviet empire"[6] the political situation in Russia has been volatile, evoking mixed feelings of apprehension, suspicion, hope, and fear. Twice tanks have rolled through the streets of Moscow and once they bombarded the Parliament. The army and air force have destroyed Grozny; Vladimir Zhyrinovski, a right-wing member of parliament, has demanded the restoration of Russia's nineteenth-century borders from Finland to Alaska. Another nationalist, General Aleksandr Lebed, and the communist Gennadi Ziuganov threaten to capture the presidency. In short, Russia remains unpredictable; one cannot blame the West for the gyrations in its moods toward Russia, from cold war, to euphoria, to "cold peace."

Russia Remains a Puzzle

The West has no option but to try to comprehend Russia, and to try to make it a faithful ally. Neither task is easy but they can be accomplished. Mistakes in these endeavors may turn out to be costly. If Russia genuinely wants to and is capable of becoming a normal, democratic country, fully integrated into the Western community, the West will acquire a powerful and faithful ally. If, on the other hand, Russia is alienated by the West's containment strategy toward her, the consequences for the West will be unfortunate.

What is it about Russia that makes her so difficult to understand? Specifically, why did Sovietology fail so miserably? Scientifically speaking, there are only two reasons for poor understanding of any given phenomenon: insufficient reliable information and inadequate processing of the information. Russia is perhaps too huge, too complex in its geographic, ethnic, religious, and cultural composition; it has also traditionally been isolated by its religion, language, lack of infrastructure, and artificially created barriers. In other words, the phenomenon of Russia may consist of too many variables to be grasped in its entirety, particularly by a compartmentalized approach. And if a large and important phenomenon is poorly understood, it may evoke strong emotional feelings that further impair scientific analysis, as Martin Malia[7] and Hedrick Smith[8] have noted.

The totalitarian system attempted to reduce the number of variables to a manageable minimum by imposing and cultivating a uniformity of production, consumption, education, and living conditions. At some point, the Sovietologists' task seemed fairly simple and their method quite obvious. That is, they had to follow several dozen key leaders in order to understand the development of the country and the entire communist bloc. Thus Sovietology degenerated into Kremlinology.[9]

The real life of the Soviet people, however, was carefully hidden by natural and artificial barriers. The Central Committee and the KGB erected a vast facade composed of false statistics, phantom plans, a smoke screen of slogans, and layers of parroted propaganda that led Westerners to erroneous conclusions.

Now these deliberate distortions have largely disappeared. At the same time, a bewildering complexity has emerged as every region and province has embarked on its own pace of development, and Russians freely criticize the government and challenge its data. To make matters worse, much of the information currently emerging from Russia is totally skewed by the suffering caused by the hardships resulting from the transition. Finally, Russia remains a highly integrated and centralized entity in which political, economic, military, social, and demographic factors are tightly intertwined and mutually dependent. Attempts to dissect this living and evolving organism can only lead to many of the same distortions and misunderstandings that plagued Sovietology.

In short, students of Russia face a phenomenon of enormous complexity and suffer from the endemic predicament of the information age: the volume of information far exceeds the capacity to process it.

The key concept of this study is "culture," and its overarching theme is cultural change. Its basic assumption is that cultures change, as do national characters (although to a lesser degree). It would be strange if cultures did not change, particularly when economic and political foundations, living and social conditions, and institutions, such as the church and the media, all rapidly change.

This study is an attempt to present the transformation of Russia in its entirety, to outline the overall picture and the cultural changes that are occurring, to grasp the major trends and understand the logic behind them. To appreciate the need for a cultural approach, one has only remind oneself that during the span of just one century Russia has lived through three totally different sociopolitical systems.

Pre-1917 Russia was a nation of peasants, ruled by a tiny class of nobles and the intelligentsia. It was a monarchy; an empire; and a society firmly based on class distinctions, Orthodox Christianity, and private ownership of property.

The Soviet Union was a nominally classless society, a dictatorship, and an empire based on an ideology transcending national boundaries and cultures. Four institutions critically important in the life of any modern society were nonexistent: private ownership of land and the means of production, independent mass media, civil society, and organized religion.

In 1996 Russia is an urbanized, industrialized, relatively homogeneous (82% of the population are ethnic Russians), secular, presidential republic, run by a technocratic elite, with private ownership and the free market, a free press and parliamentarism.

The sociopolitical, economic, and ideological differences among these three incarnations of Russia are so vast that it is difficult to recognize that beneath them there exists the same people, national character and, in fact, the same thousand-year-old culture. Any study aspiring to make reasonable forecasts of Russia's future has to explain these tectonic movements in Russia's cultural foundation.

This book begins with a theoretical framework that attempts to integrate two key ingredients of any political event: people and institutions. Two concepts—mentality and different forms of social power—are introduced.

The social composition of the Soviet Union on the brink of its break-up is then analyzed, as are the mentality and aspirations for power of the old and emerging new elites on the brink of the revolution.

Next, the book examines several personalities who can justly be called the founding fathers of the new Russia. Boris Yeltsin, of course, is a central figure of the book, which uses cognitive psychology to provide insights into his personality, mentality, operational style, political evolution, personal constancy, and place in history.

Next, we document the new Russian elite's political struggle with the entrenched communist *nomenklatura* and its attempt to reform old institutions and create new ones. This period of acute struggle came to an end in December 1993 with the adoption of a new constitution.

Following this, we examine the transformation taking place in the economy, including the processes of privatization, conversion of the defense industry to civilian production, the reform of agriculture, and the creation of the infrastructure of a market economy.

Next, we consider the changes that have occurred in social conditions: inflation, crime, corruption, unemployment, social stratification, and the question of living standards. We discuss the problem of the middle class and the culture of consumerism and consider how they are related to social peace and stability. The major social trends are examined in an attempt to estimate the acceptance of reforms by the population.

The book then outlines the new political structure as it emerged in 1994; the federalist system, the role of authoritarianism, the distribution of power between the center (Moscow) and the provinces. We assess the political system's cohesiveness and overall stability, arguing that the new system was tested during the crisis in Chechnia, which revealed a number of problems, such as an imbalance of power between different branches of government and serious structural distortions in Russia's current federalist system.

Finally, the book analyzes Russia's shifting national character and ongoing cultural change in an attempt to measure the prospects for the viability and longevity of the democratic system in Russia.

One of the major surprises of this study for many analysts may be the conclusion that Russians have turned out to be not that different from other peoples. In my opinion, Western political science greatly underestimated the impact that totalitarianism had on the behavior of Russians and, at the same time, overestimated its influence in making permanent changes in their mentality and national character. The Soviet totalitarian regime was considered by many to be a sort of overblown administrative power that, by the 1960s, had softened its grip sufficiently to allow for its "convergence" and eventual prospective merger with capitalism, which, in turn, was supposedly evolving toward socialism. In fact, totalitarian power affected each and every aspect of life and dictated its own laws of behavior for both individuals and institutions.[10] As a powerful gravitational force, it twisted and distorted not only the Russian economy but also the social and spiritual aspects of life. When it disappeared, new forces filled the vacuum of power and began to shape life. As one British journalist noted, Russians "found capitalism in their genes," and the government is now concerned "that those animal spirits may be proving uncontrollable."[11] New rules of behavior have quickly been established by newly independent forms of power: financial, industrial, media, and political.

The speed with which this transformation has occurred suggests that the twentieth century has significantly influenced Russian's mentality and prepared them for the modern age of democracy and technology.

CHAPTER 1

Historical Overview
and Theoretical Framework

Momentous political events, such as the disintegration of the communist bloc, always catch analysts by surprise. When the principal institutions of power collapse, values and ideologies are rejected, national identity and cultural norms are questioned, the moral fabric of society disintegrates, and the economic structure falls apart, yet society somehow survives and manages to rebuild itself, social scientists have a rare opportunity to rethink their approaches toward people and culture.

Following a brief historical overview of the processes that led to the creation of a new political, economic, and social system in Russia, I will outline the theoretical framework within which I will analyze them.

Historical Overview

The dismantling of the totalitarian system of power in Russia extended over three decades, although at the end it accelerated at an exponentially increasing pace. In retrospect, it is easy to discern several distinct stages of different duration and thrust.

First, there was a three-decade-long stage of *ideological* erosion. From 1956 to 1986 there was a period of gradual yet inexorable softening, erosion, and decomposition of the ideological base of totalitarian power. Alternative ideas were smuggled in via radio, television, movies, and audio tapes. They prepared the ground for the ultimate bankruptcy of the ideology of communism.

At the end of this period, after Gorbachev introduced *glasnost* in 1986, the war of ideas that had been raging in the *samizdat* (the clandestine press) emerged into the open. The battle between democratic ideals and totalitarian ideology was swift and conclusive. Within two years, communist ideology lay in ruins. The passing of the Law on the Press in July 1990 formally institutionalized the fact that the Communist Party had abdicated its

monopoly on information. This development marked the end of the ideological stage of the second Russian revolution; information had been the
first component of political power to escape totalitarian control.

In the spring of 1989, when Gorbachev permitted the first partly free
elections to the Supreme Soviet, the *political* stage of the revolution began.
Although only about one-quarter of the people's deputies of the USSR Supreme Soviet were elected on a competitive basis, this was sufficient to
create an unprecedented democratic beachhead in the existing political system of power. The Supreme Soviet became the main platform through which
the intelligentsia's demand for a share of political power was broadcast far
and wide. The confrontation between the intelligentsia and the *apparatchiks*,
which was brought into the nation's homes every day by the then largely
independent media, conclusively demonstrated the bankruptcy of communist ideology, as well as the appalling state of society, and hence the managerial ineptitude of the party *nomenklatura*.

The inescapable conclusion was that politics, industry, education, media, science, and the arts should be run by professionals, not the party's
functionaries. The legitimacy of the Communist Party suffered a mortal
blow; Article Six of the constitution, which had enshrined its rule over society, became indefensible and was quickly removed. The Soviet political
system became, de jure, a multiparty system. Formally speaking, it was at
this point that the political component of totalitarian power was vanquished.

The administrative structure of the regime split in two soon afterwards,
when the Russian Federation, under Yeltsin's leadership, declared its independence from the center.

The political stage of the revolution ended in December 1993, when a
new constitution was adopted and free elections were held for the parliament. In the new political and administrative system, power was divided
among the executive, legislative, and judicial branches. The media and the
Church became totally independent institutions.

In 1992 the *economic* stage of the revolution began. First, the state
ceded control over commodities and goods by relinquishing its monopoly
on trade and the control it had exercised over prices, currency-exchange
rates, and so on. Next, a significant portion of the means of production was
transferred from the state into private hands. Finally, the redistribution of
property and financial power began to proceed according to the laws of the
market.

We can see from this brief overview that the dismantling of totalitarian
power in Russia did not occur all at once. The party's ideological, political,

and economic monopolies on power were dismantled in stages and by different social groups.

The intelligentsia played the leading role in the ideological stage because it saw itself as the brain and soul of the nation, and because it was concerned with the informational, spiritual, and moral aspects of power. Other social groups were more interested in the political, financial, or industrial aspects of power, so they were particularly active in dismantling these components of totalitarian power. In addition, there was a lateral movement of power from the center to the provinces.

Each stage in the transformation was marked by the appearance of new independent institutions of power and corresponding power elites.[1] Although these elites have come mostly from the former *nomenklatura*, they had and have distinctly different group preferences, aspirations, and ways of exerting power. Moreover, the appearance of new independent institutions of power was accompanied by a vigorous jockeying for position among the elites, further complicating the picture. Previously nonexistent elites and social groups such as professional politicians, bankers, entrepreneurs, and entertainment and media moguls appeared and immediately entered the political process.

All social groups felt oppressed by and had reasons to unite against the totalitarian system. When they triumphed, however, they became competitors and even antagonists. New alliances and conflicts emerged, and some previously unthinkable combinations began to appear.

Questions Raised by the Revolution in Russia

Revolutions have traditionally been described as a struggle for power among classes, social groups, and elites, resulting in a radical realignment of institutions. Usually they are presented as the result of the creative efforts of elites and personalities who pursue certain social ideals, or as spontaneous uprisings of people against the status quo. Sometimes, as in the cases of Germany and Japan after World War II, revolutions have been imposed by an occupying power. In these cases, the transformations have been conducted according to blueprints provided by an outside power, based on its firmly established culture.

In the case of Russia, however, the revolution arose from within and was not the result of a military defeat or a popular uprising. Nor was the transformation imposed by an outside power. Society transformed itself. Moreover, all its entities changed more or less simultaneously, which tremendously complicates the analysis. The elites' mindsets, aspirations, and roles also changed in the process, and fairly rapidly. Plans and blueprints have been reconsidered and altered along the way; the architects of change have themselves been changed many times.

The complexity and speed of these changes and their intertwining nature raise many questions. What do people do when practically all laws, written and unwritten rules, implicit and explicit restrictions disappear or are not enforced? Does the resultant explosion of immorality, crime and hatred destroy society? Or do some higher moral dictums and restraints quickly fill the void? How do people behave when all of a sudden they lose their jobs, means of livelihood, institutional status, and national identities? How do institutions react when they are threatened or forced to change? Do they behave like living entities? Do they fight each other for scarce resources or form alliances. De they reform themselves or quietly die, deprived of resources and a power base?

The simultaneous transformation of institutions, social groups, and elites that is occurring in Russia makes it necessary to carefully examine the boundaries between these groups and the nature of the relationships among them.

Political actors have unique personalities, yet they are to some degree predictable because they represent certain social groups and institutions. Conversely, social groups tend to generate their own elites, who rely on specific institutions as tools of power. These elites and leading personalities run the institutions, sometimes rebel against and change them, create new ones, use them to advance their personal and group goals, and leave them. Institutions grow, gain power, and tend to acquire a life of their own. They can grow; merge; engulf other institutions; subjugate, mold, and create men, even reject and sometimes destroy their creators.

Institutions can vastly multiply an individual's power, or they can enslave individuals. They can dominate men or endow them with enormous power.[2] On the other hand, some individuals not only challenge institutions, they change and mold them, become institutions in their own right, and play a hand in shaping political events. Where a leader's personality ends and the institution begins, to what extent does an individual represent his or her social group, elite or institution, and at what point does the institution acquire a life of its own?

There is also the very important question of the extent to which one's political mentality can change. Political scientists usually assume that a person's political views are formed by adulthood and remain largely unchanged throughout his life. According to cognitive psychology, however the mentality of a mature person can evolve, and in a dramatically changing world it can change dramatically.[3] For post-totalitarian societies, this question of the malleability of the mentalities of individuals and social groups is very important, because it has a direct bearing on the tempo of transformation and social peace. How easily can people in Russia accept and internalize the previously taboo concepts of checks and balances in government and private property? Political science lags greatly behind cognitive psychology in exploring such phenomena.

Finally, there is the cardinal question of culture. The totalitarian system, particularly in the case of Russia, existed long enough and withstood enough severe tests to support belief in its ideological and structural cohesiveness. Did a stabilizing symbiosis exist between traditional Russian authoritarian culture and the totalitarian Soviet one? Alternatively, were contradictions between the two the main reason for the rapid and relatively unopposed collapse of Soviet communism?

As institutions change, new elites emerge, new rules are established, new values supplant the old ones and take hold, and new ethical systems emerge. What happens then to the "national character," "national mind," and the nation's self-identity? What are the constants that remain basically intact and guarantee a nation's identity? For example, the symbols, traditions, and cultural values of pre-1917 Russia are reemerging. Do they have a chance of penetrating the consciousness of people after 75 years of repression? What about the totally new demands and mores of the technological age? How, in general, can people of an established culture strive to create a new one?

A Theoretical Framework for Analyzing These Questions

I believe strongly that the above mentioned questions cannot be adequately addressed without a strong theoretical framework based on a "radically new analytical apparatus."[4] Along with some other political scientists I see the need to rethink the traditional approaches to political analysis.[5] It seems imperative to strictly differentiate decision making from the implementation of the decision. This means separating mental processes from physical action. Action occurs when power is applied, according to a preconceived plan. That is, decision making involves information processing, while action involves applying energy.

Based on this differentiation, two concepts might be suggested that could provide a theoretical framework for analyzing events in Russia: the concept of mentality and the concept of different forms of social power. Mentality relates to how one perceives reality, constructs strategies, and makes choices; social power is concerned with the tools and means by which society can be altered. The concept of mentality applies mostly to individuals the concept of different forms of social power applies mostly to institutions.

Decision making is undertaken by individuals who possess a mentality, which consists of subjective and objective components. The subjective component reflects the individual's idiosyncratic tendencies, whereas the objective component reflects the relatively predictable attributes of the social group of which the individual is a member.

Institutions can be viewed as the mechanisms of social groups and individuals. Various institutions possess great power, relative to which the personal power of most individuals is negligible; however, institutions lack a mentality per se. Instead, they are guided by the mentality of the individuals and social groups who lead them.

The merger of the two concepts of power and mentality occurs within social groups, because they possess both a group mentality and institutional power. This makes social groups the focal point of political analysis and brings us back to traditional political theories. Instead of group interests, however, we can now talk about group mentalities and aspirations, as well as the forms of power available to groups in the pursuit of their interests.

Power

The concept of power has been recognized as central to political analyses by most thinkers. Bertrand Russell argued that every ambition could be directly linked to the craving for one or another form of power.[6] Hans Morgenthau wrote that whatever man does, he tries to maximize his power— that is, his "control over the minds and actions of other men."[7] There has, however, been much misunderstanding and vulgarization of the concept of power, as epitomized by Lord Acton's maxim that "power tends to corrupt and absolute power corrupts absolutely."

In the 1960s power began to be viewed in a much more balanced and objective way. Power can either corrupt men or bring out the best in them. The absence of power was recognized to be as damaging and corrupting as an excess of power.[8] Power came to be understood as a vitally important and inalienable attribute of an individual: it can be defined as the ability to change one's environment through the delivery and application of concentrated energy so as to enhance one's safety.[9] As we now know, possession of sufficient personal power is considered to be imperative for mental and physical health.[10] In totalitarian systems, where people were deprived of most forms of personal power, this was a particularly important concern.

Social power can be defined as the ability to influence other people's behavior. There are many ways to influence people: by coercion, reward, persuasion, manipulation, and affection.[11] Similarly, one can distinguish between physical, military, technological, economic, financial, political, administrative, intellectual, and spiritual or moral forms of social power. What might be called the conducive types of power are information intensive. They require much communication and exchange of information. The coercive forms of power, on the contrary, do not.

In the same way that different forms of energy can be transformed into one another, most forms of social power are also transmutable. For example, the power of persuasion can be translated into political and financial power. Nevertheless, the different forms of power are accumulated, delivered, and exercised by different ways and means. It is important to note that some forms of power can belong only to individuals, such as the power of love or power derived from one's talent, while others can belong only to institutions, such as bureaucratic power. Different cultures and subcultures seem to foster and even cultivate particular attitudes toward power. Different social groups also perceive power differently and tend to prefer some forms to others.

Perhaps the key aspect of democracy is the fact that the different forms of power—military, financial, religious, political, moral, and intellectual—are controlled by independent elites. Although the separation of elites is never complete, in mature democracies they are fairly independent of each other and jealously guard their own turf. Thus, when someone tries to translate his political power into financial power, or vice versa, or religious power into political or financial power, or military power into political power, this violates the unwritten laws of society; other elites usually find a way to block such ambitions.

In a democracy, most social groups are interested in preventing the merger of different forms of power; because if enough of them merge in one institution, a qualitatively different form of social power—which could be called totalitarian power[12]—would appear. It is superior to the singular forms of power and gives the institution possessing it tremendous advantages.

The Soviet Union was designed and built around the concept of totalitarian power. At least in theory, it aspired to combine all forms of power in the hands of one institution. Accordingly, the Soviet Union was an extremely integrated, highly organized, and structured body with the seat of power located at its center. All institutions of power—finance, industry, property, the military and security forces, the church, education, agriculture, and the trade and distribution system—were relegated to the roles of organs in the body and were tightly controlled by the nation's "brain," the Central Committee of the Communist Party.

Mentality

Enormous strides in cognitive psychology during the last decade or so[13] have made it impossible to talk about political behavior, or more specifically, decision making, without analyzing a political actor's ways of processing information, based on his or her mentality. It is now well established that even simple decisions involve much deeper layers of mental structure than political preferences, stereotypes, prejudices, and conventional beliefs. The existence of a system of basic assumptions about the world and the tremendous role that it plays in decision making is no longer debated.[14] These assumptions are known to be subconscious, that is, they are not verbalized and are very often denied. However, they serve as both a filter for incoming signals, turning them into perceptions, and as the ultimate criteria upon which choices are made.[15] They constitute schemata, a congruent system[16] that makes our theorizing and explanation of the events possible.[17] Without understanding a person's or a group's schemata, which give their theories "cognitive consistency,"[18] no explanation of political behavior is possible. Hence I have chosen the concept of mentality as the main tool for analyzing the behavior of individuals and groups.

I distinguish between basic and sociopolitical mentalities. Basic mentality is one's most primitive mental picture of the world. Sociopolitical mentality is one's picture of the human world. Both consist of axioms. Basic mentality, of course, encompasses sociopolitical mentality.

Basic Mentality. The issue of which axioms should be included in basic mentality remains a subject of debate. Different authors suggest including assumptions about time, space, man, the physical environment, the nature of life, God, life after death, symmetry, and harmony. However, as we now know, the ultimate judgment made by humans is quite simple: Is something good for me or bad?[19] Hence the number of basic assumptions should be very small. Many authors—Ole Holsti,[20] Milton Rokeach,[21] Thomas Sowell,[22] Erich Fromm,[23] Clyde Kluckhohn,[24] James Glass,[25] Edward Hall,[26] Rollo May,[27] Abraham H. Maslow,[28] Carl R. Rogers,[29] Edward C.

Stewart,[30] and Brian Lancaster,[31]—agree on the pivotal role of three assumptions: those about the physical environment, man, and the nature of life. I am disinclined to add assumptions about God and life after death, although some authors argue for their inclusion.[32]

Because the criteria for evaluating situations are fundamentally binary (danger/safety; pain/pleasure; hostile/friendly),[33] the axioms must be binary too. Thus man can be seen as good or evil, the environment as friendly or hostile, an option as good or bad for one's survival. The basic mentality of different peoples can thus be an assortment of either positive or negative assumptions, each of which can occupy a different spot on the continuum from totally negative to totally positive. Different cultures also tend to promote certain assumptions. For example, the Japanese[34] and Indians[35] have positive assumptions about the natural environment and life after death, and their assumptions about time are totally different from those of Europeans.[36]

One extreme system of beliefs can be called Hobbesian: in this view, "the life of man [is] solitary, poor, nasty, brutish, and short."[37] In this view, life is an incessant struggle for survival with not only the evil forces of nature but also the evil of other men, since one must compete with others for power. Life does not necessarily improve; it can improve or deteriorate.

The opposite system of beliefs is based on very positive assumptions and can be called Confucian or humanitarian: humanists have been its strongest proponents.[38] For the purpose of convenience I will call it liberal. In the humanists' view, the deeper in the subconsciousness we go, the more god-like qualities we find—spirituality, compassion, imagination, creativity, conscience, altruism, feelings of harmony and love.[39] Man is seen as fundamentally good and friendly and therefore can be trusted to pursue his own interests. The physical environment is basically safe and benign; life consists of the pursuit of happiness.[40]

There are, of course, many intermediate gradations between these two extreme outlooks, but the two extremes delineate fundamentally different ways of viewing and approaching life.

Sociopolitical Mentality. A number of cognitive psychologists argue that basic assumptions about the world and oneself predispose one to certain sociopolitical views,[41] or, according to James Glass, to a certain "political philosophy."[42] Others have found a correlation between one's basic assumptions and attitudes toward justice, freedom, equality, morality, compromise, conflict, cooperation, duty, patriotism, and sacrifice.[43]

Indeed, this connectedness can be easily demonstrated. If "universal conflict is seen as the normal condition of existence,"[44] and fear dominates life, then the striving for personal survival becomes the fundamental motivation of a person's behavior. Hence power is all that really matters, and any means of obtaining and using it is good if it furthers the chances of one's survival. If life is a mortal struggle, then harmony between man and nature and among men is impossible; there can only be an enforced and inherently unfair order. To subdue the evil forces of chaos, man has to impose on them a structure of his own. He can do so through technological means or through the mobilization of others, that is, by means of political power. But evil, selfish, and unruly men can be organized only by coercive means: force, intimidation, or indoctrination.[45] Hence the Hobbesian basic mentality seems to lead to preference for coercive forms of power.

If a person sees men as selfish and greedy but not so evil, he will tend to try to purchase their cooperation or attempt to manipulate them. If he sees them as basically good and altruistic, he will think that they can be persuaded to cooperate by a calm appeal to reason. In this case, he relies more on the exchange of information than coercive power. He will also be inclined to share power with other people rather than take it from them, because information does not diminish during exchange.

Hence fundamental assumptions about the nature of man are intrinsically connected to one's preference for either conducive or coercive forms of power. Moreover, these assumptions lead to a preference for either a rigidly organized social structure supported by mostly coercive forms of power, or for a loosely structured and flexible system based on mostly conducive forms of power.

Thus assumptions about the world influence assumptions about forms of social power; these, in turn, correlate with one's vision of the correct structure of a polity. Individuals and social groups tend to have positive attitudes toward some forms of power, negative attitudes toward others, and very negative attitudes toward yet others. Bankers might criticize the military and the bureaucratic forms of power, for example, but praise the financial and industrial forms of power. Intellectuals, on the other hand, as a rule, have a negative attitude toward all forms of power except the power of ideas. The choice of means of influencing others depends on one's preferences and the perception of one's capacities vis-a-vis the world.

In sum, an individual's and a group's sociopolitical mentality consists of the fundamental attitudes toward different forms of power and their distribution in society. In other words, one's preferred form of polity correlates with one's perception of personal power potential. An individual sees himself within a social group, which occupies a certain place in the overall social structure of the nation, while the nation is seen as occupying a certain place in the world community. All of this appears within the picture of the world as a whole.

How the Theory Applies to Russia

A revolutionary environment is a natural laboratory for studying individual and group behavior in stressful and fluid circumstances in which social groups and institutions are assaulted, eliminated, and replaced.

According to our theoretical framework, the essence of the Russian revolution of the 1990s was the devolution of totalitarian power through the separation and distribution of its components: financial, political, industrial, media, scientific, and other forms of power. This was accompanied by the disintegration of the ruling Soviet *nomenklatura* and the emergence of numerous elites. The new elites have been taking over the institutions of power in Russia and becoming largely autonomous. Thus a stratification of the elites has been occurring, reminiscent of the process of the stratification of elites that occurred decades earlier in Western Europe.

I believe that the basic mentality of all social groups in Russia varied only slightly, although they visualized quite different models of the polity and saw themselves possessing different forms of power. These differences have been surfacing as changes in the power structure of society occurred; this is why different groups have played prominent roles during different stages of the revolution. Their mentalities themselves have begun to change as a result of the new distribution of power, leading to a further readjustment in the balance of power and in the mentalities of different individuals and social groups.

One must also allow for extraordinary personalities, who can rise above the limitations of institutions, social groups, and perhaps even of culture. Boris Yeltsin is such a personality. Due to his background, professional training, career, and conflict with the party, he belongs to three social groups at once: he is afflicted with the industrialists, *apparatchiks*, and democrats. He participated in all stages of the revolution except the ideological. Moreover, as every outstanding personality tends to become an institution, so has Yeltsin. He has become so powerful, in fact, that his preeminence threatens the fledgling democratic system in Russia, which is still relatively weak.

This is why an understanding of Yeltsin's personality, his vision of a proper polity for Russia, his perception of his place in it, and the actual balance of power in Russia in 1996 are necessary if we are to gain a reliable glimpse of Russia's fate in the immediate future.

Finally, there is the cardinal question of culture. The transformation of Russia can be considered a revolution because it has led to fundamental changes in the underlying culture of the country.[46] The main bearer of culture is the people, the masses or *narod*, as Russians call the ordinary people. My contention is that although the elites launched the restructuring movement that led to the revolution, shaking up existing institutions, creating new ones, and rewriting rules, the real fundamental force behind the revolution was the *narod*. It kept the transformation on track toward a maximization of individual freedom, well-being and security.

However, like all other social groups, the *narod* itself has been transformed. One might say that it has ceased to exist in its traditional sense as an entity antagonistic to both the establishment and the intelligentsia. It has turned into "the masses," and largely come to resemble people in the Western democracies. This transformation fits with the general trend of the social revolution in Russia, which can be characterized as a movement toward a culture of professionalism, and it is by no means unique. Its main features can be observed to different degrees in developing countries like India, Brazil, or China; the transformation recapitulates earlier occurrences in the United States and Western Europe.

It is within this theoretical framework that we will analyze the transformation of Russian society. We will consider the social composition of the Soviet Union at the threshold of the revolution, and the mindsets, aspirations, and roles of various elites. We will examine the dynamics of competition among the institutions of power and their realignment four years after the beginning of the revolution. We will pay special attention to Boris Yeltsin, whose personality and background enabled him to become a central focus of the main elites' interaction and competition. We will assess the economic, political and social changes that have occurred in Russia and sketch the most probable direction of changes in the future.

CHAPTER 2

SOVIET POLITICAL ELITES ON THE THRESHOLD OF THE REVOLUTION

Introduction

A widely popular view in Russia holds that the second Russian Revolution was conceived and initially led by the intelligentsia and then hijacked by the *apparatchiks*. Indeed, the intelligentsia successfully destroyed the ideology of communism, won a beachhead in the totalitarian power structure, repelled the *partocrats'* (party bureaucrats') counterattack, took over power, and launched the post-communist transformation of Russia. Four years later, however, the presidential and governmental structures are dominated by former *apparatchiks* and "red directors" with few of the original democrats remaining. So it appears as if the reforms and reformers have suffered a setback[1] and that the *apparatchiks* successfully launched a revanche and reclaimed most of their power,[2] as has happened in many other former communist countries.

In the view of some, Yeltsin has himself abandoned his initial flirtation with democracy, reverted to acting according to his party *apparatchik*'s nature and become "a highly unpopular autocrat."[3] Other analysts believe that from the beginning Yeltsin has sought to advance the interests of the *nomenklatura* and that the entire revolution was a scam designed to transfer real power from the *partocrats* to it.[4]

I believe that these theories greatly oversimplify the complex and profound interplay of social groups and elites in Russia, their expectations, and the actual roles that they played on the eve and after the collapse of communism.

To support this claim, in this chapter I will analyze the social picture of the Soviet Union at the threshold of the revolution so as to lay a firmer foundation for an analysis of developments in Russia in August 1991 and thereafter. The theoretical framework outlined in the previous chapter will be used to gain a better understanding the frustrations and aspirations of major groups of elites on the eve of the revolution, their craving for power, as well as their search for a new role, place, and sense of identity in the new sociopolitical and economic system that began to emerge.

The Social Composition of the Soviet Union in 1991

Having proclaimed the goal of building a "brand new world, without inequality and exploitation," the Bolsheviks had to eliminate the "old world's" institutions, elites, and sociopolitical structure. Taking over the power structure turned out to be relatively easy, but the creation of a new social structure took many decades. First, the "exploiting classes" were "liquidated"— killed, exiled, and deprived of all means of power. Then came the turn of the "bourgeois servants"—the "ideologues," and other *spets* (bourgeois specialists). As a Soviet textbook stated, they were mostly "reeducated by combined compulsion and painstaking educational work."[5] By the late 1930s this process culminated in the elimination of the elites of such "friendly" classes as the peasantry and workers.

Along with the elimination of traditional classes and elites, a massive drive to create a new intelligentsia "with the right class conscience" (that is, originating from the workers and peasants) was undertaken. By World War II a new social composition had emerged. In many ways it was reminiscent of the old one, consisting of the *narod*, the intelligentsia, and the ruling elite (now the party *nomenklatura*). However, in several ways it was very different.

Now all classes possessed essentially the same social background and therefore the same basic mentality. The cultural gap between them was much less dramatic than before. The massive educational drive and breakneck process of industrialization dramatically raised the educational level of the *narod*, while that of the intelligentsia was equally drastically lowered. The gap in living conditions was also narrowed by an order of magnitude, because of the party's deliberate policy of leveling off the intelligentsia's and workers' living standards. In short, under Stalin the communists managed to approximate the ideal of a classless society, to the extent that it was perhaps possible to do so.

This fairly flat and simple social structure did not last very long. First the industrialization drive, then the war, and later the nuclear arms race led to a rapid and radical structural differentiation of all social groups.[6] In the 1950s the initially uniform Stalinist *nomenklatura* began to coalesce into subgroups that later crystallized into separate, distinct elites: industrial, scientific, military, party, and cultural. They were distinguished by occupation, mentality, and the forms of power with which they were associated.

The process of stratification continued, and not only among the intelligentsia. By the 1990s, the *narod* consisted of several distinct subgroups: unskilled manual workers and peasants, "semi-skilled and skilled" workers, and highly skilled specialists. In 1985 the latter two categories constituted 51 percent of all workers.[7]

The intelligentsia also evolved into distinct subgroups such as the "creative intelligentsia," the technical intelligentsia, and the social intelligentsia. The *tvorcheskaia* (creative) intelligentsia, the literati, was composed of artists, writers, journalists, actors, filmmakers, musicians, and scholars of the humanities—about 1 million people altogether.[8] The *tekhnicheskaia* (technical) intelligentsia, also known as the technocrats,[9] consisted of hard scientists, engineers, architects, agronomists, and some of the military. The third category, the social intelligentsia, included specialists in the service sector: doctors, librarians, economists, accountants, teachers, and the like.

Finally, about three million party *apparatchiks* were also split into three groups—the top party elite, the *partocrats*; the rank and file professional party functionaries, the *apparatchiks*; and the industrial and agricultural managers—the red directors or industrialists.

This chapter will concentrate on the composition and mentality of these elites, leaving a discussion of the *narod* and related questions of culture and national character to the concluding chapters.

It is critical to remember that each elite wielded a different form of power. The *partocrats* controlled the central levers of the machinery of totalitarian power; the *apparatchiks* handled the routine work of the party apparatus; the red directors maintained and ran the agro-industrial-military complex; the literati oversaw the mass media and culture; the technocrats were responsible for scientific and technological progress; and the social intelligentsia was charged with maintaining the mental and physical health of the nation.[10]

By virtue of occupying different niches, performing different functions, and enjoying different relationships with the totalitarian machinery, the elites developed distinct perspectives on the overall architecture of the state, its endemic flaws, problems, and prospects. Accordingly, their participation in and reaction to the revolution differed widely. To understand these different reactions and roles we must briefly sketch out the social, material, and psychological conditions of the elites on the brink on the revolution.

The Psychological Travail and Despair of the Intelligentsia

By the early 1990s the Soviet intelligentsia comprised almost 30 percent of the country's 150 million-person workforce.[11] It was the second largest social group and was involved in every aspect of life. It penetrated every institution of power, including the party, the KGB, and the army.[12] In the words of Milovan Djilas, the "ground has already been prepared for the creation of a new social stratum—a special middle class . . . [of] specialists of all kinds. . . . This is the class of the future."[13] This class, however, was composed of distinct social groups with different mentalities and aspirations.

The Russian intelligentsia has been always much more than just educated people involved in mental work; it also saw itself in a missionary role. Since its inception, as a result of Peter the Great's drive to westernize Russia, the intelligentsia was perceived and has perceived itself as the only tiny beacon of light, knowledge, and progress in a sea of "poverty and gloom, savagery and oppression."[14] The intelligentsia felt that its calling was to enlighten and liberate the *narod*, and then "to realize social justice in human society, not only in Russia but in the whole world."[15]

These roles and missions were, however, usurped by the Communist Party, which claimed to be the only keeper of what it claimed was the definitive science and technology of social development. The proud and elitist intelligentsia was forced, if it wished to engage in intellectual work, to serve in the ideological department of the totalitarian machinery, under the day-to-day guidance of party functionaries. Aleksandr Fadeyev's letter written before his suicide encapsulated the situation in which the Russian intelligentsia found itself: "After the death of Lenin, we were reduced to the level of boys, we were exterminated, blackmailed, humiliated by what became known as *partiynost'*. . . Primitive, illiterate, and arrogant [*apparatchiks*] reduced us to the position of society's pariahs."[16]

The technical and social intelligentsia naturally grew and developed as technological and industrial progress proceeded. Beginning in the 1960s they began to look, talk, and think much like their fellow professionals in the industrialized nations, except for the fact that they did not enjoy the financial and political power, status, and freedom of their Western counterparts.

By Western standards, the Soviet intelligentsia's living conditions were appalling, and its members were painfully aware of this.[17] By the 1980s, with the exception of the top, thin layer of the literati, which belonged to the *nomenklatura*, the living standards of the Soviet intelligentsia were only slightly higher than those of the workers. The gap between the two was shrinking, not expanding. The salaries of teachers, 90 percent of scientists, doctors, and engineers; and thousands of artists and journalists were quite often even lower than those of many industrial workers.[18] They lived in the same communal apartments or drab apartment complexes as the *narod* that they were supposed to teach and guide. They used the same public transportation, on which they were physically abused and humiliated; they stood in the same lines for cigarettes and sausages; and they suffered heavily from the humiliation of being part of the faceless masses.

Yet as Yeltsin's future press secretary Viacheslav Kostikov wrote, "the tragedy of the Russian intelligentsia was not so much that it was deprived of both bread and paints, but that the very essence of its existence was taken away from it; that is, freedom of thought, independence from the ruling power, participation in world culture, spiritual internationalism, and freedom from dogmatic mentalities."[19]

In our terms, the real tragedy of the intelligentsia was rooted in its split conscience, its powerlessness, and the systematic lying in which it was forced to engage.

The Pain of the Tvorcheskaia Intelligentsia

It has always been difficult for Western students of the Soviet Union to fully understand the devastating effects upon the intelligentsia of this forced lying. This is perhaps because in Western sociology, a certain level of "white lying" is considered instrumental for the functioning of society, since it smooths out the minor frictions of life.[20] The Soviet intelligentsia was coerced to undertake a much more blatant and systematic form of lying, which, as political psychologists know, tends to turn into "constant and deliberate mental torture."[21]

According to many astute students of the Soviet Union, the duality of life and consciousness was the most characteristic feature of Soviet culture, perhaps its essence.[22] Robert Tucker wrote about "the suppressed and little-known unofficial life of the artist, thinker, and writer. . . ,the underground creative life over which the state had no control."[23] But complete escape was not possible for the creative intelligentsia as long as its livelihood depended on the party. Hence, a member of the Soviet literati had to "pretend to believe in mythological values and images, and, at the same time, to keep his mind sane and able to direct his behavior in the 'real material world.'"[24]

There are good reasons to think that the literati suffered from the forced duality of life and consciousness more than any other social group.[25]

Indeed, while others were forced only to say one thing and do another, the intelligentsia had to think, talk, and act contrary to their beliefs and desires.[26] A member of the literati was forced to renounce his convictions and principles, to sell out to his oppressor, to betray the finest representatives of his own group and to praise his oppressor. Moreover, he was even forced to participate in creating the ideology which then was used to oppress him and insult his intelligence.

In extreme cases, such an acute sense of guilt and powerlessness has been known to lead to a split personality, as James Glass has shown.[27] Indeed, as one member of the literati admitted, "the corrupting and debasing spiritual disease of a split personality accounts for the predicament of the intelligentsia both in Tsarist and Soviet times."[28]

By the 1990s, however, a special subgroup of the young intelligentsia had appeared that was free of many of these predicaments and pains. By social background, they were the children of the intelligentsia and the *nomenklatura*, the "golden youth." By training and occupation, they belonged both to the technocrats and the social intelligentsia.

They were different from their fathers, in terms of both their basic and sociopolitical mentalities.[29] Born mostly in the mid-1950s that is, after the death of Stalin—a decade after World War II, they escaped the most horrific psychological, mental and material hardships endured by the previous generation of both *apparatchiks* and intelligentsia. They were nurtured in the greenhouse of relative freedom and prosperity of the 1960s.[30] They did not live through the agony of first adoring Stalin and then experiencing the bitter disillusionment of de-Stalinization. They were teenagers when anti communist philosophy began to spread around the country after the invasion of Czechoslovakia in 1968. Thus they were much better prepared to accept the free market revolution that swept the world in the 1980s.

I will call them liberal democrats, hoping that Vladimir Zhyrinovsky's appropriation of this name for his ultra nationalist party will not confuse the issue. This group was so mentally and emotionally divorced from the communist regime, so completely liberated from the illusions and trappings of communist ideology including the ideologies of communism "with a human face" that it felt nothing but contempt and disgust toward the communist regime. Its adherents did not suffer from a split personality syndrome, inferiority complex, acute sense of insecurity, or the pangs of conscience so characteristic of the old intelligentsia.

The liberal democrats deserve particular attention not because of their numerical strength but because of their special role in the second Russian revolution. They seemed to represent and speak for the fledgling class of professionals to whom this revolution and the future of the country belongs.

The Privileges and Despair of the *Apparatchiks*

A very popular view among political writers holds that the *nomenklatura* was the real master of the Soviet Union. It was the actual owner of natural resources and the means of production, and it was in charge of the machinery that oppressed every other social group. The *nomenklatura* was deemed to be the only social group that was content with communism and therefore its staunchest protector. According to this view, which is strongly imprinted in the intelligentsia's psyche, the class of *apparatchiks* was nothing but an enemy of progress, democracy, and freedom. It sabotaged *perestroika*, fought for a restoration of the totalitarian system in August 1991, and staged a creeping counter-revolution two years later. It was an "enemy exceptionally skilled, experienced, inspired by its deep personal interest, merciless in the defense of its right to exist."[31]

But this simplistic theory is unfair toward a complex and important social group, and it distorts and trivializes the dynamics of the processes that occurred in the Soviet Union from the late 1980s through 1991. First, it is necessary to distinguish between the older *partocrats* of Brezhnev's generation and the younger, more professional party *apparatchiks* of Gorbachev's generation. The twenty-year age gap between the two groups accounts for important differences in their views and aspirations. Unlike the older *partocrats*, who mostly came from a poor peasant background and did not attend university, the younger generation of *apparatchiks* consisted of well-educated urbanites.[32] They had the good fortune to miss the most bloody and violent period of Soviet history and they had to deal with a totalitarian apparatus that had been significantly softened by Stalin's successors.

The *Apparatchiks*: Happy Mediocrities?

The intelligentsia referred to the communist regime as the "dictatorship of mediocrity."[33] It ridiculed and demonized the *apparatchiks* as talentless clerks without a soul. According to Yuri Afanasiev, they are "twenty million almost totally corrupt clerks who seek additional opportunities for bribes and form the black market."[34]

Although the *apparatchiks* certainly had their share of craven human beings, this unidimensional caricature says more about the intelligentsia's own state of mind than it does about this important social group in the late 1980s. In fact, the Soviet bureaucrats and *apparatchiks* were hardly different in their outlook from other educated social groups in the USSR.

It is important to remember that bureaucracy is an essential attribute of any modern society;[35] careful observers would admit that bureaucrats are "neither more or less efficient, honest, hard-working, thorough, public-spirited, and generally worthy of admiration than non bureaucrats."[36] Under democratic conditions, bureaucratic institutions tend to attract an "adaptive personality type who is inclined to play by 'tough-minded' organizational rules" and who easily accepts the "good of the organization as his highest value."[37] In a democracy, these are the people who, in Erich Fromm's words, willingly "escape from freedom" into the security of an institution. In contrast, the nonconformist personality types have other choices: to join private institutes, to avoid any institutional affiliations, or even to form their own institutions—companies, political parties, or movements. Because those who choose to join a democratic bureaucracy do so as part of a process of natural selection, they may be called "natural *apparatchiks.*"

The totalitarian system was not a normal bureaucracy. It maintained the most pervasive system of control over all human activities known to mankind. If Karl Marx characterized the second French Empire as "an appalling parasitic body, which enmeshes the body of French society like a net and chokes all its pores,"[38] one wonders what he would have said about the Soviet bureaucratic machine, which contained double, triple, and even quadruple mechanisms of control with a maddening maze of rules, regulations, restrictions, and laws.

The majority of the *apparatchiks* were not notably mediocre, as the intelligentsia claimed. The conventional wisdom was that those who failed in their profession chose a party career as the last refuge of the talentless.[39] Indeed, many future *apparatchiks* were mediocre students, but they were actively involved in Komsomol and party activities (like Gorbachev), as opposed to the intelligentsia, which spent more time in libraries and laboratories. But there were also many *apparatchiks* who excelled at university studies and in professional careers and only later joined the party bureaucracy: Yeltsin is the most prominent example of such a type.

Thus even many inherently non-conformist personality types were forced to join the system. For this reason, many Soviet bureaucrats were actually "unnatural bureaucrats." Indeed, the choices for an ambitious person were to belong, dissent, or pretend to play along. Those who chose not to rebel, and who could not genuinely belong due to the absurdity of the system, had to pretend to believe like everyone else and suffer inwardly (not unlike the intelligentsia). Even the most bureaucratic of all known regimes, the totalitarian system, was not capable of completely eliminating the human side of its clerks.[40]

The *apparatchiks* were the operators of the party-state machinery but they were its first victims as well. They were often torn between two sets of contradictory rules and regulations—those of the party and the state. In addition, the standards of their professions, and the requirements of dignity, common sense, and humanity were often quite different from the requirements of the party.

Thus, the apparatchiks suffered not only from the normal dichotomy between an individual's humanity and his role as a cog in an impersonal machine, but also from the inherent duality between the dictates of their conscience and those of the party.

They were chained to the system no matter how far they were allowed to go, no matter how invisible the chains were to outsiders.[41] Anatoly Fedoseyev, a rebel who defected to the West and can hardly be suspected of being an apologist for the top *nomenklatura*, wrote: the *apparatchiks* "also lived under very heavy and extensive constraints which are contrary to their human common sense and insulting to them as creative and active human beings."[42]

Moreover (and this is a critical point, which distinguishes this analysis from a conventional view)[43] the *apparatchiks* did not actually possess power, because totalitarian power cannot belong to any person in particular. Instead, the *apparatchiks* were merely able to use the system's power illegally for their personal advantage. This point merits further discussion.

The Material Conditions and Insecurity of the *Apparatchiks*

In addition to the mental and psychological discomfort that they experienced, the *apparatchiks* of the later days of the communist regime were not properly compensated financially and did not enjoy a particularly high social status.

Again, it is important to distinguish between the several hundred *partocrats* at the pinnacle of power and the mass of *apparatchiks*. While the former did enjoy tremendous privileges (such as access to special stores, hospitals, and resorts; travel to the West; and so on),[44] for the two million or so rank-and-file Soviet *apparatchiks*, material conditions were less luxurious than was usually assumed. Their official salaries were ridiculously small.[45] Even with added bonuses (60 to 70 percent of their salary) the official income of a party *apparatchik* at the regional level was not much higher than that of a blue-collar worker.[46] Thus *apparatchiks* were placed in a position in which they had to fend for themselves; that is, to use the power of their offices, particularly their power over the system of distribution, to extort money or goods from others. Thus *kolkhozes* were obliged to feed *apparatchiks*, factories to build their *dachas* and provide other tribute.[47] Not all *apparatchiks*, though, received such treatment.[48]

Moreover, such practices were illegal and were occasionally punished.[49] So keeping the *nomenklatura* on a meager diet but tacitly allowing it to supplement its living by using the power of the party-state machine for its personal gain caused it to feel both privileged and wary at the same time: the *nomanklatura* lived better than others but was always conscious the law and party rules could turn career and life into a shambles at any moment.

It was the deliberate policy of the party leadership to keep the mass of *apparatchiks* in a state of fear. According to historian Roy Medvedev, "Lenin was often heard to say, 'Bureaucracy is our chief enemy.'"[50] Indeed, in the words of Gavriil Popov, all of Soviet history consisted of the continuous build-up of the greatest bureaucratic machine of all time, on the one hand, and a ceaseless "struggle against bureaucracy" on the other.[51]

Gorbachev only continued this time-honored tradition. Under his policy of *glasnost,* the press was given the green light to expose corruption among the *apparatchiks*. In 1986 alone, this led to indictment proceedings against 200,000 officials.[52] Only a few hundred top *partocrats* could be assured of immunity from prosecution, as long as they played by the party rules. But when Gorbachev needed to weed out the Brezhnevites, he tacitly encouraged the so called "Churbanov affair." In 1988 Brezhnev's son-in-law Yuri Churbanov was arrested and tried for corruption.[53] The trials of Churbanov and other *partocrats* demonstrated that even they were losing immunity from prosecution.

Even top Soviet officials did not possess the same means of personal power as their Western counterparts; thus they could not translate their immense power within the apparatus into a secure form of personal power. They were painfully aware of this vulnerability. Despite their pomposity and authoritarian image, *partocrats* suffered from a profound sense of insecurity and an inferiority complex, particularly toward Western officials with whom they had to deal: Yeltsin himself has said as much.

In summary, the *apparatchiks* suffered from the inherent duality of their positions, from guilt and inferiority complexes, and from fear of expulsion from the party and prosecution. They were also acutely aware of the widespread popular resentment of their illegitimate privileges. Although they ran the machinery of totalitarian power, they were more its clerks than its masters. They were as stifled by it, albeit in a different way, as other social groups. For these reasons, they were complacent or at least ambivalent about the dismemberment of the communist regime.

The Life and Despair of the *Technocrats*

The third major elite of the Soviet Union was the industrial and agricultural managers, the red directors or industrialists. They deserve the utmost attention because of their role in shaping the economic structure and policy of the new Russia after the initial strides of the revolution.

In the early 1930s an English writer of Russian origin described a first generation Soviet technocrat this way: "He comes from the earth itself, from the masses. He has no soulfulness, no delicacy, no artistry. He is unkempt, uncouth, unshaven . . . talks endlessly and with passion of smokestacks, tractor engines, dynamos, cities, machines . . ."[54] Two generations later, this unsophisticated but socially loyal technical intelligentsia had become a highly educated "second dynamic force in the USSR" that was hostile toward the "totalitarian political bureaucrats."[55]   In many ways, the technocrats are a hybrid between the intelligentsia and the *apparatchiks*.

There are reasons to agree with one of their prominent representatives, Federal Council Chairman Vladimir Shumeiko, who claimed that the technocrats were "an entirely particular stratum, a particular social group."[56] Indeed, their specific characteristics place the technocrats apart from both the *apparatchiks* and the intelligentsia. They were highly educated[57] and generally very intelligent and capable, part of the technical intelligentsia. They enjoyed much higher living standards than those of the literati and the social intelligentsia, and even many rank and file *apparatchiks*. They were managers of research, development, and production, not party functionaries concerned with party affairs.

The directors of large enterprises, the red directors, were responsible for practically all aspects of the lives of tens of thousands of people. The scope of their duties and responsibilities would sound incredible to the president of a Western corporation. This is how Vladimir Shumeiko, himself a former "red director" described them: "The general director had his normal professional concerns with production, productivity, costs, raw materials and parts supplies"; at the same time he was forced by the system to "designate people to gather the harvest, to construct houses and to clean city streets . . ., to assign transportation to perform municipal services, to take care of the enterprise's preschools, apartment houses, children's establishments, auxiliary farms, recreation centers . . ."[58]

The red directors and industrialists also had to cope with the gap between real life and often absurd party instructions. The director of an enterprise was responsible to the state apparatus—the relevant ministry and the State Supply Agency (Gossnab)—as well as the party.[59] While carrying an enormous burden of responsibilities, as Shumeiko has noted, the directors were always "second-class" executives. "Party leaders" were supposed to teach and direct the "business executives."[60] As a professional, the red director had certain ethics, values, and standards that often contradicted those of the party, with which he nevertheless had to comply. This situation caused him considerable psychological and mental tension, as some political scientists realized.[61]

Still, on balance, the technocrats, industrial managers, and red directors were the least psychologically tormented group among the Soviet elites. Their lives were dominated by the real problems of production, construction, finance, and social and human conditions; on a day-to-day basis they could completely ignore ideology and propaganda. Accordingly, the industrialists did not suffer greatly from doubts, guilt, or other psychological complexes so characteristic of the inner life of the literati.

Another important aspect of the technocrats' condition under the communist regime explains their belated arrival on the political scene of the revolution. They led a rather politically isolated life, because many of them were sequestered by the party (they lived in "closed cities") and banned from having any contacts with foreigners or even the creative intelligentsia. Most of them were never allowed to travel to capitalist countries and had no opportunity to read the underground press. So they lagged behind the other groups of the intelligentsia in their knowledge of social and political trends. When their world was finally opened up, they had a lot of catching up to do. As a rule, however, the technocrats were intelligent and open-minded; thus it was easier for them to accept the free market and political pluralism than the creative intelligentsia assumed.

For these reasons, in words of Shumeiko, "the vast majority of [the technocrats] did, indeed, feel that they were 'released from their shackles' when communism collapsed."[62] Later, when Westerners came to know the red directors closely, they found them to be "competent, intelligent, and flexible."[63]

Summary

By the mid-1980s, the social structure of the Soviet Union had evolved into a complex composition of various social groups and subgroups. All of them suffered from being forced to various degrees to live a double life—which was psychologically, mentally, and morally debilitating—and from a sense of powerlessness vis-a-vis totalitarian power. Moreover, when the productive potential of the system had been exhausted, the regime lost its ability to sustain the decent living standards let alone the privileges of the elites. The regime was simply not working. Yuri Skokov, who was widely regarded a spokesman for the *apparatchiks*, later said: "Everybody was against the life we had, and that is why everyone wanted change and why Yeltsin was a hero."[64]

Observers of the second Russian revolution do not dispute that all social groups and elites wanted to redistribute power. Only the intelligentsia are exempted from this generalization; according to a widespread view, the intelligentsia did not care about power.[65] Igor Yefimov, for example, wrote that the struggle between the *apparatchiks* and the intelligentsia was not for power, but "a fight for the control of information and information exchange."[66] But if this were so, why was there such bitterness on the part of those "who bore the brunt of the struggle against the regime," but then were "jettisoned from power"?[67] Significantly, other members of the intelligentsia argued that it did "cherish dreams of seizing power and using it as a lever to transform society,"[68] that it had become a revolutionary class whose destiny was to rule society.[69]

Whether the intelligentsia really wanted power and struggled for it with the *apparatchiks* and red directors thus becomes an intriguing and pivotal question. It can be answered by examining events in light of the different forms of social power and the different mentalities of various strata of the elite. Doing so will help us understand the aspirations, expectations, and striving for power of the social groups of the Soviet Union on the advent of the revolution.

The Mentality of the Main Soviet Elites

An analysis must begin by examining the basic mentality of the Soviet elites, their *miro-oshchushchenie* or how they sensed the world (their affective orientation), because it is connected to their *miro-vozzrenie*, or conceptualization of the world (cognitive orientation), and thus, in the final analysis, their style of decision making.[70]

The mentalities of Soviet social groups fit into a continuum between two extremes: the Hobbesian and humanist mentalities. No social group truly possessed either extreme mentality, although the *partocrats* and democrats came closest to the respective extremes. All other Russian social groups fell in between these two extremes.

The Totalitarian Basic Mentality

The *partocrats* of Brezhnev's generation came mostly from a poor peasant background, which seemed to foster what is, essentially, a Hobbesian world view incorporating the following beliefs:

- the physical environment is hostile and dangerous;
- man is basically evil;
- life is an incessant struggle for survival;
- God and life after death do not exist.[71]

The negative assumptions about God and life after death may have been introduced into the *partocrats'* world view by the aggressively anti religious ideology of communism. Furthermore, one has to remember that all prominent Russian politicians born around the turn of the century lived through the horrors of civil war, famine, collectivization, another famine, and purges during their formative years. It would be hard to see how they could have anything but a Hobbesian mentality reinforced by their negative assumptions about God and life after death.

Many Soviet scientists and writers noted that the communist utopia was based on a profound mistrust of man. "The whole atmosphere" of life under communism, wrote Boris Vasiliev, "was saturated with malice and cruelty,"[72] stemming from "malicious hatred toward fellow human beings"[73] and the assumption that "the struggle of all against all forms the basis of human life."[74] Some Western analysts have argued that this mindset was particularly typical among the Soviet *partocrats*. Thus Nathan Leites wrote that they "seem to prefer the following construction: I am human, consequently I am hated. I am hated, so no confidence is felt in me. . . "[75]

The Liberal Basic Mentality

The opposite mentality, composed of exclusively positive assumptions, is a rare phenomenon in any society, especially in Russia. The closest approximation to it, however, can be found among the liberal democrats of the Gaidar generation and those who are younger. The core assumptions of this liberal mentality are the following:

- the physical environment is not so threatening;
- the social environment is basically safe;
- life consists of the pursuit of happiness through self-fulfillment;
- God and life after death do not exist.

Instead of fear of nature, there is a tremendous pride in man's power and his mastery of nature. Man is seen as capable of changing the geography of land and the very chemistry of the ocean and atmosphere.

The liberal democrat's view of man's nature is close to that of Confucius, who said: "I believe that people are born good, and that learning and knowledge will keep them good." This is also the view of Locke and Rousseau. By nature, all men are free and have equal rights to life, liberty, and the pursuit of happiness.

Many quotations from the democrats reflect this perception of human nature—especially their discussions of the *narod*.[76] The best proof of their trust in the innate goodness of man can be found in their passionate desire to restore "natural human values such as the motivation to work, the concept of honor, dignity, morality; respect for knowledge and professional skills," which, in the words of Gennadi Burbulis, "were turned upside down by the totalitarian regime."[77] The liberal democrats' faith in the *narod* is such that they have even been reproached by older members of the intelligentsia for having too much trust in the people.[78]

The humanist philosophy of Soviet philosopher Merab Mamardashvili seemed to have left a deep imprint on some leading liberal democrats.[79] Mamardashvili maintained that the ultimate goal of life is to free oneself from inner slavery and acquire "inner freedom." He spoke about self-realization and creating one's own spiritual world, thereby escaping the grip of totalitarian culture. He spoke about the stifling psychological effects caused by viewing life as a struggle.[80]

Finally, like the *partocrats*, the overwhelming majority of liberal democrats do not believe in God or life after death.[81]

The Totalitarian Sociopolitical Mentality

A Hobbesian basic mentality naturally leads to a totalitarian sociopolitical mentality, based on the following beliefs:

- personal power is evil, institutional power is good;
- the essence of relationships between people is a struggle for power;
- totalitarian power is supreme;
- social structures should be pyramidal and hierarchical;

- society's needs are superior to those of the individual;
- morality is dual, i.e., different for friends and enemies.

A Hobbesian basic mentality predisposes a person toward coercive forms of power and a higher need for order, structure, and hierarchy.[82] Hobbes himself asserted that "Covenants without the sword are but words, and no strength to secure a man at all." Indeed, if man is evil, then personal power serves evil, and harmony is not possible. Only superior organized force can restrain evil forces and prevent chaos.[83] Hence there is a preference for coercive and institutional forms of power, and an acceptance of society's supremacy over individual needs, desires, and goals.

The totalitarian basic mentality leads to a need for a rigid societal structure that keeps individual evil under control and directs human activities toward the goals of the group or society as a whole. Otherwise, chaos can engulf the nation.

However, as Edmund Burke argued, coercive power is weak, because its effects are temporary. To make it lasting, one has to supplement the threat of violence with ideological persuasion. This, in turn, requires control over the educational system and the mass media. Continuing this logic, one arrives at the need "to overcome the division between all formal and informal devices of power, formal and informal methods of social control," thus creating a universal form of power.[84] Hence totalitarian power is the most pervasive form of power because, by necessity, it must include and incorporate all other forms of power—political, military, social, spiritual, economic, and so on.

When power is mostly coercive, it is also scarce, which means that competition for it is not only inevitable but natural. If several individuals wish to act together as a group, they have to establish a strict hierarchy. It follows, then, not only that the existence of a singular leader is imperative, but that the relationships within a group must be those of subordination and competition at the same time. Partnership is impossible. Friendship is another matter, yet even in friendship there is hierarchy.

Fear of freedom. The totalitarian mentality fears any uncontrolled, individual forms of power, particularly the financial power of property. This is manifested in a fear of freedom, which, as was perceptively noted by Hedrick Smith, amounts to the fear that "others will use their freedom against me."[85] Accordingly, democracy is perceived as a license for evil.

Dual Morality. In a world of perpetual struggle of all against all, morality is intrinsically dual—there is one morality for one's friends, and another for enemies. Lenin, Stalin, and all official communist sources have never been shy about admitting this.[86] The *partocrats'* morality was codified in the Moral Code of the Builder of Communism, which emphasized the ability to distinguish friends and comrades from enemies, an ability derived from class consciousness.[87]

Striving for Dominance in the Group. Because personal safety is deemed possible only within a group, the struggle for attaining the dominant position within a group is the essence of human relationships. In order to achieve the desired dominance, one must constantly project one's superior power through the aggressive demonstration of physical prowess, psychological astuteness, strength of convictions, and a monopolization of the truth. Because there can be only one leader in a group, there can be no sharing of power. Compromise is accordingly a manifestation of weakness, indicative of an inability to attain dominance.

A Hobbesian mentality, when coupled with a low opinion of oneself, results in a "low threshold of insecurity" and is known to lead to conspiratorial thinking—the presumption of plots and conspiracies.[88] The *partocrats* were not a particularly happy social group, contrary to popular belief.

The Totalitarian Model of the Polity

A totalitarian sociopolitical mentality naturally leads to a preference for a totalitarian polity. In this view, because there are many irreconcilable differences among competing social groups, justice can be achieved only by the leadership control over the highly elaborate and rigid sociopolitical structure.

Indeed, the *partocrats* of Stalin's generation saw the polity as a kind of machine, an assembly of highly specialized parts that are interconnected and activated and coordinated by a single "brain" and energy source. If one part of the machine breaks down, the entire apparatus comes to a halt.

As Jeffry Klugman correctly observed, the *apparatchik*'s, and particularly the *partocrat*'s, style of thinking is deductive; that is, it proceeds from the general to the specific.[89] It starts with an overall picture of the world polity and proceeds top-down to deal with individuals.

For the previous generation of *partocrats,* the international environment was an arena of mortal struggle between two blocs representing two irreconcilable ideologies: "Every right-minded person can see clearly that the basic question of ideology can be resolved only by struggle and only by the victory of one doctrine over the other," Nikita Khrushchev wrote.[90] The struggle for domination defines international relations: "As a nation, we cannot deal with others equally. Either we are more powerful or they are."[91] Eventually, the world will be shaped in a similar strictly hierarchical way, with one nation dominating it. This will bring an end to infighting and will achieve stability and prosperity for all.

However, this type of totalitarian thinking became outdated; and in the 1980s it was supplanted by the *apparatchik*'s variation of the model of polity, which we will discuss below. This mental shift was partially responsible for the fact that in March 1985 the CPSU Politburo voted for the archetypal *apparatchik* Gorbachev, and not for a *partocrat* such as Grishin or Romanov.

The Liberal Sociopolitical Mentality

The liberal, or optimistic, basic mentality predisposes a person to a democratic sociopolitical philosophy based on the following beliefs:

- cooperation is more beneficial than confrontation;
- personal power is good;
- institutional power can be either good or bad;
- conducive forms of power are preferable;
- organizations are based on a contract between the individual and society;
- morality is absolute and universal.

The liberal democrats' sociopolitical mentality was formed during the most liberal period of Soviet history, which happened to coincide with the counterculture revolution in the West. The flood of alternative social and political ideas from Berkeley, Paris, and Prague penetrated homes in Moscow and Leningrad and was routinely discussed in the families of the *nomenklatura* and the intelligentsia.

Cooperation vs. Confrontation

Men are assumed to be basically good, it follows that they should be able to negotiate reasonably about their differences and conflicting interests and eventually arrive at a mutually satisfying compromise. The most effective means of conflict resolution, therefore, is reasoning and discussion leading to a mutual compromise.

In the information age, many forms of power, most importantly financial power, can be accumulated through knowledge. Because cooperation is seen as the best way to gain reliable information, bitter competition, so central to totalitarian thinking, is not considered to be the most advantageous way to gain power.

Personal Power is Good; Institutional Power is Suspect

The uniqueness of human individuality is a cornerstone of liberal thinking. A human being is accorded an absolute value superior to anything else.[92] Forms of power originating from the individual are assessed positively; institutional forms of power are suspect. Not only is the private possession of power deemed to be acceptable, but so is a considerable concentration of power in private hands. The individual is considered to be entitled to use power to influence and even change the sociopolitical environment.

The other side of this coin is the liberal's active dislike for coercive forms of power, especially power wielded by the military and the police.[93] Liberals also share a deep distaste for the highly structured and formalized administrative power incarnated in bureaucracies,[94] because such power eliminates or overshadows the power of individuals. We will see how this inherently suspicious attitude toward both administrative and coercive forms of power caused panic among liberal democrats on October 3, 1993.

Their distrustful attitude toward institutional power leads liberal democrats to embrace mechanisms that prevent the merger or amalgamation of the different forms of power. For example, the principle of the separation of church and state is self-evident to the liberal mind, because power over the mind or spiritual life should reside with the individual and not with an administrative entity.

The Role of Government

Understandably, a person with a liberal mentality "does not believe in the organizing role of the state and a strict social hierarchy."[95] Government is seen as an inevitable evil, which unfortunately formalizes human relationships. Hence the relationship between the government and the people should be based on a social contract, in which the government is cast in the modest role of the protector of individual rights.[96] "Only private interest can be the real motivating force of progress. We have one strategic goal: freeing enterprising people from the state's fetters."[97] "Everybody must acquire the sense of economic freedom, freedom to shape his own life."[98] Hence "Russia has to be the most liberal country in the world."[99]

The Liberal Model of the Polity

The liberal democrat's model of the polity stems from the theory of homeostasis, which was taught in Soviet universities as part of cybernetics; it was one of the most popular disciplines of the 1960s. If the theory of homeostasis is applied to society, the nation is viewed as a complex, self-contained system that has the ability to regulate itself and maintain its inner balance. It is seen as a highly organized and integrated whole, whose parts live primarily for themselves, pursuing their safety and growth. In order to do that successfully, however, they have to cooperate with other parts, which benefits society as a whole. Although social groups and institutions compete for power, this only enhances society's capacity to adapt and remain viable. Significant change in one area disturbs the existing balance, leading to readjustments in many other functions of the corporate body.[100] Such a structure is stable, because damage to one part can be compensated for by growth in other areas.

The liberal style of thinking is inductive. It starts with the individual's needs and aspirations and works upward to designs for the institutions of power, the government, and the world. As Kozyrev stated: "Our main goal is to help our people achieve the life a person is worthy of, to help the Russian people regain pride in their country and the ability to fully use the tremendous potential wealth of the Russian lands..., to give more happiness to the well-fed Russian people."[101] This sounds similar to Jeremy Bentham's formulation of the ultimate purpose of the state: to achieve "the greatest happiness of the greatest number."[102]

The Mentalities of Other Elites

A full analysis of the variations in the mentalities of all the social groups and elites in the Soviet Union in 1991 would be an extremely interesting and important undertaking. However, we must limit ourselves to only a few key aspects of the sociopolitical mentality that distinguished various elites at the threshold of the revolution. We will see the *miro-vozzrenie* and aspirations that the Russian elites brought to the revolution.

The basic mentality of all social groups, with the exception of the *partocrats* and the liberal democrats, did not differ much. Their mentality was significantly more benign than the totalitarian one but not so optimistic as the liberal mentality; life was seen as a struggle in a hostile environment, but it was not viewed as a hopeless or all-consuming struggle against the elements. Particularly the technocrats tended to have tremendous pride in man's power and mastery over nature, his ability to transform and exploit the natural environment. The literati's attitude toward nature, on the other

hand, was a more sentimental mixture of fear and awe, which often manifested itself in an attitude of almost worshipping nature and seeking to protect it from man.

Attitude Toward the Narod

In the nineteenth century, one's attitude toward the *narod* was a central
issue in the debate between the Slavophile and the Westernizer branches of
the Russian intelligentsia. The heavily emotional question of love for the
narod was considered critical for the direction of Russian sociopolitical
and economic reforms; then as now, one's perception of the *narod*, is intimately connected with one's preferred model of polity.

For the Bolsheviks and the early *partocrats,* the *narod* was a dark,
reactionary, and dangerous mass capable of evil.[103] Only the working class,
which was not tainted by the evil of property, was seen as a constructive
force—if it was educated and controlled by the party. This perception led
logically to a coercive polity.

The *apparatchiks* and the literati perceived the *narod* in a more positive light. After all, the *narod* had defeated the Nazi military machine and
bore the brunt of the industrialization of the country. Still, it was seen as
inert and passive.[104] The *narod* was seen as having an anarchic, atavistic
soul and an unruly, unpredictable character, which had to be carefully and
painstakingly shaped; the *narod* needed to be stimulated, educated and improved morally. This was the job of the creative intelligentsia—the "engineers of the human soul," as Stalin put it. A Soviet textbook, written not by
the *apparatchiks* but by the creative intelligentsia, stated that propaganda
should inculcate "certain positive traits or, on the contrary, change the personality structure in order to lead the individual to desirable activity or
behavior It exerts an ideological influence on the individual, remolds class
psychology by bringing out and consolidating those traits that make staunch
and invincible fighters."[105]

The liberal democrats' positive and trusting attitude toward the *narod*
manifested itself in their critique of the literati's arrogant, snobbish attitude.[106] Thus Gaidar said: "The intelligentsia in Russia has always been
afraid of the *narod*. It often loved it, worshipped it, and deified it, but in
actual fact it was afraid of it."[107] Indeed, the creative intelligentsia's suspicious attitude toward the *narod* kept it in perpetual expectation of a Russian *bunt*—a reign of delirious cruelty, senseless destruction, and chaos.

However, the bulk of the Soviet intelligentsia, the technical and social
intelligentsia, developed a rather benign, although not totally positive attitude toward the *narod*. After all, they not only lived among the *narod*, they

also worked and socialized with it. In the years of *glasnost*, they met the *narod* in informal clubs, associations, and movements, where they discovered that there was no huge philosophical or political gap between them and the *narod*. In 1990-91, the intelligentsia organized and led the *narod* in gigantic anti communist rallies. Up to 700,000 people participated in some of them, and they did not behave like an unruly mob. The *narod*, as the technical and social intelligentsia discovered, was reasonable, restrained, and tolerant in short, surprisingly civilized. Thus, although the technical and social intelligentsia had no illusions about the *narod*, neither did they fear it.

Attitude Toward Different Forms of Power

As discussed above, the *partocrats* had an instinctive penchant for totalitarian power, while the *apparatchiks* preferred an administrative form of power. The *apparatchiks* associated administrative power with an orderly, balanced, dispassionate social process capable of restraining evil forces. Only such a competent administrative power could be entrusted with control over the military and police, as well as technological power, which otherwise might spin out of control.[108] The *apparatchik* believes that only administrative power can serve society as a whole; the other forms of power —financial, political, and even intellectual—serve the selfish interests of individuals and groups.

The Russian intelligentsia's perception of and attitude toward power deserve special attention because, on the one hand, they played such a crucial role in the revolution, and, on the other hand, because intellectuals, "tend to deny and renounce power,"[109] and even claim that "intellectuals and power are incompatible."[110] The differentiation between various subgroups of the intelligentsia and their respective preferences for different forms of power allows us to throw new light on this paradox.

The intelligentsia is very averse toward coercive forms of power such as physical, military, and administrative power, to say nothing of totalitarian power. It is suspicious of financial, political, and even religious forms of power.

The creative intelligentsia claims that it desires only to influence society through ideas, images, music, knowledge, and love. However, this does not mean that it is not interested in power. In fact, the intelligentsia's power of persuasion is perhaps the most potent form of power. Nevertheless, transforming the power inherent in an idea into an actual force is an arduous and not always gratifying or certain process, upon which intellectuals are typically reluctant to embark; to develop their ideas, they need financial support; to disseminate their ideas, they need independent media and easy access to them; to implement their ideas, they need administrative power.

In short, the creative intelligentsia is not against bureaucratic power, it is against bureaucrats being in charge of it. It welcomes the redistributive and protective role of the state and secretly yearns to direct it. Hence, despite all their disclaimers, deep in their hearts many Russian, as well as Western, intellectuals are inherently statist and socialistic.

The Russian literati's attitude toward technological progress seems to illustrate this point. In the 1970s the Russian intelligentsia initiated and led the first informal environmental movement, which sought to protect Lake Baikal from pollution, to stop the party's gigantic projects aimed at reversing the flow of the northern rivers in order to save the Caspian and Aral seas, and so on. Apart from the hidden political overtones inherent in a protest against the totalitarian system, the intellectuals were genuinely frightened by the threat to nature that industrialization was presenting. The Chernobyl nuclear accident reinforced their fear of technological power. They called for tighter administrative control over technological and scientific pursuits. This seemed to indicate that the literati were more suspicious of technological power than administrative power.

The technical and social intelligentsia are scornful of religious power. For example, during the consideration of the rebuilding of the Cathedral of Christ the Savior in Moscow (the largest cathedral in Russia, which Stalin had destroyed), the greatest criticism came from the technocrats and democrats, who claimed that the very expensive project would serve only to satisfy the statist aspirations of the new power establishment.[111] The literati, however, were supportive of this and similar projects, because they are statists opposed to the Western-style separation of church and state.

Private Property and the Market

We are now prepared to consider the attitudes of different Russian social groups at the brink of the revolution regarding concepts such as private ownership of the means of production and land, the free market, and the separation of powers. Doing so will help us understand why many of the original "fathers of *perestroika*" and its supporters criticized the reforms after their launching in January 1992, while many of the opponents of *perestroika* supported them.

A penchant for a particular form of power manifests itself in one's vision of which power—administrative, financial, or spiritual—should reign supreme. This vision, in turn, leads to one's perception of a proper model for the polity. To put it differently, if an elite believes that spiritual power should be superior, it is likely to espouse a state built on religious precepts. If, on the other hand, an elite believes in the superiority of financial power, it will advocate the primacy of the free market and private property. If an elite favors administrative power, it will advocate a bureaucratic system.

An aversion toward private property and the market has deep historical roots, and not only in Russia. Schools of thought as varied as those represented by the Hebrew prophets, some branches of Christianity, and Marxism reject the right to private property, particularly the ownership of land, as a source of evil, injustice, and exploitation. The Russian creative intelligentsia inherited this attitude, which in the nineteenth century made it especially susceptible to communism. As one analyst noted, "In the sense of utopian ideals, the Bolsheviks were of the same flesh and blood as the Russian intelligentsia."[112] For the literati, the suggestion that anonymous, chaotic market forces should determine the value of their talents and efforts is morally repulsive.

Hence, in the 1980s, when the literati claimed that the *narod* was not ready for the market, that people preferred a guaranteed salary,[113] and opposed the private ownership of land,[114] they were really speaking about themselves. It was they who were unsympathetic to private property and were appalled by the prospect of being forced to make a living by subjecting their talents and imagination to the whims of the marketplace.

En masse, the Soviet industrialists and *apparatchiks* were ambivalent toward, and often opposed to dismantling the existing administrative system and replacing it with the market, where financial and political forces would freely compete.

Other elites in the Soviet Union were more positively disposed toward private property and the market, particularly the technical intelligentsia. The technocrats, or course, worship technological forms of power and tend to assume that technology, given administrative and financial support, is capable of solving most problems. Such support can come either from the state or from the market. The explosive technological advances in the market economies convinced the technocrats of the market's superiority.

Finally, the social intelligentsia, specialists in the service sector, saw in the market an opportunity to translate their professional skills into the material benefits that their Western counterparts enjoyed.

Model of the Polity
These perceptions usually coalesce into a coherent system, a political philosophy, which manifests itself in a preferred form of the polity. This

model and one's vision of one's place in it basically define one's political aspirations.

Apart from the *partocrats* and the liberal democrats, all the other elites shared the same model of the polity, which can be referred to as the *derzhava*—an organic conception in which each social group represents a specialized organ. The means of production (industrial power) form the skeleton. The military and police are the muscles. The brain reconciles inner contradictions and orchestrates harmonious interaction among all the social groups.

For an *apparatchik*, the ideal image of the *derzhava* is a gladiator, a perfect fighter with a strong frame, powerful muscles, perfect coordination, and the best possible tools for warfare.[115] It has to be physically and mentally healthy, and highly motivated. For the *apparatchiks*, the circulatory and nervous systems of the Soviet *derzhava* were the party.[116] Later, they came to argue that the state bureaucracy, or even the secret police could fill this role.[117] During *glasnost* the party was totally discredited, so Gorbachev decided to shift power from the party structure to the state and KGB, which were directly subordinated to him as president.[118]

For the intelligentsia, the *derzhava* had warmer overtones. It was a world unto itself, a higher-order organism which had reached the most advanced stage of evolution. It would continue to grow and become a center of gravity for smaller nations, peoples, and states. The intelligentsia saw itself as the *derzhava*'s brain, the depository of its "dignity, pride, conscience, and soul."[119]

Attitudes Toward International Affairs

The perception of the international environment and the *derzhava*'s place in it differed significantly among the major social groups of the Soviet Union. For an *apparatchik* in the 1980s, the world was a loose, amorphous conglomerate of nations, tribes, colonies, and peoples. Driven by divisive class, ethnic, religious, political, and economic interests, mankind was in a state of flux and creation. At the same time, a more definite, stable, and firmly bound structure was taking shape. Eventually, a "new world order" would evolve with only one nation at its helm. That preeminent *derzhava* would be the richest and strongest nation, the one that had managed to maximize its power by harnessing all its forces due to its inner cohesiveness and coordination. Other nations, at least those with developed cultures and strong social structures, would play crucial roles in the world.[120] One *apparatchik* put it eloquently: "Russia does not pretend to be a superpower, but rather to be one of five leading *derzhava*s. Maybe in the future it will achieve even a higher place . . ."[121]

For the intelligentsia, the international environment is an arena of peaceful competition among cultures, in which Russia has a unique role to play, "worthy of historical significance as a great nation."[122] What this role is, is not entirely clear. Different representatives of the intelligentsia have held different views about Russia's mission. The great nineteenth century Russian thinker Vladimir Soloviov thought that it was to unite in harmony the European and Oriental cultures.[123] Nikolai Berdyaev thought that Russia should be the defender of weak, particularly Slavic, states, and the center of the Slavic world in its competition with the Germanic and Latin cultures.[124] Sergei Stankevich, a former adviser to President Yeltsin, argued that Russia should harmonize different cultural principles "into a historic symphony."[125]

In any case, in the words of Vladimir Shumeiko, "Russia should occupy the place in the world that corresponds to it, a leading place."[126] This should "not [be] because of the size of its population and nuclear arsenal," added Russian Foreign Minister Andrei Kozyrev, but because of Russia's "spiritual richness."[127]

The Aspirations of the Elites

The "improvers of socialism," as Anatoli Streliany poignantly called the literati,[128] wished to create socialism with a human face. As the prominent intellectual Nikolai Amosov suggested, society should make use of evil instincts such as greed and the desire to dominate and exploit one's fellow humans. Evil can be productive, creative, and useful, he believed, but only if it is tightly controlled. Rather than try to suppress these instincts and remake human nature, Amosov said, society should exploit them.[129] The evil impulses will generate wealth, which the government should then distribute evenly and justly.[130]

While sharing essentially the same model of the polity, the elites had different aspirations for themselves. While the *apparatchiks* and technocrats cared about the strength of the nation, the intelligentsia cared more about its soul. The creative intelligentsia saw itself as the guardian of morality and spirituality. It saw itself setting standards, formulating and propagating cultural values, writing laws, and caring about the nation's mental health.

The role of the *derzhava*'s self-appointed strategists, the *partocrats*, was contested by the *apparatchiks*, the literati, and the technocrats. In fact, the entire intelligentsia suffered from what Friedrich Hayek called *the fatal conceit.* As he wrote, intellectuals are prone to think that if they are given enough information, they can regulate the allocation of society's resources and otherwise control societal development.[131] This propensity to construct elaborate strategies was particularly pronounced among the literati and the *apparatchiks*. After the reforms of 1992 were launched, they criticized the liberal democrats for lacking a thoroughly calculated strategy and not fore-seeing all the consequences of the reforms. Academician Leonid Abalkin insisted that "in economics there are strict rules that allow one to forecast the development of a situation and its long-term tendencies unambigu-ously."[132] Academician Oleg Bogomolov even called for "the rebirth of the most elementary functions of Gosplan [the state planning agency]."[133] Other literati insisted that a "long-term national strategy" was necessary in order to successfully compete in the international arena.[134] The *apparatchiks* also deplored the lack of strategy and planning.[135] Without such strategies and a state regulatory role, argued first deputy prime minister Oleg Soskovets, even the most market-oriented economies would have "plunged into chaos."[136]

To summarize, in the 1980s, neither the *apparatchiks* nor the creative intelligentsia, in one analyst's words, "really wanted radical changes. All they wanted was some liberalization, freedom to travel to the West, more intelligent censorship, more delicate bureaucracy..., but not the collapse of the system."[137]

The Beginning of Shifts in Mentality

After *perestroika* began in 1986, significant shifts in the mentalities of the elites took place. Not only was the ideology of communism demolished, but the dismemberment of totalitarian power opened new opportunities for all social groups. The liberation of the mass media gave the creative intelli-gentsia a chance to capture the power of the "fourth estate." Free elections to the parliament helped some of them discover the power of popular sup-port. The opportunity to acquire property, and the independence and self-esteem that often accompany it, quickly began to affect their attitudes.

The lifting of restrictions on travel abroad allowed many intellectuals and lower-ranking *apparatchiks* to make their first trips to the capitalist world. They were struck by the independence that their Western counter-parts had from the state, and the sense of personal security and self-confi-dence that private property instilled in Western officials and the business elite. At home, they were greatly impressed that some of their former col-leagues had joined the ranks of the new Russians and become fabulously wealthy. Thus what had previously been a purely theoretical, rather abstract, discussion suddenly took on a practical dimension.

In the end, the abolition of the state monopoly on financial power, which was vigorously advocated by the democrats, met little resistance from most *apparatchiks* and the intelligentsia. Only small subgroups continued to rage against private property, the nouveau riche, and the vulgarity of the market place. Their attitude was exemplified by actor Mikhail Ulianov, who said: "[In culture] currently the upper hand belongs to a pushy, indiscriminate public, people without conscience who are guided by primitive principles: grab, devour, drink, and do not agonize about the methods . . ."[138]

Conclusion

Under the totalitarian system, all elites lived double life, with dual consciousnesses; at the same time they were both professionals and clerks. All social groups, including the top *nomenklatura*, were, to varying degrees, unhappy, because they suffered from the humiliation of powerlessness vis-a-vis the totalitarian system. So they directly, indirectly, or inadvertently participated in its dismemberment. When the system collapsed, each individual had to choose among his several identities, or to abandon them altogether in favor of a new one. The massive devolution of totalitarian power opened up immense opportunities. Each person and each social group pursued these opportunities in line with their potential, mindset, and preferred model of the polity.

We will see in the forthcoming chapters that the old Soviet elites soon began to become new elites, each fully in charge of a specific area—finance, trade, educational institutions, political parties, religious affairs, the arts, the media, and so on. This process of forming new elites was very rapid because it involved the redistribution of power and not its creation. In essence, it was not very different from what had happened in the United States a century or so earlier.[139]

The sudden collapse of the totalitarian system opened up a floodgate of creativity. The revolution began to acquire its own momentum and direction. The liberated forces soon began to shape society beyond the initial aspirations of the elites.

Chapter 3

Yeltsin

Introduction

The social composition and mindset of the Soviet elites at the threshold of the revolution, as described in the previous chapter, cannot fully explain the events that took place in Russia, because they do not take into account the role of personalities. A number of remarkable personalities have played key roles in the revolution. Although they represented their social groups, by virtue of their talent, charisma, and original thinking they often transcended the limits of their social group's mentality. These leaders recruited followers, created institutions, and through them influenced political events. In addition, these outstanding personalities typically possessed an above average capacity for change, which allowed them to evolve along with the rapidly changing political climate. For example, an air force colonel became a member of the parliament, then vice-president, then a leader of an uprising against the president, a prisoner, and finally a leader of an opposition party and presidential candidate.

Each leading personality invites and deserves study. But there is one person without whom a study of the second Russian revolution is simply impossible. Boris Yeltsin is the paramount actor in the modern history of Russia, an extraordinary personality. His role in the destruction of the communist system and the transformation of Russia is impossible to overestimate. I can only hope to outline some of the most intriguing and important aspects of his political personality, which influenced all forces and processes leading to the new Russia.

For many reasons the study of Yeltsin's political personality is very difficult. First of all, by training, institutional affiliations, and career pattern, he has belonged to practically all the social groups described in the previous chapter. Secondly, he has played many widely varying social roles. Thirdly, he possesses a unique combination of rare qualities. Finally, his actions elicit very strong responses, because they affect tens of millions of people who themselves are going through an agonizingly difficult period. His every action generates a burst of emotional responses, which make an objective judgment very difficult, if not impossible.

Extensive information is available about Yeltsin. Yeltsin is the second leader in Russian history after Gorbachev whose political behavior has been carefully scrutinized, openly discussed, and documented. However, this deluge of information immensely complicates an objective analysis, because much of it is highly unreliable. For this reason, one should rely primarily on first-hand sources—Yeltsin's own pronouncements and writings, as well as the views of his closest associates. Fortunately, Yeltsin has provided us with two books about himself, which contain a wealth of information about his inner world. These books, which have been described as "personal, candid, and at times merciless toward the author and others,"[1] are a source of precious information for political psychologists.

Yeltsin has played at least four major roles in totally different environments. By training and in his initial career, he was a construction engineer and the manager of major construction projects. Next, he was a party *apparatchik*. After rising to the highest levels within the party, he became a dissenter and then the leader of the opposition. Then he became the designer and chief architect of the new Russia. Finally, he is now the chief executive officer of an authoritarian system of power created largely by him and under him.[2] No other politician in modern history has played this many political roles. In contrast, Mikhail Gorbachev played only one social role: that of an "*apparatchik* with a human face" and a catalyst of change. He softened the totalitarian system, thus triggering major events. But he soon lost control over them and was forced from the political scene. Yeltsin, in contrast, has remained on top of events throughout all stages of the revolution, and he is likely to remain the key political figure of the new Russia for years to come.

The case of Yeltsin also raises an intriguing question about the relationship between personality and culture. Yeltsin, as some analysts have noted, incorporates many if not most of the qualities of the so-called "Russian national character."[3] He is "perhaps the most Russian of all the czars and revolutionaries of this century."[4] On the other hand, for much of his life he was a paragon of Bolshevik culture, which in many ways is the antithesis of traditional Russian culture. But since then he has embarked on the restoration of traditional culture and started to build a new one, which, most analysts believe, has no roots in Russian soil.

In order to better understand Yeltsin's mentality, I will analyze his career in terms of the social groups and elites discussed in the previous chapter. Then, using contemporary studies of personality, I will examine aspects of Yeltsin's character that, together with his evolving mentality, have defined his operational style. This investigation should help us understand the events in Russia that have occurred since August 1991, to which the next chapter will be devoted.

Yeltsin's Background and Basic Mentality

Experts largely agree that a person's basic mentality is shaped by early childhood and adolescent experiences. The natural and man-made environment; his relationships in the family, in the community, in school, Russian literature; and the media have all participated in molding Yeltsin's view of the world, his basic mentality. His basic mentality was the foundation upon which his sociopolitical mentality was later constructed, based on his education, the mass media, career experiences, institutional affiliations, etc.

It is illuminating to compare Yeltsin's basic mentality with Gorbachev's, if only because many political analysts assume that the two leaders belonged to the same generation and had identical social backgrounds. There were important differences, however, in their childhood environments, which caused subtle but significant differences between their basic mentalities.

Both Gorbachev and Yeltsin were born to peasant families in the winter of 1931. Peasant life then was intimately linked to the elements, the natural rather than the man-made environment. So nature probably had a formative impact on their world views, just as it had on their ancestors.

The Stavropol region, where Gorbachev was born and raised, consists of monotonously flat steppes with few forests and no major rivers. But it is endowed with a rich, highly fertile soil ideal for agriculture. The climate of the area is continental, but it is still the mildest in Russia.

In contrast, Yeltsin grew up a thousand miles further north, in the very harsh climate and rugged landscape of the Urals. As a teenager, Yeltsin had an encounter with nature that almost cost him his life. He and his friends were lost in the wilderness and almost died from starvation and sickness.[5] This experience endowed him with a deep respect for and fear of natural forces. Such a harsh natural environment seems to promote a confrontational attitude: either man conquers and subdues it, or he perishes.[6] Thus such an environment encourages and rewards strength, endurance, and long-range planning.

Another important difference between Yeltsin's and Gorbachev's childhood experiences is that Yeltsin witnessed at first hand a massive demonstration of the power of man and technology in the Urals under Stalin. When Boris was four years old, his parents moved to the industrial center of the Urals, Berezniki, where during World War II and afterwards, unprecedented construction and development took place. Four hundred thirty-seven factories complete with skilled personnel and scientific institutions were relocated from European Russia to Sverdlovsk province ahead of Hitler's advancing armies.[7] The new cities, roads, and factories were built in the wilderness, vividly demonstrating the aggressive and superior power of man over nature. In the 1980s Sverdlovsk *oblast* was one of the most urbanized and industrialized in the country.[8]

Although the social origins of Yeltsin and Gorbachev were identical, their social experiences in childhood were very different. Both boys' grandfathers were well-to-do peasants who were persecuted during the 1930s. Although Yeltsin's grandfather was deported, he managed to escape. Nevertheless, he had to move from place to place to hide from the authorities. This rebellious man played a significant role in Yeltsin's upbringing.

In addition, Yeltsin's father, Nikolai Ignatievich, was arrested in 1934, in the early stages of the purges. He refused to cooperate with the KGB (another evidence of rebelliousness in Yeltsin's family), yet he survived and lived to the age of 72.[9]

Both boys lived with very authoritarian parents: Gorbachev's mother and Yeltsin's grandfather, and particularly his father, were rough, uncompromising, independent-minded people and strict disciplinarians of their children. But the social conditions of the areas in which they grew up differed. Before the October Revolution, the North Caucasus was the most prosperous region of Russia. Its people, the Cossacks, were the staunchest opponents of Bolsheviks and for this reason they were systematically subjected to a decades-long genocide. An undeclared war was waged against them with the help of a man-made famine, massive arrests, deportations, and collectivization.[10] In addition, the area was devastated by World War II, the indigenous peoples—the Chechens, the Ingush, and others—were deported to Siberia and Kazakhstan.

Gorbachev's relatives and perhaps young Misha himself witnessed at least some of the unprecedented brutality, violence, atrocities (including mass starvation and cannibalism), to which the area was subjected; according to some estimates, the results were a halving of the population of Stavropolski Krai[11] and the destruction of traditional culture. Many of Gorbachev's relatives perished as a result of starvation and the persecutions.[12] The mental and emotional impact of such experiences is known to be devastating, resulting in humiliation, a sense of total helplessness, insecurity, and the adoption of a Hobbesian attitude toward the world and other people.[13]

Yeltsin's childhood was also difficult but devoid of atrocities and destruction. The Sverdlovsk area was not devastated by famine, deportations, occupation by the Nazis, or wholesale destruction, as was the European part of Russia. On the contrary, it experienced tremendous growth and a massive influx of educated people, particularly technical specialists, who were evacuated from European cities.

The living conditions of Yeltsin's family were primitive. In the wooden barrack in which he lived from the age of four to fourteen, his entire family lived in one room separated by thin partitions from others. There was no indoor plumbing, and water was drawn from a well. Boris, his parents, grandfather, and two siblings slept on the floor. On particularly cold nights the children huddled around a goat for warmth. Later Yeltsin characterized this life style as unnatural and humiliating; as party leader of the province, he resolved to eliminate barracks and move their inhabitants into separate apartments. Yet he also retained warm memories of the camaraderie and friendship that he experienced during these years. For example, he insisted that during the ritual Russian "wall-to-wall" fights, in which he participated, men never maliciously intended to kill or maim others, although he himself received a heavy blow from a stick that broke the bridge of his nose.[14] It was a rough way to have fun, but a far cry from the executions and cannibalism that people experienced in Gorbachev's area.

Such a crowded and impoverished life can have a devastating effect on the psyche of a young person.[15] Or, on the contrary, it can make him sensitive and responsive to people's sufferings and needs. The latter happened in Yeltsin's case. He was an extrovert and a natural leader, always organizing games and after-school activities, some of them very dangerous. His exceptional courage, quick wits, tenacity, and impressive physical strength made him a leader.

To sum up, Gorbachev grew up under the cloud of a reign of terror and destruction. Very early on, he internalized the attitude that survival can be found only in an organization—the more powerful, the better. He learned to draw his strength and confidence from the power of organizations.

Yeltsin grew up in the atmosphere of the struggle of man against nature. He internalized an attitude of respect and admiration for the power of man rooted in science, technology, and professional expertise. He learned to draw his strength mostly from within.

Yeltsin's Basic Mentality

All this allows us to infer with some confidence the basic mentalities of Gorbachev and Yeltsin. Without conclusive first-hand evidence, of course, these inferences must remain working hypotheses; nevertheless, they are supported by a content analysis of Gorbachev's and Yeltsin's own pronouncements.

Gorbachev's basic mentality was Hobbesian, as described in Chapter 1.[16]

Yeltsin's basic mentality was more optimistic. He has consistently expressed trust in the innate goodness of people.[17] Later, he came to embrace the thought that the communist experience corrupted people's attitudes and habits. He believes that life is a struggle against both the natural environment and enemies. Yeltsin's characterization of one period of his life is very indicative in this regard: "It was a constant fight, not a single month, not a single week, could I work in peace anywhere at any time. Everywhere there was a fight with someone, and, of course, it embitters a person."[18]

Neither Gorbachev nor Yeltsin believes in God[19] or life after death. However, Yeltsin's fatalism comes close to a belief in a supernatural, omnipotent power. He has expressed belief in some "inexplicable" superior forces, that guide and protect him and Russia.[20] He feels that "something mysterious in nature knows everything in advance."[21]

Yeltsin's fatalist attitude toward life is an archetypical feature of the Russian "national character." In much of Dostoevski and Chekhov, one can read passages similar to this statement by Yeltsin: "The debilitating bouts of depression, the grave thoughts, the insomnia and headaches in the middle of the night, despair and bitterness at the vision of impoverished Moscow and other cities, the daily flood of criticism from the pages of newspapers and television screens, the hounds at the Congress sessions, the heavy burden of the decisions, the hurt from the people close to me who failed to support me, who did not hold firm and betrayed me—I have had to bear all of this."[22]

Yeltsin's attitude toward death appears to be rather contradictory. His insistence that he does not think much about death because he is "too busy"[23] can be interpreted as a subliminal belief that death is not the end of personality. His recurrent depressions, mentioned so many times in both books, are accompanied by a sense and fear of impending doom.[24] But he is very concerned with the legacy that he will leave after his death. Thus he believes in cultural immortality, and fears that his legacy may not prove to be lasting.

Yeltsin's Political Career
Professional

The Hobbesian mentality of Gorbachev led him to seek a close affiliation with the organs of totalitarian power.[25] He headed Komsomol organizations for fourteen years and earned a reputation as a zealous Komsomol leader.[26] He joined the party as soon as he became eligible, and he chose to enter the law department of the elite Moscow State University when Stalinist law was nothing more than a tool for imposing the party's dominance on a reluctant society.[27]

Yeltsin's basic mentality directed him toward enhancing his physical strength and pursuing excellence in a professional career. In 1949 Boris graduated from high school; following in his father's footsteps, he entered the Construction Department of the Urals Polytechnic Institute of Sverdlovsk. With its 30,000 students, it was one of the largest schools in the Soviet Union. It had notably high academic standards, due to the many fine professors who had been exiled in the 1930s from Moscow and Leningrad to the Urals. His education focused on mathematics, physics, drawing, and *sopromat* (the resistance of materials), not on ideology. Yeltsin excelled in sciences despite the heavy load imposed on his time by his pursuit of a professional career in volleyball. For his diploma, for example, he single-handedly designed one of the first television towers in the Soviet Union.

Yeltsin graduated with a "red diploma" (top honors); for this reason was granted the privilege of remaining in Sverdlovsk rather than being sent to remote areas. His first job assignment was typical for the institute's graduates: he was a foreman of a construction site. However, Yeltsin declined the position, and made a very unusual request—to work for one year as a simple worker in twelve different trades: carpenter, truck driver, painter, bricklayer, and so on. He thought that he needed on-the-job training in the practical skills of construction, and he was determined to learn one skill a month for a year. (This decision to master basic skills recalls Peter the Great's decision to go to Holland in order to learn at first hand the knowledge needed to build ships for the Russian Navy.) Thus Yeltsin voluntarily imposed on himself the burden of excellence in order to achieve the highest standards of his profession. Within a few years he had distinguished himself as a construction engineer.

Red Director

Yeltsin's honest and selfless attitude, the relentless drive and enormous energy that he put into his work, as well as his competence in finding innovative technical solutions resulted in a successful career. In 1961 he became the chief engineer of a factory making prefabricated housing, which employed twenty thousand employees. Two years later, he became the general director of the factory.

As director he was responsible not only for meeting the requirements of the plan, raising productivity, securing the flow of supplies, and maintaining quality standards. He was also responsible for the life and well-being of all the factory's employees, including their housing, training, vacations, living conditions, food supplies, preschools, auxiliary farms, recreational activities, and much more. Yeltsin evidently succeeded in handling these responsibilities:[28] in 1969 he was invited to head the construction department of the Sverdlovsk provincial party committee, at which time he became a party *apparatchik*.

If education is included, as it should be, Yeltsin's life as a technocrat and red director spanned twenty years. Thus technical and managerial experience were first and foremost in his life; we can safely assume that they had the greatest impact on his sociopolitical mentality.

Party Career

Few analysts have noted how different the party careers of Gorbachev and Yeltsin were.[29] Gorbachev's career followed the classic pattern of an *apparatchik* par excellence: from Komsomol leader to *oblast* party chief, then Secretary of the Central Committee, candidate member of the Politburo, full member, and then, finally, General Secretary. Gorbachev entered the party in 1952, during the beginning of Stalin's massive new purge. In fact, Gorbachev was very late to repudiate Stalin. Even in late 1987, when Stalin was widely seen as a bloody tyrant, Gorbachev praised him for his "incontestable contribution to the struggle for socialism," particularly his acceleration of industrialization and collectivization.[30]

Yeltsin joined the party unusually late in life, in 1961, when his career had reached the ceiling set for non-party members,[31] and in an entirely different political climate. Yeltsin took his invitation to join the party seriously. He "carefully studied the party statutes, program, and even the classics: Marx, Engels and Lenin,"[32] which very few people bothered to do.

In 1961 the atmosphere in the country and within the party was very different from what it had been ten years earlier. In the late 1950s the party, under Khrushchev's leadership, had tried to shed its Stalinist legacy and return to its original mission to act as a vanguard for society. The struggle of antagonistic classes was declared to be over and to have been supplanted by the unity of the fraternal classes of workers, peasants, and the strata of the intelligentsia. The party put forward a new program with an emphasis on raising the quality of life, with the aim of surpassing the wealthiest capitalist countries and thus proving the superiority of the socialist system.

To a professional, the party's new policy of the concrete improvement of life seemed to remove the traditional ideological antagonism between the *partocrats* and the professionals. Soviet triumphs in the exploration of space seemed to support the claim of the superiority of socialism over capitalism and to legitimize the leading role of the party. In this atmosphere of renewed hopes and expectations, Yeltsin's decision to join the party was not a Faustian bargain; it was in line with a popular movement at that time among the intelligentsia to join the party in order to raise its quality and humanize it.

Yeltsin accepted the offer to become head of the Sverdlovsk Oblast Party Committee's department of construction, but not without reservations. He sensed that his career was about to change fundamentally: instead of being an industrial manager he would now become a party *apparatchik*. However, he could not turn down the opportunity. His duties were not political: he was to supervise all construction projects in the third most industrialized region of the Soviet Union.[33]

One might say that during this period of his career, which lasted seven years, he combined the roles of a technocrat-industrialist and an *apparatchik*.

Yeltsin became a full-time party functionary in 1976, when Leonid Brezhnev appointed him first secretary of Sverdlovsk Oblast's Communist Party. The appointment of a person with brief party experience, over the head of the second secretary, was very unusual. It can only be explained by the overall weakening of the totalitarian system and by Brezhnev's personal reluctance to burden himself with provincial matters.

Sverdlovsk Oblast, with its 4.7 million people, was the capital of the Urals' military-industrial complex. It is important to point out that a first secretary of the party had much broader responsibilities and power than a governor of a state in the United States. As was the case when he was a factory director, Yeltsin was responsible for practically all aspects of life in the province: production, construction, and social conditions (including the food supply, education, science and even cultural life).

Yeltsin was a tough taskmaster, relentless in driving himself and others. A workaholic himself, he demanded the same fanatical devotion to work from his subordinates, often making their lives impossible.[34] As eyewitnesses testified, "he would set industrial enterprises such huge, fantastic tasks that anyone—even the fittest director—could have a seizure."[35]

Yelstin's career in the party was marked by occasional harshness. In 1979, as party leader, he was guilty of a cover-up when anthrax virus leaked from a biological weapon factory.[36] In the same year he showed little mercy toward a group of students of his alma mater who demanded freedom for political prisoners, and he put them in prison.[37] He also showed unusual zeal in carrying out the orders of the Politburo to demolish the Ipatiev House, where the Tsar's family had been executed.

Despite all this, Yeltsin was the first party leader to earn broad popularity in the region. He was credited with a number of accomplishments in the *oblast*: he constructed new roads and a city metro, he liquidated the barracks and replaced them with apartment complexes, and he improved the food situation.[38] More than anything else, however, *oblast* residents have good things to say about Yeltsin's humane attitude toward ordinary people[39] and his relentless campaign against the privileges of and corruption among the *nomenklatura*.

Yeltsin's open style of leadership was unprecedented. He met regularly with students, members of the intelligentsia, and workers; he honestly answered questions they submitted, making sure that none was left unanswered. He was the first regional party leader to address the people regularly on television.[40] He would personally raid local stores, factories and canteens, forcing them to release hoarded goods to the public. He also often traveled by public transportation rather than in a limousine with a police escort.

Yeltsin's leadership was a radical departure from that of previous party barons, who were insulated from the people and from reality. Yeltsin's down-to-earth style caused people to think that he was one of them.

A month after Gorbachev became General Secretary, central committee secretary Vladimir Dolgikh called Yeltsin and conveyed to him the Politburo's offer to head the Central Committee's department of construction. Yeltsin politely refused. He preferred to remain in his native land, where he was popular. He then received a call from his former friend Gorbachev. Only the tacit understanding that his assignment would be temporary induced Yeltsin to change his mind and accept the position.

On April 12, 1985, Yeltsin moved to Moscow. On December 22, 1985, he was appointed first secretary of the Moscow city Communist Party; soon afterwards he became a nonvoting member of the Politburo. One must remember that under party statutes, all members of the top party *nomenklatura* who lived in Moscow belonged to the Moscow party organization, that is, they were at least nominally subordinate to Yeltsin. This power was given to him by his fellow provincial Gorbachev in order to cleanse the arrogant and corrupt party organization of the capital.

Primarily to eradicate those loyal to Grishin, who had been Gorbachev's rival for the post of General Secretary.[41] Gorbachev needed Yeltsin to shake up the Moscow party establishment (and consequently the entire country) and to awaken it from Brezhnev's "era of stagnation."

As usual, Yeltsin took his job very seriously. He wasted no time in launching the same sort of campaign against privileges and corruption that he had waged in Sverdlovsk. Traveling by public transport, he personally inspected shops and factories, met and talked to ordinary people. He dismissed many managers and 60 percent of the party *apparatchiks*. He earnestly promoted *glasnost*: freedom of the press, political associations, and assemblies.

The Maverick and Rebel

Many Russian and foreign analysts maintain that Yeltsin carried "within him too much of the baggage of a party apparatchik."[42] But Yeltsin never became a typical *apparatchik* and never adopted predictable views, complexes, and allegiances.

In the words of one party veteran, Yeltsin's "political immaturity stemmed from the fact that he entered the party too late and was not hardened by sufficiently long party work."[43] Indeed, Yeltsin's extremely successful professional and party career, particularly his meteoric rise to the uppermost position in the province, allowed him to skip a critically important part of the process of integration into the party's organizational culture: he was never forced to adopt the humiliating posture of total submissiveness and the denigrating requirement to please one's superior by all possible means.[44] As Yeltsin forcefully stated in his memoirs, he was never anyone's deputy; that is, he never occupied a position in which he was someone's immediate subordinate.[45] (The devastating effect of total submissiveness on a person's psyche has been well studied both in the West, most notably by Erich Fromm,[46] and by Soviet psychologists.[47]) As Morton Kaplan noted, a longtime *apparatchik*, forced by fear and humiliation to bend "his behavior to the inconsistent requirements of a constantly shifting set of external pressures," can eventually lose his sense of identity and consistency in behavior.[48] Yeltsin , however, did not become a typical *apparatchik*.

It is also important to remember that during the last years of Brezhnev and the subsequent succession of four general secretaries in three years, the provincial party leaders enjoyed relative freedom in running their fiefdoms. As Yeltsin wrote, "The power of the first secretary was practically limitless. . . . The first secretary was both Tsar and God. His view and decision on practically any question was final."[49] This situation obviously suited Yeltsin's personality type perfectly. As he later confessed, "Those ten years in the post of Sverdlovsk Party secretary were the best period of my life."[50]

Having avoided the "hardening of the character" typical of the party, Yeltsin retained and developed a self-confidence quite extraordinary for an *apparatchik*. Independent minded and lacking any trace of servility, Yeltsin was a maverick and a misfit in the party. This is why "he so easily gave up his communist past," wrote a journalist.[51]

As a party bureaucrat, Yeltsin belonged, (in Anthony Downs's definition) to the category of zealots. Downs wrote that zealots, driven by the desire to bring about institutional change, "must launch vociferous attacks on the *status quo*. . . They attract attention to existing or future deficiencies . . . and help to generate and focus enormous amounts of energy to overcome bureaucratic inertia. In the process, they antagonize other officials."[52] The methods that proved successful in Sverdlovsk, however, were useless in Yeltsin's struggle with the central apparatus. He antagonized the party establishment and Gorbachev, but he failed to bring about a further democratization of the party or to curb its power.

Dissenter and Popular Hero

Three years in the inner sanctum of the totalitarian system allowed Yeltsin to understand its nature, raison d'etre, and mechanics.

He was appalled by the stifling ineptitude of the totalitarian machinery and by the luxurious life style of the top *partocrats*, which struck him as not only immoral but absurd. The cruelty of an utterly dehumanized *apparat* and the cynicism of the socialist slogans of freedom, equality, and brotherhood (in light of top party leadership's life-style and corruption) led him to conclude that the system needed radical reform.

At the October 1987 Central Committee Plenum, Yeltsin accused Gorbachev of playing at *glasnost* and *perestroika* rather than pursuing real reforms. This was an open rebellion unheard of in the top party ranks since the time of Lenin. Party rules required that Yeltsin be punished by expulsion from the party and cast into oblivion. Gorbachev had no choice but to give the "go-ahead" to the top party establishment's decision to conduct a typical "party trial." Twenty-seven members of the Central Committee took part in a ritual of "character assassination" that Yeltsin compared to "execution by words." The goal was to destroy Yeltsin's dignity and pride by forcing him to make a humiliating, self-flagellating confession of errors and repentance. Instead, he apologized only for tactical mistakes and inconveniences that he had caused. After the session Yeltsin was hospitalized, suffering from a nervous breakdown. Yet three weeks later, on November 11, 1987, he was brought back from the hospital for the second round of his "trial."[53] The procedure was repeated again in February 1988. In the end Yeltsin was stripped of his position as Moscow first secretary and expelled from the Politburo.

Although Yeltsin's "trial" and punishment were in the spirit of Gorbachev's *glasnost* (half hearted and extremely mild, by the standards of the 1930s), the ordeal caused a major "psychological break." His pains, agony, and doubts were almost a textbook description of the symptoms of Post-Traumatic Stress Disorder.[54] Even five years later he wrote about that time as "the most painful period of [his] life."[55] He felt betrayed by his colleagues and friends; he fought a "battle with [him]self;" and for months of sleepless nights he subjected himself to merciless analysis, examining his entire life as a professional and an *apparatchik*. He tried to understand what mistakes and flaws in his personality had led him to such a debacle and the crashing end of all his ambitions.[56]

Yeltsin's conclusion was that he was right and the system wrong. But he still retained the faint hope that he could persuade the party to reform itself. After all, there were intelligent and sensible people in the Politburo, such as Aleksandr Yakovlev and Eduard Shevardnadze. He decided to try one more time, during the nineteenth party conference in June 1988. At the conference Yeltsin argued that the Soviet political system needed major revamping and offered a program of democratization for the party. He also asked the leadership to "rehabilitate him during his lifetime."[57] However, the party establishment rejected both his arguments and his conciliatory gesture. This led him to conclude that "it was impossible to reform the CPSU and the system of soviets."[58]

Thus ended Yeltsin's career as an *apparatchik*. In fact, the conference, which was televised nationwide, closed a chapter in the life of the party itself. It demonstrated to the nation that the party had exhausted its capacity for rejuvenation and self-reform. In the eyes of Yeltsin and a large portion of the population, the party had become atavistic, a drag on the nation's progress.

Becoming a Democrat and the Leader of the Opposition

After the conference Yeltsin was showered with thousands of letters from ordinary people. This "fantastic support"[59] revealed that Yeltsin had a tremendous following, not only among party members. So when Gorbachev ventured to expand the system of alternative elections into the Congress of People's Deputies, Yeltsin embarked on yet another major gamble—to re-enter the Soviet political scene despite the fierce resistance of the party *nomenklatura* and in defiance of Gorbachev's own promise not to allow him back into politics. He gambled on his tremendous popularity among the *narod*, challenged the power of the totalitarian system, and won.

A new Yeltsin was born on March 26, 1989, when he received 89.6 percent of the votes of Muscovites in the first contested elections to the Congress of People's Deputies. His victory over the party establishment revealed two things: the weakness of the totalitarian machinery and the growing power of the democratic forces. However, the struggle ahead of him seemed to provide little chance for success. If only out of the instinct for self-preservation, the totalitarian system was likely eventually to find the strength to brutally reassert its domination over society. Thus Yeltsin embarked on the path of open dissent, upon which so many brave people before him had perished.

Yeltsin's election to the Supreme Soviet, the permanent body of the congress, was skillfully blocked by the party machinery; only the sacrifice by a provincial lawyer, Yuri Kazannik, who conceded his seat to Yeltsin, allowed him to become a member of the Supreme Soviet. This was yet another victory over the failing Soviet system and its weak leader.

From the first televised session of the Supreme Soviet, Yeltsin became one of the leaders of the opposition. Out of 2250 People's Deputies, 362 formed an opposition group known as the Interregional Group of Deputies. Yeltsin, Yuri Afanasiev, Viktor Palm, Gavriil Popov, and Andrei Sakharov became its rotating co-chairmen. Yeltsin was elected to be its chairman for the first year. The Coordinating Committee of the Interregional Group met for the first time in July 1989. When Andrei Sakharov died on December 14, 1989, Yeltsin became the unchallenged leader of the democrats and their permanent representative in the Supreme Soviet. Out of the five co-chairmen, only Yeltsin was a member of the Supreme Soviet.

In March 1990 Yeltsin was elected to the Supreme Soviet of the Russian Federation. Then, on May 29, despite tremendous efforts by Gorbachev to stop him, Yeltsin was narrowly elected its chairman.[60] His election as chairman signified the beginning of yet another chapter in Yeltsin's political biography; ending his short career as a dissident and the leader of the Soviet parliamentary opposition.

To sum up, the longest and the most profound experience in Yeltsin's career was as a technocrat and manager. He was also an *apparatchik*; but he became one only late in life, so he did not become a typical *apparatchik*, obedient and conformist, full of inferiority complexes and fears. He remained a rebel and a maverick. This made his open confrontation with the totalitarian establishment inevitable; this clash with the system greatly accelerated the evolution of his sociopolitical mentality, leading him to an accept the basic principles of democracy and the free market.

A number of analysts have noted that Yeltsin tends "to fall into apathy after winning a fight, to retreat when he should be advancing to consummate his victory,"[61] that great events in Yeltsin's life are always followed by "periods of lassitude."[62] But a different interpretation of Yeltsin's tendency to go into seclusion after major events is possible. I would argue that these supposed retreats marked major shifts in his life, the ends of epochs and the beginnings of new social roles. Twice after such events he took the time to write autobiographical books, indicating his desire to contemplate what had happened and what lay ahead. What is thought of as apathy actually reveals an understandable need for introspect.[63]

The Evolution of Yeltsin's Political Views

Four years of Yeltsin's life—from 1985 to 1989—were years in which a provincial technocrat was educated in the principles and values of democratic thinking. Yeltsin had to internalize several principal concepts before he came to embrace a democratic sociopolitical philosophy.

Understanding the Nature of Totalitarianism

Yeltsin confessed that when he joined the party he honestly believed that it was the guardian of the ideals of social justice,[64] hence that it had the moral right to lead the *narod*. Yeltsin's experience in the party *apparat* taught him that it was a Kafkaesque "terrible, impersonal machine," which autonomously and anonymously made fateful decisions for which no one was personally responsible.[65] It subjugated not only the *narod* but also the *nomenklatura* itself and became the real owner and master of everything, including the *apparatchiks*. "It was an ingenious way" to keep the *apparatchiks* obedient and paralyzed by fear. "They did not possess anything." They were allowed to use all the wonderful *dachas* at the sea, cars, and so on, but these belonged to the system, which could revoke their privileges at any time. Finally, and what is most important, the *apparat* of totalitarian power had become flagrantly inefficient.[66] Thus Yeltsin concluded that the communist system was fundamentally flawed.[67]

Discovering the Narod—a New Source of Power

While in Moscow, Yeltsin experienced another major discovery—the power of the *narod*. Yeltsin had always been sensitive to the concerns of ordinary people.[68] But when the policy of *glasnost*, legalized informal groups, associations, discussion clubs, and meetings, he discovered that the *narod* was not a passive mass that had to be organized, led, and inspired. It could also be a potent source of political power: "The time has changed. Now a General Secretary can say 'I will not let you back in politics,' but the people can decide otherwise and return you there."[69]

During a five-year period, beginning in 1988, Yeltsin has had five formal confirmations of his popular mandate—his elections to the party conference in 1988, to the Congress of People's Deputies in March 1989, and to the Russian Supreme Soviet in March 1990; his election as President of Russia in June 1991; and the referendum in April 1993. He won a popular mandate from the people during three different stages in his political career: as a rebel, as head of the opposition, and as the leader of the new Russia. These experiences fed his belief in the fundamental goodness of man and reinforced his resolve to rely on popular support as a source of power. He came to appreciate the supremacy of the power of persuasion over the coercive forms of power.

Once Yeltsin began to rely on democratic power, other aspects of the democratic mentality followed in turn.[70] If the ultimate source of power is believed to reside in the people, it makes sense to grant them more freedom and specifically to permit them to acquire private property. Thus in 1990, while many intellectuals were still debating the question of the ownership of land, Yeltsin not only insisted that without it sufficient food could not be produced,[71] but he also urged the Russian Supreme Soviet to adopt the appropriate laws.

A major influence on Yeltsin's sociopolitical mentality was his trip to the United States in September 19 had been was quite limited. Unlike the well-traveled Gorbachev, Yeltsin did not travel to the West until 1986. Nor did he have much chance to meet foreigners in the USSR, because Sverdlovsk was off limits to them until 1991. His short trip to West Germany in May 1986 and particularly his 1989 visit to the United States "opened up the entire world."[72] He was led to reconsider a number of previously sacrosanct political clichés. In Germany he "was shocked by the quality of life of the workers.[73] In the United States he was shocked by a typical grocery store in Texas: "I felt, quite frankly, sick with despair for the Soviet people." Yeltsin explained: "For more than 50 years they pounded in my head the idea that capitalism was rotting away . . . I was told that Americans were wicked, harmful, badly behaved . . ."[74] And now, he said, "I've seen that capitalism is flourishing. . . . In just a day and a half, my views have been turned around by one hundred and eighty degrees."[75]

Although he was ridiculed for this turnaround by both Russian and Western intellectuals, the experience of other Russian technocrats showed that Yeltsin's reaction was typical.[76] As a technocrat, he was particularly impressed by the fact that technological progress in the West manifests itself in consumer goods above all. All technological innovations were immediately incorporated into and even driven by the consumer market. By contrast, in the Soviet Union the latest technology served the strategic goals of the party, while people had to wait for decades to benefit from the advances.

These experiences completed the transformation of Yeltsin's sociopolitical mentality. He accepted all the basic concepts of democratic political philosophy. "He has changed in his innermost self," wrote a political writer, "even his language, mannerisms, and appearance have changed."[77]

Yeltsin's Sociopolitical Mentality

I believe that Yeltsin understands Russia in terms of an architectural metaphor. He seems to conceive of it as a house that is constantly expanding and improving. It needs a firm foundation and a solid roof. It should be strong enough to withstand all storms and earthquakes but also aesthetically pleasing, and most of all, comfortable to live in. The inhabitants should feel safe and happy. New additions are being made, it expands and grows, but it does not seek to fight or conquer other people.

Thus Yeltsin has now come to recognize the supremacy of the individual human being over the state. However, he also believes that the interests of society are ultimately superior to those of an individual or a group.[78] He sees the president as the head of the household who looks after the interests of society as a whole and acts as the guarantor of social peace.[79]

Numerous critics, including his associates, have accused Yeltsin of lacking vision and a clear program of reforms.[80] But since 1989 Yeltsin has consistently reaffirmed his newly adopted political philosophy and his vision of Russia's future, both at home and abroad. In the fall of 1990, under his guidance, a first draft of a new Russian constitution was written. Its basic principles were firmly rooted in the Universal Declaration of Human Rights and the comparable constitutions of democratic states, notably that of the United States. In his inaugural speech as newly elected President of the Russian Federation in June 1991, Yeltsin pledged to undo all the damage done to Russia by the Communist regime.[81] Three months later, as a young reformer said, "it was Yeltsin who declared the goal of building democratic capitalism, although he did not call it such."[82]

Yeltsin's Personality Traits

Political actors can have similar cognitive structures yet perceive identical circumstances in totally different ways. They can perceive the same situation either as dangerous or as beneficial, depending on their perception of their personal power relative to that of the environment—that is, according to their level of self-confidence. How they approach problems is also strictly individual. Their attempts to solve problems depends on their energy level and their ability to utilize both the personal and societal resources that are available. With these considerations in mind, we should consider some peculiarities of Yeltsin as a person.

Yeltsin's Physical Condition

Personality has been defined as the sum total of "recurring regularities that mark the style of a person and distinguish him from others."[83] An obvious element distinguishing one person from another is his bodily characteristics and experience, which are known to affect "our understanding of balanced personalities, balanced views, balanced systems, balanced equations, the balance of power, the balance of justice, and so on."[84] For example, Franklin D. Roosevelt's physical disability and suffering have lately been acknowledged as far more important to his view of the world and political behavior than was previously recognized.[85]

Yeltsin's physical prowess has been so extraordinary throughout his life that one cannot ignore it without missing a crucial link between his mentality and his operational style. In fact, his robust health, remarkable athleticism, and utterly reckless attitude toward physical danger in a way mirror his political style.

Yeltsin is tall (6'2") and strongly built. He likes swimming and has swum in the icy waters of a Siberian river just to demonstrate to a group of coal miners that he was not corrupted by the soft life in the Politburo;[86] he has also "taken a dip" in the 45-50 degree water of the Black Sea in March[87] because he likes the shocking sensation of icy water.[88] Throughout his life Yeltsin has maintained the habit of starting the day with a cold shower.[89] Until recently, he played tennis twice a week, even in bad weather, and daily during vacation.[90]

A little known but significant fact about Yeltsin's life is that he has grown potatoes for his family's consumption all his life, even after becoming president of Russia.[91] Once he became director of a major enterprise there was obviously no economic need for him to do so. Potato gathering is a tough physical job, often requiring hefting 120-pound sacks of potatoes. Why would a 62-year-old man voluntarily engage in such labor? He explained simply that it was a habit. However, this unlikely habit must satisfy some important psychological need. It may enable Yeltsin to escape from incessant political struggle, to keep in touch with nature, or to satisfy his need to "constantly prove [his] physical strength."[92] Whatever the answer, this habit shows how firmly Yeltsin's feet are planted on the ground.

Athletic Experience

Few analysts have noted the importance of volleyball in Yeltsin's life.[93] He has played volleyball since his teenage years, playing in the top professional league when he was a student in the Polytechnic institute. It is noteworthy that he did so despite missing two fingers on his left hand, which he lost while handling a grenade as a teenager. One has to be extraordinarily persistent in pursuit of excellence to overcome such a handicap and be competitive in the top professional ranks.

A volleyball player at this level must not only be a strong person with excellent physical coordination; he must also react exceptionally quickly, because of the speed the ball travels and the limited size of the court. To play professional volleyball one must keep track of twelve fast-moving people and a ball simultaneously; one learns to orient oneself quickly in a fluid environment. A good volleyball player also develops an aptitude and taste for highly coordinated, synchronized teamwork. Finally, volleyball is a game in which ties do not exist. One can only win or lose in volleyball, not accidentally, as Yeltsin admitted, in politics he also always plays to win.[94]

Yeltsin's exceptional athletic talents have not diminished as he has aged. In 1988 he started to learn to play tennis; by his sixtieth birthday he had become a good player with a powerful serve.[95] His coach noted that Yeltsin always plays best when he is behind.[96] "When we are losing, Yeltsin does not make any mistakes," his regular partner said.[97]

In politics, too, he has done best in highly critical situations, because of his propensity to mobilize his resources when losing.

Health

Rumors about Yeltsin's failing health have circulated in the Russian and Western media since 1987.[98] In addition, political observers and journalists have continuously speculated about his reported drinking problem.[99] In the words of Richard Nixon, such rumors always "make fascinating theater and newspaper copy;"[100] however, Yeltsin has himself contributed to these speculations by suddenly canceling meetings with foreign dignitaries, changing his schedules abruptly, and from time to time disappearing from sight.

Yeltsin has never taken these rumors seriously, refusing to discuss them. Once, irritated by the persistent rumors, he forcefully stressed: "I wish every person could be as healthy as I am at my age. Can someone who constantly plays tennis very hard for an hour and a half at a time (mind you, playing against honored masters of sports;) and swims in the Black Sea in March . . . be in poor health? [I am} someone who works 16-18 hours a day, virtually without days off. You have got to envy me!"[101]

The truth appears to reside in the middle. Yeltsin, as does any 64-year-old has the usual health problems. He has a slipped disk in his lower back[102] for which he has undergone surgery.[103] He has also had several other operations: for "some intestinal ailment"[104] and on his middle ear.[105] He has been involved in a car accident[106] and once had a bad case of pneumonia.[107] Yet all the evidence (including examinations by Russian and Western doctors) shows that his physical health is good.[108] On the other hand, since the age of 19, he has had valvular insufficiency (a heart condition) and lately he has acquired ischemia (a partial coronary blockage) which resulted in two mild heart attacks in 1995. Still, his heart condition and migraine headaches are related more to his stressful life rather than to the inherent physical problems. Sometimes his mercilessness toward his body backfires, resulting in nervous exhaustion.[109] "He is an animated person," prone to "letting his emotions pour out"[110] or taking too many drinks during social gatherings; but contrary to a popular contention, he does not indulge periodically in bouts of heavy drinking.

All these problems notwithstanding, Yeltsin has been endowed with good health. His health problems stem from his reckless attitude toward his body. All his life, he has behaved like a person who does not know the limits of his body's abilities.[111] In the words of his brother Mikhail, "he always lived on the edge of possibilities,"[112] as if experimenting with his body by putting himself in difficult and sometimes impossible situations.[113] He enjoys challenging his and others' capacities to handle risks.[114] He is extremely competitive, as he has admitted.[115] Many observers and Yeltsin's associates unanimously confirm that he has extraordinary energy and "enormous capacity for work,"[116] that "his daily schedule would make a normal man collapse,"[117] and that "very few people are blessed with his ability to withstand such a level of effort."[118] In the process, he often overexerts himself.

This may eventually endanger his health, if he does not to observe the limits imposed by natural biological processes.[119]

In sum, Yeltsin's overall physical fitness has shaped his bold political style. His tendency to push his body to the limit, extremely high energy level, athletic achievements, admiration for strength, and need for action—all shaped his self confidence, which borders on arrogance.

Curiosity, Information Processing, and Learning Capacities

Our potential for change seems to be defined by our level of curiosity and our information-processing capacity, as well as our ability to absorb new facts and concepts. An examination of this aspect of Yeltsin's personality is crucial for understanding both his past and his likely future evolution.

Yeltsin has displayed unusual curiosity all his life. As a teenager he attempted to find out how a grenade worked and blew off two fingers. When he was nineteen, he undertook a grueling and dangerous three-month-long journey across the huge expanse of Russia, without money, on the roofs of rail cars.[120]

Later in life, while in Moscow, Yeltsin demonstrated a similar hunger for new ideas and people. Unlike Gorbachev, he did not betray an instinctive need to dominate meetings by speaking constantly. On the contrary, he preferred to listen and absorb information.[121] When he came to the United States, his eagerness to learn as much as possible was remarkable. Driven by the insatiable desire to learn as much about America as he could, he decided to reduce his normal four to five hours of sleep per night to two hours.[122]

Yeltsin processes an enormous volume of information. Remembering the experience of Gorbachev, who fell victim to one-sided information fed to him by the KGB,[123] Yeltsin has made sure to receive information from as many alternative sources as possible. He has referred to fourteen different sources upon which he has relied. Moreover, he has deliberately made it known to each source that it was competing with others.[124] In this way he eliminates incentives to skew the information that they provide.[125] In addition to news summaries and executive briefings prepared by the Center for Prompt Information and other agencies, he receives about two thousand letters[126] daily and reads between ten to twelve newspapers each day.[127] He is surely one of the best informed persons in the country.

In short, Yeltsin's curiosity about new information and ideas is and has always been remarkable. It is backed by an extraordinary capacity for information processing and an excellent memory.[128]

Yeltsin's Value System

Yeltsin has stated that three historic personalities have inspired him most of all: Andrei Sakharov, a true democrat and a beacon of morality; Margaret Thatcher, a willful and decisive politician, and Peter the Great, "who has done more for Russia than anybody."[129] This statement, coupled with Yeltsin's amazingly honest self-assessments and the judgments of others (with which his books abound) allows us to reconstruct his value system with a high degree of certainty.

In Yeltsin's value system, one quality appears to be paramount: strength. It overshadows any other human quality. He regards all the other qualities that he values honesty, energy, courage, dependability, reliability, straightforwardness, and a principled mode of conduct (*printsypialnost*)[130] as derivatives of strength. In his eyes, only a strong man can afford to have these qualities. Accordingly, he despises duplicity, weakness, and cowardice. He disparaged Gorbachev both "as a former politician and as a human being"[131] for his weakness, for which, Yeltsin thought, Gorbachev tried to compensate with cunning and waffling.

Curiously, although Yeltsin is compassionate, he has never praised kindness in other people. One can speculate that, for him, kindness is not a primary quality. In his mind, a strong, honest, and conscientious person is automatically kind. Finally, he likes to surround himself with optimistic people who generate a *joie de vivre* around them[132] and feels uncomfortable with people who have negative attitudes, particularly those whose suspicion borders on paranoia.[133]

Yeltsin's honesty and integrity have been recognized by both friend and foe. People as different as Adam Michnik, the Polish philosopher,[134] Aleksandr Solzhenitsyn[135] and Richard Nixon[136] have testified to this. But the best evidence of his honesty and integrity can be found in Yeltsin's books, particularly the second one. In the words of a journalist, Yeltsin is too big and too strong for hypocrisy, duplicity, or vanity.[137] For the same reason he is totally indifferent toward money; he has no need or desire for this form of power.

How Yeltsin Projects His Image

A person's mentality and value system are reflected in the ideal image of himself that he would like to project to others. That image hinges on one's assumptions about national psychology, society's needs, and what it admires in and expects of a leader.

Yeltsin "is not lacking in acting ability," one veteran television producer has noted.[138] However, as Burbulis put it, Yeltsin does not so much act as live his roles, and "he is his own script writer, stage director, and performer."[139] For this reason, all the attempts of his close associates to modify his image have failed.[140]

Many of his aides and supporters have criticized Yeltsin for appearing on television too infrequently.[141] Yeltsin has admitted that he does not like the way he looks on television,[142] but this is not the reason for the infrequency of his television appearances. On the contrary, he made the conscious decision to appear on television "only when he felt he had something very important to say."[143]

Yeltsin has been fully aware of the power of the media since Gorbachev initiated his policy of *glasnost*. After the nineteenth party conference in 1988, which was televised, Yeltsin realized that popular support could be translated into political power. It was at his insistence that the first Congress of People's Deputies in May 1989 was broadcast live on television.

He was also keenly aware of the crucial importance of projecting one's image correctly. Yeltsin believes that the Russian *narod* will not respect an authority figure who is too familiar or accessible. In his mind, politicians who talk too much are trying to compensate for their inner weakness and, sooner or later, will lose the respect of the people, as did Khrushchev and Gorbachev.[144] Anatoly Lysenko summed up Yeltsin's attitude in this way: he "does not care about pleasing anyone, but he is afraid of not appearing serious enough in front of the people."[145]

Yeltsin's various images have naturally changed as his social roles have changed. However, they have also reflected the genuine facets of his personality.

During his relatively brief struggle with the Soviet regime, Yeltsin wished to project the image of a Russian folk hero who "doesn't burn and bites the bullet," who manages to escape from any predicament unscathed because he is strong and enjoys heavenly protection. According to Josef Dzialoshynski, president of the Russian Institute of the Press and Mass Media, this image fits Russian folk mythology, which holds in popular affection three types of characters: the knight, saint, and entrepreneur (*delovoi chelovek*).[146] Yeltsin's personality, according to Dzialoshynski, ideally fits the image of a knight: a strong, bold *narodny zastupnik* (defender of the poor), a Russian version of Robin Hood, who can single-handedly confront the establishment and win.[147]

Later, after Yeltsin embarked on the task of putting Russia's house in order, he began to project the image of the master of the house who guarantees order, stability, and prosperity. He said that he did not like the way the media had portrayed him as "a hard-boiled, tough and rigid man";[148] instead he preferred to be seen as a "willful, decisive, tough politician."[149]

When Yeltsin addresses the Russian people, he deliberately speaks slowly, in a low and measured voice. He believes that by projecting strength and confidence he can instill the sense of security and stability that he believes the Russian people need most of all. For this reason, in December 1991 he made the decision to move from the White House into the Kremlin, which is associated in people's minds with "stability, duration and lasting reforms."[150] The highly unflattering photograph on the cover of the Russian-language edition of his second book was also meant to convey an image of strength. It was taken on the heels of the Supreme Soviet's uprising of October 1993. With the Kremlin in the background, he is pointing his finger like Uncle Sam, with an angry expression on his face. He seems to chastise Russia's enemies for their attempts to destabilize the country and wishes to assure the people that he will not allow them to succeed. In general, while in 1991 he appeared as "our lovable hero," he now often appears as a demanding leader. It seems that he cares less about being loved than being respected.

Abroad, Yeltsin also projects power and reliability. But he adds what he thinks the Western democratic mentality appreciates: the quick wits, optimism, sociability, and innovativeness of a creative statesman.[151] As one Russian observer wrote, during his summit with President Clinton, Yeltsin "was energetic, lively, and relaxed in his dealings with his audience. Unlike Clinton, who smiled more than he told jokes, Yeltsin made broad use of irony and sarcasm."[152] This behavior comes to Yeltsin naturally, because he does not like to stick to a script too closely.[153] Instead, he likes to improvise and surprise his audience.[154] This behavior delights the media but often creates anxiety and uneasiness in the regimented world of diplomacy and statecraft, giving the impression that Yeltsin is unpredictable and unreliable.

Temperament: Self-Confident, Aggressive, and Adventurous

During his entire adult life, Yeltsin has slept only four to five hours per day, and yet he has never had enough time. He is locked in a perpetual race against time, and the phrase "So many things must be done!" has been his life's refrain. His eagerness to see results is a source of his perpetual dissatisfaction with himself. His definition of happiness is synonymous with a sense of accomplishment.[155] However, his impatience goes hand in hand with the rare stubbornness of someone who would not quit, no matter what.

Yeltsin's temperament would be classified by psychologists as self-confident, adventurous, and aggressive.[156] Adventurous and self-confident types hate routine and drudgery. They like spontaneous improvisations in which they can rely on their wits and ingenuity. This description fits Yeltsin, who is recognized as a "talented improvisor who likes to stun the audience, puzzle his partners and aides, and only then elaborate his concept."[157] Furthermore, according to John M. Oldham and Lois B. Morris, a typical aggressive type thrives on competition and "competes with the supreme confidence of a champion."[158] This describes Yeltsin too, although his aggressive behavior is not directed against other people. It does not stem from a need for confrontation, as some have argued,[159] but from a need for action and accomplishment, a need to reaffirm his power and maintain mastery of events.[160]

In my view, Yeltsin's relentless drive and preemptive operational style are another side of his fear of being overtaken by events and enemies. This is reflected in the nature of his worst nightmares, which involve the sensation of being trapped in situations and powerless to get out.[161] When he feels trapped in real life, his solution is to resort to "sharp actions."[162]

Finally, there is an evident paradox between Yeltsin's bearish physical appearance and his soft, almost delicate inner constitution, as some analysts have noted.[163] As his books make abundantly clear, on the one hand, he is superbly confident and aggressive, but on the other hand, he is tormented by self-doubts, by the "terrible premonition of being doomed."[164] He often experiences "exhausting bouts of depression, sleepless nights accompanied by headaches, desperation, and bitterness."[165] These are typical syndromes, according to Ernest Hartman, of "persons with thin boundaries" who are unusually open because they are strong and confident. As a result, however, they are also vulnerable to attack. They are easily hurt, because they tend to take conflicts too personally. Consequently, they suffer from migraine headaches, sleepless nights, and nightmares.[166] Indeed, as a self-confident type, Yeltsin feels that he is strong enough to openly discuss his ambitions, weaknesses and mistakes.[167] By opening himself to others, he invites them to examine his intimate world, as if he were looking for help understanding his persona. Naturally, too often he is unintentionally or deliberately hurt.

After having experienced this many times, Yeltsin has begun to learn to guard his inner world more closely. He admitted in his last book that, regrettably, he has become more reclusive and reluctant to let others into his inner sanctum.[168]

Yeltsin's Operational Style

A politician's actions are the most visible aspect of his political behavior. When a political actor's decisions directly or indirectly affect the lives of tens of millions of people, an objective analysis of his operational style becomes exceedingly difficult. Yeltsin's operational style has been the subject of so many myths, controversies, and misunderstandings that to address all of them would require a separate study. His operational style can be deduced from his mentality, personality, and ethical system, which we described earlier.

In assessing a political actor's behavior, one has to clearly discriminate between two processes: decision making and implementation. One involves mental processes and information and therefore one's sociopolitical mentality; the other, physical action, which involves energy. The decision-making process involves the choice among various means, which is dependent on an actor's ethical system; the actor's temperamental type and level of energy are reflected in his implementation of decisions.

In the case of Yeltsin, it seems justified to conclude that he possesses a technocratic and democratic mentality, on the one hand, but also the style of a leader and a hero. As a technocrat and democrat, Yeltsin is receptive to different views, while as a long-time leader and heroic personality type, he has a propensity to employ authoritarian and forceful means.

Decision-making Style

Despite Yeltsin's repeated claims that he personally makes "all cardinal decisions,"[169] his many critics are enamored of the theory that he is constantly influenced and even manipulated by different people. Yeltsin's close friends, aides, and associates vehemently dispute this theory, insisting that the "president is not swayed by particular individuals."[170] They note, though, that one can argue with Yeltsin and even persuade him,[171] that "he will listen, sift it all through his mind and do it in his own, characteristic way."[172] Oleg Lobov stated that "he prefers to obtain information from different sources, but to make decisions independently. It is no accident that these decisions are sometimes unpredictable."[173] "He observes the balance of forces in his entourage, not allowing anyone even among his closest assistants to completely control him."[174] Our analysis of Yeltsin's information-processing style corroborates the comments made by Yeltsin's associates.

He is simply too well informed to be manipulated by an aide or a body-guard.

It is true, however, that on a number of occasions Yeltsin has changed his decisions repeatedly which has been interpreted by some as evidence of outside influences. One such case involved the activities of Western banks in Russia. Russian banks were asking for two years of protection from foreign competition in order to allow them time to gain the strength and expertise needed to compete with their powerful Western counterparts. On the other hand, the overall philosophy of opening Russia to world financial markets and introducing competition required that Western banks have free access to the Russian market. In July 1993 Yeltsin opposed the Supreme Soviet's decision to impose such limits. On November 17, 1993, however, under the influence of Fedorov and Gaidar, he introduced some restrictions on the operations of Western banks. Finally, he eased them in June 1994 under the influence of Gerashchenko[175] and again in May 1995, at the recommendation of Aleksandr Livshits.[176] Similar policy changes occurred in the process of privatization. However, in these instances the issues were extremely complex, requiring technical expertise exceeding Yeltsin's own, while expert opinions were split. In such cases Yeltsin chooses to take decisions and, if needed, to amend or even reverse them later. He also readily delegates the power of decision making and does not indulge in "petty tutelage," as many of his associates have testified.[177]

During his tenure as party leader in Sverdlovsk and in Moscow, Yeltsin clearly showed a penchant for populism. Many of his actions were aimed at gaining popularity. This can easily be explained by his need to be admired. For more than a decade, his populism served no practical purpose; only later did it begin to bring him unexpected dividends. After Yeltsin became president, however, all traces of populism have disappeared; in the words of an American observer, his "major political decisions were fully consistent with his beliefs,"[178] even if they were unpopular. And Yeltsin has made many unpopular decisions.[179]

Nor does Yeltsin's mingling with crowds support the thesis that he is a populist. He genuinely desires to probe people's sentiments, not to gain publicity.[180] His contacts with crowds have kept Yeltsin in touch with "the movements of Russian history," as one analyst wrote,[181] by assessing the mood and hopes of the people first-hand.

Many intellectuals, both bitter critics and ardent supporters of Yeltsin, have criticized him for neglecting to fashion a long-term strategy,[182] for tending to "oversimplify the situation and reduce it to a dichotomy of friends

versus enemies,"[183] and for preferring "straightforward, single-move decisions rather than multi-move combinations and stages."[184] And yet they
admit that Yeltsin has had "devilish intuition. Sometimes he made willful
decisions that we thought were crazy, yet he turned out to be right."[185]

Indeed, Yeltsin does not suffer from the intelligentsia's fatal conceit, the
propensity to construct elaborate strategies. Yeltsin explains: "Sometimes
more harm is done by excessive concentration on routine work, by endless
coordination, by the desire to take into account all nuances and shades of
opinions without exception."[186] As an aggressive type, Yeltsin likes taking
decisions, and does so easily and quickly.[187]

At the same time, Yeltsin prepares major decisions carefully. He never
signs documents without reading and correcting them, sometimes even catching misspellings or grammatical mistakes.[188] "He will check the text [of a
major speech] three or four times and make amendments, deleting some
things and adding others. He tells us which bits don't work and which parts
need to be developed and rewritten more emotionally,"[189] according to an
aide. His meticulous preparations for foreign trips involve reading about
the geography, people, and history of the country; learning its current political and economic situation; studying its leading politicians; and examining the documents that are to be discussed and signed. On a trip abroad he
may carry a suitcase full of documents to study.[190]

Style of Action

Once Yeltsin has made a decision, he is not tormented by doubts or
second thoughts.[191] Instead he focuses on the implementation of his decision and tends to attack the problem head on. As an experienced leader, he
knows how to put an end to a discussion and issue an order: "I told them:
Just do what I'm saying! And left without saying good-bye."[192]

Yeltsin's major operational flaw and the main source of his errors lie in
his tendency to be overly optimistic about how quickly things can be achieved.
He is prone, for example, to create a group and assign it to investigate an
alleged financial plot in three days. He appears to have seriously miscalcu-
lated how long it might take to "clear the territory of Chechnia of illegal
bandit formations." However, when his miscalculation has been revealed,
Yeltsin is able to adjust his timetable, bring in additional resources, improvise, and stubbornly see the problem through to a conclusion. Then he
takes a respite, selects another problem, studies it, chooses a team of different people, and launches an attack on it.

Yeltsin can also be reproached for his tendency to disregard the cost of achieving a goal, both to himself and others.[193] He prefers to finish a job and repair the damage later. Yet this ability to focus all his attention and energy is what has made "Yeltsin so impressive in dramatic situations."[194]

Conclusion

On the surface, Yeltsin's mentality and style of action seem incompatible. As Yeltsin's adviser Satarov noted: "Unfortunately, Yeltsin is mixing the style of a volleyball player with that of a chess player."[195] However, it is precisely this ability to combine the style of a chess master when making decisions with the style of a volleyball player in implementing them that has made Yeltsin's operational style so effective. The next chapter will review the major engagements on the political battlefield that Yeltsin has waged and won.

If Yeltsin's operational style had been more orderly, punctilious, and scrupulously attentive to details, he would not have been so effective in the extraordinary circumstances of the second Russian revolution.[196] In this respect the contrast with Gorbachev is most illuminating. Gorbachev's operational style was almost diametrically opposed to that of Yeltsin. First of all, he was difficult to persuade. As he admitted: "I'm capable of self-analysis, but so far I haven't heard any arguments that make me want to change my position."[197] Second, he loved the exploratory stage of decision making, and instinctively shied away from the responsibility of making a final decision. His motto was to "be bold and decisive, yet balanced and careful."[198] In practice, this operational style resulted in bold ideas but flawed semi-decisions: endless discussions and wobbly execution.

As Richard Nixon wrote, "Yeltsin cannot be judged as if he were the president of a stable democracy with an established constitutional order."[199] In the extraordinary environment of the revolution and transition, Yeltsin's operational style has been effective.

But Yeltsin's operational style may become a major problem if Russia achieves a stable environment and a fully functional and effective democratic system. The operational style of a political actor tends not to change easily. Will Yeltsin's operational style be able to change enough to adapt to the more stable and orderly environment of the new Russia that he has worked so hard to build? This question will be examined after we reflect on what has happened to Russia and its society since the revolution.

CHAPTER 4

THE STRUGGLE
FOR A DEMOCRATIC RUSSIA

Overview of the Struggle: 1989 - 1991

The collapse of the Soviet totalitarian system began on March 26, 1989, when the first multi-candidate elections in more than seventy years, for the Congress of People's Deputies of the Soviet Union, were held.[1] Many representatives of the intelligentsia were elected, while hundreds of *partocrats* and *apparatchiks*, including 38 *obkom* secretaries, were defeated—even dozens who ran unopposed.[2] Although the elections did little to change the formal structure of power, they became a referendum on the party; and this marked the beginning of the end of totalitarianism in the USSR.

Then, in May-June of 1989, during the First Congress of People's Deputies, the entire Soviet Union came to a halt: for two weeks everyone was glued to television sets watching the fascinating spectacle of the Communist Party's legacy being publicly demolished. The bankruptcy of the ideology of communism, which had been revealed during three years of *glasnost*, was now officially confirmed from the highest political rostrum of the nation. One people's deputy after another exposed the horrible state of affairs in the country. The principal point of criticism was the miserable and humiliating living conditions of workers and peasants on whose behalf the party was allegedly ruling, on the one hand; and the appalling degradation and corruption among the *nomenklatura*, on the other. As several particularly courageous deputies, Yeltsin among them, pointed out, this flagrantly unfair system was upheld by a monstrous apparatus of repression. Yeltsin pointed out that the KGB had such enormous power that it could shape society.[3] The deputies demanded a drastic overhaul of this "state within the state," placing it under the control of the Supreme Soviet and curbing the power of the party. This last demand was expressed in Andrei Sakharov's proposal to eliminate article six from the Soviet Union's constitution, which asserted the Communist Party's sole prerogative to rule.

After the congress, the country changed. A poll by the highly respected sociologist Tatiana Zaslavskaia determined that only 10 to 20 percent of the population supported socialism, and 48 percent wanted to adopt the best features of capitalism.[4] Perhaps the most important result of the first Congress of People's Deputies was the dissipation of people's fear of the regime, particularly when no massive repressions followed the congress. The following year, 1.8 million people left the CPSU,[5] and millions of others suspended their membership. A wave of strikes, demonstrations, rallies, terrorist attacks, and ethnic conflicts began to sweep the Soviet Union.

In the fall of 1989 a short and mostly bloodless anti-Communist revolution occurred in six East European nations. For the highly integrated economic system of the communist bloc, the loss of these territories, with a combined population of 113 million people, was a serious economic blow. But the main impact of the revolution in Eastern Europe was political and psychological. It demonstrated that the totalitarian system was not immortal and that liberation was possible. This gave a powerful impulse to liberation movements in the Soviet republics, particularly in the Baltics.

Many analysts were surprised that under Yeltsin's leadership Russia displayed little desire to maintain its empire at any cost. The Russian people were indifferent and even sympathetic toward other peoples' quests for liberation from communism. Moreover, Russia soon became the leader of the anti communist movement in the USSR. During 1990 to 1991 when Gorbachev attempted to stymie the drive for independence in various republics, first by an economic blockade and then by force, the Russian parliament protested. On February 19, 1991, in a television address, Yeltsin demanded Gorbachev's resignation; soon he went to the Baltic republics to personally express Russia's solidarity with and support for them. Russia helped to breach the economic embargo imposed by Gorbachev's regime on the Balts by delivering energy and other commodities to them. The principal motivation behind Russia's stance was its people's own desire for liberation from communism; hence they looked favorably upon any movement or discord that weakened the totalitarian system.

In the spring of 1990 elections to the Congress of People's Deputies of Russia and to the municipal governments created a new political situation. Democrats won about 35 percent of the seats to the Congress[6] and a majority of seats in local governments in such major industrial and cultural centers as Moscow, Leningrad, Sverdlovsk, Volgograd, Gorki, Kuibushev, Donetsk, and Lvov. Two months later Boris Yeltsin became the Chairman of the Supreme Soviet of the Russian Federation. June 12, 1990, when, by an overwhelming majority of votes, the Congress of People's Deputies of Russia declared Russia a sovereign state, can be considered the day when the demise of the Soviet Union became inevitable. In July 1990 Yeltsin demonstratively left the Communist Party and declared the goal of building a democratic, free-market Russia.

The Yeltsin-led Russian parliament then began a systematic attack on the institutions of the communist regime. The Russian Supreme Soviet soon announced its intention to form a Russian security service,[7] and it passed a law making a citizen's cooperation with the all-union KGB a criminal offense.[8] In December 1990 the Supreme Soviet of Russia cut Russia's contribution to the federal budget by 80 percent. Because Russian payments came to about 70 percent of the Soviet Union's budget, this step seriously undercut the financial base of the Soviet system. The passing of a law on the press led to the emergence of democratic newspapers and radio stations. A Russian Ministry of Foreign Affairs was created, and the young democrat Andrei Kozyrev became its minister. In May 1991 the creation of the Russian KGB was announced.[9]

On June 12, 1991, Yeltsin received 71.5 percent of the votes and became the first popularly elected president and head of state of the Russian Federation. The Soviet Union was scheduled officially to cease to exist on August 20, 1991, when the Union Treaty was to be signed by the presidents of nine former republics and Gorbachev. It was nicknamed the "nine-plus-one treaty." This formula emphasized Gorbachev's agreement to become a largely nominal head of a loose confederation of nine independent states.

Days after Yeltsin's presidential inauguration on July 10, the Russian State Council was formed, and Gennadi Burbulis became Secretary of State with the power to supervise the formation of the RSFSR Foreign Ministry, Interior Ministry, and KGB.[10] Yeltsin and his allies intensified attacks on the center, chipping away its power, piece by piece. They brought the Russian coal industry under their jurisdiction and were planning to do the same with defense factories. Yeltsin issued a decree outlawing party cells in the KGB, armed forces, and police and state enterprises in the RSFSR.[11] He demanded veto power over decisions involving strategic nuclear forces. He began to build his administrative structure by appointing representatives in the provinces with a mandate to see that his decisions were implemented. Thus Yeltsin and Burbulis moved to circumvent the power of the soviets and the party both in the center and in the provinces. Various initiatives by the Russian government followed in rapid succession, giving the center not a day of respite. The slow, utterly bureaucratized machinery of the communist regime was constantly facing *faits accomplis* to which it could not respond promptly and adequately.

At this point, only very drastic repressive measures, such as the imposition of emergency rule, could have saved the Soviet Union. However, Gorbachev had just reached the pinnacle of his international fame as a liberal and almost a democratic leader. In June 1991, he attended the G-7 summit in London, to which he was invited as an honored guest, and he managed to place himself at center stage during the meeting of the leaders of the major democracies of the world. He was voted the "Man of the Decade" by *Time* magazine and was a serious candidate for the Nobel Peace Prize. Politically and psychologically, it was impossible for him to take drastic coercive measures and thus to turn himself into a Russian Pinochet. In addition, Yeltsin persuaded him that he did not covet Gorbachev's job and that the post of the head of the Union of Sovereign States would be reserved for Gorbachev.

The top Soviet leadership, however, had everything to lose were the Soviet Union to become a confederation of nine states. For several months the leadership urged Gorbachev to prevent the looming destruction of the USSR by introducing a state of emergency and rule by martial law. The leadership drew its inspiration from the successful imposition of martial law in Poland in December of 1981, which managed to delay the collapse of the communist regime there by eight years. When the putschists' emissaries journeyed to Gorbachev's summer resort in an eleventh-hour attempt to persuade him to declare a state of emergency, Gorbachev's position was utterly confusing. He reportedly shouted at them and called their plans to use the army idiotic. They then suggested that he would feign illness, so that Vice President Gennadi Yanayev could temporarily assume power. He rejected this plan, too, out of fear that his close associates might try to get rid of him. At the same time he hinted that he might join them if they managed to pull off the crackdown on their own.

This evasive and confusing behavior by Gorbachev condemned the coup to failure. Unlike General Woyciech Yaruzelski in 1981, Gorbachev could not force himself to initiate a crackdown. Neither could he abdicate his power in favor of the vice president even temporarily. He chose a "wait-and-see" policy and undertook no attempts to actively intervene in events as they unfolded.

The conspirators were left without a legitimate leader and no one among these party *apparatchiks* was capable of assuming such a role. Furthermore, Gorbachev's evasiveness confused them and fatally crippled their plans. Instead of openly deposing Gorbachev, they pronounced him temporarily incapacitated by illness, yet they failed to present any evidence that he was ill. They claimed that Gorbachev was with them and would soon return to his duties, yet they could not provide any proof, such as a statement by him endorsing the imposition of a state of emergency. Moreover, unsure of his further actions, they had to limit his lines of communications. Thus, against their original intentions, the declaration of emergency turned into an attempted *coup d'etat* against the legitimate president and the General Secretary of the CPSU. The formerly legitimate top government officials had now become putschists.

As obedient *apparatchiks*, they were afraid to use violence in Moscow without the sanction of the president and general secretary. Instead they hoped to achieve their goal by relying on the people's inherent fear of the regime. They chose a show of force and intimidation rather than a swift and decisive crackdown. The army was not initially provided with live munitions and was reluctant to roll its tanks over unarmed civilians. A number of army officers informed Yeltsin of their units' movements and delayed action. Even the KGB, which led the putsch, contained many who sympathized with Yeltsin, both secretly and openly. For example, they provided Yeltsin's team with a printing press to publish its leaflets.[12] Soon people realized that the putschists was using scare tactics rather than launching a bloody crackdown. The remnants of their fear of the repressive machine vanished. They did everything to prevent the tanks from moving toward the White House. When the KGB elite team, the alpha unit, was ordered to storm the White House, the men refused.

In contrast with the wobbly putschists, the democrats were enthusiastic and determined. They kept the initiative firmly in their hands and were always one or two steps ahead of their enemies. Boris Yeltsin was fearless, decisive, and uncompromising. He declared the putschists' actions criminal and, as the legitimately elected president of Russia, assumed the role of supreme commander of the Russian armed forces and security services. Many democratic leaders went to meet the advancing tank columns and urged their commanding officers to obey the orders of the president of Russia.

When the coup collapsed, its leaders did not flee the country but flew to Gorbachev to plead for forgiveness and protection. Instead they were arrested by Russian security forces, and two of them committed suicide. Gorbachev was thus "liberated" from his semi-voluntary exile in Foros.

Yeltsin was perfectly aware of Gorbachev's duplicitous game, but he kept this secret to himself[13] in exchange for Gorbachev's acquiescence to

Yeltsin's leadership. The humiliated Gorbachev was soon seen on the television screens of the world, humbly obeying Yeltsin in a meeting before the Russian Supreme Soviet.

Later, during their trial, the coup leaders had good reasons to accuse Gorbachev of betrayal and to blame him for their failure to prevent the collapse of communism. Indeed, had a more decisive and ruthless leader occupied Gorbachev's position, it would have been possible to crush the democrats and preserve the communist regime for another decade or so.

Consolidating Power

Yeltsin described the shock and bewilderment caused by the sudden collapse of the totalitarian regime in the following words: when we woke up on August 22, "we found ourselves in a completely different country;"[14] "a new era began, and hardly anybody knew what it would be."[15] Yeltsin and his comrades in arms were prepared for years of struggle against the totalitarian regime, only to see it falter and fold in three days.

In the aftermath of the putsch, the democrats were determined not to repeat the failure of the provisional government of Kerensky to consolidate power and secure the gains of the democratic revolution of February 1917.

The State Council of Russia quickly assumed a great deal of power by simple fiat. For two months, it became the de facto governing body of Russia. Its narrow circle of members allowed effective decision-making and expedient execution. Not only were the institutions of the Soviet Union paralyzed, but, in the words of one commentator, "there was little left for the [Russian] parliament to do."[16] On August 22, the State Council sealed the headquarters of the CPSU Central Committee and the KGB, in part to prevent mobs from ransacking the buildings and destroying the archives.

Thus the brain of the totalitarian organism was destroyed. Its body remained practically intact, however, although in a state of shock. The totalitarian leadership reckoned that its days were numbered and began to look for a way to reverse this situation. For many weeks following the putsch there was a real danger that the KGB's military units would take decisive action. Indeed, in September 1991 the media reported troop movements toward and around Moscow. When the issue was raised in the Supreme Soviet, the explanation was given that the troops were being brought in to harvest potatoes and prepare for the November 7 parade on Red Square. They then returned to their barracks.

The democrats' first priority was to dismantle, or at least to cripple, the backbone of the totalitarian regime, the KGB machine. Gorbachev's immediate impulse, however, was quite the opposite. He replaced the head of the

KGB, Vladimir Kriuchkov, who was in Lefortovo prison, with one of his deputies. Yeltsin, however, vetoed this decision and insisted on the appointment of Vadim Bakatin, a liberal and the respected former head of the Interior Ministry. Moreover, a democrat and a former associate of Andrei Sakharov, Yevgeni Sevastianov, was appointed to the critically important position of head of the Moscow branch of the KGB.[17] The democrats demanded that Bakatin be given a clear mandate to begin a radical reorganization of the KGB.[18] Indeed, Bakatin, with the advice of former KGB general and dissenter Oleg Kalugin, began to radically reform the organization. Many departments were turned over to the Russian KGB, some were disbanded, and the military units were transferred to other ministries, mostly to the Ministry of Defense. In October the KGB of the USSR ceased to exist altogether.

In the weeks following the putsch, Yeltsin and Burbulis took other measures to emasculate and dismantle the power of the center. On Yeltsin's demand, the Prosecutor General, who had supported the putsch, was dismissed. The USSR Supreme Soviet Committees for defense, security, and fighting crime were disbanded. The State Supply and Distribution Agency, Gossnab, critically important for maintaining centralized control of the economy, was abolished.[19] Of greatest importance, the functioning of the Russian Communist Party was suspended,[20] and on November 6, by the Russian president's decree, the Communist Party of the Soviet Union and the Communist Party of Russia were banned and ordered to dissolve their organizational structures. Simultaneously, Yeltsin's regime was transferring such powerful institutions as the Federal State Bank, the Finance Ministry, and the Customs Committee to the jurisdiction of Russia.[21] In August 1991 about 80 percent of the 88 provincial governments, the soviets, supported the putschists.[22] So to consolidate his control over the provinces, Yeltsin appointed personal plenipotentiaries and, wherever possible, heads of local administrations who were loyal to him.

Thus in three months Yeltsin and his associates managed to consolidate their power and effectively end the existence of the Soviet Union. The "time had come for the most decisive actions not only in politics but also in the economy."[23] The transformation of Russia into a "normal state" became Yeltsin's priority; it was a totally different task of enormous dimensions.

Yeltsin, Burbulis, and the Liberal Democrats

Westerners have greatly underestimated the role that Gennadi Burbulis played in the second Russian revolution. In contrast, some Russian analysts have viewed the union between Yeltsin and Burbulis as the most significant event of the second Russian revolution,[24] because it symbolized a compromise between the reform-minded *apparatchiks* and the most liberal-minded and constructive part of the intelligentsia.[25] For several years Burbulis was the second most powerful politician in Russia. He was the architect of the power structure of Russia during the first transitional years. Burbulis was, de facto, the first prime minister of post-communist Russia, and it was under his stewardship that the government of "Young Turks" transformed the economic system of Russia.

The alliance of Yeltsin and the radical democrats that Burbulis orchestrated predetermined the direction of the transformation of Russia, its speed and character, as well as the pains and setbacks that have occurred during the transition.

Yeltsin and the Intelligentsia

The first question that must be asked is why Yeltsin did not rely entirely on the powerful class of the intelligentsia, which had led the revolution.

Yeltsin's "relationship with the intelligentsia was at first very difficult," as he has admitted.[26] During his short tenure as Moscow party leader, the intellectual elite of Moscow considered him to be one of "them"—a *partocrat*,[27] a clumsy neo-Bolshevik.[28] They preferred a more intellectual member of the Politburo, Aleksandr Yakovlev, the godfather of *glasnost*, and the smooth and diplomatic Gorbachev.[29] After Yeltsin was expelled from the party Olympus and became the *narodny geroi* (people's hero), the intelligentsia snubbed him, labeling him as a demagogue and a populist who was good only at inciting the masses against Gorbachev, while the latter was waging a noble and difficult struggle with the *partocrats* in the Politburo. However, the Interregional Group of Deputies brought Yeltsin and the intelligentsia together, and they discovered one another. The intellectual elite was particularly pleased that Yeltsin was eager to listen and learn from them.

However, at this time Yeltsin's sociopolitical mentality was quickly evolving in the direction of laissez-faire capitalism, while the intelligentsia, especially most literati, still cherished the idea of socialism with a human face,[30] or, at best, a Swedish style of social-democratic capitalism. They argued that "the *narod*, en masse, [was] not yet ready for the market,"[31] that people did not want to own land.[32] In fact, in 1990 only 35 percent of democrats favored unrestricted private ownership of land, while 57 percent opposed the right to sell land. Only 29 percent of them advocated the unlimited use of hired labor, while 47 percent were in favor of allowing only a limited number of hired employees.[33]

At the same time, Yeltsin's political views were evolving rapidly. In the fall of 1989 he had seemed to support Gorbachev's efforts to build "socialism with a human face," but only one year later, the draft of a new Russian constitution written by a Constitutional Commission headed by Yeltsin called on Russia to embrace Western-style democratic capitalism. The rapid change in Yeltsin's political beliefs can, to some extent, be attributed to the influence of Burbulis, as Yeltsin himself[34] and close associates have admitted.[35]

Gennadi Burbulis

Burbulis was born near Sverdlovsk (now Ekaterinburg) on August 4, 1945. Although his ancestors on his father's side were Lithuanians, Burbulis grew up in a Russian cultural atmosphere. He served three years in the Strategic Rocket Forces, graduated from Ural State University in Sverdlovsk, received a Ph. D. in philosophy and taught philosophy at local institutes until 1989, when he was elected a People's Deputy of the USSR. Although the scholarly interests of Burbulis were in the area of cognitive psychology —man's "interests and motivations and the nature of mental processes"[36] —he was not a typical academic, a closet theoretician. He always pursued his scholarly interests with an eye to their practical implications, exploring how they were connected to "problems of morality and politics," actual conditions, and the sociopolitical system.[37] As a cognitive psychologist, he diagnosed Soviet society as mentally, morally, and economically ill: "The insanity of [totalitarian] society was in the fact that the majority of the population had twisted perceptions of natural human values such as the motivation to work, the concept of honor, dignity, and morality; respect for knowledge and professional skills used to be turned upside down."[38] In Burbulis' view, society needed a drastic cure, and he sought it in the liberation of the creative potential of people which, in his mind, far outweighed their evil inclinations. He was convinced that "everyone must acquire a sense of economic freedom, freedom to shape his own life," and that society as a whole would benefit from this.[39]

Burbulis also proved to be a uniquely talented organizer. The list of his organizational achievements is perhaps longer than that of anyone else in Russia, with the exception of Yeltsin himself. He has organized discussion clubs, political parties, movements, election campaigns, paramilitary organizations, councils, and ministries. In 1988 he organized and led the Discussion Tribune, one of the first democratic forums in Sverdlovsk and an extremely popular one.[40] In May 1990 Burbulis was one of the organizers and co-chairmen of the Democratic Party of Russia,[41] which nominated Yeltsin to be president of Russia. Burbulis helped Yeltsin win the post of

Chairman of the Supreme Soviet of Russia and became his personal representative in Sverdlovsk *oblast*. The next year, Burbulis managed Yeltsin's victorious presidential campaign.[42]

Burbulis' rare combination of theoretical and practical skills suddenly received "the rarest opportunity—to be able to materialize into reality what [he] knew and had thought through."[43]

Yeltsin and Burbulis

Yeltsin and Burbulis have as different personalities as two people can have. One is a philosopher and an organizer. The other is a builder, a former party leader, *narodny zastupnik* (defender of the *narod*) and an experienced political fighter. One speaks of kindness, beauty, harmony, creativity, freedom, and spirituality.[44] The other's speech is laconic, straightforward, full of concrete, practical ideas and such words as strength, struggle, and so on.

However, Yeltsin and Burbulis have much in common as well. To start with, both are from Sverdlovsk. The Sverdlovsk province differs from Moscow as much as the Rocky Mountains region differs from the East Coast. Sverdlovsk was arguably the least corrupt province of Russia.[45] Its remoteness, severe climate, majestic landscape, and the natural riches of the land had, for centuries, attracted a certain human type: strong survivors yet romantics, spiritually independent, pragmatic idealists. This natural selection was compounded by the effects of the exile of many rebels and nonconformists to the Urals under both tsars and communists.

Both Yeltsin and Burbulis are physically strong and fit. Both were professional-level athletes and have remained devoted to sports their entire lives.[46] Yeltsin carried a sick and starving friend when they were lost in the mountains; Burbulis jumped into the icy waters of the Baltic sea to save people thrown into the water after an explosion on a yacht.[47] Both are ambitious, strong-willed, and aggressive personality types.

Although Yeltsin and Burbulis had never met, until March 1989, when they did meet, they felt an affinity as fellow provincials struggling to establish themselves in one of the largest metropolises of the world, the cultural and political center of an empire. In the Interregional Group, both were initially overshadowed by such outspoken superstars as Andrei Sakharov, Anatoli Sobchak, Gavriil Popov, Yuri Afanasiev, Galina Starovoitova, and others. They did not speak out much but they absorbed a lot, and they talked to each other. While most intellectuals were skeptical of Yeltsin, Burbulis recognized the tremendous political potential in Yeltsin's operational style, enormous energy, and firm resolve. He was the first to realize what a powerful opponent of the totalitarian regime Yeltsin could be.[48]

Burbulis persuaded Yeltsin to run for the Congress of People's Deputies of Russia. The idea of building his power base in Russia, rather then trying to compete with Gorbachev at the all-Union level, was very bold. At the time the republics' supreme soviets were not taken seriously, because of their traditionally decorative status. To most prominent politicians, provincial politics was a stagnant backwater. Yet Burbulis and Yeltsin sensed that the advent of multi-candidate elections provided the opportunity to turn this heretofore moribund institution into a real power base for the democrats. Indeed, the democrats captured a much greater share of seats in the Russian parliament than they did in the USSR Congress of People's Deputies, causing it to look very democratic when compared to the USSR Supreme Soviet.

Burbulis was a visionary who, in the words of a cabinet member, was "perhaps the only [member of the government] who possessed a vision of the future Russia."[49] As early as the spring of 1991 Burbulis spoke of "building a society based on the laws of beauty, kindness, and freedom."[50] He argued that a perfect democracy had not been implemented completely anywhere; for this reason Russians "should not replicate existing systems." He stressed that only "radical economic, political, and cultural reforms" could lead to Russia's recovery from decades of grave illness, but he added that the methods pursued should be devoid of any violence or coercion.[51]

Burbulis quickly earned the reputation of being a political genius. He was equally good at the strategy and tactics of politics, which he regarded as "the highest form of creativity."[52] He demonstrated so much skill and ingenuity in subtle political intrigues that at some point he was thought to be behind every major political event in Russia.[53] He was called "the chief theorist of the destruction of the Soviet totalitarian system,"[54] the author of all the "victories of the democrats,"[55] and a true father of the reforms.[56]

These descriptions certainly exaggerate Burbulis' role; nevertheless, without any doubt, during the years of struggle with the totalitarian regime, Burbulis' political talents were absolutely crucial. Following June 1991, "every decision was taken at the level of Yeltsin and Burbulis."[57] During the August putsch, Burbulis' office in the Russian White House became the "sociopolitical headquarters" in which political aspects of the battle were determined.[58] Burbulis orchestrated the demise of the Soviet regime through the process of sovereignization of the republics. By 1992, in the words of one political observer, "Burbulis concentrated truly immense power in his hands."[59] He became the second most powerful politician in Russia; incidentally, he was the one who occupied Gorbachev's office in the Kremlin.

Choosing An Economic Program And Its Implementers

Yeltsin was ready to embrace the most radical and speedy reforms. However, choosing a specific program and the right people to implement it was not easy, as he admitted.[60] Discussions of economic reform had been going on for several years. There were, according to one analyst's calculation, eleven major economic reform programs,[61] and two dozen economists competed for the job of overseeing the process. Witnesses emphasized the chaos ensuing from the number of individuals and groups that surrounded Yeltsin in September 1991.[62] Contrary to popular belief, Yeltsin did not fall into a state of apathy when he went to Sochi for his now famous vacation in September 1991. Yeltsin purposefully absented himself from the crowd of contenders surrounding him and sought out the seclusion of the resort in order to make some of the most fateful decisions of his life: to choose an economic program and the people to run it.[63]

The aspirants for the job represented all the major elites: the industrialists, the *apparatchiks*, the technocrats, and the literati. Among them there were many household names, such as several members of the Presidential Council, which had been created specifically to advise Yeltsin on broad strategic questions.[64] There were economists in the cabinet of Prime Minister Ivan Silayev such as Yevgeni Saburov, and well-known economists who did not belong to the inner circle: academicians Stanislav Shatalin and Nikolai Petrakov, and the rising star Grigori Yavlinsky. Ruslan Khazbulatov, a defender of the White House who would eventually become a bitter enemy of Yeltsin, was also an economist.

However, as Alexei Golovkov, who was helping Burbulis review the candidates, noted, despite the great number of candidates, very few were qualified to undertake the job of reforming the economic system. Some excellent economists simply were not eager to engage in practical, political activities; others did not possess an adequate understanding of the market;[65] others did not have a team with them. Yevgeni Saburov advocated a gradual process of reforms in coordination with other republics. Academician Yuri Ryzhov, a member of the Presidential Council, did not believe in the sudden liberalization of prices and painted apocalyptic scenarios of the social explosions to which he believed it would lead.[66] Others, like Grigori Yavlinsky and Mikhail Malei, were highly opinionated and domineering personalities, which made them ill-suited for cooperative efforts; they also insisted on preserving the Soviet Union.[67]

Initially Yeltsin favored professor Yevgeni Yasin, a first-class economist and a leading voice during the discussion of privatization in the early

1990s,[68] as a deputy prime minister responsible for the economy[69] and Yuri Skokov, his well-tested stalwart, as prime minister. But their programs were not radical enough for Yeltsin's temperament. Indeed, the economic program presented by Russian prime minister Ivan Silaev in April 1991 was even more radical than the famous "500-day Plan" of Shatalin and Yavlinsky.[70]

There was also a group of little known young economists who represented the fledgling class of professionals, the most selfless and spirited defenders of the nascent Russian democracy in August 1991.[71] They did not belong to any elite; nevertheless, Burbulis, who was making most of the ministerial appointments,[72] actively promoted them. He and his chief of staff Alexei Golovkov did everything that they could to present Yegor Gaidar's group in the best light.

Golovkov has been a member of the Gaidar group for many years. Beginning in the mid-1980s these young economists from Leningrad and Moscow held informal seminars devoted to the problem of a transition from a command-administrative system to a market economy.[73] During the putsch, Gaidar, who was at the time director of a research institute, brought most of his associates to the White House.[74] Golovkov introduced them to Burbulis.[75]

Yegor Gaidar

Yegor Gaidar was born on March 19, 1956, in Moscow. His grandfather was a legendary Bolshevik commander who later became a famous writer of children's books. Gaider's father was a Soviet admiral. Gaider had a phenomenal memory for numbers, and even as a 12-year-old he was interested in philosophy. He graduated from high school with honors and immediately entered Moscow State University's economics faculty, which was headed by Gavriil Popov. Two of his professors there were Stanislav Shatalin and Nikolai Petrakov. He graduated with a red diploma of excellence. In 1988 he defended his doctoral dissertation, which analyzed the state of the Soviet economy prior to 1985 and the reforms that had been pursued in Eastern Europe. Gaidar's fluency in English allowed him to communicate with the leading economists of the world specializing in transitions to a market economy. Due to his knowledge of Serbo-Croatian, he was able to closely observe Yugoslavia's experiments of managing factories with worker's collectives.[76] His knowledge of Spanish helped him become one of Russia's leading experts on Latin American transitions to a free market. The experience that was most pertinent to Russia, however, was that of Poland. Thanks to his contacts and friendship with Leszek

Barcelowicz, Gaidar was intimately familiar with the "shock therapy" that Poland had undergone in 1990. He wrote many articles and several books on the subject of the transition to a market economy. At least one of his books, *Economic Reforms and Hierarchical Structures*, was recognized as "the best Soviet academic book in economics."[77]

In 1990-1991, Gaidar became a founder and director of the Institute of Economic Policy, which specialized in the problems the Soviet Union would have to face in switching to a market economy. The institute was fairly sizable, with 70 employees.

Yeltsin gravitated toward the most radical economic reform because of his personality type rather than his knowledge of economic theory. His attitude toward the nation was reminiscent of his attitude toward his own body, as was discussed in the previous chapter. To him, a recovery from a prolonged illness was not possible without pain, and the sooner the pain is experienced, the sooner the patient will be able to recover his strength[78] — that is, if he does not die. But Yeltsin was as sure of Russia's vitality as he had always been certain of his own.[79] Gaidar was able to back up Yeltsin's gut feeling with lessons drawn from the experience of other countries, which seemed to indicate that more radical reforms would yield a more successful transition. Yeltsin, Burbulis, and Gaidar believed that it was better to unleash spontaneous creativity than to impose a carefully calculated strategy of transformation. Hence the credo of the radical reforms, formulated by one Gaidarian: "Russia has to be the most [economically] liberal country in the world."[80]

Yeltsin had reservations about the youth and purely academic background of the Gaidarians.[81] In addition, along with many other democrats,[82] he entertained the hope that some sort of union of the former republics would survive; he therefore believed that the reforms in Russia needed to be coordinated with reforms in the other republics. However, the work on the Economic Community treaty bogged down due to disputes over the internal and external debts, the size of the former republics' contributions to the central budget, and so on. Gaidar and Burbulis argued that radical economic reforms "could only be implemented at the republican level,"[83] that the work on the economic union could only delay Russian economic reform,[84] and that the union would cost Russia more than $30 billion annually in subsidies to other former republics. Thus Gaidar and the other democrats were not only opposed to keeping the other republics together by force, they were also against a subsidized union. Instead they believed that Russia should "become an attractive example of [the democratic free-market system] and turn into a center of attraction" to other former republics.[85]

Burbulis asked Gaidar to write an economic program with an emphasis on the go-it-alone scenario, which he did by the end of September.[86] The plan looked convincing to Yeltsin and he incorporated it into his address to the Fifth Congress of People's Deputies on October 28, 1991.[87]

Foreign advisers endorsed the Gaidar group as "the best and the brightest of Russia's young economists."[88] In addition to their professional excellence, Yeltsin was impressed with their self-confidence and independent-mindness; he thought that they were "people without any hang-ups, daring independent thinkers," not the yes-men so typical among *apparatchiks*.[89] In his eyes, they were a new breed who technically did not belong either to the *nomenklatura* or to the dissidents.[90] As Gaidar said, "We were not marginals or dissidents, nor did we belong to the industrialists bound by myriad ties to the old system."[91] Yeltsin could not help but admire their personal courage, which impelled them to come to the White House on the eve of its expected storming. Above all, "they [were] young, strong and full of a burning desire to implement the program that they had prepared."[92] Finally, they were a closely knit group, a cohesive team[93] of people who shared "the same understanding of macroeconomic logic."[94] From both Burbulis' and Yeltsin's points of view, this was a decisive factor ensuring productive and speedy work.

Thus Yeltsin made his choice in favor of Gaidar and his team; by doing this, in the words of Burbulis, he "committed perhaps the most important and meaningful act of his political career."[95]

During the Congress of People's Deputies of Russia, after presenting his radical economic reform plan, Yeltsin asked to be given the emergency power to rule by decree. Because a social upheaval was thought to be inevitable, he was granted such a prerogative for one year.[96] Yeltsin's first use of this power was to establish a new structure for the government consisting of a president, vice-president, state advisers, state council, security council, federation council and a cabinet composed of about twenty ministries.[97] Burbulis became First Deputy Chairman of the Council of Ministers, while Shokhin and Gaidar became deputy chairmen.[98]

The presidential *apparat*, the secretariat, had been created earlier and was filled with Yeltsin's old aides, associates, and colleagues.[99] It was headed by Yuri Petrov, a long-time associate of Yeltsin. The power ministries—the Russian KGB, the Ministry of Interior, and the Ministry of Defense—remained under direct presidential control.

Yeltsin gave the Burbulis-Gaidar government virtual *carte blanche* in charting the strategy and tactics of reforms, as well as the power to implement them in practice.[100] The vice president's post did not have administrative power, and Aleksandr Rutskoi was deeply offended by this. He told an interviewer: "You do not have enough fingers to count all the responsibilities Gaidar carries. He supervises ministries of economy and finance, industry, transport, energy, trade, material resources, and housing, as well as committees of state property, architecture, anti-monopoly, etc."[101] Indeed, Gaidar concentrated in his hands practically all the economic power of a prime minister.

Very few analysts have fully appreciated how politically risky Yeltsin's decision was, and what a dire price he had to pay for it during the next two years. By choosing such young and scarcely known economists, Yeltsin angered and antagonized virtually all elites: the literati, professors, industrialists, and *apparatchiks*, as well as many senior advisers and close associates. Mikhail Malei, who was widely regarded as a spokesman for the military-industrial complex, said: "The president offended a number of people. I myself felt insulted for about six weeks."[102] Yevgeni Yasin admitted that he had been very disappointed: "For a while I wouldn't shake hands with Gaidar."[103] Anatoli Sobchak accused Yeltsin of jettisoning the "people of the first democratic wave, those who had borne the brunt of the struggle against the regime."[104]

Almost immediately after the Fifth Congress of People's Deputies of Russia, the government of Burbulis-Gaidar and its economic reform program, became the focus of the struggle between the president and the Supreme Soviet. The chairman of the Supreme Soviet Ruslan Khazbulatov, called the Gaidar cabinet totally incompetent "kids in pink shorts." In April 1992 four prominent academicians launched what became known as the "academicians' mutiny."[105] Such notable authorities as Georgy Arbatov, Sviatoslav Fedorov, Nikolai Petrakov, Oleg Bogomolov, and later even the "godfather of reformers" Stanislav Shatalin subjected the president and his government to the most furious criticism from the podium of the Supreme Soviet.[106]

The furious attack on the Gaidar cabinet was reflected in the nickname it received—the "kamikaze government." It was expected to survive for only a few months. And yet the Gaidar government managed to survive long enough to give the reforms an irreversible momentum. Yeltsin fought stubbornly for it, he maneuvered, compromised, and made real and false concessions to the Supreme Soviet and elites; in short, he did everything to ensure that a market mechanism took hold in the Russian economy and started to determine its life.

The Abolition of the Soviet Union

By late 1991 the existence of the Soviet Union had become largely symbolic. All former republics had declared total independence and embarked on securing their sovereignty. They were confronted with many difficult issues and disputes. Some problems were highly sensitive; potentially catastrophic conflicts loomed, considering that some former republics had chemical and nuclear weapons, and even the means to deliver them thousands of miles across the globe. The Soviet Union looked more like "a grab-bag of unpredictable little countries," as one State Department official put it, and the president of the Soviet Union had no power over them. In fact, two of the former republics, Armenia and Azerbaijan, were already locked in a bloody war over the Nagorny Karabakh. Moldova, Tadjikistan, and Georgia were in a state of civil war or on the brink of it, and no effective borders separated them from Russia. The main danger stemmed from potential conflicts between Russia and Ukraine. The military conflict between the two largest Slavic states was everyone's worst nightmare. The situation was precarious, marked by fears of famine, mass epidemics, civil war, conflicts among former republics, and the influx of millions of refugees.

Meanwhile, Gorbachev, Shevardnadze, and many prominent democrats, Sobchak and Yavlinsky among them, argued that the dissolution of the Soviet Union would lead to a Yugoslavia-like war,[107] and that it was not feasible because of the many economic and political problems that it would create.[108] However, the Gorbachev-sponsored negotiation of a new Union Treaty, which was supposed to save the Soviet Union in some form, ran into roadblocks. Finally, after the referendum in Ukraine on December, 1, 1991, which favored independence, and the rejection by Ukrainian president Kravchuk of participation in any further talks about the Union Treaty, the abolition of the Soviet Union became a *fait accompli.*

Yeltsin and his associates brought a formal end to the USSR. On December 8, 1991, the presidents of the three Slavic states met and agreed to create the Commonwealth of Independent States (CIS). Its first function was psychological: to be a political forum in which mutual suspicion and fears could be discussed and defused. Secondly, it provided a "mechanism for the civilized divorce" of the sovereign states. A set of procedures and a mechanism for resolving outstanding issues and problems among its members was established. And there were many problems, such as mutual financial debts, territorial claims, the status of ethnic minorities within their territories, as well as disputes over the Soviet Union's external debts and property, customs and visa arrangements, the proper division of the armed forces, etc. Kazakhstan immediately joined the CIS, and then seven other former republics followed.

The logic of the founding fathers of the CIS was simple: the Soviet Union had been an artificial creation kept together by a totalitarian system. If some kind of union of its component nations was desirable and possible, and they believed that it was, then they had to separate first; only after having consolidated their statehoods could they consider some form of reintegration. But reintegration had to be a natural process based on the organic economic, social, and cultural ties among them.

Naturally, the creation of the CIS could not automatically resolve the many problems and disputes dividing its members. Doing so would require years of patient work. However, several immediate benefits soon became apparent. Perhaps the most important aspect of the creation of the CIS was the establishment of a united military.[109] This removed the immediate danger of military conflict between CIS members, particularly between Russia and Ukraine, which, in the fall of 1991, was considered by some to be inevitable. It also removed the incentives for the outburst of a new arms race. To further ameliorate the fears and concerns that the former republics had about Russia, and to forestall an arms race, Yeltsin pledged that Russia would be the "last of the former republics to set up its own armed forces, if she is compelled to do so."[110]

On December 25, 1991, the red flag of the Soviet Union over the Kremlin was taken down and the white, blue, and red flag of Russia was raised. In Yeltsin's words, Russia re-embarked on a journey that had been interrupted in October 1917, that is, the journey toward becoming a "normal society." Yeltsin confessed that he felt "a sensation of freedom and lightness" that only comes with liberation.[111]

The Legacy of Communism

The legacy of seventy-four years of communist rule was so appalling that many analysts believed that "the chances of a successful transition [for Russia were] all but impossible."[112]

By 1920 the Bolsheviks had nationalized all means of production and land, abolished the free press and political parties, and thus replaced all institutions of power with a single unified bureaucracy. These measures effectively turned the country into one single company with the population as its employees. But the people remained largely unruly; to subdue them, particularly the peasants, Lenin took over control of the entire food supply in the country and distributed food according to people's loyalty to the regime. This policy led to a famine but managed to subdue the country. Finally, in the late 1920s the communist party completed the construction of a strictly hierarchical bureaucratic machine, a backbone of the totalitarian system.

After the Second World War, the Soviet Union became a multilayered empire, much like a Russian *matrioshka* doll. The outer layer consisted of client states, such as Cuba, North Korea, Vietnam and others. Next was the Eurasian layer of the empire, which stretched from the Elbe River in East Germany to the Pacific, with a combined population of 405 million people. In 1989 the Soviet empire lost its European layer of states, and in 1991 Russia led the liberation of the 14 republics comprising the inner layer. What remained in 1991 was a country composed of 60 percent of the territory and 51 percent of the population of the Soviet Union. Russia itself was a country of more than a hundred peoples, 21 of which were regarded as autonomous.

In the fall of 1991 the economically vital areas were amputated from the core of the empire, and the economic ties between former satellites and republics were severed. Thus centralized control over the highly monopolized economy was effectively lost. The "parade of sovereignties" threatened the very existence of Russia as an integral state. Indeed, on the heels of the failed coup, several autonomous republics declared themselves independent states with their own constitutions, presidents, councils of ministers, and in some cases even armed forces. Several provinces declared themselves republics. Many provinces united and declared themselves superrepublics, such as the Ural, Don, Maritime, and Siberian Republics. Some provinces continued to regulate prices even after economic reforms were started, and some even attempted to issue their own currencies, set up customs barriers, and control the flow of goods. In at least one province the head of the administration began his market reforms by abolishing price controls before the rest of the country had done so.[113] Several provinces refused to pay taxes to the federal treasury. In short, as one political analyst observed, "the process of sovereignization acquired a spontaneous, unmanageable quality and was destroying the whole."[114]

Social conditions at this time were worse than they had been since the end of World War II. Stores were absolutely empty, and long lines of people waited for hours to buy cigarettes, vodka, and food, creating a real threat that spontaneous protests would result in riots and looting. As one of the key architects of economic reform noted, "The country was fraught with a destructive social upheaval";[115] in a land filled with nuclear, chemical, and biological weapons, and 16 nuclear power reactors similar to the infamous Chernobyl reactor, such an outburst could have led to a catastrophe of global proportions.

The liberalization of prices, announced to begin on January 2, 1992, was universally expected to trigger such a social upheaval.[116] All this explains why, as insiders later confessed, for about one year the government lived in a state of "an oppressive agonizing feeling that a social explosion was about to occur";[117] it was feared that neo-Nazis, Russian chauvinists, or communist hard-liners would try to seize power in an attempt to "bring at least some clarity to the economic and political situation, and stop the disintegration process."[118]

One American analyst summed up Russia's psychological state in these words: "Buried within a federation within a federation, the Russian 'nation' experienced the same sense of peril that smaller peoples of the Soviet Union felt. The nation was in danger, its heritage squandered, its monuments crumbling, the memory of its past distorted almost beyond recovery."[119] It was then that the brilliant Russian humorist Mikhail Zhvanetski coined his famous parable with regard to the challenge facing Russia: Everyone can turn an aquarium into fish soup. But how does one turn fish soup back into an aquarium?

A prominent historian, Richard Pipes, noted that the task that the Yeltsin government faced in 1991 knew no parallels,[120] while leading political scientist, Zbigniew Brzezinski indicated that "no prescription of how to transform a statist corrupt totalitarian system into a pluralistic democracy based on a free market" existed.[121]

The Pains of the Transition to Democracy

Indeed, how does one even start to approach the task of building a democratic political system out of the ruins of a totalitarian one? By canceling the old constitution and liquidating the existing institutions of power? By writing a new constitution and constructing new institutions? Such a process could take many years, creating confusion and instability and impeding progress toward better living conditions. Perhaps it is best to reform and transform the existing institutions rather than eliminate them? But can institutions die quietly or be relied upon to submit to reform? Or should one fear that they will sabotage the planned changes? Should the old institutions be purged and staffed with new people? But where would one find qualified new people? Should new institutions be built and for a while coexist with the old ones?

Intellectuals are inherently prone to strategizing, and many of them reproached the Yeltsin government for not taking the time to devise a comprehensive strategic plan of transformation. It is true that the reformers had no strategic plan, and no time to work one out. There were, however, several guiding principles to which they were determined to adhere, as well as several requirements that they intended to observe. The transformation had to be peaceful and evolutionary, and life had to proceed in as uninterrupted a fashion as possible. This meant that the economic reform should not unduly hamper ongoing economic life, that the process of creating a new legal system should not halt, even temporarily, the fight against crime, that the process of creating checks and balances should not paralyze the governmental power structure, and that the redistribution of state assets into private hands should not turn into wholesale thievery. Above all, the methods should be nonviolent, the process as organic as possible and yet rapid because, as democrats strongly felt, Russia had lost several years of precious time under Gorbachev. Yeltsin, Burbulis, Gaidar, Shakhrai, and Kozyrev agreed upon these principles as we shall see, they tried very hard to observe them.

To Purge or not to Purge?

Some radical democrats have insisted that, following the examples of Czechoslovakia and Germany, the Russian government should have purged about 200,000 members of the former *nomenklatura*. The majority of the democrats, however, felt that purges were morally repulsive as well as impractical. Even former political prisoners and human rights champions argued against purges and purification campaigns.[122] Yeltsin felt that such witch hunts could divide society into "the clean and the unclean"[123] and create fear and anxiety in Russian society reminiscent of the nightmarish events of the 1930s. He felt that society should focus on constructive work instead of recriminations, which might open a Pandora's box of mutual accusations, infighting, and resignations.

Moreover, there were no reliable criteria to distinguish "the clean" from "the unclean," because under the totalitarian regime every member of society was, to some extent, compromised by his or her cooperation with the system. To strictly define the parameters of guilt was, with the exception of several hundred obvious cases, simply impossible.

For the Bolsheviks, one's social origin and profession were sufficient criteria to determine who was ideologically loyal and who was not. In 1991, however, the social roots of all elites were fairly similar, and many people claimed to possess democratic views. Thus, there were neither the criteria nor an established process to establish people's ideological loyalty. Moreover, even the certified democrats, who were tested during the mass rallies and at the White House barricades in August, disagreed on practically all ideological principles and policy questions, including the existence of the Soviet Union, policies toward autonomous republics and other entities, attitude toward the old *nomenklatura*, and the best methods of achieving economic reform. Such ideological disunity existed even among Yeltsin's circle of close associates, which consisted of such future bitter antagonists as Burbulis, Gaidar, Shakhrai, Poltoranin, and Kozyrev, on the one hand, and Rutskoi, Khazbulatov, Makashov, and Sterligov on the other.

The Question of Elections

Another question that had to be faced immediately was whether elections to the new parliament should be held, as some democrats had suggested.[124] After all, elections are the process in which the people select their leaders. Later, in August 1993, Yeltsin expressed doubts about his decision not to hold elections to the Supreme Soviet and for local organs of government immediately after the failed putsch. At the time, however, Yeltsin was convinced that elections were a "luxury the country could not afford"; he thought that to have an "election campaign and conduct serious economic reforms simultaneously was impossible."[125]

In retrospect there are compelling reasons to think that Yeltsin was right in 1991, and not in 1993. The principal reason was the nonexistence at the time of an effective multiparty system. All the political parties except one were essentially narrow circles of friends who had rallied around one or two prominent personalities, enjoying only a thousand or so followers. The only well-organized, national party was the Communist Party, whose members controlled the local media and the entire electoral infrastructure and process. In such conditions, holding elections could easily have led to a political catastrophe. In 1990, for example, in the first truly free elections for People's Deputies of Russia, members of the CPSU won 86.3 percent of the seats—20 percent more than in the 1985 elections![126] Even in 1993, after the soviets had been eliminated, the elections for the parliament were reportedly rigged by the local *nomenklatura*.[127] In 1991 the chances for the *nomenklatura* to gain a revanche by legal methods—through "popular elections"—were considerable. If this had happened, economic and political reforms would have become even more problematic, if not impossible.

Authoritarianism

Thus purges were deemed morally repulsive and impractical; elections were thought politically risky; both were very difficult to implement. Why then did Yeltsin not just dissolve governmental bodies at all levels, so as to establish "wise authoritarianism and rule entirely without the constraints of a parliament," as one BBC correspondent suggested? Yeltsin categorically rejected such an option: "No. I am a democrat, and we shall find answers to all our problems through consultations. Consultation with parliament, with the Supreme Soviet, and with other institutions."[128] In fact, as we shall see, after two years of honest attempts to govern by the democratic methods of consultation and compromise, Yeltsin did resort to "wise authoritarianism."

Yeltsin and Burbulis "consciously chose the policy of compromise in order to let the *nomenklatura* peacefully, evolutionarily grow into a new regime, a new system."[129] Under the communist regime, as Yeltsin explained, "there was a certain system of selection. The institutions of power absorbed many intelligent people, and they did not disappear."[130] As Yeltsin said, the democrats and former *apparatchiks* should work together "contributing to the strategy and tactics of reforms different approaches—as long as they share an overall strategy."[131] The democrats would chart the course,[132] while the *apparatchiks* would implement it.[133]

Thus the reformers decided against "revolutionary earth-shaking,"[134] reforms opting instead for a simultaneous transformation of all institutions in which all the major elites of Russia could and should participate.

The Strategy of Parallel Structures

The decision to work with the "defeated enemies"[135] has been the most frequently and vehemently criticized strategic decision made by the Yeltsin-Burbulis government.[136] Indeed, it enormously complicated the transition.

The strategy of dual institutions was a logical consequence of the policy of compromise between the elites. The key principle of this strategy was to use the existing institutions wherever possible,[137] to create new institutions, if necessary, and to gradually transfer power from the old institutions to the new ones.

To assert control in the provinces, the Yeltsin government resorted to a bold and controversial tactic: it created regional administrations directly subordinated to the president in place of the former provincial party committees. Because they were overwhelmingly staffed by the former *nomenklatura*, to many democrats this idea appeared ludicrous or dangerous. However, this tactic enabled Yeltsin and Burbulis to "create a vertical structure of power" and "achieve the stability of the power structure," as Yeltsin explained.[138] Being appointed by the president, the heads of the administration had a vested interest in the survival of the institution of the presidency. To further assure their loyalty, on August 31, 1991, Yeltsin began to appoint plenipotentiaries. Recruited mostly from locally known democrats, the plenipotentiaries had no administrative power; however, they had direct access to the presidential administration. Thus they served effectively as Yeltsin's watchdogs, supervising the implementation of the president's decisions in the provinces.[139] The allegiance of the local soviets was naturally to the Supreme Soviet.

This triarchy of power in the provinces proved to be an effective mechanism for the transitional period. Most heads of administrations soon became supporters of Yeltsin and his policies.[140] However, the heads of administration did not enjoy the legitimacy of the soviets, which had been elected in 1990 during fairly free elections. Soon the war between the legislative and the executive branches was raging in all but three *oblasts*.[141] In this war, the heads of administrations needed the support of the president's plenipotentiaries, despite the fact that even the most democratic and reform-minded of them did not like the existence of plenipotentiaries.[142] This triarchy of mutually suspicious and openly antagonistic institutions unquestionably impeded reforms in the provinces. At the same time, it proved to be effective in forestalling an open revolt against Moscow during the two-year-long tug of war between the president and Supreme Soviet. Thus, during the second putsch in October 1993, very few provinces openly sided with the Supreme Soviet.

Many institutions were created by the leadership or with its approval. Faced with a deluge of pressing problems, Yeltsin and Burbulis assigned tasks to individuals and gave them a free hand to create the necessary institutions.[143] New committees, commissions, departments, and ministries were created when a specific problem had to be solved. Naturally, not all of them proved to be viable. Some institutions turned out to be stillborn, others had no further purpose once their task had been accomplished, and still others stood the test of time.

There were also continuing efforts to adapt and reform existing institutions. Many of the old institutions and their administrators were honestly trying to change, and some managed to do so for the better. A few existing institutions even became more effective than the newly created ones. For example, the administrative *apparat* of the president was perhaps the most effective institution in the new power structure; not surprisingly, it had the least turnover among all governmental institutions.[144] In the volatile economic environment, very few people were willing voluntarily to leave the government. They tried to justify their continued existence in government by developing new roles for their institutions. To remove unsuitable individuals from the government, entire institutions had to be eliminated. But the existence of some of these institutions was engraved in the constitution. The best known example was the case of former Vice President Aleksandr Rutskoi. He did not fit in with the presidential team from an ideological point of view, or in terms of his personality. However, as a man of great energy and ambition, he could not resign himself to being an idle bystander. He mistakenly thought that the vice presidency would be the second most powerful post in the government hierarchy, ascribed his misfortunes to Burbulis' intrigues, and fought for his share of power to the bitter end. Rutskoi launched a full-scale offensive against the democrats, accusing almost every member of the government of monstrous corruption. Counter charges followed. However, neither the leading democrats nor Rutskoi were found guilty of corruption. Needless to say, these internal squabbles disrupted the creation of a new political and economic system.

The strategy of dual institutions led to "an extraordinary proliferation of presidential councils, committees, think tanks, and agencies — all with overlapping authorities":[145] bloated governmental structure. Thus by November 1993 the number of ministries and committees had grown to 96,[146] and there were 15-20 percent more employees in the Russian governmental apparatus than there had been in the former USSR.[147] Enormous organizational complexities were created.[148] For example, three entities were responsible for the formulation of foreign policy: the Committee on Foreign Affairs of the Supreme Soviet, the Ministry of Foreign Affairs, and the Security Council. As Gennadi Burbulis admitted, they overestimated the usefulness of "the method of parallel structures."[149]

The Problem of Turnover

Many analysts have noted the extraordinary fluidity among political actors in the new Russia, particularly the very high level of rotation among people in the government.[150] Some have sought explanations of this phenomenon in the nature of Yeltsin's personality and operational style; others in the traditionally Byzantine nature of politics in Russia. Yeltsin was said by some to whimsically fire and hire people because of his uneven temper and the command-administrative style to which he had become accustomed as a former *apparatchik*. Others sought an explanation in Yeltsin's lack of democratic managerial skills and his general mistrust of people and sense of insecurity.[151]

These explanations, however, oversimplify the much more profound process at work. Among the objective forces behind the phenomenon of the high turnover was the fact that none of the elites was capable of taking the reins of power firmly in its hands and leading a simultaneous transformation of all institutions. Each of the three major elites had its shortcomings as well as its strong points.

Burbulis described the democrats who brought down the communist system as "courageous people who proved resourceful and active during the toppling of the totalitarian system, [who were] now less active, given a much more favorable situation."[152] But as one close associate of Yeltsin added tellingly, they "didn't know anything about how to run a country."[153] They were successful in organizing mass rallies and movements, but not always successful in creating viable institutions or administering and re-forming the existing institutions. They lacked the experience and habits of working within institutions, discipline, punctuality, and a sense of respect for the chain of command.[154] They tended to argue and endlessly discuss options, even when emergency actions were needed. As Yeltsin found out, most young democrats were not effective in implementing decisions that required tenacity and toughness.[155] Some of them, like Anatoli Chubais and Sergei Shakhrai, turned out to be very effective in implementing their ideas and plans, but the overwhelming majority of the liberal democrats were ill suited for bureaucratic work. In addition, the intelligent and soft-spoken democrats were incapable of conveying an aura of authority to impress the hard-boiled *apparatchiks*. They did not project the imposing toughness and strength that the *apparatchiks* and local managers were used to expecting from the leadership.

The *apparatchiks* had their own weaknesses. A considerable propor-tion of them, in the words of Yeltsin, did not "wish to accept the new social system. They have a vicious hatred for democracy, which presupposes [per-sonal] responsibility."[156] On the other hand, as a rule, they were educated and intelligent people.[157] For example, in 1994, in the Council of Ministers and the office of the president, 97.4 percent of the staff had advanced de-grees, and almost half had scientific degrees in economics or science and engineering.[158] Their operational style was based on respect for subordina-tion, diligence, and an aversion to risk change. However, the principal ideas of the democratic reforms—the diffusion of power, compromise, tolerance toward other views, and a reliance on methods of persuasion to win support—were alien to them. They saw reforms as the destruction of the only effective system of government that they knew—a centralized, strictly hierarchical system based on unconditional obedience to orders from above.

The coexistence between the democrats and the *apparatchiks* was more a tug of war than genuine cooperation. The independent-minded democrats spoke their mind. They were impatient to see results and blamed the *apparatchiks* for sabotaging their decisions. They were determined to control the administrative organs and enjoy full power, which they felt they deserved. They used the media, which was overwhelmingly democratic, to keep the *apparatchiks* under constant fire. The unnerving media campaigns against Petrov, Lobov, Skokov and others kept them under constant pressure to resign. Burbulis, according to Yeltsin, had a particularly "childish, infantile," confrontational attitude toward the *apparatchiks*.[159]

In May 1992 Burbulis succeeded in transferring several functions from the administrative apparatus of the president to the apparatus of the government headed by Golovkov.[160] The president's chief of staff Yuri Petrov complained: "I am not happy about the appetites of the government's apparatus," and he handed Yeltsin his letter of resignation.[161] However, Yeltsin thought that the democrats were ineffective in administrative work, and he resisted their pressure. Finally, in January 1993 he removed both Petrov and Golovkov.[162]

There was a large pool of professional competence and managerial talent with which Yeltsin was intimately familiar. This was the corps of red directors, factory managers, as Yeltsin himself had been before he became an *apparatchik*. Many of the red directors were extremely capable people, who possessed both scientific degrees and important practical experience. Some of them had had extraordinarily successful careers. For example, Chernomyrdin, Shumeiko, Soskovets, and Skokov had scientific accomplishments to their credit and had become general directors of major enterprises before the age of forty.[163] Yeltsin admired their reliability, tenacity, and work ethic. Moreover, they knew how to deal with the directors and managers of industry.[164]

Yeltsin began to look for cadres among this managerial stratum as early as the winter of 1991.[165] However, the red directors were relatively slow in embracing both the ideas and operational methods of democracy and the market, and they were, as a rule, reluctant to engage in politics. Initially, most industrialists were strongly anti-reformist: the abolition of state control and patronage of factories and their replacement by a largely nonexistent market whose most prominent characteristic was runaway inflation appeared to them to be an erroneous if not outright criminal course of action.

However, as early as the summer of 1992 a significant number of red directors began to favor a market system. Thus, in the words of former National Security Council staff member Stephen Sestanovich, "Yeltsin's government managed to co-opt Soviet-style industrial managers without adopting their anti-reform program."[166]

To keep the red directors and *apparatchiks* in line with his program, in the words of one political analyst, "Yeltsin created a powerful political fist,"[167] which included Gennadi Burbulis, Yegor Gaidar, Sergei Shakhrai, Alexandr Shokhin, Mikhail Poltoranin, Alexei Golovkov, Andrei Kozyrev, Anatoly Chubais, and other reformers. These exceptionally intelligent and articulate people could take on any opponents of their democratic philosophy and prevail in an open discussion. They were, in effect, the ideologists and strategists of the reforms, and they were very effective at that task. In addition, at least during the initial appointments of various red directors to the government, Yeltsin consulted with the democrats, asking for their endorsements of the candidates.[168] For more than a year, young reformers dominated the strategic and even operational aspects of decision making in the government, not allowing the *apparatchiks* and red directors to deviate from the course that they and Yeltsin had prescribed.

The ultimate guarantor of the strategic direction of reforms, however, was Yeltsin himself. He did a great deal to promote understanding and cooperation among the different groups and personalities.

Yeltsin often combined in one task force young democrats, red directors and *apparatchiks*, so that they would learn to work together. This tactic was not always successful and led to a number of controversial decisions, yet he persevered in order to promote cooperation among groups with different views. In addition, he encouraged informal and semiformal social contacts and exchanges of ideas between the various groups. Thus in May 1992 representatives of *apparatchiks* and the "young Turks" created an "informal group in support of democracy and reforms," in which they could exchange of views."[169] Later, Yeltsin created the "presidential tennis club," in which government officials were able to meet socially with "scientists, journalists, politicians, businessmen, and cultural figures," have fun, relax, and get to know one another better.[170] A number of former *apparatchiks* proved capable of adopting the ideology of democracy.[171] Others, like Yuri Petrov, Yuri Skokov, and Aleksandr Rutskoi, could not adopt the new ideas and methods. At the same time, in some cases democrats turned into very conservative *gosudarstvennik* (state supremacists) and joined forces with Aleksandr Rutskoi.[172]

Naturally, ordinary human weaknesses and vices, such as vanity, envy, pride, and fear of losing status and the perquisites of office have unavoidably affected political life in Russia, as they do anywhere. Personal biases, sympathies, and animosities played their own role in conflicts within the government and contributed to the turnover among top officials. However, the role of these factors was highly exaggerated by Kremlin watchers. The objective reasons behind the high turnover among cadres in the top echelon of Russia during the transition phase have far outweighed them.

Yeltsin emphatically said that he had no intention to rotate people, but that "life was doing it, the nature of power."[173] How then did he characterize his cadres policy? During the first three years, Yeltsin often operated in emergency circumstances. The process of selecting cadres was necessarily very subjective. Yeltsin formulated the principles of his appointments in this way: "First, they should be professionals; second they should be younger than me; third, they should support reforms; fourth, they should be loyal to the President."[174]

Not surprisingly, Yeltsin committed his share of mistakes. On several occasions, he dismissed capable professionals on the spur of the moment.[175] More significant changes, however, were dictated by the change in priorities as the transition evolved.

Yeltsin has a characteristically single-minded operational style. That is, he has tended, at any given moment, to focus on a single task: the struggle with the Communist center, economic reforms and financial stabilization, the struggle with the Supreme Soviet, promoting the new constitution, resolving the Chechen crisis, etc. Each major task has required people with different expertise and knowledge, as Oleg Lobov explained, and this has elevated to prominence "people with different backgrounds, experience, and skills."[176] For example, when Yeltsin decided that diplomatic and political options had been exhausted and that a military solution was the only effective option left in the Chechen crisis, his civilian advisers were supplanted by military and security officers.[177] To many insiders and the outside observers, these changes in focus and personnel appeared as changes in Yeltsin's strategic direction. They were mistakenly attributed to Yeltsin's pliability and the exaggerated influence of specific individuals, such as Korzhakov (the chief of his security service).

Months after the reforms were launched, Yeltsin's administration began to emphasize professional competence and managerial skills rather than "political affiliation."[178] However, professional excellence, operational skills, and managerial talents, which are so crucial if governmental structures are to function effectively, can be tested and improved only by practical experience. A number of democrats lacked these talents.[179] In addition, many could not cope with the turbulent and tense political environment of the transition.[180] Some young democrats, such as Chubais, Kozyrev, Filatov, and Shakhrai, proved their administrative capabilities and remained in government through the years of transition. However, the majority of young democrats left government to return to scientific careers or to pursue other interests that were opening up to them in business, finance, and politics.

In sum, the incredible pace of changes and accompanying uncertainty, the collapse of old institutions and the launching of new ones, and the extremely stressful environment of political turmoil were mainly responsible for the high turnover of political cadres in Russia thus far during the transition.

The Struggle with the Soviets

The two-year-long struggle between the president and the Supreme Soviet encapsulated all the problems that elites, institutions, and individuals had to cope with during Russia's monumental transition.

Some analysts tended to see this struggle as a conflict between ambitious and impetuous personalities. Others saw in it a conflict between the legislative and executive branches of the government. Still others thought of this conflict as a continuation of the struggle between the Communist Party and an emerging democratic Russia.

Human factors did significantly affect the character of the conflict. Pride, vanity, ambition, and personal prejudice all played a role and were perhaps responsible for the dramatic conclusion of the conflict. However, the ideological and institutional aspects underlying the conflict were far more important, because they reflected the profound forces that were shaping the transformation of society.

The institution of the presidency was a new phenomenon in Russian political history. The concept of the presidency originated during the struggle between the intelligentsia and the Communist Party. In 1990 the intelligentsia promoted the institution of the presidency as an alternative source of power to that of the party. It hoped that after acquiring his own source of power Gorbachev would abandon the backbone of the totalitarian system, the Communist Party. Indeed, in his first address to the Presidential Council, Gorbachev did not mention the words "Communist Party" once.[181] However, later, in typical Gorbachevian style, he changed his mind; he not only refused to disband the Communist Party but remained its General Secretary.

The Russian Congress of People's Deputies created the institution of the Russian presidency in the spring of 1991 as a counterweight to the communist center. Its creation allowed Yeltsin to launch a frontal attack on the communist regime and bring it down. However, the role and structure of the Russian presidency were fully defined, shaped and crystallized only in the fall of 1991. The new institution as endorsed by the Congress of People's Deputies and endowed with emergency powers to rule by decree for one year.

The rivalry between the presidency and the Supreme Soviet began immediately after the Fifth Congress of People's Deputies. Apart from personal ambition, two institutions' competing quests to accumulate power was promoted by the power vacuum that followed the collapse of the totalitarian system. In the absence of an appropriate constitutional framework and strictly defined rules and boundaries, the two institutions were inevitably engaged in a contest to extend their control into uncharted territory. They began to compete for executive, judicial, financial, and legislative forms of power.

Both institutions thought that their claims to power were legitimate, although Brezhnev's 1977 constitution had been amended about 300 times since 1990, its main premise remained intact. According to it, the Congress of People's Deputies of Russia was the supreme legislative body of the country, and its permanent organ, the Supreme Soviet, was "the supreme body of state power."[182] However, the Congress of People's Deputies of Russia, with 1026 members and two or three short sessions annually, could not be an effective legislative body. It tended to endorse the laws and resolutions of the Supreme Soviet. Hence the Supreme Soviet was, de facto, the supreme governing body of the country. At least this is how its chairman, Ruslan Khazbulatov, perceived its role and power.

According to the amended constitution, the president headed the apparatus of executive power. However, the president had been elected by direct popular vote just a few months earlier, and presidential power was greatly enhanced by the fifth Congress of People's Deputies. Naturally, the president felt entitled to full power as well.

The struggle between the two institutions quickly spread into all areas: foreign policy, privatization, finances, defense industry conversion, as well as design of the constitution. Soon both branches were involved in both legislative and executive matters, issuing conflicting orders and laws: a situation that had to eventually lead to an open confrontation.[183]

Clearly defined ideological boundaries soon appeared. The Supreme Soviet became the stronghold of all those who opposed radical, rapid privatization; opposed a radical scaling down of the armed forces; supported large subsidies to collective farms and the defense industry; advocated Russia's pressure on the former republics; supported pro-Russian movements in the Crimea, Moldova, and Abkhazia; and opposed the pro-Western foreign policy of Yeltsin and Kozyrev. In addition, the Supreme Soviet was the ally of the conservative forces in the provinces.

The duality of power in the center was replicated in most provinces, paralyzing local power structures and impeding reforms. In one province, for example, there were two heads of administration for six months.[184] In another, the head of administration disbanded the soviets by force.[185]

Boris Yeltsin was criticized for vacillating, compromising with the Supreme Soviet, not working with it, and, at the end, for using excessive force against it.[186]

His close advisers from the ranks of the radical democrats urged him "to disband that idle talking-shop," the parliament, by means of a presidential decree, even if such an action meant violating the constitution.[187] Yeltsin admitted that for a long time he resisted "the temptation to resolve the internal disputes and differences with the use of arms."[188] He did threaten several times to resort to raw power;[189] however, in reality, he stubbornly pursued a policy of negotiations, concessions, and compromise with the Supreme Soviet.[190] At the same time Yeltsin was luring the reform-minded members of the Supreme Soviet into his administration. About 70 members of the Supreme Soviet joined the presidential and governmental structures. As one political observer wrote, this policy allowed Yeltsin to bleed his main enemy and build up both the executive and administrative organs.[191] However, the critics claimed that this tactic led to a lowering of the level of professionalism of the Supreme Soviet and pushed it to oppose reforms still more.[192] As one analyst wrote, "The legislative branch became a place for losers in the race for influence."[193]

Indeed, the confrontation was growing sharper. The struggle between the two institutions became an open public confrontation on April 11, 1992, when the sixth Congress of People's Deputies demanded that Yeltsin eliminate the institution of his personal representatives. The Burbulis-Gaidar government collectively threatened to resign under the barrage of vicious criticism. In July 1992 the Supreme Soviet passed, over the veto of the president, a highly inflationary budget that seriously undermined the reform efforts of Gaidar. In December 1992 the confrontation took a dramatic turn when Yeltsin had to resort to the threat of using force. Instead, in the end, he made concessions, replaced Gaidar with Chernomyrdin, and agreed to hold a referendum on the strategy of reforms. In March 1993 Yeltsin barely escaped impeachment. In response, he issued an executive order suspending the work of the Supreme Soviet. However, this move met resistance among Yeltsin's close associates: Vice-President Rutskoi, the Chairman of the Constitutional Court Valeri Zorkin, Vice-Premier Khizha, and Skokov. Yeltsin backed off.

Yeltsin's decisive victory in the April 1993 referendum created a new political situation. Surprisingly, the Russian population, which was widely thought to be disillusioned with both democracy and reforms, spoke clearly in support of Yeltsin and his reforms, not the Supreme Soviet. This was the fifth confirmation of the people's trust in Yeltsin since 1988. Naturally, he perceived it as a popular mandate for pushing the political and economic transformation of Russia into a truly democratic and free market system. He concentrated all his attention and energy on the task of working out a draft of a new Russian constitution and having it adopted. He organized a constitutional conference to hammer out the draft and create societal consensus for its adoption. All prominent individuals, all formal and informal political parties, movements, and institutions were invited to participate in the conference. However, by August 1993 it became obvious that the Supreme Soviet and the Congress of People's Deputies had no desire to vote themselves out of existence by adopting the new constitution.

Thus, as French President De Gaulle did in 1962, Yeltsin reached the point when he had to resolve the stalemate by crossing the boundaries of the existing constitution. In his typical manner he decided to take the initiative, knowing that "the November 17 session of the Congress of People's Deputies will invariably end up with impeachment of the president and resignation of the government," as Shumeiko later admitted.[194] On September 21, 1993, President Yeltsin issued a decree dissolving the Supreme Soviet, suspending the further work of the Constitutional Court, and setting the date for general elections for a two-chamber Russian Parliament for Dec. 11-12, 1993. Until the new parliament could begin functioning, the president was to rule by decree, restrained only by public opinion and the media.

Contrary to some views, Yeltsin's move was not a gamble,[195] but a well-prepared strategy worked out many months in advance.[196] In the words of Shumeiko: "Before directly signing this decree [the president] conferred with and consulted all the leaders of the state and government... The idea was worked out gradually, and every time a compromise was proposed, every time it was proposed to find some other option, some other way, every time this was refused, something would be added to this draft."[197] Yeltsin dismissed those who objected to his attempt to dissolve the Supreme Soviet in March. He relieved Vice-President Rutskoi of all his duties and even barred him from the Kremlin; he appointed a new Minister of Security, brought Gaidar back to the government, and raised the salaries of the military by 80 percent.[198] Finally, Yeltsin informed the United States government of his decision.[199]

Why then did such a carefully planned operation turn violent and cost 145 human lives?[200] As Gennadi Burbulis said: "Yeltsin could perhaps be blamed for his failure to use power but certainly not for any 'abuse' of power."[201] Indeed, Yeltsin had done everything to avoid violence. The blockade of the Supreme Soviet was enforced by unarmed police to prevent the accidental use of firearms. A special office was set up to find employment for defecting Supreme Soviet members. Yeltsin hoped that the legislators would prefer to abandon the confrontation and join the election campaign for the upcoming elections to the Federal Assembly.[202] Indeed, by September 30, 586 people left the White House.[203] Eighty-five legislators accepted monetary compensation and a job offer. Out of two hundred People's Deputies who were in the White House, only twelve flatly refused to take the offer.[204]

The plan seemed to work. By October 2, only about a hundred legislators remained in the White House. The negotiations, under the auspices of the Russian Orthodox Church, were progressing and seemed to be approaching a peaceful resolution of the conflict. On October 2, a compromise was worked out: the Supreme Soviet would disarm its paramilitary units in return for turning on the electricity and hot water in the White House and other measures to lessen the severity of the blockade.[205] Indeed, the blockade of the Supreme Soviet was considerably eased.[206] However, Rutskoi and Khazbulatov were misled by deputy speaker Yuri Voronin, who led the Supreme Soviet's delegation at the negotiations and interpreted Yeltsin's eagerness to compromise as a sign of weakness.[207] They refused to disarm the militia and instead called for a popular uprising. Mobs attacked the mayoral office and the Ostankino television station.

Rutskoi and Khazbulatov's forces consisted of more than a thousand men armed with 1900 automatic weapons, 2000 pistols, 38 machine guns, and 15 grenade launchers,[208] which was more than sufficient to prevail over police armed with handguns. The army and special purpose units were reluctant to get involved in putting down the riots, as they had been two years earlier. If the mutineers had succeeded in appealing to the nation in a televised address, they could have received the support of renegade military commanders. Thus, on October 3, 1993, Russia faced a serious threat of descending into civil war.

Yeltsin had to take personal responsibility for the use of the army in downtown Moscow, and he did so. Once the decision to storm the White House was made, the operation was well implemented. Tanks fired only twelve shots, enough to produce the needed psychological effect on the besieged, and the defense soon crumbled. In the battle for the White House, less than a hundred people died, including a number of spectators who, in thousands, chose to stay to watch the spectacle despite the danger. There was no popular support for the mutineers. Not a single People's Deputy was killed or arrested.[209] Thus "the fledgling fire of a civil war was put down."[210]

The period of dual power in Russia ended; a short period of authoritarianism followed. For about three months, Yeltsin ruled the country without any institutional restraints. Yet he managed to refrain from abuses of power. Yeltsin eliminated the Supreme Soviet; they died, as one analyst noted, surprisingly uneventfully, which demonstrated that they had indeed outlived their usefulness.[211] The attempt of Yeltsin's right-hand man Vladimir Shumeiko to ban the radical opposition newspapers was short lived; the attempt to restrict political parties that opposed the adoption of the constitution was canceled by the president under the pressure of public opinion. However, Yeltsin did take the opportunity to introduce new clauses into the final draft of the constitution that gave greater power to the presidency; thus he turned Russia into a presidential republic.

Summary

From a political point of view, the totalitarian system was designed and built like a military machine, an extremely well-organized and rigid structure kept together by the all-embracing party-KGB machine. Such a structure turned out to be very brittle and prone to sudden breakdown when the effects of its main social "glue"—systematic terror—evaporated. The totalitarian system did not possess the capacity for adjustment and self-renewal that allows democracies to absorb economic crises and social unrest.

When, in the fall of 1991, the controlling mechanism of the totalitarian system was switched off, the system of power came to a halt and became moribund. However, new sources of power and vitality began to fill the void, surprisingly quickly.

The underground economy, informal cultural life, illegal activities, and private life, all of which had begun to flourish during *glasnost* and *perestroika*, provided the nation with great energy and vitality and kept society alive.

In the fall of 1991 very few visionaries like Yeltsin, Burbulis, and Gaidar believed in the nation's ability to survive what many thought was a looming economic, social, and political catastrophe. The minority of optimists turned out to be right.

Another lesson of the transitional period pertains to the division of power. Two institutions of power emerged to replace the totalitarian system; this division quickly evolved into a dyarchy that proved not only ineffective but mortally dangerous to the nation's survival.

CHAPTER 5

ECONOMIC REFORM

Introduction

From an economic point of view, the Soviet Union was designed as if it were one gigantic company. Resources, production facilities, labor, capital, and distribution were all fully controlled by a single bureaucratic machine, run by the *nomenklatura*. Accordingly, the livelihood of its employees and employers was, at least in theory, completely dependent on centralized supplies of the staples of life.

The transformation of such an economic system into a varied array of markets, therefore, required splitting the finance, production, accounting, and other departments of the company into independent entities—and doing this with a minimum amount of disruption in order not to cause undue hardships for employees. What such a breakdown of centralized control can mean for a complex contemporary society was demonstrated during the 1977 blackout in New York City. During only a 25-hour-long electrical blackout, the city plunged into total chaos and suffered disruptions comparable to those caused by a major natural disaster. Police protecting transportation, and water supplies were paralyzed; looting and robbery were rampant. The overall cost of damages and losses was estimated at several billion dollars.[1]

A total breakdown of the systems of distribution of food, electricity, gas, and water as well as a paralysis of transportation and communications in the Soviet Union would have been disastrous.[2] For generations, the Soviet people were conditioned to expect the central authorities to provide them with the basics of life. At the same time, following the liberalization of the system under Gorbachev, they lost their fear of the repressive apparatus and were not afraid to voice their demands, as the massive rallies and strikes that helped topple the communist regime demonstrated.

Thus the transformation of the economic system had to be accomplished with minimal interruption of the functioning of vitally important institutions. But how is it possible to reform working institutions, all at once, without interrupting their functions, even temporarily?

The Debate About the Model of the Transformation

From 1989 to 1991 a heated debate about transforming the Soviet economy took place. Three major philosophies and approaches emerged. They agreed that "administrative price controls should be abolished, and [that] the currency should become freely convertible,"[3] but they disagreed on the tempo of price liberalization and the privatization of state property as well as their order. One group of distinguished academicians supported a gradual and tightly controlled process, arguing that radical changes would cause famine and social turmoil that would lead to a right-wing coup and a return to dictatorship.[4] They called for a gradual liberalization of prices and the privatization of state property sector by sector and factory by factory, depending on their size and condition.[5] They counted on massive Western assistance, primarily in the form of credits for consumer goods and food purchases, to ameliorate the anger and frustration of the population. Even when the transformation was well advanced, an authority on the Soviet economic system like Harvard professor Marshall Goldman thought that "Russian culture, the seventy years of communism, and its creation of new mind-sets and gigantomanian institutions made rapid economic reform impossible."[6]

Another school of thought was inspired by China's highly successful agricultural reforms.[7] The most notable Russian leader of this school was Arkadi Volski, a former Central Committee member, who was considered a spokesman for the former *nomenklatura*. The rationale was to eliminate restrictions on the use of land and thereby enable the nation to feed itself first; only then would reform be extended into other sectors of the economy. China's experience with the development of special economic zones was considered so successful that during Gorbachev's tenure many regions of the Soviet Union strove to obtain such a status.[8]

China's method was perhaps sensible in a country in which 80 percent of the population was involved in agriculture and was prepared to switch to independent, market-oriented production, which facilitated the subsequent reforms in industry. Because China's agriculture was overwhelmingly based on the manual cultivation of tiny plots, peasants were able to switch to a market system without the state having to investment much in infrastructure.

The free economic zones along the coast of China were also a manifestly Chinese phenomenon that was difficult to replicate. The cities and industries in them were mostly built from scratch and financed by wealthy overseas Chinese. And their freedom had limits. They were fenced off from the rest of the country and the lucky Chinese who settled in these zones enjoyed much higher living standards and the basic freedoms of a market economy.

Such a gradual course of reform, and particularly the artificial division of a country into zones living under vastly different systems, are fraught with serious sociopolitical ramifications. These conditions could be implemented only with the help of a party-state machinery that exerted tight control over the political and economic life of the nation.

In Russia the situation was almost precisely the opposite of that in China. First of all, the communist regime had been overthrown by a popular movement; a power vacuum followed it. Secondly, only 26 percent of the population lived in the countryside. Russian agriculture was monopolistic and industrialized; that is, it was highly integrated with and dependent upon other industries. Perhaps it would have been possible to launch agricultural reforms first and then gradually extend them throughout the economy in 1985, when the regime still in controlled the political situation. However, Gorbachev was reluctant to cede control of the food supply for fear of angering the *nomenklatura*.[9]

The creation of special zones in the three Baltic states and perhaps the Kaliningrad *oblast* was also possible until 1991. However, Gorbachev was reluctant to grant the Balts special status for fear of setting a precedent and promoting the disintegration of the country.

In 1991, when the food situation deteriorated sharply, the USSR's monetary reserves were exhausted, political control had been lost, and more decisive and comprehensive measures were required than permitting the farming of private plots or gradually lessening central planning. The split of the Soviet bloc into twenty-two pieces and "the breakdown of economic ties [among them] undermined [the Russian] economy and the very ability of economic structures to function," as one expert wrote.[10] Thus the opportunity to pursue partial and gradual reforms was lost.

Later, the creation of special zones within Russia, fenced off from the rest of the country as in China, would have been economically costly, morally repulsive, and politically unacceptable to the Russian democrats. Besides, Russia did not have a wealthy diaspora that could finance the construction of industries within such zones.

By the fall of 1991, however, the first positive indicators began to emerge from Poland, where reformers had introduced "shock therapy," that is, a radical liberalization of prices and trade. Russian reformers and their Western advisers both regarded Poland as the example that was most relevant to

Russia. "Shock therapy" proved to be capable of quickly alleviating the most pressing problem in the former communist states: the endemic shortage of food and consumer goods, which was accompanied by depressing and socially explosive half-mile-long lines of tired and angry citizens. However, the inevitable inflation that would follow shock therapy was deemed to be particularly dangerous in Russia, because the Russian leadership did not enjoy the support of a powerful nationwide organization such as Solidarity in Poland.[11]

Eventually Russia opted for a quintessentially Russian-style economic reform. It was more radical than in Hungary, to say nothing of the Ukraine, the privatization drive was much more robust than in Poland, and unlike China, the reforms affected the entire economy, not one sector or specially designated zones.

Only time will conclusively prove which model of reform was better; however, considering the size and peculiarities of Russia, it seemed sensible for its leadership not to try to emulate other countries' reforms in toto.

Reforms

For a proper perspective on the enormous financial costs required by the economic transformation of Russia, one need only look at the price that West Germany paid for reunifying with East Germany, whose economy was only one tenth of the West German economy. It cost $430 billion to revamp and expand the infrastructure of the market economy in eastern Germany.[12] In the words of CIA experts, "the reunification pushed western Germany into its deepest recession since World War II," which lasted almost four years, resulting in 10 percent unemployment, 2 percent decline of GNP,[13] and social tensions manifested in violence against *gastarbeiters* (guest workers).

Considering the size and much worse state of the infrastructure in Russia, an equivalent financial cost would have been 3.8 trillion dollars. Such a huge amount of capital was not available even if the entire community of industrialized countries were to have mobilized all its available resources.

The Liberalization of Trade and Commodity Markets
Prikhvatizatsia ("grabization")

Surprisingly, the necessary resources were unearthed in Russia's own backyard through the mechanism of "privatization and free trade."[14] Even in Stalin's Soviet Union, as Robert Tucker noted, "a life of underground private enterprise in various forms" existed.[15] Later it developed into what

Janos Kornai called the "informal private economy."[16] Gorbachev's relaxation of the rules governing private and cooperative economic activities gave the informal private economy a powerful boost. In 1988 the so-called "spontaneous privatization,"[17] began and by 1991 it had led to the emergence of 268,000 small enterprises[18] and two thousand joint ventures with foreign companies.

The flourishing informal economy provided great help to state-owned enterprises that were left without a centralized supply of parts and materials. Another aspect of the Soviet economic system also facilitated this process. For generations, the highly sporadic system of distribution of resources through *Gossnab* (the State Committee for Material and Technical Supply) had promoted the enormous hoarding of everything that both citizens and enterprises could lay their hands on. Warehouses, storage facilities, the backyards of factories, collective farms, military installations, and the closets of citizens were stocked with food, consumer goods, fuel, equipment, spare parts, raw materials, commodities, and all sort of liquid assets.[19] The amount of liquid assets that the nation had accumulated by 1991 was impossible to estimate accurately (because most were unaccounted for and even forgotten),[20] but it might have amounted to about $700 billion worth of goods according to the official exchange rate.[21] At the same time, money that both enterprises and individuals secreted in banking accounts and under mattresses was estimated to amount to approximately 700 billion rubles.[22]

Yeltsin's advisers argued that these resources "should belong to the producer . . . and he has the right to set prices."[23] Accordingly, a presidential decree of November 10, 1991, abolished *Gossnab* and liberalized domestic and foreign trade.[24] This act had an explosive effect on the informal private economy by bringing a huge amount of resources into circulation. The liquid assets idling and perishing in the country's backyards were uncovered, repaired, packaged, and thus turned into commodities. Commodity exchanges soon opened in every industrial town, their number growing to 650 in 1992. In 1992 alone, according to estimates of economists in the Russian Academy of Sciences, $80 billion worth of commodities and goods were exported from Russia,[25] which is about the amount the United States invested under the Marshall Plan from 1948 to 1952.[26]

This process was popularly nicknamed *prikhvatizatsia* ("grabization"). Critics of the government called it "the greatest swindle of the century,"[27] legalized thievery, and a scheme designed to enrich the *nomenklatura*. The people resented its flagrant unfairness—the fact that only a small group of former members of the *nomenklatura* and swindlers with direct access to these resources benefited from selling them off. This criticism was, to a large degree, justified. Indeed, many of the red directors, *apparatchiks,* and wheeler-dealers of the shadow economy personally profited tremendously from *prikhvatizatia.*

I believe that, from the start, enterprises should have been transformed into joint stock companies. Had that been done, the collectives could have inherited the bulk of both liquid and illiquid assets.[28] Nevertheless, the liberalization of state control over the prices of commodities and consumer goods, as well as the legalization of both domestic and foreign trade, played a life-saving role that has never been fully appreciated by either Russian or Western economists. It provided vital relief for the economy and consumers of Russia. The opportunities to profit generated a tremendous burst of energy among the entrepreneurs who later became known as "new Russians." The red directors also desperately needed the market of commodities and parts to keep their enterprises afloat after the central supply system disappeared.[29]

Reformers philosophically referred to this spontaneous privatization as the unavoidable "era of the initial accumulation of capital," which allowed them to saturate the consumer market with goods and build the infrastructure of a market economy and a functioning monetary system.

Of course, many red directors and wheeler-dealers made tens of billions of dollars and stashed them away in foreign banks. Still, a large portion of this money returned to Russia in the form of consumer goods, parts, and equipment that otherwise would not have been available. This money helped pay employees and avoid massive layoffs, and it fueled a boom in private housing construction. This process promoted the reorientation of production from fulfilling state orders to satisfying consumers. In addition, a large segment of entrepreneurially minded people, including members of the *nomenklatura,* received their first lessons in rudimentary capitalism. The participants developed basic skills such as finding markets, advertising, and solving numerous logistical problems pertaining to supply.

Later the *Economist* wrote that the participants of this gold rush were "risk-taking free-marketeers. . . [who] were just the sort of persons who were to create new companies and new wealth."[30]

Creating the Monetary System
By the standards of free-market economies, the communist monetary system was exceptionally stable. Prices and currency-exchange rates were fixed by decree and did not officially change for decades. Inflation was

allegedly eliminated, once and for all, which facilitated long-term projections and planning.

All this, however, was nothing but an illusion. In reality there was no true monetary system. The ruble was a mysterious entity unrecognized as money outside the country. There were several ruble/dollar exchange rates: one for tourists, one for commercial transactions, one for officials traveling abroad and the one in the black market. The disparity among them approached two orders of magnitude.[31] Apart from the ordinary ruble, there was another *beznalichny* (non-cash) ruble used for transactions between enterprises. The latter was worth roughly half the cash ruble. There were also numerous *sertifikaty* (coupons) that were more valuable than the ruble. The most precious was the *valiutny sertifikat* (a hard-currency coupon), which at one point could be traded for ten ordinary rubles, because it could be used at the notorious *Beriozka* stores reserved for foreign tourists. Foreign financial operations, meanwhile, had their own exchange rates— one for socialist countries, one for the Third World, and another for capitalist countries. Finally, hard currency circulated in the country and was highly desirable, although Soviet citizens were strictly forbidden from possessing it.

In the last days of the communist regime, the ruble itself could buy very few things, and for this reason it was scornfully nicknamed *derevianny* (made of wood). In 1991 the unsatisfied demand for consumer goods was estimated to be as high as $200 billion.[32]

Such was the reality behind the edifice of an allegedly solid financial system.

The absence of a real monetary system made an evaluation of national wealth, productivity, military expenditures, inflation, and the quality of life totally impossible.

In fact, the Soviet monetary system "was patently unstable," because there were fifteen central banks issuing one currency.[33] Only strict political control could maintain the monetary equilibrium. When the totalitarian regime expired in August 1991, the monetary system collapsed. Barter became the principal form of economic exchange.[34]

Hence the reforms did not destroy a stable financial system, as some critics have maintained.[35] Instead they destroyed the distributive system of socialism and the myth of monetary stability. They also introduced a market mechanism that made possible the creation of a true monetary system. As Burbulis correctly remarked, "the deranged financial and monetary system was the main drawback" to a functioning market system;[36] if money is the "economy's blood circulation, then we have been stricken with economic leukemia."[37]

By abandoning price controls and liberalizing domestic and foreign trade, the reformers let the genie of supply and demand out of the bottle. Money began to circulate immediately. In three years the turnover of money tripled.[38] The emergence of the Moscow International Currency Exchange in 1992, and its subsequent rapid growth, made possible by with the lifting of restrictions on currency possession and exchange eliminated the black market in hard currency, which disappeared by 1994. By 1995 the ruble's purchasing power relative to the dollar increased from twelve to fifteen times.[39]

Contrary to most economists' predictions, the construction of the monetary system in Russia was basically complete by 1994.[40] In the words of a Western specialist this Russian "financial revolution" accomplished what the West took several decades to do.[41]

The Creation of the Principal Markets

Anders Aslund correctly pointed out that "a normal market economy has millions of markets," but the principal markets are the "product, labor, capital, and property markets."[42] On January 2, 1992, the state relinquished its control over 90 percent of consumer prices and 80 percent of producer prices, and abolished most wage control.[43] Thus, the reformers started by creating the principal markets, which could be formed relatively easily.

By liberalizing domestic and foreign trade, and liquidating state production quotas, the reformers immediately created commodity and consumer goods markets.

By lifting wage controls and restrictions on the population's choice of residence (except in Moscow and St. Petersburg), the reformers triggered the evolution of a mobile labor market.

By freeing the currency-exchange rate and lifting restrictions on private banking activities, the reformers laid the foundation for the emergence of a financial market. Money became a commodity that could be sold or bought.

While a number of markets were created in a matter of several months, the creation of a market in the means of production turned out to be much more complicated.

It could not function before numerous institutions of a market economy were in place.

Banking, insurance, and mortgage systems, commodity and securities markets, mutual and pension funds, social security networks providing for unemployment insurance, and job-retraining programs all had to be built, from scratch. The laws regulating a market economy had to be written, and a mechanism for enforcing them had to be created.

Privatizing State Property

The creation of a market in the means of production through the privatization of state property was the single most revolutionary element of the economic and social transformation of Russia, just as the nationalization of private property had been for the communist regime in the 1920s. Privatization is far more significant for the future of the country than is suggested by the economists' notion of "allocation of property rights." The means of production, land included, are the main sources of financial power, which, as discussed previously, is the most universal form of power. In other words, financial power is translatable into most other forms of power and therefore affects the distribution of power in practically all spheres of life; it therefore has a profound impact on the nature of a culture.

Although Russian public opinion accepted the need for private ownership of factories and land surprisingly quickly, the methods for redistributing state property into private hands, as well as its timing, were hotly debated for several years. Russia had the most monopolized[44] and militarized economy of all the former communist countries, and there were no ready prescriptions or easy formulas for disaggregating it.

There were several competing theories about the way in which privatization should be accomplished. The primary disagreement was, as usual, between the gradualists and the "shock therapists." Most Westerners advocated a gradual and expensive British-style privatization that would minimize the pain and shock of abandoning the alleged security of life under socialism.[45] The gradualists insisted on selling state property to whoever could pay for it, so that the state would have the resources to sustain a social safety net. They claimed that "the state cannot and should not give property away free of charge, because people do not value free property; it has to be earned."[46]

Another school of thought believed that the property had already been "earned" and advocated quickly returning the bulk of it to the people free of charge. They argued that a democratic government had neither the moral authority nor the legal right to sell property that had been usurped by an illegal regime using coercive methods, often including the extermination of owners. The most prominent and vocal advocates of this philosophy were Larisa Piasheva and Vasili Seliunin.[47]

Yeltsin shared what might be called the give-away philosophy and thought that privatization could be accomplished in a few months through the corporatization of enterprises. Before he came to know Gaidar and other young reformers, Yeltsin spoke about turning enterprises into joint stock companies and compensating older people for their past exploitation.[48] In his seminal speech at the Fifth Congress of People's Deputies of Russia in October 1991, Yeltsin promised that "in the next months, the rapid and massive process of transforming enterprises into joint stock companies will begin. The shares will be distributed between the working collectives and the state. In the next stage, the shares held by the state will be sold to all who are willing to buy them at the market price."[49]

However, Yeltsin's privatization proposal was not implemented, due to a lack of consensus and because "debates over various variations of reforms within the frameworks of socialist illusions have complicated it," as Burbulis later explained.[50]

The actual process of privatization was much delayed and eventually took a very different form. Petr Filippov, one of the most radical democrats, and an influential economic adviser of the president,[51] introduced the concept of voucher privatization.[52] He, like Anatoli Chubais, argued that giving property to collectives would be like creating new communes, because people value only property that they have paid for;[53] he feared that the collectives would veto tough austerity and modernization measures. The latter argument was very prominent in the radical democrats' thinking.

The Role of Anatoli Chubais

In November 1991 Anatoli Chubais, a close associate of Yegor Gaidar, was appointed minister of privatization and chairman of the State Committee for the Management of State Property (GKI). This 36-year-old economist was destined to play a paramount role in Russia's unprecedentedly rapid and large-scale privatization of property.

Anders Aslund characterized him this way: "Anatoli Chubais is an amazing politician who has smoothly done everything right, to the extent that rarely happens. He has combined ideological principles with execution of his ideas."[54] Chubais had the organizational talent to create the GKI from scratch; he skillfully navigated through the rifts of conflicting political and economic interests. He demonstrated rare determination and staying power to see this grandiose project though to its conclusion.[55]

Chubais insisted on the fastest possible privatization, admitting that he "was ready to make many compromises for the sake of this."[56] He had no desire to enrich the state or enhance the power of the bureaucracy by selling off property. He resolutely favored giving property away. However, like most other young reformers, he was highly suspicious of giving property to collectives. He mistook the corporatization of enterprises for collective ownership. He often referred to the negative experience that Yugoslavia had had with workers' management and called successful American experiments with employee-owned enterprises "a fairy tale."[57] He believed that ownership shares should be evenly distributed initially and that the process of natural selection would eventually concentrate property in the hands of the "10-15 percent of intelligent and dedicated" people who were "willing to become efficient owners." He believed that the market would correct all initial injustices and errors.[58]

The Actual Process of Privatization

Russia's privatization was a liberalized version of the voucher program adopted by Czechoslovakia. Russia's program entitled each citizen, including children, to one voucher with a face value of 10,000 rubles, for which they paid a nominal 25 rubles. In addition, because Russian vouchers were transferable, they could be freely sold for cash.[59]

However, the allocation of shares of enterprises in exchange for vouchers and cash became the focal point of many battles in the Supreme Soviet. At the end of an arduous two-year-long process of bargaining among many interest groups, the initial program was significantly amended. Gaidar explained: "We are not the authors of the privatization program. We proposed a different program that did not contain such privileges for working collectives... However, decisions were made by the Supreme Soviet, often contrary to our opinion. As a result, we have a compromise version of the program with many flaws. We cannot change the rules of the game now without running the risk of major social conflict. This is why we should conduct the current privatization to the end and change the rules gradually."[60]

In the final analysis, Russian privatization incorporated many different forms of privatization: self-privatization via conversion to a joint-stock company, buy-outs by employees, auction sales, and a three-option voucher-based privatization in which citizens traded vouchers for shares of their own and other enterprises.

The principal method used for the privatization of small enterprises in Russia was collective buy-outs. By 1995 41,000 retail trade enterprises

(72 percent of the total), and 10,700 enterprises catering to the public (78.3 percent of the total) had been privatized.[61] By 1995 75.2 percent of all enterprises in trade, those catering to the public, and domestic services were privatized.[62] The privatized trade enterprises accounted for 85 percent of retail sales.[63] Altogether, by July 1994 90,000 small businesses (80 percent of enterprises with less than 200 employees) had been sold.[64]

The principal method for the privatization of middle- and large-sized enterprises was corporatizaton. By June 1994 70 percent of Russian large- and mid-sized industrial enterprises were privatized,[65] including several seaports;[66] major airports;[67] and enterprises in the transportation energy, defense,[68] and metallurgy sectors.[69] Altogether, by October 1995 118,500 enterprises were privatized.[70]

After the most painful, controversial, and politically dangerous stage of privatization was concluded, on July 1, 1994, the second stage of privatization began. Companies were now obliged to sell about 25 percent of their shares on the stock exchange for cash, to whoever wanted to buy them, including foreign investors.[71] Seven thousand auctions were held in Russia in 1995.[72]

Fifty-one percent of the earnings from the sales of shares were to go to the companies' investment funds. On the other hand, these newly privatized firms now face the threat of bankruptcy,[73] in which the crucial role would belong to institutional investors—investment funds, holding companies, and mutual and pension funds—that can acquire many shares. The Damoclean sword of bankruptcy hangs over the heads of company executives, forcing them to strive for efficiency and competitiveness or lose their jobs. Simulta- neously, the existing 650 investment funds[74] were limited to owning no more than 10 percent of the shares of any company (not 20 percent as in the Czech Republic). This restriction prevents the overconcentration of owner- ship and increases competition among financial institutions. "Thus, the sec- ond phase of privatization has begun in Russia with many good signs," one analyst observed.[75]

Mistakes and Their Potential Ramifications

Critics of Russian privatization have claimed that it failed to improve efficiency, create a social safety net, promote financial stability, attract for- eign investments, and increase ownership by entrepreneurs.[76] This criticism is misplaced, because the privatization initially aimed only at transferring property into private hands, thereby creating the necessary preconditions for achieving the other goals. On the other hand, the privatizers can be reproached for real mistakes concerning the sociopolitical aspects of privatization.

First, one must dispel the popular misconception that holds that the party-state *nomenklatura* possessed all the means of production, capital, and land. In fact, the property of the Soviet state did not belong to anyone in particular. If anything, the Communist Party owned it collectively. The members of the *nomenklatura*, to use Anders Aslund's terms, were only skimming rent from the property that they managed.[77] Nor did Russia have any previous owners from the pre-Soviet era who could claim property rights. These two facts made it much easier for the leadership to distribute state assets than was the case in Poland, Hungary, or the Baltic states. At the same time, those who were already managing property had tremendous advantages. First the "informal privatization" and *prikhvatizatsia*, and later the introduction of the 5-percent quota of stocks for management turned the privatization into "*nomenklatura* privatization."

This was not the privatization that Yeltsin had in mind initially. In fact, in his key speech on October 28, 1991, Yeltsin strongly emphasized the need to stop the "personal privatization actively pursued by the party-state elite." In my view, Yeltsin's concept of privatization through turning enterprises into joint-stock companies was the correct way to prevent "*nomenklatura* privatization."[78] The main defect of the voucher system was that it was grossly unfair to give the same amount of investment money in the form of vouchers to a newborn baby and to a 50-year-old father of three who had invested his entire life in an enterprise.

The pragmatists among the democrats argued that the members of the former *nomenklatura* should be given a second chance to find their place in commercial structures and be transformed by (in Burbulis' words) "the objective logic of a competitive economy,"[79] so as to "become allies of reform, not its enemy."[80] Indeed, many ambitious and capable people were in the *nomenklatura*, and they deserved the opportunity to have a business career. However, ordinary people were perfectly aware that the managers had used the illegitimate political power of a totalitarian regime to attain commanding positions in their enterprises, and they did not want them to profit from their positions.

In the eyes of ordinary people, it was equally wrong to give wheeler-dealers on the black market and outright criminals the opportunity to legally launder dirty money through the sales of small enterprises at auctions. After all, most black-marketeers violated not only questionable communist laws but common ethical standards as well. Ninety percent of the buyouts of restaurants, shops, and other service-related enterprises were, in fact, "sponsored by large investors,"[81] that is, by the sharks of the black market.

Unlike the *nomenklatura* and black-marketeers, the majority of people under the communist regime preferred relative passivity to the active pursuit of a career, which required demeaning political and moral compromises. They were more scrupulous about participating in dirty financial or political games. This is why the "Chubais privatization" that privileged the managers and benefited black-marketeers and criminals struck many people who had tried to maintain their integrity under communism as morally wrong.

One can only hope that the reformers were right, and that the market system will lead the former members of the *nomenklatura* and blackmarketeers to change their methods, that competition will force them to cultivate good reputations by serving their customers.

Unfortunately, the greatest damage to the market economy and the social climate in Russia resulted from an injustice done to the nascent middle class, a large portion of which was concentrated in the military-industrial complex. The eight million or so of these highly skilled professionals were the nation's depository of professional expertise and moral integrity. They (particularly those trapped in the military-industrial complex) were humiliated and dispirited by voucher privatization.

The little savings that they had were wiped out by inflation. In general, their only compensation for decades of exploitation was a modest two-room apartment. Nor did they have the political power or the connections enjoyed by the *nomenklatura* whose members were able to obtain the credit needed to purchase large quantities of vouchers.

As a result the middle class turned bitter and frustrated. It was they to whom Yeltsin referred when he conceded that "not only bandits and political gamblers took to the streets [in October, 1993]. There were other people among the protesters who had lost hope and despaired."[82] Later, many of these frustrated professionals cast protest votes for Zhyrinovsky.[83]

These regrettable mistakes of the privatization process could have been prevented; the professional class could have received its due share of property if the privatization process had distributed shares differently. The distribution of shares among employees would have rewarded people for their contribution to the well-being of society in the past. The number of shares could have been adjusted to take into account employees' age, their tenure on the job, professional skills, and the size of their families.[84]

Such a remuneration of the professional strata would not only have been fair, it would also have been pragmatic. The skilled professionals would have had the greatest vested interest in the survival of their enterprises, and they also knew better than anyone else how to ensure it. They knew best how to improve the quality of their products and how to increase productivity; they knew what new products could be quickly launched into production. Any plan that did not tap their energy and expertise was flawed in its very foundation.

Results

These mistakes and shortcomings notwithstanding, foreigners (both academics[85] and businessmen with hands-on experience in Russia)[86] have termed Russia's privatization "the most successful part of the economic reforms,"[87] which put Russia ahead of almost all other former communist states,[88] including those with a head start, like Poland,[89] Hungary[90] and Slovakia.[91] These countries have privatized only profitable enterprises because their principal method was sales at auction. As a result, they were stuck with the bulk of loss-generating enterprises, which no one would buy.

Two people, Yeltsin and Chubais, deserve full credit for the radical and speedier privatization in Russia. Both of them demonstrated a rare resolve in relentlessly pushing the program forward, [92] and they continue to do so. In 1994 Russian reformers liberalized the rules of land ownership for companies. According to the presidential decree of July 22, 1994, companies can now purchase land for a very low price (only three times the rent that they formerly paid the state for the use of the land).[93] This measure, in the words of Dmitry Vasiliev, gives ailing factories "chances to attract investments" because "they [can] now mortgage the land or sell the extra land and use the money for restructuring."[94] The Russian government intends to further reduce property owned by the state to only 10 percent of all holding.[95]

In 1988 there were only 214,000 enterprises in Russia, with 43,320 of them being industrial enterprises,[96] compared to about fifteen million businesses in the United States. In the 1990s the number of newly created small businesses exploded, by 1995 it had grown to 1,038,000.[97] The total number of enterprises, including those in the agricultural and service sectors, grew to 2.5 million.[98]

Thus in very short period of time a broad, diverse, and viable economic base has been created as tens of millions of people have become owners of property. The private sector of the economy produces as much as 65 percent of Russia's GNP.[99] The leader of Russia's communists, Ziuganov, has bitterly remarked: "There is 100 times more socialism in modern France than in Yeltsin's Russia."[100]

Reforming Russian Agriculture

Food has always been the most important commodity. Land was fought over because it was the source of food. Navies were built to find new land and secure food shipments. Slavery was used to produce food. Huge subsidies and high tariffs on imported food have been used by governments to sustain the unprofitable domestic production of food. Lately, of course, oil and other energy resources have become equally crucial strategic commodities; in part, however, this is because without them machines could not run and food would not be produced. Even the most advanced economies cannot treat food as a negligible commodity.

Russia's communist experiment with agriculture taught an extremely important lesson from both the philosophical and practical points of view. It was an attempt to create a large-scale, highly mechanized, and centrally run agricultural industry. It had both noble and sinister underpinnings. It was a massive effort to liberate man from dependency on natural elements, to free him from being tied to the land and the slavery of round-the-clock labor, and to release him from the drudgery of rural life. At the same time, the communist agricultural system was designed as one of the principal instruments of totalitarian power. The system of central food production and distribution enabled the party to control not only the life and labor of the peasants but the food supply of the entire nation.

The Historical Perspective

Pre-1917 Russia was an agricultural country.[101] The questions of land and food largely defined its economy and internal politics. The reforms of 1861 by Czar Alexander II were a half-hearted but important step toward liberating the peasantry, which had been confined by serfdom. In 1906 Prime Minister Petr Stolypin took another important step forward, establishing private ownership of land in place of the communal system of land possession. As a result, before World War I Russia developed a significant class of landowners—about 14 million households.[102] By 1914 annual grain production had increased by 65 percent, making Russia responsible for about 30 percent of the world trade in grain.[103]

After 1929 the history of Soviet agriculture was the concerted attempt to increase the size of farms and reduce their number to a minimum, so that they could be controlled from the center, as industry was. This *ukrupnenie*, or enlargement, was considered the key to progress in agricultural working and living conditions. Whereas in the United States, enlargement led to more economical forms of production, in the Soviet Union, "the cult of bigness . . . ha[d] its ideological roots in the orthodox Marxist doctrine of economic concentration, which stresses the similarity, as far as large-scale methods of production are concerned, between agriculture and manufacturing."[104] By 1935, 25 million small peasant farms were transformed into a network of 245,400 collective farms. This process was further advanced during the 1950s and 1960s when the number of collective farms was reduced by more than 75 percent[105] to only 46,000 farms in the late 1970s.[106] Under Gorbachev, centralization continued, and the role and scope of responsibility of the State Supply Agency (*Gossnab*) were increased accordingly.[107]

Soviet agriculture was also one of the most mechanized in the world. It employed more people and used more machinery and arable land than American agriculture. The cultivated area in the USSR was 40 percent larger than that in the United States. The capital stock per unit of farm output was 3.5 times higher than in the United States. The Soviet labor force involved in agriculture was nine times that of the American agricultural labor force.[108] It used 2.5-3 times more fuel for one unit of land than American or Canadian farmers.[109] Soviet agriculture used 50 percent more mineral fertilizers (81 kg. per hectare)[110] than did American farmers. In short, the communist leadership succeeded in creating a large-scale, highly mechanized and centrally run agricultural industry. However, the results, when measured in terms of the balance of exports and imports and food production, were dismal.

Average U.S. grain production was 25 percent higher than that of the USSR,[111] and the productivity of the average Soviet farmer was only about one-eighth that of the average American farmer. The United States has been the world's largest grain exporter, while the USSR was the largest grain importer. Thus in 1990 the Soviet Union imported 40 million tons of grain, spending about $14.7 billion to do so.

The Achilles' heel of Soviet agriculture was not production but the deficiencies of the extremely centralized system of storage, processing, and distribution, as well as inefficient use of the produce. In the United States, 60 percent of storage facilities are located on farms, and losses of produce do not exceed 3 percent;[112] by contrast, only 40 percent of all farms in the Soviet Union had food storage facilities. Most Soviet farms had to transport grain 100 to 300 miles to the nearest grain elevator.[113] Produce was trucked to a railroad station, unloaded, stored, then loaded in the railroad cars, shipped hundreds or even thousands of miles, unloaded, stored, and then trucked to a food processing plant. Huge amounts of food, perhaps as much as 60 percent of the total, were lost in transit from the field to the grocery store. For example, in 1989 as much as 50 million tons of grain were estimated to have been lost or to have rotted in the fields and on the roads.[114] During the record harvest of 1990 the USSR grew more grain than the United States, but at least 70 million tons of it was lost.

In addition, the use of grain was highly inefficient. For example, in Russia, bread grain constituted 55.6 percent of grain production, compared to only 23.4 percent in the United States. As a result, wheat was often used for feeding livestock.[115]

All these inefficiencies were a direct result of the bureaucratized control and the alienation of the producers from the means of production and the fruit of their labor. Yet Gorbachev's program of transition toward a market economy contained provisions for "state control over key staples such as bread, meat, dairy products, etc."[116] A very elaborate "structure including food packages, food coupons, and so on," was elaborated to feed the population;[117] yet by 1990 the food crisis had reached near-famine proportions.[118] The Soviet government appealed to Western governments for emergency food deliveries, and special KGB units were ordered to handle the distribution of foreign food aid. Even in Moscow, 50 percent of all state grocery stores had no meat for sale,[119] and even problems with bread supplies developed.[120] A headline in the December 4, 1991, edition of *Izvestia* read: "The Government of Moscow Considers the Food Situation Catastrophic."

Radical Changes in the Nature of Agriculture

Yeltsin knew perfectly well that "the power of party officials lay in their monopoly over agriculture, and this is why they were reluctant to give it up."[121] Under his leadership, starting in 1990 the RSFSR Supreme Soviet passed much legislation to facilitate private land-holding and farming. The Law On Private Ownership of Land and Farming, adopted by the Russian Parliament in December 1990, opened the way to private farming, although it continued to place major limits on the use and sale of land.

In October 1991 the RSFSR Congress of People's Deputies imposed a ten-year delay before land could be resold or repurchased.[122] But in December 1991 Yeltsin signed two decrees: "On the Acceleration of Privatization" and "On Urgent Measures for the Realization of Land Reform in the RSFSR."[123] They removed important stumbling blocks that hindered privatization of land and private farming.[124] The decree instructed all farms to reorganize by January 1, 1992. They were given several options: to disband and divide up their land and equipment, to become joint-stock companies, or to remain cooperative enterprises.[125] Eventually, 40 percent of collective farms chose to become associations, 32 percent became joint-stock companies, 21 percent became cooperatives, and 7 percent remained collective farms with full ownership of land. Two thousand, six hundred loss-generating farms were disbanded, and their land and equipment were sold at auction.[126]

Initially the democrats were tempted to immediately disband the hateful collective-farm system by decree. For example, Petr Filippov, a presidential economic adviser, promoted the idea of the mandatory splitting of collective farms into small units employing no more than 30 people.[127] The radical democrats placed great emphasis on the creation of family farms, and at one point they anticipated that in several years Russia would have about one million of them. Indeed, initially the growth of private farms in Russia exceeded all expectations: their number increased from 8,931 in March 1991 to 50,000 in December 1991, 150,000 in July 1992,[128] and 290,000 in November 1994.[129] Initially, the idealism of those seeking a return to the soil also played a significant role in the reemergence of family farming. Thus more than half of new farmers came from the cities and the military.[130] However, by 1994 31,200 family farms had disappeared,[131] and the creation of new farms has since slowed down. The total number of family farms has seemed to recede below the 290,000 mark.

A number of people, most prominently a powerful collective-farm lobby, but also some American agro-industrialists, argued against the "complete privatization of the agrarian sector."[132] They believed that the former collective farms should be given a second chance, that private ownership and liberation from the yoke of the central plan would radically change their incentives and make them more efficient. They believed that if large Russian collective farms owned their produce and were free to sell it at the best market price, they might quickly become more efficient and profitable. They pointed to the experience of the United States, where large agricultural firms were more productive and efficient than small family farms. In Poland, too, small family farms were experiencing difficulties. These arguments prompted Yeltsin to reject the forced disbandment of collective farms and to seek a solution that could incorporate many types of farms.[133]

All collective farms were given a choice; even those farms operating at a loss were only urged to disband rather than being forced to do so.

The leader of the Agrarian party, Mikhail Lapshin, perhaps the most vocal advocate of collectivized farms and a consistent critic of the government, described the allegedly coercive methods of the reformers in the following way: "Look at recent events in Nizhni Novgorod *oblast*. Temptations were offered to the leaders of six *kolkhozes*. They were taken on trips abroad, a major advertising campaign was launched, people got carried away, and these farms ceased to exist. People find it difficult to resist such propaganda pressures."[134] Indeed, thousands of Russian farmers were trained in Germany, the Netherlands, Sweden, and the United States.[135] Thousands of Western farmers also visited Russia to share their expertise and experience.

Since 1991 significant changes have occurred. Prices have been freed, and the obligatory deliveries of grain to the state have been abolished. Grain prices are now determined by the market. After his October 1993 victory over the Supreme Soviet, President Yeltsin signed a historic decree permitting land to be sold.[136] Thus Yeltsin used the short period of his authoritarian rule to remove the last obstacle to profound reforms in Russian agriculture. This decree allowed people to buy and sell land and to use it as collateral, thus laying the foundation for a mortgage system and private investments. These measures have drastically improved attitudes and motivations even in the large agribusiness companies.

By the middle of 1995 Russia had a rather diverse agricultural industry: from small family farms with an average 42 hectares of land;[137] to midsized farms specializing in poultry, hogs, dairy, and vegetables; to huge agribusinesses. Eighty-five percent of arable land in Russia is in private hands.[138] Now the forces of market competition will determine their future. In addition, the influx of hundreds of thousands of highly skilled Russians from the former republics who settle mostly in the countryside gives Russian agriculture its first real chance for revival after generations of drainage and exploitation.[139]

Explaining the Food Paradox
From 1986 to 1990, Russia produced, on average, 105 million tons of grain per year.[140] From 1991 to 1994 average annual production declined by 10.5 percent, to 94 million tons, and to only 69 million tons in 1995.[141] Nevertheless, the food situation in Russia is better than at any time since World War I. The abundance and variety of food products is astonishing by Russian standards. How can one explain this paradox?

Losses are Declining
The main factor has been a decline in the previously huge loss of produce, which was caused by the poor infrastructure and the lack of motivation pervading the system.

After produce became a freely traded commodity owned by the producer, the incentive to ensure that the harvest was delivered to market was greatly enhanced. Analysts have estimated that losses have dramatically declined by as much as 25 percent.[142] In addition, the use of bread grain for animal feed fell drastically.[143]

However, losses still remain too high by the standards of developed countries. The poor infrastructure remains the main reason. The leadership is aware of this and has sought to ameliorate the problem by introducing private enterprise into "the entire system governing the transportation, storage, and processing of farm produce."[144]

Of course, the entire existing infrastructure cannot be thoroughly improved in a few years. Infrastructure development is currently one of the most rapidly growing business sectors in Russia;[145] entrepreneurs are building small and mid-size storage facilities, grain dryers, and food-processing factories, and they are developing a packaging industry.[146] But it will take several years before the situation can change dramatically in this sector.

Another endemic problem is in technical support infrastructure. Russia has a huge mass of agricultural machinery. However, on average, up to 40 percent of it has historically set idle due to a lack of spare parts.[147] The industry was plagued by low quality and a lack of professional service. Now this situation, too, has begun to gradually change. Russia has one of the biggest pools of mechanics in the world. They have now begun to form companies specializing in servicing agricultural machinery. Some of them have also offered their services in sowing and harvesting, and a growing number of large and small farms have hired these mechanized firms.[148]

All these factors have significantly increased the efficiency of agricultural firms. In 1993 the agro-industry of Omsk *oblast*, for example, used less than half as much machinery and fuel as in 1970, yet it was just as productive.[149]

Private Plots

The tilling of tiny private plots by families has always been an important part of Russian agriculture. Every third family was involved in growing potatoes or vegetables, raising pigs, or keeping chickens. In May 1985 Gorbachev allowed the additional allocation of about one million private plots per year.[150] However, all restrictions on the private ownership of plots were removed only under Russian leadership. In 1993 there appeared to be about 50 million private plots, and they accounted for perhaps as much as 40 percent of gross agricultural production.[151] In addition, the number of private greenhouses increased to about 25 million[152] and the family-held livestock increased by an average 45 percent.[153]

Grain Self-Sufficiency Achieved

All these factors contributed to a dramatic reduction in grain imports. Centralized grain imports fell from 27 million tons in 1992[154] to 11 million in 1993, to about 2.5 million tons in 1994.[155] Only 1.7-2 million tons of grain are likely to have been imported by Russia in 1995.[156] In addition, "In 1993 Russia stopped all imports of potatoes, vegetables, and wool,"[157] and imports of sugar fell by 28 percent to 1.2 million tons.[158]

At the same time, "in 1994 Russia [became] the most active supplier of grain to the former USSR republics," with no less than three million tons of grain to be shipped in 1995.[159] Even Ukraine, the former breadbasket of the USSR, imported more grain from Russia than it exported to it. Only with Kazakhstan was the balance of trade in grain negative for Russia.[160] In addition, Russia managed to export 1.5 million tons of grain to countries outside the CIS from the 1994 harvest,[161] including 400,000 tons of barley and 700,000 tons of wheat.[162] Thus, despite a poor harvest in 1994, Russia has already became a net grain exporter.

In sum, four years after the reform of agriculture was launched, not only has Russia reached self-sufficiency in the traditional staple, grain, but it is increasingly clear that in several years Russia will take its place among the major world exporters of grain.

At the same time, Russian imports of meat, poultry, and butter are growing[163] and are likely to continue to do so, as the diet of Russians becomes more diversified and sophisticated.

Conclusion

The transformation of Russia from a food importer under communism system to a food exporter today proves that, given modern technology and the incentive provided in a free-market system by ownership of the means of production and land, any nation with a suitable geographic endowment can feed itself. Speaking more broadly, food is losing its paramount role as a strategic commodity that governments are obliged to secure by all means. A developed nation should rather concentrate on securing access to information and supplies of cheap energy.

Defense Industry Conversion

The radical democrats regarded the military-industrial complex of the Soviet Union as the most monstrous creation of the totalitarian regime and the principal impediment blocking the transformation to a market economy.

Indeed, as discussed earlier, the Soviet Union was conceived as a fighting machine. In the words of one analyst, "the Soviet Union did not have a military-industrial complex (MIC), it was one."[164] The MIC was the basis of the Soviet Union's claim to superpower status, as well as the second largest source of its hard-currency earnings.[165]

The entire economy was geared to the production of superior weapons. This orientation was reinforced during World War II, when another totalitarian regime demonstrated its technical superiority. By the end of Brezhnev's era of stagnation, the MIC had begun to falter and could not meet the new challenge from the United States. In response the Politburo elected Gorbachev to the post of General Secretary with the mandate to invigorate the Soviet military-industrial complex and make it more competitive.[166]

The enormity of "this largest military-industrial complex of all time"[167] can be grasped by comparing its output with that of the United States. In 1989 the Soviet MIC manufactured 1,700 tanks (2.3 times as many as the United States), 300 multiple rocket launchers (6.2 times as many as the United States), 750 units of self-propelled artillery (19 times as many as the United States), 5,700 armored fighting vehicles (8.8 times as many as the United States), and 140 ICBMs (11.1 times as many as the United States).[168] Between 1965 and 1990 the Soviet MIC manufactured 100,000 tanks— more than the rest of the entire world combined[169]—and 243 nuclear-powered submarines, 22 more than were produced by the rest of the world.[170]

In addition to producing weapons, the defense industry had long been a major source of civilian goods, producing all of the former Soviet Union's civilian aircraft, radios, cameras, television sets, sewing machines, and VCRs; 93 percent of the refrigerators; 80 percent of food processing and medical equipment; and a large share of the country's industrial equipment.[171]

Russia inherited more than 60 percent of the USSR's military-industrial enterprises, capital stock, and research and development facilities. Estimates of the relative size of the defense industry in the Russian economy vary. Thus, according to former prime minister of Russia Ivan Silaev, 75 percent of Russian industry was military-related;[172] according to Anatoli Chubais, 63 percent.[173] Other analysts estimated that the MIC consumed up to 80 percent of Russia's raw materials and technical, financial, and intellectual resources.[174] In 1992 the Committee for the Defense Industry of the Supreme Soviet supervised 1,750 factories.[175] By the middle of 1993 the Russian MIC still employed 6 million people and had 1,400 factories and 967 research institutes.[176]

The democrats were convinced that Russia faced no immediate external threat and therefore that the lion's share of the MIC's production "was not vitally necessary:"[177] in place of six incapable divisions Russia needed "only one fully equipped and ready to fight."[178] Gaidar promised "to cut arms procurement with the utmost severity"[179] and to force the MIC "to produce more television sets;"[180] he was true to his word.[181]

In 1991 the Gaidar government slashed military orders by 32 percent and by 68 percent in 1992 (compared with the previous year).[182] This led to a 24-26 percent fall in the production of military hardware in 1993.[183] Some areas in which the defense industry was particularly highly concentrated were hit even harder—for example, in Udmurdia, where 80 percent of industry was military-related. By the end of 1994 military orders had dropped to 10-12 percent of total industrial production.[184]

This policy continued in 1993 when Chernomyrdin became prime minister.[185] He once bluntly told the arms manufacturers: "Listen, we don't need more cannons." At the same time the democratic government stopped selling Russian weapons to the Soviet government's traditional clients, such as Libya, Iraq, and Yugoslavia. Arms sales dropped from $11 billion in 1989 to $4 billion in 1992,[186] and to less than $2 billion in 1993.

Military Doctrine and Conversion

Many defense contractors in the Soviet Union duplicated one another's efforts; such duplication was much higher than that in the United States. It was clear that this redundancy needed to be eliminated by defense conversion. In 1993, according to the League of Defense Factories, the majority of defense enterprises opted to become private enterprises serving civilian needs.[187]

The problem of converting the Russian defense industry to civilian production was complicated by the need to reconsider the country's place in the world and to redefine its role on the continent and its relationships with its immediate neighbors. This could not be done until Russia's existence as an integral state was secured and its economic potential established. Until then, any attempts to redefine the nation's military doctrine (and consequently the state's policy toward the defense industry) could not be founded in political and economic realities. Specifically, until such a doctrine was formulated, it was impossible to decide which plants should be converted to serve civilian needs and which should remain under state control.

Only in the autumn of 1993 was the government able to define its new military doctrine. It was then decided that only 454 defense factories were to remain fully state-owned by the end of 1995;[188] this number was to be further reduced to 430.[189] For example, 71 out of 128 aerospace industrial enterprises were scheduled to be privatized by 1996.[190]

In 1993 900 defense factories were in the process of conversion to civilian production,[191] and by August 1994 half of them had become joint stock companies.[192] However, by then the consumer market was largely saturated with domestic and foreign goods; as a result, it was hard for the converted firms to compete.

Conversion from military to civilian production is difficult everywhere. Many American defense contractors are currently in trouble, and it seems likely that a number of them will disappear. Although it has declined somewhat, the U.S. defense budget has remained relatively steady, so that conversion can be stretched over a period of many years and its impact softened. The Russian defense industry had no such cushion because of the lack of resources. Defense conversion adviser Mikhail Malei estimated in 1993 that $150 billion dollars would be needed during the next 15 years to convert the Russian MIC to civilian production.[193] In reality, in 1992 only 77 billion rubles (about $260 million according to the average exchange rate) were allocated for conversion of the defense industry; in 1993 300 billion rubles (or $370 million) were allocated,[194] and in 1994 900 billion rubles ($400 million).[195] The salary of an average worker in a missile factory in late 1992 was only 5,000 rubles a month, while the average salary in industry was 10,373 rubles.[196] Moreover, very often salaries were not paid for two months or longer.[197] From 1992 to 1993, 1.5 million specialists left the defense industry.[198] Mikhail Malei sarcastically called this process not conversion but "a spontaneous dying down."[199]

During the first two years the defense plants had one advantage: a seemingly insatiable demand for consumer goods and a lack of competition. Many defense enterprises expanded their production of consumer goods. Thus, in 1992 the production of many durable consumer goods increased, on average, by 12 percent.[200] In the first ten months of 1993 the production of refrigerators increased by 17 percent, freezers by 60 percent, automated kitchen appliances by 42 percent, color television sets by 7 percent, and small electric motors by 10 percent.[201]

By 1994, however, this window of opportunity disappeared, because of the increase in imports resulting from the reformers' free trade policy. The Russian consumer goods market was soon filled by foreign electronics and home appliances of generally better quality and design. Hence a number of defense factories that were given the green light for conversion in late 1993 found themselves in a particularly difficult position. Not only did they have to convert, but they now had to face well-entrenched competition, both domestic and foreign. As a result, in 1994 the production of consumer goods by defense enterprises fell by 35 percent.[202]

By 1994 examples of successful conversion were nevertheless plentiful.[203] Lipetsk's Stinol refrigerators are said to be world class.[204] Yaroslavl's

"Mashpribor" produces camcorders and Rybinsk's "Instrument-making Plant" produces air conditioners and refrigerators.[205] Rail cars formerly produced in Riga were replaced by Tverv's factory, and electric motors from a Tallinn factory were replaced by a factory in Voronezh. Hungarian Ikarus buses and Lvov buses were replaced by the "Sukhoi" factory of Saratov, Tushino's machine-building factory,[206] and the "Sokol" factory of Moscow.[207] As a result, the production of city buses increased from 500 in 1993 to 3,600 in 1995.[208] The loss of Georgia's electromotive production and Czechoslovakian Skoda locomotives is being compensated for by the Novocherkassk locomotive factory with the help of the American ABB company.[209] The ship-building plant "Sevmash" builds oil platforms[210] and oil tankers.[211]

Arzamas' Machine Building plan—the manufacturer of Armed Personnel Carriers—has expanded production by adapting its military vehicle to logging, mining, and agricultural needs. It has also started producing spare parts for Russian automobile factories that used to receive them from neighboring countries."[212] Instead of producing tanks and heavy tractors, Tikhvin's "Transmash" now produces high-speed locomotives.[213] Five years ago, Tomsk's "Instrument" plant was a super-secret defense factory and 90 percent defense-oriented. In July 1994 defense contracts comprised only 10 percent of its total production. Among its new products are medical equipment, water meters, and incubators.[214] Saratov's "Reflektor" plant was able to survive by converting from the production of electronic equipment used for MIG-29 fighters to the production of home electronics.[215] "Leninets" of St. Petersburg has developed gas pumps which were previously not manufactured by Russian industry.[216] The Design Bureau Khimavtomatika (KBKhA) in Voronezh, a leading designer and producer of liquid-propellant rocket engines, now produces equipment for oil, gas, water purification, and food processing. It has quadrupled its production of chemical pumps for the treatment of oil wells.[217] State orders fell by 78 percent for Kursk's "Elektroagregat" plant. Nevertheless, it survived by dramatically expanding its production of portable power stations, transformers for welding, pumps and other equipment for agriculture.[218]

The conversion of what are known as city-factories, however, was immeasurably more difficult. Seventy-four such city-plants, some having a population of about 100,000 people, existed.[219] They were devoted to the production of missiles, nuclear or chemical weapons, tanks, airplanes, nuclear submarines, and artillery.[220] Many of them, like Arzamas-16, exclusively fulfilled defense contracts.[221] As Shumeiko eloquently put it, "Some plants are not only state-owned. They were built as part of the state itself from the outset. Cities and whole infrastructures totally depending on them rose around such plants. To reconstruct such plants means to reconstruct the old political system where they are located. This is difficult."[222] Conversion of these city-plants into ordinary cities is likely to be a long and agonizing process.

Results

Nevertheless, contrary to the doubts of some skeptics,[223] the Russian MIC has already undergone a radical transformation. First of all, it has been dramatically scaled down, as is reflected in the decline of the defense budget from at least 30 percent of GNP under the communist regime to 4.73 percent of GNP in 1992, 4.4 percent in 1993, and 4.9 percent in 1994.[224] Moreover, it is projected to further decline to 3.6 percent of GNP in 1996.[225] The production of all weapons was reduced by six times[226] and the production of certain weapons (such as chemical weapons, strategic bombers, and tactical nuclear warheads) has stopped altogether. Secondly, the MIC has ceased to dominate and define the rest of the economy. Instead, it must now live according to the laws of supply and demand. In the judgment of Anders Aslund and Viktor Glukhikh, Chairman of the Duma Committee for Defense Industry, it has "generally adapted to market conditions."[227]

The change in the mindset of many red directors of the former MIC supports this assertion. They seem to have acquired a taste for life under market conditions. Thus, in December 1994 the League of Defense Industry factories suggested that of the 680 defense plants still fully owned by the state, 60 percent should be privatized.[228] This recommendation corresponds with the assessment of the general director of "Saturn" Scientific Industrial Complex, V. Chepkin. He stated in October 1994 that 25-30 percent of all factories of the MIC had adapted to market conditions, 30-40 percent had begun to adapt, and 30-35 percent had not yet begun to adapt.[229]

Concerns about the brain drain from the MIC also need to be qualified. According to some estimates, 600,000 scientists and one million workers have left the MIC, while 70,000 scientists have emigrated.[230] These statistics may appear to signal the death of the research and development base of the MIC. In fact, however, many employees did not really leave the defense enterprises; instead they formed small private firms affiliated with them, often on the same premises.[231] For example, almost all of Russia's 1,000 manufacturers of personal computer makers were affiliated with defense factories. In 1994 they produced about 400,000 personal computers, mostly assembled from imported components.[232]

Conclusion

The MIC was the sector of the Russian economy that was hit hardest by the transformation to a market economy. The reformers treated it more ruthlessly than any other sector of the economy. State orders and subsidies were mercilessly cut, including funds for conversion. The status of many defense factories was not defined during almost two years of reforms, and they were the last to become privatized and enter the market.

It is therefore amazing that the former MIC has resisted the reforms only mildly. For example, none of the defense city-plants exploded in social unrest, no Russian nuclear scientists migrated to rogue states that are seeking to develop their own nuclear programs, and no nuclear devices or material was smuggled out of Russia to terrorist states or groups.[233]

The conversion of the defense industry will be a long and painful process, but the most critical and politically dangerous stage of it seems to have been completed. Instead of being a hindrance to the free market, Russia's former defense industry can provide a powerful impetus for technological progress.

The Emerging Market Economy

One American expert noted that "while the popular press was focused on stories of chaos and corruption, Russia was building the financial infrastructure it needs for a modern market economy."[234] As the president of Overseas Private Investment Corporation (OPIC), Ruth Harkin, admitted, "Russia is moving faster toward the free market than anyone had expected."[235]

Indeed, in just three years the edifice of a viable economic system was erected on the ruins of the centrally run distributive system of socialism. The entire network of private and government institutions that compose a market economy was built from scratch, including 2,500 insurance companies, 2,543 banks,[236] 646 investment funds,[237] 1000 private pension funds,[238] and 93 stock and commodity exchanges.[239]

All the basic government institutions essential for the functioning of a market economy were created. The unemployment and taxation systems were built anew[240] while the state customs services were radically rebuilt. The Chamber of Commerce, the Agency of International Cooperation and Development, the State Investment Corporation, the Financial Corporation, and the International Agency for Insuring Foreign Investments were created.[241] International arbitrage was introduced.[242]

Of greatest importance, a civil code governing the market economy and property relationships has been adopted by the parliament, becoming the law of the land at the end of 1994.[243] Consisting of 650 articles, the Russian Federal Civil Code includes all the basic rules regulating investment, ownership, and shareholding laws characteristic of free-market economies.

In the view of Western specialists, this code was a "significant advance in Russian economic law,"[244] which introduced strict rules governing business practices in Russia that were said to be beginning "to catch on."[245] "Russia has created a solid, credible foundation that will facilitate investment vehicles and opportunities."[246] In short, Russia began to move from the stage of wild ruthless capitalism to a "period of stable, productive, and civilized entrepreneurship."[247]

During the course of a few years, the Russian people were introduced to the brand new world of capitalist finances. To understand this development it is important to remember that the Soviet economy was a cash economy. Although Soviet citizens had savings accounts in state bank branches, they paid cash for everything: rent, utilities, consumer goods, and services. In 1990 only a few members of the *nomenklatura* had checking accounts and credit cards. Soviet citizens were amazed to learn from the press that Mrs. Raisa Gorbachev used the American Express Card on her shopping sprees in London.

By 1995, however, Russian citizens were familiar with the institutions of a contemporary financial system: commercial savings and investment banks, investment, mutual and pension funds, mortgages, stocks, dividends, checking accounts, security deposits, government bonds, and other securities.[248] They have come to appreciate the security of having home, health, car, and life insurance, as well as the convenience of shopping with "plastic money" and using automatic-teller machines.[249] Out of thousands of Russian commercial banks, several dozen have emerged that offer services approaching those of Western banks,[250] which has made possible a Russian "credit card boom."[251] By mid-1995, there were several hundred thousand card holders; the number of credit card users is projected to grow to about 5 million in a few years.[252] Russian credit cards have entered a cooperative relationship with VISA and are beginning to be accepted in Europe, Israel, and other countries.[253]

A "most striking development has been the rapid emergence of a capital market," as one Western observer noted.[254] Indeed, "Russia's stock market has emerged with astonishing speed."[255] In the spring of 1994 a boom on the stock market began.[256] Although later in the year it somewhat subsided, it regained momentum in 1995, primarily because foreign and domestic investors realized that the property that the state was selling at auction was greatly undervalued. For example, Kaluga's "Turbine Plant," which employed more than 11,000 people and produced world class turbines, was sold for $1.5 million.[257] This realization increasingly prompted foreign investors to purchase Russian stocks,[258] while Russian banks began "investing in industry, manufacturing, and construction," as one Russian real estate developer noted,[259] and engaging in friendly and hostile takeovers.[260]

"Since 1993, Russian treasury bills and security markets have grown extremely quickly";[261] by the middle of 1995 the Russian equity market was fully formed and resembled its Western counterparts. Russian financial and equity markets now respond to governmental regulatory activities (such as the Central Bank's changes in interest rates)[262] and they react to political news, both domestic and foreign.[263]

The Structural Revolution

Along with the construction of a market system, the Russian economy underwent fundamental structural changes. Soviet industry, built to serve the strategic goals of the Communist Party, was distorted by a heavy industry that consumed its own products and, in the words of Gaidar, "generated negative value-added for our entire industry."[264] The folklore reflected this expert observation in a popular joke: we dig coal and ore, burn the coal and make steel, which we use to make machines to dig more coal and ore, and so on.

Creating a market economy led to the downfall of heavy industry and the reorientation of the economy toward the consumer market. The production of tractors has fallen to one-sixth its previous level.[265] The production of heavy trucks fell sharply,[266] while the production of small utility trucks increased manyfold,[267] as did the production of popular midsized cars.[268] The production of automobile spare parts,[269] machine tools,[270] and personal computers exploded. In three years, several Russian producers of personal computers grew into sizable companies capable of competing with foreign producers.[271]

The explosive growth of the service economy was not confined to banking. In three years the number of small trade and service companies quadrupled.[272] Two hundred eighty-six private air companies,[273] up to 8,500 travel agencies,[274] and a thousand or so commercial advertising companies emerged.[275] From 1992 to 1994 the number of commercial restaurants grew six-fold, while the total number of restaurants, cafes, and bars grew 3.5 times to 45,000.[276] The car servicing business expanded by several hundred percent.[277]

The overall share of the service sector expanded from 32-35 percent of the economy in 1990 to 53.3 percent in 1994.[278] The volume of services grew in 1994 by 37 percent.[279] The structure of consumption and accumulation changed radically. The share of national consumption increased from 50 percent of GNP in 1992 to 66 percent of GNP in 1994, quickly approaching European standards.[280] The share of private consumption grew to 58 percent of GNP,[281] as opposed to less than 40 percent in 1985.[282]

In short, in the words of Yakov Urinson, First Deputy Minister of the Economy, "Russia's economy underwent a grandiose transformation toward normality."[283] This "qualitatively new economy," to use Chernomyrdin's phrase,[284] is driven by the consumer-goods market rather than by the state's strategic goals. The demilitarization of the economy and its conversion to the production of civilian goods to meet the needs of the population was a painful but healthy phenomenon.

Conclusion

The evidence supports the reformers' claim that "the grandiose task of the creation of a market economy out of a totally centralized and monopolized one was successfully accomplished."[285] The Russian economy has begun to operate largely by the laws of the market, responding to interest rates and other financial levers.[286]

Discussion

Some critics have called "shock therapy" a cold-blooded experiment by monetarists on the living body of the nation. Others maintain that there was no shock therapy, because the liberalization of prices was too gradual and subsidies to inefficient industries remained too large.[287] Still others claim that there was a "big shock, [but] little therapy,"[288] which resulted in "a collapse unprecedented for peacetime"[289] and the "almost total destruction of Russia's economy."[290]

How Much Did the Russian Economy Shrink?

Critics point out that in 1990 Russia's GNP was estimated to be $1,268 billion (that is, 23 percent that of the United States'), while in 1994 Russian GNP shrank to R630 trillion[291] or $170 billion according to the average dollar/ruble exchange rate (about 3 percent of U.S. GNP). Other economists, however, believe that this shrinkage is "a typical delusion";[292] they claim that "cumulative falls in reported GDP have been grossly exaggerated"[293] and point to the relatively small decline in electric power consumption that occurred during this time.[294] The aggregate fall calculated on the basis of Goskomstat data is about a 70 percent shrinkage of the economy.[295]

But to put these figures in perspective, one has to clarify some misconceptions about the Soviet economy. The Soviet Union used its own statistical methods of calculating the Gross *Material* Product, which differed from the United Nations Statistic Commission's methodology of calculating the Gross *National* Product (used by most Western countries since 1968).[296] The Soviet method was flawed by double counting, on the one hand, and the failure to take into account the service sector, on the other.[297] The defense sector was carefully hidden from everyone's eyes, and even top Soviet officials did not know its exact budget.[298] Soviet official data became even worse when the economy began to decline under Gorbachev.[299] In addition, the size of the Soviet Gross Material Product was valued in rubles, the true exchange rate of which was a mystery.

On top of all this, production data were seriously tampered with at both the grassroots and the top level. Enterprise directors were forced to exaggerate their economic performance and understate their production, while the leadership inflated the performance of the economy to prove the cornerstone ideological claim that the socialist system was superior to the capitalist one.

Unfortunately, this distorted picture of the Soviet economy was accepted and even promoted by most Western scholars,[300] as Martin Malia has shown.[301] The few Western economists (most notably Warren Nutter) who drew attention to the flagrant inconsistencies of Soviet official data were ignored and ostracized.[302] For example, the CIA estimated that Soviet GNP was 55 to 60 percent of that of the United States, and Soviet per capita GNP was estimated to be only slightly lower than that of Britain.[303] These miscalculations were costly not only ideologically, but financially too, as was demonstrated during the reunification of the two Germanies. In the West, East Germany's per capita GNP had been estimated to be 12 percent higher than that of Britain, and only 10 percent lower than that of Sweden.[304] This gross miscalculation cost West Germany dearly.[305]

With the beginning of reform, the reliability of Russian statistics deteriorated even further. Although the incentives to exaggerate output have disappeared, the incentives to present the situation in a gloomy light have increased sharply.[306] By understating production and sales state-owned enterprises could solicit state subsidies,[307] while private firms can avoid paying taxes.[308] It was estimated, for example, that most small enterprises have underestimated their production, and at least one-third of them are ignored by the official statistics.[309] As much as 40 percent of agricultural production on private plots and up to 50 percent of retail trade are thought to have been under reported.310 A large portion of trade between former republics has also been under reported.310 Even statistics on foreign trade have been off the mark by many billions of dollars.[312]

In 1994, however, things began to improve. First of all, world statistical methods were adopted by the Goskomstat and became fully operational in 1995.[313] "The reliability of Russian price statistics was recognized by the IMF."[314] Secondly, after the end of privatization paid for through vouchers and the beginning of privatization paid for in cash, the motivation to intentionally depreciate a company's performance has lessened. Both managers and "brokers are realizing the need for Western-style auditing and disclosure if they are going to play the market."[315] The threats of bankruptcy and hostile takeovers also discourage managers from painting a dismal picture of their companies' financial situations.

In short, as is the case of all transitional economies, the size of the economy before the changeover and the extent of the collapse of the state sector after the reform were exaggerated,[316] while the growth in the private sector was greatly underestimated.

However, another factor is more important in explaining why the economy appears to have collapsed completely. Paradoxically, the explanation lies in the opening of the country to the international market. Foreign buyers are not likely to import products from a newly opened economy. New market niches have to be carved out with the help of better and cheaper products. Soviet-made products, however, were notorious for their poor quality, bad design, shoddy packaging, and miserable maintenance. Hence, when Russia entered the international market it had very few goods and commodities worth buying.

The wrenching reorientation of the Russian economy from the production of tanks and submarines to services and the production of consumer goods made a steep drop in economic production inevitable, in the short run. But this contraction was the necessary precursor to healthy economic growth.

The actual fall in the Russian economy's material production probably did not exceed 20 percent.[317] On the other hand, the market value of the country's output was indeed very low, and it fell even further when the production of heavy industry declined sharply. However, the rapid development of the service sectors has begun to restore the market value of the Russian economy. For example, better packaging and marketing alone can significantly increase the value of many Russian products. In fact, the increase has already taken place: Russia's GNP, if calculated according to the ruble/dollar exchange rate, will grow from $170 billion in 1992 to a projected $500 billion by 1996.[318] An illusion of a total collapse would then be followed by the illusion of incredible growth.

Nor have reforms bankrupted Russia. On the contrary, in 1991 the Soviet Union was bankrupt. The budget deficit was about 20 percent of GNP,[319] gold and currency reserves were worth less than $100 million,[320] and Vneshekonombank of the USSR suspended its payments on hard-currency accounts.

Russia's positive balance of trade doubled from $10 billion in 1992 to $20 billion in 1994.[321] The gold and hard-currency reserves of Russia have steadily risen, and in August 1995 they reached $12.4 billion:[322] enough to stop the ruble's fall against the dollar. Although Russia's foreign debt is estimated to be $112.7 billion, other countries owed Russia $147 billion.[323]

Was there a "shock therapy?"

Yeltsin, Burbulis, Gaidar, and Chubais were guided by this principle: the faster one "sow[s] normal seeds of new property relations, the more reliable and calm will be the intellectual, social, and political climate in Russia."[324] However, the welfare mentality of the nation, cultivated over several generations, prevented the reformers from totally liberalizing prices, which could have made the transition faster and simpler.

Friedrich Hayek argued fifty years ago that "if prices are to be fixed by the central authority, they have to be fixed in every individual case," across every industry.[325] The opposite is also true. If markets are being created, as many as possible have to be allowed to develop simultaneously, because they stimulate, promote, and mutually aid one another. Free markets tend to cleanse the system, to use Aslund's phrase, "of distortions and corruptions."[326]

This analyst believes that the high inflation, the destruction of the central distribution system, and the introduction of a broad variety of markets in place of the paternalistic state were indeed a shocking experience for the population. The transition forced every member of society to reconsider his or her source of livelihood and place in society. And yet it is my belief that if pain was inevitable, it should have been administered even more quickly. For example, the delayed privatization of the energy and defense industries, and the gradual liberalization of energy prices only prolonged the agonizing uncertainty in these sectors and the economy at large.

Summary

Many reputable analysts, when evaluating the results of the first three years of economic reforms in Russia, have focused on "instability, when almost anything seems possible,"[327] and claimed that reforms failed and a great opportunity was lost.[328] Their propensity to overlook the incredible economic accomplishments resulting from the reforms is extraordinary.

In this analyst's view, however, the accomplishments of the reformers are enormous and the magnitude of the changes that have occurred boggles the mind. Indeed, in an extremely short period of time, the Russian economy was effectively demilitarized, decentralized, de-monopolized, privatized, monetarized, and reoriented toward consumers' needs. In the words of an American investment banker, it is amazing "how rapidly the [capitalist] economy is evolving in a country where investment bankers were considered capitalist evil incarnate just a few years ago";[329] significantly, this is happening without a massive infusion of capital and resources from outside. In fact, "The word reform does not capture the magnitude of change" in Russia, as one Western analyst has noted.[330] It was a quiet revolution that unleashed new forces, which are now "transforming the entire culture."[331] The economic transformation is yielding social, political and cultural ramifications for the future of Russia that will undoubtedly be enormous.

CHAPTER 6

A Social Portrait of Russia in 1995

Introduction: Pessimists vs Optimists

The economic reforms have dramatically changed the Russian way of life. Everything has changed: how people earn a living, buy things, address one another, choose their homes and vacations, educate themselves, seek medical assistance, and socialize. The changes have been greater for some than for others. Social status, living standards, and the quality of life are now defined differently; different social problems, ills, and fears now preoccupy people. But have these changes been for better or worse? A great debate rages on this issue.

Four years is long enough to assess the lasting impact of the transformation on social conditions in Russia. However, analysts are trying to detect trends, and they have come to staggeringly different conclusions.

One group of analysts is convinced that the price paid by Russian society as a whole has been exorbitant, and that only about 10 percent of the population has benefited from reforms, while the rest of the population has suffered physically and psychologically.[1] Opposition leaders claim that "the results of the democrats' reforms are nothing but a monstrosity,"[2] that they have ruined "a great nation,"[3] subjected its people to genocide,[4] and implanted "universal helplessness and hopelessness".[5]

Characterizing Russian society, one American journalist wrote: "The bulk of the people are doing worse under freedom than ever before. People forget how primitive Russia is—it's the Third World. Russians are dreaming about indoor plumbing, having a little car, not living with their parents. They can now travel, but have no money. They can now vote, but for whom? They can now say what they want, but so what? They are not better off."[6] In 1995 the American Embassy in Moscow published a booklet "How to Survive in Russia," which painted such an apocalyptic picture of Russia that one Russian journalist sarcastically wrote: "I experience a feeling of sincere admiration for our citizens who in this hell are alive by some miracle, and in some places are healthy and cheerful from time to time."[7]

Another side of this picture, as some critical observers have perceived, is the conspicuously luxurious and decadent life-style of the *nouveaux-riches*, or the so-called new Russians. Journalists endlessly write about "members only" clubs and the proliferating casinos in Moscow,[8] where the new Russians easily lose what for ordinary Russians would be a fortune;[9] the thousands of Mercedes-Benzes that roam the streets of Moscow; and the construction of "huge brick villas, trimmed with granite and marble," which "even by Western standards are expensive."[10] The new Russians who "make rich Arabs look like paupers,"[11] have seemingly introduced a fresh cast of characters to the ongoing Western television program "Life-styles of the Rich and Famous."

Many reputable analysts have bolstered this picture of increasing social degradation and polarization.[12] They point to the explosion of social ills such as inflation, unemployment, crime, corruption, increases in drinking and infectious diseases, higher suicide and mortality rates, the fall in life expectancy, and a population decrease. They argue that "growing social disintegration" and the developing chasm between the rich and the poor are creating a highly explosive situation.[13] They worry that the resultant envy, resentment, and hatred may exhaust even the legendary patience of ordinary Russians and create a political maelstrom.[14] Hence it is claimed that the world should brace itself for the direst consequences.

However, a number of other journalists, businessmen, and analysts, both Russian and foreign, argue that this picture of a depressed and dying Russia "doesn't measure up to [their] experiences,"[15] that "things are not as bad as they once looked."[16] Moreover, they "feel the surge of energy in Russia"[17] and see unmistakable signs of "moral and spiritual revival."[18] They argue that behind the crumbling facade of the communist world there is the emerging reality of prosperous private lives that is reshaping Russia into "a fairly normal, democratic, and not so unpredictable country."[19]

So where is the truth? Russian officials concede that social problems and ills have increased. However, they insist that new mechanisms for solving these problems have now been created and that things are bound to improve, because these mechanisms have worked in many different cultures and countries. They believe that Russia can gradually overcome its most pernicious problems with the help of the "invisible hand of the market" and open democratic processes, which allow and encourage broad social participation.

It is surprising that this debate overlooks many critically important social processes in transitional societies. Four years of reforms have already proved the most apocalyptic (and some of the optimistic) predictions wrong. All the important forces, processes, and trends shaping the new Russia must be considered.

Reforms and Social Ills

Before we attempt to assess the societal health of the new Russia, we should recall that, the official Soviet view was that many social ills (such as unemployment, prostitution, drug addiction, and organized crime) did not even exist in the USSR. Until 1986 statistics on many negative social phenomena were kept secret, while other data were completely distorted.[20] In addition, totalitarian methods for resolving social problems were practiced to cleanse society of "unhealthy phenomena." Homeless people, prostitutes, vagrants, and beggars were labeled social parasites and hidden from the public and from foreigners behind the walls of labor camps. Handicapped people were confined to special clinics. Drunkards were collected by the police into prison-like centers in which they were treated inhumanely. In short, the official portrait of a healthy and constantly progressing society was maintained by massive deception and harsh police measures.

When Gorbachev eased the pressures of totalitarian control in 1986 and lifted the restrictions on the mass media, the real picture of Soviet society that soon emerged was shocking. There were revelations of narcomania; prostitution; organized crime; inflation; homelessness; appalling corruption;[21] brutality on the part of the police, the army, and the prison system;[22] rampant poverty among the peasantry; and horrible living conditions suffered by miners. The famous 1990 documentary by Stanislav Govorukhin, "We Must Not Live Like This," painted such a horrible social portrait of the nation that it shocked even the top party elite. Its portrait of a degenerate, despondent, and decaying society resonated tremendously in the Soviet Union and emboldened the Russian parliament to push for radical change.

Soviet society was profoundly ill.[23] The symptoms of the disease, however, had been suppressed by totalitarian power and simply denied. But the relaxation of totalitarian methods did not do much to cure the social ills; instead, it sped up the process of degradation and disintegration.

It was to this diseased society that "shock therapy" was applied. The main component of the shock therapy was the abolition of price controls, which immediately triggered rapid inflation.

Inflation

Critics claim that Russian reformers will never be "forgiven for the fact that prices jumped 1,000 times,"[24] because the inflation utterly impoverished the population and destroyed the existing way of life. Indeed, inflation did eliminate the old economic order; for years it has been the chief concern of the Russian population.[25] Paradoxically, however, the inflation also had effects that improved Russia's economy and society.

First, it should be recalled that inflation was introduced into Soviet life before the reforms. In 1990 it was estimated to be 50 percent annually;[26] in 1991 it surged to 230 percent,[27] and then to a shocking 2,400 percent in 1992. After that, it began to subside, to 840 percent in 1993 and 240 percent in 1994.[28] Inflation surged again to 17.8 percent a month in January 1995, due to the war in Chechnia, and then subsided to 5.5 percent a month in the summer of 1995. The government hopes to bring it to a 1-2 percent monthly level by the end of 1995, and to about 1 percent monthly in 1996.

Although Russian inflation was not by any means unprecedented and never reached the 50 percent per month barrier that defines hyper-inflation (which equals percent per year), five years of high inflation have had a profound psychological effect on society, generating uncertainty, anxiety, and insecurity.

Suddenly the Russian people felt that the state had abandoned them and thrown them to the mercy of a chaotic market. Viktor Chernomyrdin perhaps best expressed public sentiment toward the market when, in 1992, he compared it to a Middle Eastern bazaar.[29] In ordinary people's minds, the market was controlled by the mafia, and they felt like hostages. Inflation also wiped out people's savings: modest as these savings were, they were the sole financial support of many elderly people.

Finally, although Russians have never regarded themselves as wealthy, high inflation and the collapse of the ruble against the dollar suddenly turned a superpower into a Third World country. Almost overnight, the average income of Russians fell to a humiliating .25 percent of that of Americans, putting Russia in the ranks of the poorest countries of the world. As a result, world-renowned Russian professors or musicians seemed like paupers compared with any American student visiting Russia with $100 in his pocket. Many Western businessmen who had failed in their own countries felt like millionaires in Russia.

The inflation occurred because a totally distorted economy and system of values had been maintained by the communist regime for political reasons for 74 years. In 1990 a man's shirt cost as much as a minimal monthly pension. The Soviet population spent 70 percent of its income on food, and in 1989 a personal computer, available only on the black market, cost the equivalent of three years of earnings for an engineer. The price of oil was about 60 times lower than on the international market, while the monthly rent for an apartment was only one-tenth that in neighboring European countries.[30] If Russia was to integrate its economy with the world economy, these huge price differentials had to be corrected, which could only be done by the market, not by the government (as many, including Western economists, advised Gorbachev).

In addition, inflation forced Russia's powerful managerial elite to find new ways of securing its future. Some managers chose to skim off superprofits through their privileged access to commodity trade and abscond with their new fortunes, but the majority of them saw an opportunity to attain security by acquiring private property. By the summer of 1992 the majority of the former *nomenklatura* supported private ownership of the means of production. They had accepted the legitimacy of separating political power from financial power—a major change in the political mentality of people whose well-being had been vested in the existence of totalitarian power. Thus the collapse of the totalitarian system and the resulting rapid inflation had the beneficial effect of converting many *apparatchiks* into potential proprietors and entrepreneurs.

The persistence of Russia's inflation has not been adequately treated even by excellent economists. Anders Aslund, for example, explained inflation persistence as a result of the inconsistencies of the reformers, who, under pressure from the populist Supreme Soviet, made too many concessions to the agrarian lobby, the MIC, and others.[31]

I find this explanation insufficient. In my view, there were several other objective and fundamental reasons responsible for the slow progress in the fight against inflation in Russia.

First of all, Russia's economy was 40 percent smaller than that of the USSR, yet she was left with the burden of its entire money supply. Secondly, the Russian government did not fully control the money supply. For two years the former Soviet republics, with the exception of the three Baltic states, had pursued their own budgetary and monetary policies, yet at the same time their branches of the Central Bank were printing rubles with little concern for the overall stability of the "ruble zone." As Jeffrey Sachs and David Lipton noted, with 13 independent central banks issuing banknotes, there was "no realistic possibility to control inflation."[32] This situation was corrected only in July 1993, when it became clear that almost all the former republics wished to introduce their own currencies. Russia then conducted a partial monetary reform by introducing new large-denomination banknotes devoid of Soviet symbols, thus protecting itself from the inflationary impact of old rubles accumulated in the former republics.

The third major reason for the relatively slow progress in subduing inflation lies in the need to secure the functioning of vitally important sectors of the economy, such as agriculture, public transportation, and energy. Providing support for these sectors of the economy contradicted the policy of stabilization based on fiscal austerity, which relied on a dramatic reduction of state subsidies. But in the short run the government had no alternative but to provide these industries with subsidies, because they had been totally dependent on a centralized supply of equipment, raw materials, parts, livestock feed, and fuel. For some time, the abolition of Gossnab had to be compensated for by subsidies, to ensure a continuing supply of food and energy and the continued functioning of transportation and communications.

Russia was also vulnerable to inflation because its defense industry almost totally monopolized the production of durable consumer goods, such as washing machines, radios, television sets, refrigerators, VCRs, and so on. Naturally, when price regulations were lifted and military orders drastically cut, the defense sector took advantage of its monopoly position and for about a year dictated the prices of many consumer goods. Nevertheless, over the course of the past four years, the prices of many of these goods have fallen, relative to the average income, by an order of magnitude. Thus their costs are now much more comparable to the costs of similar merchandise in other countries.

Considering all the peculiarities of the Russian economic situation at the onset of reforms, it is actually surprising that, after the first two months, inflation did not metastastize into hyper-inflation, as it has in many other transitional economies.

Conclusion

It was not the reformers' fault that Russia inherited the largest welfare state in history. Abolishing it in one stroke would have meant a virtual death warrant for millions of people who were totally dependent on heavily subsidized public transportation, fuel, and food. By printing money and subsidizing vitally important sectors of the economy and social network, the Russian government spread the pains of the transition more or less evenly across the entire nation. This understandable policy was the key source of inflation.

Inflation created insecurity and instability, it undermined the conventional value system and forced every member of society to reconsider his social position and means of earning a living. But at the same time it accomplished important purgatory, mobilizing, and correctional functions. It inaugurated the new system and created new gauges for measuring the value of material things as well as human creativity, energy, and talent. It supplanted the old criteria of success and established new and more realistic appraisals of effort, talent, labor, and goods. The current Russian system of prices is much more in line with European standards — a necessary precondition for and, indeed, the beginning of Russia's integration into the community of advanced nations.

Crime and Corruption

Another prominent subject in the mass media has been the surge of criminality in Russia. According to critics, the reforms have unleashed criminal forces that have swept the country. Organized crime is said to be threatening to take over all the institutions of power.[33] Corruption is said to have taken on unprecedented dimensions: "Russia and its reforms are sinking into an abyss of contract killings, arms smuggling, extortion, drug trafficking, money laundering, and bank fraud."[34] Some politicians have gone so far as to claim that "in many ways control in Russia has already shifted to the new criminal network, which has replaced the old Communist structure,"[35] and controls up to 70% of the economy.[36] In other words, "Russia today has become the world's first major Mafia state."[37]

Indeed, social surveys have unambiguously shown crime to be a major concern for the Russian population.[38] However, the nature, magnitude, and causes of rising criminality deserve a more objective analysis. I will accordingly offer a few considerations missing from most discussions of crime and corruption in the new Russia.

According to Marxist ideology, private property is the main source of criminality. Because private property was eliminated in the Soviet Union, criminal behavior was supposed have been eradicated as well. The last attempt to prove this romantic claim of communist ideology was made in the early 1960s, when Nikita Khrushchev promised to eliminate criminality in the Soviet Union altogether. In fact, he even promised to "publicly display the last criminal of the nation."

Crime did not disappear, of course, because the Soviet repressive system itself induced criminal behavior. The Soviet government found a solution to this problem in falsified statistics. The statistics on crime were manipulated to maintain the myth that a low rate of crime was one of the greatest advantages of the communist system over the "dangerous world of capitalism, where citizens were deprived of security and protection."[39] Many forms of crime were allegedly eradicated altogether.[40] The statistical methods involved were highly suspicious. For example, police claimed to have achieved a 90-95 percent rate of successful investigations. In the words of Aleksei Iliushenko, Acting Procurator General, "MVD personnel have knowingly kept crimes off the record books and falsified materials on citizens' complains in order to show a decline in the crime rate."[41]

When *glasnost* was launched, a different picture began to emerge, and it was appalling. Official statistics showed an explosion of crime.[42] For example, from 1987 to 1989 the number of premeditated murders was said to have increased by 130 percent; rapes were said to have increased by 120 percent; and cases of serious bodily injury were alleged to have risen by 150 percent.[43] The Soviet press was filled with reports of arson and sabotage.[44] Soviet officials claimed apocalyptically that the growth of organized crime was threatening the regime.[45] KGB chairman Vladimir Kryuchkov spoke about "terrorism reaching appalling proportions" and insisted on a crackdown on the political opposition.[46] Thus, according to one analyst, the KGB "used the scarecrow of civil war and terrorism as a tool of social intimidation."[47]

The democratic opposition, on the other hand, used its newly acquired freedom to prove that the communist regime was totally corrupt and criminal.[48] In 1988 one author wrote that "[t]he mafia does not simply grow, it becomes integrated into the pyramid of state power... whole regions of the country are being run essentially by criminals."[49] Others noted that the mafia has its "courts, banks, mutual funds, [and] strict hierarchical system,"[50] and that some of its "members occupy very high positions."[51]

These assertions reflected the fact that the totalitarian regime was installed and maintained by a party that operated like a criminal syndicate. As Sergei Shakhrai wrote, the "party [was] a mafia-like structure with a cruel mechanism of governing."[52] Moreover, the stability of the regime depended on its ability to corrupt the entire society by driving people to act illegally.[53]

The rules of survival forced the population to lie, cheat, and steal; practically everyone was guilty of at least some of these transgressions. Such forms of crime as speculation in consumer goods and currency, theft of state property, and running illegal private businesses resulted mainly from the communist ban on the pursuit of private economic interests. On the other hand, general societal mores deemed crimes against state property acceptable, bribery was a way of life. Consequently, crimes against state property and bribery were widespread but greatly under-reported. Due to a profound mistrust of the authorities, most crimes against individuals, such as hooliganism, rape, and petty theft were also grossly under-reported.[54]

Some forms of criminal behavior—such as vandalism and hooliganism—were motivated by sheer frustration and hatred, stemming from a sense of helplessness.[55] These crimes were also mostly under-reported. Thus, according to one survey, 85 percent of people admitted having committed a criminal offense,[56] while only 15 percent of the adult population of the Soviet Union had criminal records.[57]

In other words, actual criminality was about six times higher than suggested by the official figures. Soviet society was profoundly corrupt and criminal; however, its criminality was very different from that in democratic and free-market societies.

The collapse of the Soviet police state could not help but boost existing criminality and introduce new forms of criminality. Open borders with the newly independent states provided sanctuary for gangsters who had regional ties. The collapse of control of the borders in many former republics greatly increased opportunities for trafficking in drugs and arms, particularly from Afghanistan. The democratic liberalization of human rights policy resulted in several amnesties and the freeing of several hundred thousand prisoners.

The lifting and then abolition of many restrictions on private economic activities created entirely new opportunities for black marketeers and criminal groups, who were psychologically and organizationally much better prepared to seize these opportunities than average citizens. Criminal elements that had managed not only to survive in a police state but to prosper were predictably in the forefront of the new entrepreneurial activities.[58] For example, the now legendary gangs of Kazan and Moscow, such as the *Liubertsy*, turned from hooliganism, hazing, and bullying to racketeering, prostitution, and extortion. Many of them went into trade, entering the gray economy by smuggling foreign cars into Russia.[59]

Cooperation between the former *nomenklatura* and organized crime became highly lucrative. The former used its old-boy networks to obtain cheap credits and licenses to sell commodities, while the latter transported them, sold them abroad, purchased consumer goods, delivered them to

Russia, and sold them. In this sense, the critics are correct in claiming that the former *nomenklatura* and organized crime have merged. The massive distribution of state property, which began in 1992, gave another impetus to economic crime and corruption.

However, after the "initial accumulation of capital" was accomplished, the paths of the former *nomenklatura* and organized crime began to diverge. The overwhelming majority of the new Russians who do not come from the criminal world (that is, 87 percent)[60] have turned mostly to legitimate business pursuits, banking, joint ventures with foreign partners and production of consumer goods, while organized crime began to launder its money through buying out small enterprises such as restaurants, shops, gas and service stations, and so on.[61] In short, the new Russians are desperately trying to distance themselves from the illegal methods that they used during the "initial accumulation of capital" and look and behave like legitimate businessmen.

It is true that the former *nomenklatura* and black marketeers captured an unfair share of the national wealth, and public opinion is well aware of this.[62] However, privatization made their enrichment almost inevitable. A different method of privatization, as was suggested in the previous chapter, could have helped avoid some abuses of power; but many of them were unavoidable, because the guiding principle of the new leadership was to place state property in private hands as soon as possible. Corruption helped commodities and consumer goods move across borders and made the establishment of banks and new construction possible. It accelerated the transformation; thus society at large has not only suffered from corruption and criminal activities but also benefited from them as well. All the invidious aspects of criminality notwithstanding, as a group of American analysts paradoxically noted, "The net impact of organized crime in Russia [was] probably beneficial."[63]

When privatization was essentially complete, and prices reached European levels, the grounds for corruption and the shadow economy began to shrink. In the words of one analyst, this shrinkage caused a crisis in the world of organized crime.[64] Two presidential decrees issued in February 1995, abolishing privileges of selected Russian exporters, have further "undermined the mighty potential for corruption," as another analyst wrote.[65]

Analysts agree that the more civilized the Russian economy becomes, the narrower the space for crime and corruption.[66] At the same time, like all other aspects of life in Russia, criminal activities are undergoing a dramatic change.

The appearance of significant private wealth gave a powerful impetus to the professionalization of crime. Professional crimes such as bank robberies, and drug- and gun-running, which were practically nonexistent in the Soviet Union, began to flourish.[67] In 1994 the number of economic crimes rose 84 percent,[68] while the overall crime rate fell 6 percent. From 1991 to 1994 the number of murders almost doubled going from 16,200 to 32,286.[69] Contraband trade has increased thirteen-fold, and drug-related crimes have increased by 40 percent.[70] During the three and a half years since the reforms started, there have been 84 attempts on bankers' lives, 46 of them successful.[71] In 1994 alone there were 562 contract murders.[72] The fact that 185 criminal kingpins and 177 businessmen were murdered[73] shows that in the absence of appropriate laws regulating business conduct, private interests resorted to their own methods of enforcing contract obligations and collecting debts.[74]

For years an effective struggle against crime was delayed by the absence of a new legislative framework and effective law enforcement agencies. The introduction of the new civil code and a new criminal code was impossible without a new constitution and new legislative organs. Finally, after the dyarchy of power was ended and a new political structure established, to use one newspaper's words, "the state [began] increasingly to engage in what should be its principal business: setting the rules of the game in the market."[75]

In April 1994 President Yeltsin issued a decree containing tough measures against organized criminal activities. In November 1994 the Duma passed the civil code, and in July 1995 a draft of a new criminal code for Russia,[76] which lists 14 new types of economic crimes punishable by either imprisonment or fines.[77]

Thus, only in 1995 have free-market activities been codified in a legal framework; only then did law-enforcement institutions receive a legal framework for guarding private property and personal safety.

To fight crime, totally new, professional, law-enforcement organs were needed. In the past, the only truly professional security force was, ironically, the notorious KGB. However, the democrats split the KGB into five security organs and did their best to emasculate them. Thousands of highly trained KGB officers retired and joined private security firms. For several years, institutional disarray and severe financial constraints prevented the government from creating highly professional law-enforcement agencies, although attempts were made. Only in 1995 have these agencies received adequate financing, which has allowed them to hire and train professional personnel[78] and modernize their equipment.[79] Finally, as one newspaper wrote, it is now evident that the "effectiveness of state protective services has become considerably greater."[80]

How powerful is the criminal world? Some analysts claim that the godfathers of the criminal world are collectively more powerful than the Russian government.[81] The estimates of the "number of enterprises and organizations with all forms of ownership controlled or used by organized crime" vary between 35,000 and 50,000, including about 400 banks.[82] Law-enforcement organs contended that 8,059 criminal groups, with a total of 35,348 members, were operating in Russia in 1995.[83] In comparison, Japan, with a similar population, has at least three times as many mobsters.[84]

Appalling as these numbers appear, they have to be evaluated in light of the huge size of the country and its economy. First of all, the overwhelming majority of criminal groups consist of amateurs and free-lancers, who have joined together in order to commit random crimes. Less than one thousand of the criminal groups possess characteristics of the mafia like a hierarchical organizational structure, substantial resources, political connections, and interregional ties; they are not, however, united into several nationwide families.[85] If they control fifty thousand businesses, that is still less than 3 percent of the total number of enterprises, and four hundred banks make up only about 14 percent of all commercial banks.

Organized crime lacks the resources to control large enterprises and banks, because it has limited capital at its disposal: 1.7 trillion rubles,[86] or less than one-third of one percent of Russia's GNP.[87] Moreover, legitimate businesses have increasingly begun to "launder their reputation" through self-policing practices well known in the West: they have formed associations that deny membership to dubious enterprises.[88] Their actions have made it more difficult for criminal organizations to launder their money.

Thus the claim that organized crime controls most of the economy and threatens to take over political power is a gross exaggeration.[89]

The biggest surge of criminal activity in Russia occurred during the five most turbulent years: from 1989 to 1993. If we are to believe the statistics, the growth rate of crime in the 1990s has been lower than it was in the late 1980s. For example, in the 1989-1991 period, the number of reported crimes grew by 75 percent, while from 1992 to 1994 it increased by 22 percent.[90] In 1993 crime grew by only 1.4 percent,[91] and in 1994, for the first time since 1987, the number of reported crimes declined by 6 percent. The decrease was particularly apparent among crimes typical of the Soviet period, such as petty theft, mugging, hooliganism, and vandalism.[92] Early indications are that in 1995 crime will have increased by about 5 percent.[93] We should also add what many analysts fail to note, that some widely anticipated sorts of crimes were not committed. For example, there were relatively few politically, racially, or religiously motivated crimes. There were no programs against Jews, and even clashes between Slavic and Caucasian organized groups in Moscow and other cities were motivated by economic conflicts rather than ethnic or racial intolerance. There were few politically motivated terrorist acts,[94] even during the eight-month-long war in Chechnia.

A group of researchers who conducted a comprehensive study of criminality in the new Russia concluded that the rise of criminality in Russia was not extraordinary, or even unusual;[95] contrary to the impressions one receives from the media, the researchers observed that by international standards, Russia has not become a leader in crime, although in some categories it is ahead of West European nations.[96] The prevalence of crime in Moscow, which is the subject of many media reports on crime, is not characteristic of the country as a whole. Moscow has twice as much crime per capita as the whole country,[97] and there are objective reasons for its high crime rate. Moscow attracted at least 180,000 people from the areas engulfed by ethnic conflicts,[98] and it has the greatest concentration of wealth in the country. As is the case everywhere in the world, displaced people commit a disproportionate share of crimes. Still, in 1993 the number of murders in Moscow was 40 percent lower than in New York.[99]

If we are to believe statistics, in 1994 there were 1,757 recorded criminal acts per 100,000 residents in Russia, compared with 5,660 in the United States[100] and 8,200 in Germany.[101] These figures are clearly the result of under-reporting in Russia[102] and the United States, and meticulous reporting in Germany. However, in countries with traditions similar to Russia's, such as Hungary, Poland, Estonia and Lithuania, crime rates are still significantly higher than in Russia.[103]

One must also realize that the term "Russian mafia" is used too broadly as a generic term for what should properly be referred to as "organized criminal groups from the former Soviet Union." These groups include Soviet emigre's who settled in the United States in the 1970s and 1980s, Balts operating in Poland and Scandinavia, Chechens killed in London, Central Asians smuggling weapons and drugs from Afghanistan and Iran, and so on.[104] Early in 1994 some journalists predicted that the Russian mafia would "occupy Europe. Nobody will have resources to stop them."[105] Two years later, however, the anticipated "offensive of Russian mafia in Western Europe has not yet occurred."[106] "Rumors of the almighty Russian mafia in Britain are exaggerated," according to one article's title.[107] The bureau chief of Interpol in Moscow has, in fact, argued that the existence of an international Russian mafia is a myth.[108]

Conclusion

I tend to agree with Prime Minister Viktor Chernomyrdin, who noted that the rise of criminality in Russia was an unfortunate but inevitable side effect of the country's economic transition;[109] yet "in spite of the widespread stereotypes, the criminal world and the criminal way of life were rejected by Russians, and society itself did not become criminal."[110]

Moreover, I would argue that, in a way, Russian society at large has been decriminalized. In the new Russia, criminality is becoming increasingly confined to a particular segment of the population, while in Soviet society everyone was guilty of unlawful deeds. Today, those who break the law choose this option consciously. The overwhelming majority of people prefer to pursue their interests within the confines of the law. This is not to deny the traditional disrespect for the law, or the widespread phenomena of bribing and tax evasion. However, once the transition is accomplished and new rules of conduct are established and enforced by laws, the resurgence of religion and the increase in social pressure should lessen these forms of criminal behavior.[111]

The new economic and political establishment of Russia has become the stoutest bulwark against criminality. As the resolution of the Congress of Russian Entrepreneurs in December 1994 stated, "No matter what the rest of the country or the world might think, the new wave of Russian entrepreneurs craves a legal order; chaos is bad for the country and bad for business."[112] Their growing influence in society is the best guarantee of an ultimately successful struggle against criminality.

In sum, it is unfortunate that the disintegration of state power and of law-enforcement institutions was not compensated for by a sudden increase of civility and self-restraint among citizens. However, the lessening of confrontations between the state and its citizens (and between Russia and the outside world), the improvement of living conditions, and the renaissance of the human spirit that is occurring in Russia should lead to an overall decline in crime.

Unemployment

The labor market is essential if a market economy is to exist. In turn, the labor market cannot exist without a reserve pool of workers. Hence the transformation of the Soviet economy into a market economy was bound to introduce the "sickness of capitalism" known as unemployment. Given the enormous inefficiencies and distortions of the Soviet economy, both the government and the opposition expected unemployment to surge to socially explosive levels. Thus the reformers thought that five to six million people would be unemployed by the end of 1992,[113] while domestic critics and some Western academics, judging from the experience of Poland, predicted up to twenty million unemployed. It was feared that unemployment would have a devastating effect on the residents of what had been the most extensive welfare state in history. Four years after the fall of communism, however, the number of officially registered unemployed amounted to only 3 percent of the workforce,[114] and there were few signs of social unrest.

The opposition explained this surprising turn of events by theorizing that massive unemployment, equivalent to about 16 percent of the workforce, does exist, but is hidden from the public eye by the government's deliberate strategy of keeping state enterprises alive and idle rather than letting them die and causing their workers to lost their jobs. They claim that this policy, cannot continue for long, so that eventually there is bound to be massive, undisguised unemployment, resulting in dire social and political consequences.[115] Some top Russian officials have admitted that they believe that the actual unemployment level is about 12 percent.[116]

In my view, however, neither Russian officials nor the opposition know the true number of unemployed, apart from those who are registered with unemployment agencies. One can only guess at the magnitude of so-called hidden unemployment, and this is where the controversy begins. A remark made by Aleksandr Livshits, Yeltsin's chief economic adviser, reveals the amount of confusion and guesswork among the top leadership on this issue: "No, I do not believe that massive unemployment in Russia exists."[117]

Meanwhile, an understanding of the true causes and dimensions of unemployment can help clarify other controversial issues, such as the size of the poor and wealthy strata of society, the productivity of the economy, the size of GNP, and so on. For example, if Russia's GNP indeed contracted by about 50 percent, why did employment decline by only 6 percent?[118]

To answer this question we must begin by dispelling yet another myth of Soviet propaganda, according to which the elimination of unemployment was one of the monumental achievements of socialism. It is true that article 40 of the Constitution of the USSR ensured the right of its citizens to employment; the centrally planned economic system did stimulate a perpetually unsatisfied demand for labor. It is also true that the residents of large cities could always find new jobs because most large and mid-sized enterprises were constantly hiring. However, the quest for additional employees was yet another symptom of the distortions of the Soviet economy; by claiming to be under-manned, directors of enterprises could ask for both more funds and smaller production quotas.

On the other hand, peasants and residents of small towns that were dependent on one or two factories had little choice of jobs, and they were kept from moving to large cities by an elaborate coercive system incorporating residence permits, the *trudovaia knizhka* (working cards), and the absence of a system of unemployment benefits. One could not, by law, stay jobless for more than three months. Such tight control over at least half of the Soviet workforce allowed planners to attract labor for new industrial projects in the remote regions of Russia. Thus the Communist Party could change the demographic balance in favor of the Slavic population, fill undesirable jobs, and maintain the appearance of full employment. Finally, low salaries made it impossible for a married couple to exist on one salary, so practically all married women had to work. All these measures combined to secure full employment and the almost total mobilization of the economically active population.

Of course, in reality unemployment did exist, because people changed jobs. According to some estimates, by the late 1980s unemployment in the Soviet Union affected up to 4 percent of the workforce.[119] It was, however, short-term unemployment, and it did not constitute a major social problem. Much more economically and psychologically damaging was the phenomenon of enormous hidden unemployment and indolence. Most factories maintained inflated payroll head counts. Many millions of security guards, union and party officials, professional athletes, social workers,[120] and other "dead souls" who did not contribute to production were kept on the payroll.[121] In the late 1980s up to one-quarter of the labor force was estimated to be redundant.[122] When *khozraschot* (self-accounting) was introduced, some factory managers were able to dismiss half of their employees, increase the salaries of the rest, and still boost factory production.

In addition, workers used to remain idle for days or weeks every month because supplies of materials and parts were sporadic. Acute shortages of food and consumer goods also forced workers to do their shopping during their working hours. This phenomenon was so pervasive that Yuri Andropov introduced policing of the streets during working hours. The police checked the identifications of citizens and questioned them about what they were doing away from their enterprises during working hours.[123] Incidentally, as General Secretary Gorbachev renewed this policy, which had been abandoned by Andropov's successor Chernenko.

In short, while the Soviet system artificially maintained the illusion of full employment for mostly ideological purposes, hidden unemployment and indolence resulted in an enormous waste of human resources and ultimately in the comatose state of the economy.

The liberalization of economic activities by the reformers gave a powerful impetus to the freer movement of labor. At the same time, the existence of unemployment was recognized and legitimized. In consequence critics were able to accuse the government of creating massive unemployment, impoverishing a large segment of the population and thus placing the country on the brink of a social explosion.[124] Indeed, by the middle of 1995, according to official data, there were 2 million people registered as unemployed; 5.7 million people were looking for jobs was 5.7 million and about 3.8 million people were working short shifts or taking unpaid vacations.[125] On the basis of these figures the "hidden unemployed" number 9.5 million or 13 percent of the workforce, total unemployment comes to about 16 percent of the workforce.[126]

In my view, however, both government officials and the opposition have overestimated the extent of hidden unemployment. They are correct in stating that most people do not bother to resister with unemployment offices and do not count on the government to find them jobs. But most people have several sources of income, which is reflected in the fact that paychecks account for only 40 percent of the monetary income of typical families.[127] When they lose their principal job, people are not idle. Instead they pursue informal ways of earning a living, most of the time in the private sector.

The current Russian economy presents ample opportunities for people who are willing to work and move to places where jobs are readily available. There have consistently been between 400,000 and 500,000 job vacancies.[128] Moscow, which has the most market-oriented economy, has the greatest labor market. In Moscow there are more job vacancies than unemployed workers.[129]

The overall situation in Russia is, in some ways, similar to that of the United States, where there are said to be about eleven million people seeking work (including the hidden unemployed);[130] nevertheless, millions of people from other countries wish to emigrate to the United States, and more than one million do so annually. Similarly, in four years the Russian economy has absorbed at least 3 million immigrants and 400,000 *gastarbeiters* (guest workers),[131] as well as about 1.1 million discharged military men.[132]

Officially, the booming private sector has generated more than three million jobs, primarily in the service sector.[133] In fact, the number is much greater. Small enterprises alone have provided full-or part-time jobs to about 30 percent of the population, and the number of small enterprises is expected to reach 2 to 2.5 million in the next couple of years, creating up to 800,000 new jobs.[134]

There are also "millions of people who officially do not work, and do not figure in the statistics, who nevertheless earn their living," as one economist pointed out.[135] And they often do not make a bad living, although frequently their labor is back-breaking. At least 3.5 million people are involved in retail trade.[136] Crucial to the working of the retail sector are the so-called "shuttlers." Several million "shuttlers" transport goods from abroad (or from one part of Russia to another)[137] carrying tens of billions of dollars worth of consumer goods each year and earning several hundred dollars a month.[138] In addition, millions are involved in small services, hand crafts, growing their own food, and so on; these activities are not recorded in any statistics.

The population of the so-called closed cities, which totals 2.5 million people,[139] has been the most badly hurt. In these city-factories, the local economy as wholly dependent on a single enterprise; closing it down would have meant putting tens of thousands of people out of work. When state orders to these enterprises were drastically cut, their directors were reluctant to fire specialists, preferring instead to give them different assignments within the enterprise. Numerous small companies were created around these giant enterprises, and they have produced equipment and consumer goods for the local communities. When the restructuring of city-factories began in earnest in 1995, these small companies absorbed many of the laid-off workers, helping to avoid an explosive surge in unemployment.

Finally, credit should be given to the Russian unemployment agency, which was created practically from scratch; yet by June 1993 it consisted of 2,500 centers with 24,000 employees.[140] During 1992 it helped to find jobs for 650,000 workers,[141] and in 1994 for more than one million.[142] The number of people retrained grew from 20,000 in 1992 to 275,000 in 1994.[143]

Conclusion

The creation of a free labor market in an utterly distorted economy and society was a major technical and psychological undertaking. However, so far this wrenching process has not caused serious sociopolitical problems. In March 1995 only one-third of all Russians expressed concern about losing their jobs,[144] although joblessness had entered their consciousness.[145] Their awareness of unemployment has not been an entirely negative phenomenon, however. The Damoclean sword of unemployment is instigating a major, positive change in Russian work habits. After all, for generations the Soviet people were conditioned to live according to this principle: "They pretend to pay us, while we pretend to work."

Four years after the beginning of the reforms, many of the phenomena that caused an enormous waste of time and energy during the Soviet era no longer exist. Gone are the morally and physically debilitating vigils in lines, for hours on end, to purchase food and consumer goods.[146] Gone are the weeks of frustrating waiting for the arrival of supplies, when one could do absolutely nothing but kill time and drink vodka. Gone are the do-nothing jobs, such as spying and reporting on others or peddling meaningless propaganda. There is no doubt that in 1995 the Russian population works harder and longer hours than it did four years ago;[147] according to psychologists, hard work usually has a positive impact on people's dignity and self-esteem.

In general, the Russian people have turned out to be more resourceful, resilient, and self-reliant than either the reformers or the opposition anticipated.

Escapism: Drinking and Drugs Abuse

Critics claim that the majority of Russians rejected the reforms and in desperation turned to heavy drinking, drugs, and suicide. They call for the reorientation of reforms to help people and the reintroduction of strict state control over the production, import, and sale of alcohol.[148]

Indeed, from 1986 to 1994 consumption of hard alcohol doubled.[149] In 1994 alone, the use of drugs was said to have increased by 40 percent.[150] In 1995, according to some studies, the number of heavy drinkers is 8-9 percent of the adult Russian population, while alcoholics make up 4-5 percent of the adult population.[151]

The drinking of distilled alcohol is a centuries-long tradition and a serious problem for Russia (as, incidentally, it is for all northern peoples, from Finland to Minnesota). Apart from such factors as climate, religion, and tradition, social conditions also contribute to the level of drinking.[152] It is estimated that Russians consume about 14 liters of alcohol per person a year, twice the average level of Scandinavian countries, which have a similar climate.[153] In the United States, for example, it is believed that there are more than ten million alcoholics (that is, about 6 percent of the adult population), although the consumption of hard liquor per capita is one-fourth that of Russia.[154]

Drinking under the communist regime had its own history. After Stalin's death, the draconian anti-drinking measures were relaxed, and after that drinking steadily rose. A 1984 study by Novosibirsk social scientists shocked the nation by revealing the catastrophic magnitude of the phenomenon. The study revealed the shocking number of 40 million alcoholics; it claimed that one out of six newborns had alcohol-related birth defects.[155] This study prompted Gorbachev to adopt harsh administrative measures to curtail drinking. The production and sale of alcohol were cut by 50 percent and the price of vodka soon tripled. Official statistics quickly obliged the leadership by showing a sharp decline in alcohol consumption and an improvement in many social indicators, with decreases in the rates of crime and accidents.

However, while Gorbachev's restrictions generated good statistics, they also yielded a number of pernicious side effects. The production and consumption of homemade vodka and the use of poisonous substitutes surged. Thus the production of homemade alcohol nearly tripled from an estimated 2.4 liters of vodka per capita in 1985 to 6.8 liters in 1990,[156] and the total amount of homemade alcohol may have equaled that of the state production.[157] Sales of sugar (a key ingredient in the production of homemade vodka) increased 20 percent, resulting in acute shortages; previously it had been one of the few readily available products.[158] In 1989 the Gorbachev government realized its mistake and relaxed its restrictive policy; however, the price of vodka did not drop.

The post-Soviet reforms removed practically all restrictions on the sale of liquor. Since 1990 the price of vodka fell four to five times,[159] and officially registered sales of alcohol increased by about 20 percent. However, data on the production of homemade vodka are not available, because the police stopped raiding private homes in search of violators of the state monopoly on alcohol production. There are compelling reasons to think that the production of homemade vodka decreased significantly for purely economic reasons; in relative terms the price of vodka has fallen many times, while that of sugar has increased.[160] Similarly, drinking eau de cologne, after-shave, and other alcohol-based cosmetological products, which was widely popular in Soviet days, no longer makes economic sense. Finally, there is no incentive to drink alcohol substitutes and outright poisonous substances such as brake fluid, methyl alcohol, and acetone, because alcoholic beverages are more affordable.

Under the totalitarian regime, there were powerful psychological motivations for drinking, which disappeared with its collapse. Under communism, the psychological strain of leading a double life was terrible.

The stultifying propaganda, the omnipresent lies, the constant need for duplicity—all placed enormous strain on people's sense of personal integrity and individuality. Drinking provided the illusion of "reconciling one's conscience with one's deed."[161] Drinking was perhaps the most popular form of escapism practiced by Soviet citizens to some extent in an ironic attempt to preserve their individuality.

The second reason for widespread drinking in the Soviet era was embedded in the nature of the relationship between personality and power. Both drinking and drug abuse are known to be linked to a sense of powerlessness and helplessness. The totalitarian system, as we discussed in Chapter Three, deprived its subjects of personal power and cultivated dependence on the party and the state. Particularly damaging for much of the population was the ban on the pursuit of economic and political power. The lack of opportunity had to be compensated for by at least the temporary illusion (provided by drunkenness) of controlling one's life.

Of course, the collapse of the Soviet welfare state has aggravated the sense of powerlessness and hopelessness among many older and dependent people. Since alcohol reduces anxiety, the stress that accompanied the transition should have increased drinking. On the other hand, new opportunities have given many more people the chance to regain a sense of power and personal integrity.

It is impossible to accurately estimate whether the overall consumption of homemade and industrially manufactured alcohol has risen or fallen. The policy of the democratic regime has made alcohol freely available and relatively affordable; the variety of alcoholic beverages is staggering to ordinary Russians. In 1994 an estimated 200,000 deciliters of vodka were consumed by the Russian population.[162] It is conceivable that drinking increased among those segments of the population who could not adjust to the new realities of competition, possible unemployment, and high inflation. Some people may also have started to drink more because vodka became cheaper and their earnings increased.[163]

There are indications, however, that drinking has decreased in the segment of the population actively involved in the private sector. For example, 67 percent of Muscovites drink the same amount of alcohol (44 percent) or less (23 percent) than they previously did.[164] The new Russians clearly drink less and much more selectively.[165] The consumption of high-quality liquor, such as French cognacs and Scotch whisky, is on the rise.[166]

In sum, drinking alcohol is a multifaceted phenomenon deeply embedded in and affected by one's cultural heritage, climate, religion, sociopolitical and economic conditions, and so on. The current Russian revolution is changing practically all these aspects of life and culture. Hence there is little doubt that Russian substance-abuse patterns are likely to change.

The traditional Russian way of drinking—sporadic consumption of huge amounts of vodka until one falls into a total stupor—is likely to evolve into more "civilized" patterns of alcohol consumption: smaller amounts yet more frequent drinking of lighter and better distilled liquor. In fact, this has already begun to happen. Whether the European style of drinking is better for one's health is debatable, but it is better suited to the functioning of a technocratic society, which Russia is quickly becoming.

Suicide

The ultimate escape is, of course, suicide. The sense of total powerlessness, hopelessness, and inability to change one's destiny are the principal psychological motivations behind the decision to terminate one's life. Hence a dramatic surge in the suicide rate is indicative of serious societal problems. The rate of suicide in Russia has grown from 24 per thousand citizens in 1989 to 30 in 1993; most victims are older people. However, some evidence indicates that suicide has declined among younger people.[167]

In sum, the sense of personal failure and hopelessness connected to the transition did not evenly affect all strata of Russian society. Among older people elsewhere, the suicide rate is about five times higher than that of people in the prime of their life. The overall suicide rate in Russia has increased only marginally. Russia has now reached the level of suicide characteristic of such prosperous and stable countries as France and Denmark,[168] and its rate remains much lower than that of Hungary (37 per thousand)[169] and Lithuania (42 per thousand).[170] Moreover, the rate of suicide remains much lower than its 1984 peak level (in what was ostensibly a more stable and prosperous time): the rate then was 52 suicides per thousand.[171] Evidently, the transition has not been so hard to cope with as the depressing stagnation of the Brezhnev era.

Life Expectancy

Longevity is perhaps the ultimate indicator of the quality of life in a nation, since it reflects the quality of health care, the extent of environmental pollution and crime, and so on.

The collapse of the socialist welfare state, particularly its health-care system, must have facilitated the proliferation of diseases, increases in cases of poisoning, and ultimately a rise in the mortality rate. Combined with the rise in deaths from accidents, suicide, and crime, these factors could be expected to have dramatically lowered the life expectancy of the population.

Indeed, statistics show an increase in various sicknesses[172] and in infant-mortality rates (which rose from 17.7 per thousand births in Russia in 1989,[173] and 22.4 per thousand births for the Soviet Union in 1990 to 27 per thousand in 1994).[174] At the same time, the overall death rate grew from 11.2 per 1,000 people in 1990 to 14.5 in 1994,[175] while the birth rate fell from 19 per thousand in 1987 (in the Soviet Union as a whole)[176] to 13 in 1994.[177] One might think that all social ills that have befallen Russia since 1989, acting in concert, should have caused a dramatic decline in life expectancy.

In reality, the decline in life expectancy has not been dramatic. It merely reflected a continuation of trends that had begun to emerge during the 1970s.[178] From 1965 to 1980 average life expectancy in the USSR fell from 70.5 to 67.7 years.[179] The pace of the decline then accelerated: from 1986 to 1992, the life expectancy for Russian men fell by 7.5 years.[180] From 1992 to 1994 overall life expectancy fell by only one year—to slightly less than 64 years.[181] Moreover, in 1994 the birth rate rose slightly,[182] and the decline of the population decreased from 308,000 in 1993 to only 124,000 in 1994.[183]

It is necessary to take into account several considerations in order to place the issue of life expectancy in proper historical context. First of all, the infant-mortality rate began to rise in 1971; soon it became so disturbing that it disappeared from Soviet reference books.[184] According to some analysts, it was under-reported by as much as 50 percent, so that the real infant-mortality rate in the Soviet Union in 1989 was probably about 33 per thousand births.[185]

The claims made by some analysts that reforms resulted in the "extraordinary phenomenon of negative population growth for an industrially developed country"[186] are either disingenuous or naive. Low birth rates, in general, are characteristic of affluent rather than poor societies. The most prosperous countries, such as West Germany, Austria, and Denmark, have experienced negative population growth. Even a change in the quality of life for the better does not automatically ensure an increase in the birth rate. Exactly the opposite trend was observed in East Germany after reunification: from 1989 to 1993 birth rates there plunged 60 percent.[187]

What, then, accounts for the drop in the birth rate? I would argue that uncertainty connected to the transition and the availability of modern birth-control techniques were primarily responsible for the decline. Under the communist regime, we must remind ourselves, abortion was a principal method of birth control, because the government deliberately did not produce or import modern contraceptives (so as to encourage population growth).[188] Since 1991 all such restrictions on modern contraceptives have been lifted, which must have lowered both the rate of abortions and the birth rate.

Conclusion

It seems that the critics have been too quick to blame the reforms for decreases in life expectancy. In reality, the few years of transition have neither improved nor dramatically worsened Russia's demographic picture. The negative trend began under the communist regime, and it will take a long period of stability and prosperity to reverse it. In 1994 "Russia has already shown some signs of reversing the downward slide of negative natural increase in the number of births."[189] In the words of one reporter, "it is too early to play requiem for the nation."[190]

Living Standards and the Quality of Life

The most prominent critique of the reforms is that they have turned the bulk of the population into the *lumpenproletariat*, while at the same time creating a tiny segment of the super-rich. Critics maintain that living standards of the mass of ordinary people have fallen 50 or even 70 percent, while the new Russians enjoy living standards equivalent to those of the upper classes in the West. What has happened to living standards and the quality of life since the reforms began?

Methodological Difficulties

Different methodologies for calculating the cost of living in Russia lead to stunningly different conclusions. If one uses official Soviet income data, taking fringe benefits into account and the ruble/dollar exchange rate, the standard of living for Soviet citizens in the 1980s was about one-third of that of Americans.[191] In 1992, according to this methodology, they fell by as much as 70 percent, and currently are at about one-tenth of the American level.

On the other hand, in December 1991, the average monthly salary in the Soviet Union was 530 rubles[192]—that is, about $5 according to the commercial exchange rate.[193] In December 1995 the average monthly wage in non-state sector of economy was 770,000 rubles ($165), while the official subsistence minimum was 298,000 rubles ($66) per month.[194] Should we then conclude, based on these data, that living standards have increased by a factor of 33, and that even the subsistence minimum in 1995 was 13 times higher than the average wage in 1991?

These paradoxes stem from the mythical value of the Soviet ruble because; under the communist regime, in the words of Robert Kaiser, even "the calculation of the relative purchasing power of the ruble and the currency of foreign states" was censored.[195]

This methodology of calculating living standards totally fails to take into account the huge disparity in the quality of life in the United States, the Soviet Union, and the new Russia. That is, the quality of goods and services, their variety, and their range and availability must also be considered.

For example, in 1989 a kilo of pork of poor quality in a state store cost 2.2 rubles, while a kilo of good quality pork in a farmers' market in Moscow was 25 rubles.[196] In August 1995 the price of one kilo of good-quality pork was about 10,500 rubles, and lesser-quality pork could be bought for 6,000 rubles. Hence better food was twelve times as expensive in 1989 and only twice as expensive in 1995. Roughly the same twelve-to-one differential existed between the official and black-market currency-exchange rates in Soviet days; in 1995, by contrast, there is only one ruble/dollar exchange rate.

Another factor complicating the calculation is access to goods and services. How can one compare the quality of life in a country in which people must travel 150 miles and queue for hours in a store to buy groceries, with that in a country in which the consumer market is saturated and one can buy whatever one wants in a matter of minutes?

The highly elaborate and covert system of distribution of material and social benefits that existed under the communist regime (when the politically favored had access to special stores, hospitals, resorts, travel to the West, and so on) obscured both incomes and the quality of goods to which people had access.[197]

The current situation is only partially better. Personal wealth is too often demonstratively displayed. However, the incomes of the majority of the population are carefully hidden from both the government and organized crime; thus the "real figures of the population's incomes are far removed from the official data,"[198] which often understate them by at least 35 percent.[199]

There are also totally unquantifiable factors that are nevertheless extremely important for the psychological well-being of people. How can one measure the life in cities in which "oxygen cocktails" had to be administered to children to combat pollution?[200] How are we to evaluate the damage to dignity, self-esteem, and productivity resulting from idling in queues for hours, or the humiliation of witnessing preferential treatment for people with party membership cards or dollars in their pockets?

The discussion of living conditions in the post-communist Russia vis-a-vis those in the Soviet Union has to include macro and micro perspectives, retrospective and contemporary looks, outside and inside views, scholarly and practitioners' assessments, both the hard data and anecdotal evidence. I can only offer a few of these.

Two Lives in One Nation

Perhaps the most characteristic feature of the new Russia is the existence of two stunningly different sorts of lives coexisting side by side.

One American journalist described the decaying communal world: "The sour monotony of enforced poverty and public neglect: the ruined villages, the unpainted wood and unpaved roads, the grasping mud and leaking toilets, the cracked plastic shoes tripping over the broken sidewalks, the scattered heaps of drunks propped up against peeling buildings, drinking rough vodka and smoking harsh tobacco, and everywhere the smell of sweat, alcohol and smoke."[201]

One Russian analyst advanced a theory that "reforms meant global redistribution of wealth from the elderly strata to the young."[202] In reality, there was no great wealth to be redistributed. The poverty, decay, and desolation described above stems from generations of waste, neglect, and stifling of creativity, as experts have conclusively demonstrated.[203] The budgetary crisis and managerial disarray that accompanied reform could only exacerbate the heart-rending poverty, drabness, and shabbiness produced by socialism—not create them.

Unfortunately, the overwhelming majority of the Russian people live in this impoverished world, and no quick solution can magically extricate them from it. Their extrication depends upon the success of the private sphere that is arising from the rubble of socialism.

Periodic visitors intimately familiar with Russia invariably notice "enormous progress and an amazing scale of positive economic changes,"[204] which manifest themselves in colorful advertising,[205] thousands of foreign-made cars, tens of thousands of restaurants,[206] dozens of American-style department stores, twelve thousand currency-exchange offices, improved roads, European-style gas stations,[207] numerous industrial and consumer fairs, art exhibits and fashion shows,[208] and even improved ecological conditions.[209]

These changes were encapsulated by one French journalist in these words: "Moscow is a living city again."[210]

Although the rest of the country lags behind Moscow, pockets of vitality and progress can be found elsewhere.[211]

Still, a legitimate question remains: Which of the two worlds is likely to triumph? It is conceivable that the decaying communal world will stifle the private one by imposing taxes, regulations, and protectionist measures. Alternatively, it is possible that the prospering private sphere will generate such wealth that it will spill over and invigorate the public sector. They may also coexist side by side for decades, as happens in many developing countries.

To predict which outcome is most likely, one must examine several major trends that now affect Russia.

The Trends

First we will try to examine the two goals toward which Russian energy today is directed: protest and struggle or constructive pursuits.

Social Peace

From 1989 to 1991 everything seemed to indicate that a major bloody upheaval was inevitable and imminent. Reformers were preparing for it, and the opposition was counting on it.[212] The country was gripped by a wave of strikes in the mining, transportation and steel industries. "To help avert possible large-scale social upheaval," Western countries sent emergency food aid.[213] Atrocities were committed on ethnic and religious grounds. Political rallies sometimes gathered up to one million participants. In 1991 alone, 1.2 million man-days were lost through strikes in Russia.[214] It seemed that violence against communists, the secret police, minorities, or the new Russians would inevitably erupt.

But thereafter the number of strike-related losses of man-days fell by 82 percent in 1992 and by 75 percent in 1993.[215] Even workers in huge factories with 30 to 40 thousand employees, who did not receive salaries for up to three months, did not go on a rampage of pogroms and destruction. In 1994 the number of strikes increased, and they rose further in 1995, however, they were largely local and sporadic, and 65 percent of them were in educational institutions.[216] Protest rallies were relatively rare, peaceful, and attended by no more than a few thousand people.[217] The behavior of Moscovites during the two day-long protest in October 1993 was indicative. First, they were confined to two places in Moscow. Secondly, they failed to attract broad participation. Thousands of people came to observe the storming of the White House out of curiosity but showed no desire to take part in the action. It is also important to note that since 1991 politically motivated terrorism has almost completely disappeared. Even the war in Chechnia did not trigger a widely anticipated wave of terrorism. The attacks on Budionovsk and Kizliar, where hostages were taken, were two notable exceptions.[218]

In fact, socially, Russia has been much calmer than other transition societies. For example, Germany experienced violence against foreigners, Poland saw massive strikes and clashes of miners with the police, and China lived through bloody peasant unrest.[219]

In sum, social peace in Russia during the transition strongly suggests that the *narod* broadly consents to reforms[220] and is directing its energies peacefully. People did not rush to the streets to vent their anger and frustration; instead, they took advantage of new opportunities to improve their private lives.

Emigration and Immigration

The second major trend that is important to note is the direction of migration. Are people escaping from a troubled Russia or, on the contrary, are they returning to their ancestors' land?

For decades "in the core areas of Central Russia, the population has been 'dying out,' as one highly respected demographer wrote.[221] In addition, since the 1970s hundreds of thousands of people have emigrated annually. Thus, in 1990, the last full year of the communist regime, 452,000 Jews, Germans, Armenians, Greeks, and others left the Soviet Union.[222] In 1991 Western and Central Europe braced themselves in anticipation of millions of refugees fleeing from the former Soviet Union.

However "the mass migration from the East . . . never actually materialized."[223] In fact, the migration was in the other direction. The opening of borders made it possible for Russians to go temporarily to Western Europe and the United States to work, and at least 100,000 Russians have done so.[224] About 90,000 Russian scientists did go abroad temporarily, nevertheless, as one newspaper wrote, "No nuclear physicists knowledgeable in weapons technology have so far left Russia permanently — in spite of the fact that Iraqi President Saddam Hussein has offered to pay up to $300,000 a year for such expertise."[225]

During 1994 1,146,000 people migrated to Russia, while 231,400 left.[226] Russia has become the only former Soviet republic with a positive migration balance.[227] Since 1992 about 3 million immigrants and *gastarbeiters* (guest workers) settled in Russia,[228] and 37 percent of immigrants to Russia were not even ethnic Russians.[229] In addition, an estimated 500,000 illegal aliens from Africa, Asia, and the Middle East have entered Russia.[230] Tens of thousands of people have sought political asylum there.[231] By 1998 Russia is preparing to absorb about 3.5 million people from the former republics,[232] and by the year 2000, up to six million.[233]

In sum, to many outsiders Russia appears to be "the most stable and peaceful" of former republics,[234] with higher living standards than the others.[235]

Signs of Recovery

Another positive trend appeared in the summer of 1995, which indicated that "the long-awaited turnaround in the economy has come."[236] Since 1992 Russia's foreign trade has been growing at a 15 to 25 percent annual rate. What is more important, Russia's positive balance of trade has doubled from $10 billion in 1992 to $20 billion in 1994;[237] it promises to reach $26 billion in 1995.[238] As for the financial situation, federal reserves of gold and hard currency have reached $12.4 billion.[239] Revenues were 40 percent higher than projected, which allowed the government to reduce the budget deficit for the 1996 fiscal year to 3.5 percent of GNP.[240]

For many years, the ruble was falling against the dollar. However, in May 1995, reflecting the strength of the economy and several years of significant positive balances in foreign trade, the ruble began to appreciate; it stabilized at around 4,600 rubles to the dollar. However, the real purchasing power of the ruble is estimated to be about 2,000 rubles to the dollar,[241] suggesting that the ruble may strengthen even more.

For many years Russians were exporting capital to safe havens abroad. By 1995 this capital was estimated to amount to some $80 billion.[242] However, in 1994 it appeared that this capital was beginning to return to Russia.[243] In 1995, with the ruble having stabilized, the preference for the dollar weakened.[244] Russians began "to keep their funds in Russian commercial banks, because they received positive interest rates from ruble accounts," as Chernomyrdin noted.[245]

Another sign of recovery is the growth of savings. In 1995 only 20 percent of the Russian adult population had no savings.[246] Total savings (both in rubles and foreign currency) were estimated to be between $45 billion [247] and $65 billion.[248] The average savings account would accordingly be worth $800 to $1,200. Forty percent of the active population plans to improve their housing in 1996.[249]

There are also many visual signs of economic recovery. Particularly conspicuous has been the boom in construction of private houses,[250] hotels and offices.[251] In 1994 housing construction in Moscow grew by 30 percent,[252] and it continued to grow at a 25 percent annual rate in 1995.[253] As one newspaper wrote, Moscow looks like one gigantic construction site.[254]

Finally, in the summer of 1995 industrial production began to grow,[255] while inflation declined to 4.6 percent in August. Comparable economic results from two years earlier in the Czech republic and Poland suggest that 1996 may become the first year of real economic growth in Russia. If such growth does occur, it will prove an extremely important point: that the emerging Russian economy possesses internal vitality.

The Technological Revolution

Another major trend is the technological revolution quietly occurring in Russia; according to specialists, this development might turn out to be "more important than [the revolution] of 1917."[256]

One must realize that in terms of the technology available to the population, the Soviet Union was decades behind the West. Soviet citizens had practically no VCRs, fax machines, cellular phones, cordless phones, answering machines, personal computers, or copiers. When Gorbachev unveiled his 1986 plan to purchase 1 million personal computers abroad, it seemed very daring project.

Nothing came of his plan, however, until computerization was initiated by private companies. Russians bought 600,000 personal computers in 1993[257] and 800,000 in 1994;[258] they were buying computers at the rate of 990,000 in 1995,[259] and sales are expected to exceed 1 million in 1996.[260] Per capita, this figure is nine times higher than that of China.[261] By 1996 the total number of personal computers in Russia may reach 3.5 million.[262]

As recently as 1989, enterprises used to lock and seal their copying machines after 5 p.m. in order to prevent their use for private purposes by employees. Today there are about 150,000 copiers in corporate and personal use.[263]

Anyone who tried to call Russia or send a fax in both 1990 and 1995 knows how dramatically the situation has improved. Calling Moscow from overseas has become as easy as calling Paris. Communication with provincial cities, on the other hand, remains difficult and sometimes impossible. However, the situation is radically improving there as well.[264] A number of major projects are currently being implemented[265] that should bring the number of telephone lines to 27 per 100 inhabitants,[266] increase the number of international telephone channels to 50,000,[267] and connect all major cities by digital fiber-optic lines.[268] According to foreign experts, by the turn of the century Russia could have the most advanced communications system in Eastern Europe,[269] and the world's most advanced system of interbank clearing.[270]

Another sign of technological progress can be seen in the rapidity with which the fledgling Russian banking system was computerized and integrated. By 1995 forty thousand central bank and commercial bank branches were linked electronically by the satellite system Bankir.[271]

Reportedly, the use of computers in manufacturing is are also becoming more frequent. For example, the American company ABB estimated that in several years the Russian market for automated industrial systems will grow to tens of billion of dollars.[272]

Finally, Russia may become the first country in the world to introduce an electronic voting system. The system *Vybory* (elections) is scheduled for testing in parliamentary elections in December 1995. Consisting of 5,800 computers and 6,700 printers, it will allow no-ballot voting, thus tremendously speeding up the process of tabulating results and also diminishing fraud.[273]

In the words of the president of an American company, "In less than six years, Russia accomplished the computer revolution, which for the United States took fifteen years."[274] Russia's feat should not be surprising, considering that the overwhelming majority of the Russian industrial elite are technocrats. Moreover, the emphasis on high technology is likely to accelerate, because technological advances are the only way for the former defense industry, which only now is entering the market arena, to compete with foreign manufacturers.[275]

All these positive trends, however, can easily be reversed if the gap between the poor and the rich is growing, if "the middle class has practically disappeared,"[276] if the tensions caused by societal splits are growing and erupt in social unrest and upheavals.

The Poor, the Rich, and the Middle Class

Is it possible that a million or so conspicuously consuming super-rich, are creating the illusion that Russia is well off while in reality most Russians are sinking deeper and deeper into poverty?

According to official statistics, 20 percent of the population lives below the poverty line—that is, their per capita income is less than 133,000 rubles ($33) a month.[277] Many pensioners and the rural elderly people belong to this group. The average pension (with additional compensations) is 200,000 rubles ($45) a month.[278] However, even among the 37 million pensioners the situation is not uniformly bad. For example, war veterans receive pensions that are higher than the average salary; at least 8 million pensioners still work.[279] In addition, pensioners enjoy state-subsidized medical service, apartments, utilities, and public transportation.

In the Russian countryside, older people have always had to rely on themselves. Until the 1970s millions of elderly peasants did not receive any pensions at all. Now all of them receive pensions; they are free to earn additional income. Some even rent their land to private farmers.

City dwellers who are still dependent on the state, particularly those employed in education, science, culture, and the arts, suffer badly if they have no supplementary income. However, with the first signs of economic recovery in the fall of 1995, workers in state owned enterprises received a 54 percent pay raise,[280] while teachers' salaries were doubled.[281]

While the existence of poverty and wealth is obvious, there is much debate about the size of the middle class, the guarantor of political stability in western democracies. The government defines the middle-income group as those earning $250 a month or more. Estimates of their number vary from 16 million[282] to about twenty million[283]—that is, about 20 percent of the adult population.[284]

By Western standards, of course, $250 a month is far below the poverty line. Nevertheless, the standard of living and buying power of this group needs to be examined carefully.

This segment of the population pays 12 percent of its income in taxes, which leaves them with about $220 per month. But if we add about 40 percent to their income (since Russians typically do not report that percentage of their income to the government, as all analysts realize), and take into account the purchasing power of the ruble, their disposable income is equivalent to about $700 a month. In addition, even the middle-income segment of the population enjoys free education; state-subsidized medical services, transportation, and utilities;[285] and so on.

The purchasing and savings patterns of the middle-income group confirm the impression that they have substantial disposable income. Indeed, when asked where would they turn for money if they wanted to buy something expensive, 20 percent of Russians responded that they would use their regular earnings or dip into their savings. The rest would have to borrow.[286] Market research conducted by producers of computers, color television sets, cars, and other expensive consumer goods consistently indicates that this segment of the population is expanding, not contracting. In short, as one seasoned American observer remarked, "The evidence that the wealthy class is no longer confined to a few streets or hotels is everywhere."[287]

Apart from income, one has to take into account the following facts: twenty six million families possess private plots of land,[288] 20 million families fully own their apartments, 42 million people own shares in companies, about 15 million families have their own cottages or *dachas*, 80 percent of Russians have savings, and 11 million own cars.

All this evidence combined seems to support the government view, seconded by foreign journalists, that "the average person is growing better off,"[289] and that the middle class is expanding.

The Emerging Consumer Society

While analysts have devoted much attention to the level of consumption in Russia, most of them have failed to notice a trend of colossal importance: the consumer-goods market has increasingly begun to define and shape economic trends.

Soviet citizens were not consumers; instead they were receivers of goods and services that were carefully distributed by the state, according to their relative importance to the state. By 1991 this "distribution system had all but fallen apart";[290] 96-97 percent of basic consumer goods were in short supply.[291]

In 1994, by contrast, the food and consumer goods markets were 91 percent saturated,[292] and the Russian people "could not even dream about such a [wide] variety of consumer goods and food."[293] With many choices available to them, Russians are in a position to choose between good and bad products, and thereby to drive companies making inferior products out of the market.

It is important to dispel the common misconception that foreign goods totally dominate the market. The situation in Moscow, where foreign goods do dominate, is unusual: in the country as a whole up to 70 percent of consumer goods and foodstuffs sold are of domestic origin.[294] After the initial surge of interest in imported food, Russian consumers are becoming more selective.[295] A survey conducted in the summer of 1995 showed that 79 percent of Russian consumers preferred Russian-made food.[296] Market research also indicates that some domestic consumer goods are not inferior to imports.[297] The preference for domestic products represents a stunning change of heart for a nation where, for generations, anything foreign was considered automatically superior to its domestic equivalents: it also indicates that domestic producers of food and goods can compete successfully.

Many critics claim that ordinary people lack money to buy goods and accordingly are acutely aware of their powerlessness, which causes them anguish. Thus one journalist wrote: "When a person has money in his pockets but there is nothing to buy with it, he apparently feels more worthy and more confident than when he is surrounded by everything, but has no money to buy anything."[298]

I believe that this theory is profoundly wrong. First of all, money that can buy nothing can add neither confidence nor self-esteem. One can feel worthy only when one has personal power and the opportunity to exercise it to enhance one's personal comfort and security. Even a poor person enjoys the hope, no matter how slim, that he may someday become rich.

Secondly, after the initial plunge in 1992 the consumption of foodstuffs and consumer goods began to rebound, which cannot be accounted for by one million rich and super-rich Russians. Thus in 1994 official statistics show that consumption of foodstuffs was up 11 percent compared to the same period in 1993.[299] Actual purchases of food, small appliances, and clothing may actually have been much greater, because up to 50 percent of retail trade is thought to be unreported.[300] Taking this trade into account, some analysts estimated that in 1994 consumption of consumer goods grew by 30-35 percent[301] and continued to grow at an 8 percent annual rate in the first half of 1995.[302] The rapid expansion of American-style "supermarkets for average people"[303] is yet more evidence of the growing power of consumers. After all, 55 percent of Russian GNP is now devoted to wages, that is, to personal consumption.[304] New-car demand in Russia is expected to soar 50 percent by the year 2000.[305]

In sum, for better or worse Russia is quickly becoming a consumer society rather than a distributive society. In a way, Russian life has become comparable to life in the West. Professional pursuits have become a main preoccupation, and professional success is the key to enjoyment of life. Excellence in one's profession almost automatically rewards one with the solution to many material problems.

Conclusion

The essence of the critics' arguments is that the reforms have awakened the evil side of human nature, encouraging greed, cruelty, and selfishness. The reforms are said to have led to inflation, a rise in crime, unemployment, the collapse of social services, a growing disparity in social conditions, and a deterioration in the overall standard of living. Frustration and a growing sense of helplessness are said to have caused a surge in alcoholism, suicide, diseases, infant mortality, abortions, and accidents. In short, they have allegedly promoted "degradation and dissolution."[306]

But the critics are wrong. To begin with, they fail to mention that many economic and social disasters did not occur. The systems of transportation and communications continue to function(albeit with difficulties); mass epidemics have been prevented.[307] Secondly, the critics understate the positive changes that have occurred or interpret them as accidental.[308] Many apocalyptic predictions were not, after all, fulfilled. As one magazine wrote: "The dates set by oracles for the disintegration and destruction [of Russia] are passing, one after another, and Russia is still standing; what is more, her success is becoming more and more evident."[309]

The communal world of universal poverty and uniformity is dying. The new world, with a mixture of modern features and traditional Russian ones, is replacing it. Modern sounds, shapes, symbols, and colors are achieving predominance;; traditional Russian forms of address, place names, symbols, heroes, songs, and festivals are having a resurgence. Modernistic buildings now appear alongside restored architectural masterpieces.[310] Entire streets are being restored to their pre-1917 look.[311] Religion is reasserting its importance: 8,000 Orthodox churches, 32 dioceses, 289 monasteries, two academies, and 23 theological colleges have opened.[312] On the other hand, public telephones accepting credit cards,[313] faxes, computers, automatic teller machines, modern gas stations, and other signs of modernization appear every day.

People can move,[314] travel abroad, and buy whatever they want if they can afford it. They have an unprecedented choice of goods, schools,[315] hospitals, services, restaurants, entertainment, sources of news, and so on.

In sum, the elimination of totalitarian control over society has awakened constructive as well as destructive instincts and forces. The intolerance and hatred cultivated by the ideology of class struggle could not disappear overnight, as if the nation had magically awakened from a nightmare. Still, a massive rehabilitation of life has occurred, and the convalescence and recovery of human nature continue. The constructive impulses should eventually prevail, because the totalitarian power's systemic support for manifestations of human evil has now been eliminated from Russian life.

If this process continues, Russia is likely to become a normal, understandable, and rather predictable country. Unfortunately, she might also lose the mystique that throughout the centuries has charmed and intrigued so many foreign observers.

CHAPTER 7

THE EVOLVING RUSSIAN CULTURE

Introduction

As was discussed earlier, the transformation of Russia has been proceeding in all areas at once. The reformers had no master plan that could prescribe, for example, an orderly sequence to be followed, such as first writing a new constitution, then creating a new political structure, then building a market economy, and subsequently, reforming social institutions. All institutions were changing simultaneously, and they mutually affected one another. Nor was this a totally spontaneous, organic process, because such powerful personalities as Yeltsin, Burbulis, Gaidar, Chubais, and Shakhrai were relentlessly shaping events. It was also an extremely rapid process. Indeed, only a few years after the birth of a new state, a totally different political and economic foundation has been created, new elites have appeared, new institutions and a new way of life has been established.

Naturally, a number of legitimate questions arise: Has this process been too hasty? How stable and viable is the new sociopolitical entity?

While the market economy in Russia is widely considered to be irreversible (because very few people really want to go back to a planned economy),[1] the viability and longevity of the democratic system in Russia is universally doubted.

These doubts are rooted in the Russian cultural legacy. Historians and political scientists have pointed out that Russian history has seen despotism, anarchy, and a totalitarian system, but that European-type democracy has no roots in Russia; for this reason they contend, all previous attempts to introduce it failed. The liberal reign of Alexander I was followed by the reactionary regime of Nicholas I, the reforms of Alexander II were stymied by the reactionary Alexander III; and the brief period of constitutional monarchy under Nicholas II was supplanted by the Bolshevik dictatorship.

Some political scientists even contend that Western democracy is alien to Russia's tradition, culture, and national character.[2] They believe that Russia's current flirtation with democracy is doomed, that it is only a matter of time before Russia relapses into some form of fascist dictatorship under Vladimir Zhyrinovski or nationalist dictatorship under someone like former general Aleksandr Lebed. At the least, they believe, Russia will fall victim to an authoritarian regime under Yeltsin or someone even worse.

The founding fathers of the new Russia, however, argue that Russia's industrialization and modernization in the twentieth century changed Russia's culture and her people to such a degree that the free market and the democratic system suit them as well as any other people. They point out that democracy has proven that it can function in totally different societies, like Argentina, Germany, India, and Japan; they argue that there is no reason to think that it cannot function in Russia as well. They point to the speedy and surprisingly peaceful transition from a totalitarian regime to a fairly democratic system as evidence of the *narod*'s support for democracy.[3]

Even the most optimistic analysts, however, cannot exclude the possibility that the so-called national patriots or the communists may seize power by capitalizing on a wave of popular disenchantment with democracy and resentment at Russia's alleged political, military, economic, and psychological humiliation by the West.[4] Thus the manifesto of one of the contenders for the presidency, retired general Aleksandr Lebed, seems to reflect the views and sentiments of a significant segment of the population, demonstrating the depth and power of these resentments, suspicions, and hatreds. "Today, a new creeping, sticky, and putrid yoke is advancing on us. And this time it is aimed against the spirit of the people. Our enemies learned in dozens of inglorious invasions that Russia can be defeated only by Russia itself, and they have decided to become invisible. You cannot cross swords with this enemy and you cannot hit him with bullets but he exists. He is shaking and destroying the foundations that our ancestors bequeathed to us, and he is replacing them with an imported surrogate that undermines national morality and the state organism. He is producing party sects and mafia clans, is preaching an English-language Christianity to Orthodox Russia, and is creating economic chaos and inciting peoples who lived in friendship for centuries to fight one another. To separate Belarus and Ukraine from Russia was the same as to tear a piece out of a living organism! And the enemy was able to do this. Today, the enemy is within us—traitors and nonentities who do not care if we have democracy or tyranny, as long as they can satisfy the insatiable requirements of their filthy lives."[5]

Where, then, does Russia's future lie: in a desperate struggle for survival with enemies, real and imagined, or in peaceful integration with the rest of the democratic world, principally Europe?

To shed some light on this centuries-old dilemma, one has to look at both the edifice and the foundation, the political structure and the culture of the new Russia.

The New Political System

The new Russian constitution took three and one-half years to work out and adopt. The old constitution contained two fundamental flaws: the Congress of People's Deputies was the supreme legislative power, and the Supreme Soviet was the supreme governing body of the country, though neither one could perform its functions. On Yeltsin's initiative, in the summer of 1990 a Constitutional Commission under Yeltsin's chairmanship was set up, in order to work out a totally new constitution for a sovereign, democratic Russia. The commission, led by executive secretary Oleg Rumiantsev, a 26-year-old lawyer, composed a draft that incorporated the basic provisions of the constitutions of the mature democracies of the West, envisioning Russia as a parliamentary republic. However, the circumstances of the time, particularly the bitter struggle with the communist center, as well as the federalist structure of Russia, called for a strong presidency. Eventually, after half a dozen drafts, endless debates,[6] and even armed clashes, on December 12, 1993, the new constitution was adopted in a nationwide referendum.[7]

By dint of their role in this process, five individuals can be considered the founding fathers of the new Russia: Sergei Shakhrai, Gennadi Burbulis, Anatoli Sobchak, Sergei Alekseyev, and Boris Yeltsin. Hundreds of people made constructive suggestions and helped work out the constitution's specific sections. Yet ultimately, in the words of Foreign Minister Andrei Kozyrev, "it was the president's constitution, just as [it is] the De Gaulle constitution in France, or the Jefferson constitution in the United States."[8] Indeed, no one invested as much thinking and energy in designing the constitution as Boris Yeltsin. And as we shall see, his role may be the source of some serious problems that Russian democracy now faces.

The new constitution of Russia has all the attributes of a typical democracy and some uniquely Russian features. Its ideological preamble derives from the Universal Charter of Human Rights adopted by the UN in 1948. It recognizes all the basic human rights: private property, freedom of speech and conscience, the separation of church and state, and so on. It also recognizes the overarching importance of the principle of the separation of powers. State power is divided among the presidency, the Federal Assembly (a bicameral legislature), the executive branch of the government, the

Constitutional Court, the Supreme Court."[T]he demarcation of their power and functions is clearly established."[9]

The Legislature

Russia's cumulative experience with parliamentarianism now amounts to eighteen years: twelve years of the State Duma, from 1906 to 1917, three years of the Russian Supreme Soviet, and two years of the Federal Assembly or Duma. All previous legislatures however, were basically forums for confrontation between the opposition and the ruling power, represented by the czar, the communist regime, or the president.

The Federal Assembly has undoubtedly been the most representative and constructive of all Russian legislatures so far. It is also the most educated and professional. Although it has its share of demagogues, eccentrics, and populists, the overwhelming majority of lawmakers are "hard-working, balanced, and very intelligent people."[10] Ninety-five percent of the Duma's deputies, for example, have college degrees, and 33 percent have scientific degrees.[11]

The Federal Assembly has also proved to be independent-minded. It offered an amnesty to the October 1993 coup leaders (against the strong objections of the president), and it overrode several presidential vetoes on the budget and some of his decrees. But the Duma has not taken a doggedly confrontational stance toward the president, as did its predecessor, the Supreme Soviet.

The Duma has turned out to be quite productive, particularly considering the huge logistical problems that it has had to face. During its first 93-day-long working session, it changed its quarters twice, yet it considered 222 bills and adopted 46 laws.[12] Its second session was three times as productive.[13] And during its spring 1995 session, the Duma passed 140 laws.[14] In two years, it also approved three federal budgets.

The Constitutional Court

The Constitutional Court can be considered pivotal for the institutional structure of Russian democracy. After President Yeltsin suspended the work of the Constitutional Court in October 1993, it did not function until March 16, 1995.[15] It took until then to nominate all of its nineteen judges and to elect its chairman. According to Chairman Vladimir Tumanov, the Constitutional Court is a totally independent body endowed with an "enormous amount of power" to interpret the constitution and to arbitrate the disagreements among the branches of government as well as between the central and local governments.[16] Like its Western counterparts,[17] it intends to "uphold the constitution and thus facilitate the work of the democratic system as a whole."[18] Its chairman has pledged to "safeguard a principled position: Everyone must hew to the Constitution and nothing else."[19] It is too early to tell if the Constitutional Court will be able to perform its role as guardian of the constitution. Its first major test was to examine the legality of President Yeltsin's decree of December 9, 1994, which sent troops to Chechnia.[20]

The Judicial System

The new judicial system of Russia was basically established by 1995, although reforms continue to be made.[21] It incorporated all the main principles of international law, such as the presumption of innocence, protection against self-incrimination, and judicial monitoring of arrests. Investigation and trial procedures are even embodied in the Constitution and detailed in the judicial reforms initiated by the president.[22] Trial by jury has been reintroduced after 75 years.[23] Citizens are now subject to laws rather than the arbitrary dictates of the state—a critically important distinction. An important precedent for the new judicial system was set in October 1995, when Minister of Defense Pavel Grachev was ordered by a prosecutor of the district court of Moscow to appear in court in connection with a civil suit filed against him by the newspaper *Moskovski Komsomolets*.[24]

The Fourth Estate: The Mass Media

Since 1990 the Russian mass media have experienced explosive growth. There are now many more types of publications, radio stations, and television stations. For example, the number of television channels in Moscow increased from three to eight, and cable and satellite reception now allows Russians to watch 12 foreign television stations.[25] The number of newspapers increased almost eleven-fold, from 2,270 in 1990 to 24,000 in June 1994.[26] Specialized publications proliferated in particular, as they do in all democratic societies. Instead of a few state-owned publishing houses, there are now more than 8,000 commercial publishers.

Instead of one state television and radio committee, there are now 457 independent television broadcasting companies. Russian television offers provocative interviews and discussions,[27] as well as pictures of crime, poverty, and violence.

Even before the collapse of communism, the press had become a significant political force. Since 1991, however, the mass media have evolved into a "truly free and influential 'fourth estate'."[28] Some analysts have even referred to the "party of the media."[29]

As in the West, the Russian media have assumed the role of a watchdog over the government. They focus on social ills such as crime, poverty, corruption, and violations of human rights. The mass media bring these issues into open forums; the media have been able to bring about changes by highlighting governmental failures. For example, media exposure of corruption in the armed forces stationed in Germany led to the ouster of the deputy defense minister.[30] When the war in Chechnia broke out, for the first time in Russian history its "ugly picture was brought to Russian homes by uncensored TV"[31] and newspapers.

The Security Forces

On the heels of their August 1991 victory, the liberal democrats were burning with desire to dismantle the KGB empire. Yeltsin also had little sympathy for the KGB, although he never displayed any paranoid fear of it. The democrats eliminated the Soviet Union's KGB; in its place the Russian Ministry of Security was created, a much smaller and relatively toothless organization. Tens of thousands of KGB officers left the security service and went into private business.[32] However, chaos and disintegration soon began to threaten the very existence of Russia. On December 19, 1991, in expectation of social unrest, Yeltsin attempted to merge the KGB and MVD into one ministry of security.[33] Many democrats, most importantly Burbulis, opposed this plan,[34] and the Constitutional Court overruled Yeltsin's decree. In January 1992 Yeltsin decreed the creation of the Federal Security Agency, staffed by 137,900 employees.[35] Since then the Russian security services have been in a state of almost constant reorganization. In December 1993 Yeltsin declared that the "Security Ministry, the body that for nearly 75 years carried out surveillance of the people, has been disbanded."[36] Indeed, it was split into five different organizations.[37] Its successor agency's personnel was cut to 76,000, and the personnel of the Military Intelligence Service (GRU) was also cut by 50 percent.[38]

In 1995 the place formerly occupied by the KGB was filled by six entities: the Federal Security Service (FSB), headed by Colonel-General Mikhail Barsukov; the Foreign Intelligence Service (SVR), led by Yevgeni Primakov; the Federal Agency for Government Communications and Information (FAPSI), headed by Colonel A. Starovoitov; the Federal Border Service, headed by Andrei Nikolayev; the Presidential Security Service (SBP), headed by Lt. General Aleksandr Korzhakov; and the Customs Service, headed by Anatoli Kruglov. In addition, there was, as before, the

Ministry of Interior headed by Anatoli Kulikov and the GRU headed by Lt. General Fedor Ladygin.

Critics claimed that all these services combined were comparable to the former KGB and concluded that "the KGB still lives, and is regaining its lost position . . . it is now reporting directly to the President. There is no public oversight."[39]

What these critics have failed to understand, however, is the fact that six separate and independent entities are not equivalent to a single organization capable of controlling all aspects of life of the country. As we discussed in chapter one, it is the synergy of many forms of power under a single authority that defines totalitarian power. The KGB employed up to 3.5 million workers[40] and its empire included institutions of education and research and development and production facilities (to say nothing about military units).

By splitting the backbone of totalitarian power into many pieces, the democrats effectively destroyed its ability to control society. Such functions of the KGB as the enforcement of ideology and political loyalty, the supervision of the defense industry, control of education and the media, strategic planning, border protection, the operation of customs services, and so on were transferred to other institutions or eliminated altogether. It is true that the majority of these successor services have been staffed by former KGB officers and employees. However, their allegiances now belong to the new institutions, which have different functions, goals, structures, budgets, and responsibilities.

Moreover, the democrats seem to have initially gone too far in emasculating the main security services. The FSB and Ministry of Interior proved to be unable to cope with organized crime, private armies, and terrorism. Hence in 1994 Yeltsin's government began to return some critically important powers to the FSB. Thus the directorate of special operations was created,[41] and the FSB again became an investigative body.[42] Finally, in August 1995 the anti terrorist group Alpha was returned to the Federal Security Service.[43] The number of special troops in the Ministry of Interior was also increased (to 52,000 men, who could be deployed rapidly.[44]

This is not to deny that problems in the security forces exist. The Presidential Security Service, for example, is too powerful, and its head, Aleksandr Korzhakov, has interpreted his agency's mission too broadly. He has intervened in purely financial matters,[45] claiming that corruption among the top business and administrative elite is one of his agency's concerns.[46] His service harassed one of the leading bankers of the country, alleging that he had ties with criminal organizations.

These disturbing facts notwithstanding, the allegations that the KGB has been recreated are baseless. However, all "power ministries" and security forces are under direct presidential supervision; the prime minister has no control over them;[47] and parliamentary oversight is ineffective. These facts point to serious problems for Russian democracy: too much power is concentrated in the hands of the president, and the other branches of government are too weak.

The Presidency

Boris Yeltsin built the institution of the presidency from scratch in the midst of a fierce political struggle, a daunting economic crisis, the disintegration of the empire, and the threatened disintegration of Russia. From the beginning, the founding fathers of the new Russia argued that Russia needed a strong presidency, because "in a multi-ethnic state such as Russia, a president elected by the entire population should be a guarantor of the unity of the state,"[48] who can "arbitrate between the parliament and the government, assist in the resolution of arguments between the center and the provinces, and be a guarantor of human rights and liberties."[49]

Every builder of institutions creates an institutional culture that more or less fits his personality and mentality. As a powerful and, indeed, aggressive personality, Yeltsin created an institution capable not only of fighting and destroying but also of building.

During his two years of struggle with the Supreme Soviet and the simultaneous construction of the foundation of the new Russia, Yeltsin managed to concentrate executive, legislative, financial, and military forms of power in the institution of the presidency.[50] As we discussed above, this merger of different forms of power is potentially problematic.

In summary, although the edifice of democracy in Russia looks fairly complete, although it includes all the familiar features of a typical Western democracy, the strength and solidity of its foundation are the subjects of heated debate. In order to resolve this critical debate, we must examine the new sociopolitical system's ability to withstand crises.

Chechnia: Democracy On Trial

Only one year after the new Russia was born, it was subjected to an extremely rigorous test. Chechnia, a tiny autonomous republic in the northern Caucasus, has had a two-century-long history of struggle against

Russia. Stalin deported the entire population of the Chechen-Ingush republic to Kazakhstan in 1944 to punish their alleged collaboration with Nazi
Germany. After his death, the Chechens were allowed to return, but the
tragedy left deep scars in their psyche.

In November 1990 the Chechen-Ingush Autonomous Republic declared
its sovereignty, which it reaffirmed in July 1991. General Dzokhar Dudayev
rigged the October 1991 elections to the local parliament and made himself
president of the Chechen Republic. The Russian Supreme Soviet (at that
time headed by fellow Chechen Ruslan Khazbulatov) annulled the results
of the elections, and the Russian president declared a state of emergency in
the Chechen-Ingush Republic.[51] In response, Dudayev declared the total
independence of Chechen republic and threatened to unleash a "holy war"
on Russia if she intervened.[52] He claimed that the Chechens were the "most
ancient people on earth" and called on other neighboring peoples to support
Chechnia.[53]

The democrats urged Yeltsin to end the state of emergency,[54] and the
Russian Supreme Soviet canceled it.[55] Russia effectively lost all control
over the Chechen Republic, which is an internationally recognized part of
the Russian Federation. In May 1992 Dudayev forced the Russian army to
withdraw from Chechnia and leave 50 percent of its armaments behind.
Thus General Dudayev acquired hundreds of tanks and armored personnel
carriers, and even several hundred airplanes.[56]

In Chechnia, Dudayev was not recognized as the undisputed leader of
the republic, partially because he did not belong to the dominant tribe.[57] At
least four Chechen leaders were entangled in a power struggle with him and
among themselves. This turned Chechnia into a no-man's land, leading to
an explosion of crime, the hijacking of airplanes, attacks on passenger and
freight trains, and so on. The Chechen mafia in Moscow became one of the
strongest. In the words of Aleksei Iliushenko, the Acting Procurator General, "Chechnia became one of the criminal forces' main bases."[58] Its
economy was brought to ruins. Thus oil output fell from 4.1 million tons in
1991 to 1.2 million tons in 1994, and oil refining fell from 11.1 million tons
in 1991 to 100,000 tons in 1994.[59] Russians constituted about 20 percent of
Chechnia's million inhabitants. Dudayev used tactics of harassment and
pressure to force Russians to leave the republic, and more than 120,000 did
so.

Until 1994 Yeltsin was too deeply entangled in more pressing problems
—enacting reforms, struggling with the Supreme Soviet, creating the constitution and warding off separatism in more powerful autonomous

republics like Tatarstan. His government hoped that Chechnia's economic difficulties and the Chechen Republic's violations of human rights would result in popular resentment and the emergence of a more pragmatic leadership opposed to separation. In May 1994, however, Yeltsin decided that he could no longer tolerate such resistance to Russian authority. His administration threw its weight behind one of the anti-Dudayev groups and provided it with financial and some military support. However, the opposition failed to unseat General Dudayev, even with half-hearted Russian military support. After the humiliating defeat of opposition forces supported by the Russian "volunteers" in November 1994, Yeltsin decided in favor of a full-scale military operation against Dudayev's forces.

However, Yeltsin made a major miscalculation, similar to those previously made by many Europeans in that part of the world. When Russian troops crossed Chechnia's border, all the local tribes put aside their quarrels and turned their arms against the common enemy. Suddenly, the previously unpopular Dudayev became the undisputed leader, who now had under his command an army of up to 30,000 well-trained and well-equipped guerrillas led by former career officers of the Soviet Army. As an Afghanistan war veteran, Dudayev skillfully fought an urban guerrilla war. The easy, victorious campaign that Russia had anticipated turned into a very bloody war. It cost Russia about $2 billion; 2,000 Russian troops were killed and 5,500 others wounded.[60] An estimated 20,000 civilians and 14,000 Chechen fighters have been killed or wounded.[61]

Yeltsin's decision to solve the crisis in Chechnia by military means created an uproar in the country and abroad. The Russian democratic community and the mass media were outraged. The majority of parliamentarians,[62] the liberals in the presidential administration,[63] some ministers,[64] and one-third of the Presidential Expert Council[65] spoke out against a direct military solution.[66] An estimated 70 percent of the population opposed a military solution.[67] Even Yeltsin's old "comrades in arms," such as Burbulis and Shumeiko, expressed their disapproval.[68]

The media were particularly merciless in criticizing the administration and the army for the destruction of Grozny, the many civilian casualties, and the violations of human rights.[69] In turn, members of the presidential administration accused the media of one-sidedness and charged that they had been bribed by Dudayev.[70] The media reacted furiously and accused the presidential appointees of lying.[71] Their charge angered Yeltsin in turn and made him repeat the allegations about payments of Chechen money to the media.[72]

From reading the media, one could think that the president's actions were opposed by all of Russia. Even his former allies claimed that he had lost his social base and became a captive of the "party of war."[73]

The war in Chechnia significantly harmed the Russian economy. It triggered a new wave of inflation, which lasted for several months, and depleted the currency reserves of the federal government.

Yet the war in Chechnia did not derail the overall recovery of the economy and failed to turn into a real political crisis for the democratic regime. There were no massive antiwar rallies or outbreaks of terrorism (except in the towns of Budionovsk and Pervomaisk). No autonomous entities openly supported Chechnia. The Federal Assembly simply exercised its power to restrain the president. It canceled the presidential decree that had declared an emergency in the Ossetia-Ingushetia area, and it forced Yeltsin to dismiss the "power ministers" (although the president gave them other government jobs).[74]

For his part, the president did not resort to repressive measures such as censorship, the cancellation of elections, the disbanding of parliament, and so on. Yeltsin did not even dismiss those of his advisers who openly criticized him during the crisis.[75] In the middle of the war campaign, he bowed to public opinion and ordered the army to use force more discretely and selectively.

When the military action was nearing its conclusion, the Constitutional Court held hearings on the actions of the president in Chechnia and ruled that the president had been entitled to use force against illegal armed formations, although it did criticize his methods.

The Problems and Perils of Russian Democracy

Chechnia exposed many problems in the security and armed forces. The conscript armed forces displayed very low morale and were ill equipped to wage military operations against a well-prepared rebel army, especially in Chechen cities. Chechnia also demonstrated that security forces should be, in Yeltsin's words, "strong, well trained, properly equipped, fully armed,"[76] and thus capable of swift action to put down disturbances.

Of greater importance, the war in Chechnia highlighted three major problems in Russia's sociopolitical system: the intrinsic flaws in the Russian federalist structure, the profound weakness of the still-emerging civil society, and the imbalance of power among the branches of the government.

Federalism

Chechnia demonstrated that Russia's federalist structure, which grants attributes of statehood to autonomous republics, is fraught with mortal danger to her integrity.

Yeltsin was highly attuned to the democratic concept of the horizontal distribution of power—from Moscow to the provinces. Having himself been a party leader of the most powerful Ural province, and having experienced the need to confront Moscow over every small issue, such as building a subway in Sverdlovsk, Yeltsin has been very receptive to the provinces' drive for "local, independent self-rule,"[77] realizing that the future of Russia depends on the prosperity of the provinces.

At the same time, in the absence of totalitarian controls, Russia's peculiar federalist system poses the danger of Balkanization. Before the 1917 revolution Russia was divided into 115 *gubernii* (provinces). Currently, there are 56 ordinary provinces (*oblasts* and *krais*), 21 autonomous entities that enjoy special status, and 12 autonomous republics whose status approaches that of independent states (that is, they have their own presidents, parliaments, and councils of ministers, their own flags and national anthems).

This system was conceived by the Bolsheviks to win support from the ethnic minorities; it aimed at mobilizing them against the White Guards who stood for the restoration of the monarchy and the preservation of the Russian empire. Lenin promised total independence to Poland, Finland, Ukraine, Georgia and other now independent states, and self-determination to the other minorities. As soon as the Bolsheviks won the civil war, however, they reoccupied the republics and deprived them of any real independence. Although Lenin bestowed the status of autonomous republic, *oblast* or *krai* to areas in which ethnic minorities predominated, he established a totalitarian regime that deprived them of any political, economic, or cultural autonomy. This pernicious system posed a tremendous problem for the democratic government when practically all the institutional bonds preserving the federation—the Communist Party, the KGB, and central economic planning disappeared.

In 1990, when the Soviet empire began to fall apart, many autonomous entities followed the lead of the East European states and then Russia and the Baltic republics, embarking on their own crusades for independence and statehood. The "parade of sovereignties" began. This led to bloody ethnic disputes throughout the entire Caucasus. Wars and civil wars resulted in ethnic cleansing and atrocities in many places: Sumgait, Nagorno-Karabakh,

Tbilisi, Baku, Southern and Northern Ossetia, Nakhichevan, and Abkhazia. In October 1992 ethnic conflict erupted on Russian territory, between the Ossetians and the Ingush, when the Ossetians decided to expel the Ingush from North Ossetia. The ensuing three-day war left 600 people dead, destroyed 3,397 houses, and created 43,000 refugees.[78] Only the separation of the warring sides by the Russian army stopped the bloodshed and ethnic cleansing.

These ethnic conflicts have demonstrated that Russia's complex mix of ethnicities, combined with its federalist structure, pose a mortal threat to Russia's existence as an integral state. There is no obvious solution for this problem in sight. Until October 1993 the government used negotiations, concessions, and the threat of economic sanctions to keep the country together. Then, on the heels of his October 4 victory, Yeltsin toughened his position and "began the restoration of control over the state."[79] A reference to republics as "sovereign states" was dropped from the constitution.[80] Yeltsin told the leaders of the regions that "the president of the Russian Federation is the guarantor of its integrity. I support the right of nations to self-determination, but I have to make one reservation, that this excludes the right to secede from Russia."[81]

Eventually a significant portion of power was transferred from the federal center to the provinces. As a result, the self-proclaimed republics of the Urals and Siberia dropped their claims to independence.[82] In February 1994 Tatarstan, the largest (with 3.6 million inhabitants) and economically strongest of all the autonomous republics,[83] signed a treaty with Russia, according to which it acknowledged itself to be an inseparable part of the Russian Federation.[84] In Yeltsin's words, the specter of the disintegration of Russia along Soviet (or even Yugoslav) lines, which had been haunting Russia for three years, has evaporated.[85] By September 1995 similar treaties with five other autonomous republics were signed.[86] At the same time, Yeltsin issued an edict suggesting that "the constituent parts of the Russian Federation remove from their constitutions, laws, statutes, and other normative legal acts any contradictions of the provisions of the Basic Law of the Russian Federation and the federal laws."[87]

Nevertheless, the issue of federalism is bound to haunt Russia, and sooner or later the federalist structure will have to be radically reformed or abolished altogether.

In 1991 the democratic strategist Gavriil Popov suggested that referendums be held and independence granted to all autonomous entities wishing to leave the Russian federation. He suggested that a new administrative structure should then be created: Russia should be divided into 10-15 provinces (North, Center, South, West Siberia, and so on), each of which would have equal status.[88]

However, the secession of autonomous republics does not seem to be feasible for Russia. Unlike other European empires, Russia does not have a clear-cut division of its territory, with Russians predominating in some places and individual ethnic groups predominating elsewhere. A cluster of the largest autonomous republics, for example, is situated in the very heart of Russia. Twenty-six million people live in Russia's autonomous entities; ten million of them are the titular indigenous peoples, Russians constitute another 11 million; and 5 million are from other ethnic groups. Only in six autonomous republics, with a combined population of about 4 million people, (Kabardino-Balkaria, Northern Ossetia, Tuva, Chechnia, and the Ingush and Chuvash republics) does the titular ethnic group constitute an absolute majority of the population.[89]

In some autonomous regions, the situation is absurd. For example, Karelians make up only 10 percent of the Karelian republic, while Russians comprise 74 percent of the population. There are more Tatars and Russians in the Bashkir republic than Bashkirs; only 5 percent of the population in the Jewish autonomous *oblast* is Jewish. Many of Russia's *oblasts* and *krais* include autonomous entities in which other ethnic groups, who could also claim the right to autonomous status, reside. The most striking example is the case of the Daghestan Autonomous Republic. Its population of 1.8 million consists of 36 nationalities, which do not all coexist peacefully. The animosities and conflicts among the ethnic groups of the Caucasus have a centuries-long history, which includes the Soviet period.[90] The removal of Russia's presence from these territories would undoubtedly lead to massive ethnic conflicts. One million Chechens, by far the largest ethnic group of the region, would become a local superpower capable of "uniting the rest of the brotherly peoples," as Dudayev has stated.

These considerations suggest that Russia's withdrawal from this and other autonomous regions would not only be impractical but also extremely destabilizing. To forestall such a possibility, Yeltsin unambiguously stated: "Not a single subject of the Russian Federation will leave Russia; one should not even raise that question. Russia is, was, and will remain indivisible."[91]

However, even if the secession of autonomous regions is out of the question, either reforming or abolishing the federalist system is going to be extremely difficult. The current system, which grants different statuses to two dozen minorities, is unfair toward other minorities, and even more so toward the majority of ethnic Russians. If the desires and demands of minorities within the autonomous regions were to be accommodated, the regions would have to be restructured so that ethnic groups could constitute a majority of the population in their territories. But this would involve a massive redrawing of borders and the large-scale resettlement of people in almost all the autonomous republics. It would also be necessary to guarantee cultural and political self-determination to the minorities within these regions. If continued to its logical conclusion, this process would lead to about 130 entities, some of which would have only several thousand inhabitants. Obviously, breaking up Russia in this way is unimaginable.

Abolishing the federalist system and establishing in its place a unified nation-state based on territorial divisions would be a radical solution but in the long run the most viable one.[92] However, this policy would require radical changes in the constitution, which, in turn, would require a two-third majority in the Duma, a three-quarters majority in the Federal Council, and the consent of three-quarters of the local governments. If this step is not taken in the near future, the autonomous republics may develop a growing national consciousness and a taste for statehood that may soon be irreversible. The inherent slowness of the democratic process may mean that "Chechnia phenomenon" will reemerge in several other autonomous regions.

To defuse this time bomb once and for all, Russia would need yet another heroic effort; if his health permits, Yeltsin seems to be the best candidate for the job.

Civil Society and the Multi-Party System

If the media were right and all of Russia opposed Yeltsin's Chechnia policy, why then was he not stopped? The Duma factions were unable to muster a majority to confront the president, and civil society did not provide them with the massive public support needed to impeach the president or force the government to resign. Civil society was clearly still too weak, and the multi-party system too ineffective. Some analysts have explained the weakness of civil society in Russia as the result of the Russian people's de-politicization, general apathy, or even its disillusionment with democracy.[93] In my view, however, the fragmentation of the political spectrum in Russia demands more profound explanation.

After the introduction of *glasnost* in 1987 there was a staggering explosion of civil energy and activity in the Soviet Union. By the fall of 1988 there were approximately 30,000 informal groups, associations, and debate societies. About 53 percent of the nation's young professionals, 66 percent of the workers, and 74 percent of the students were involved in at least one informal group.[94] However, since the multi-party system in Russia was legalized in 1989, all attempts to create large, viable political parties have failed. Instead the number of parties has grown exponentially: from less than a dozen parties in 1991, to 31 in 1993, to about 250 in 1995.[95] Only a few of them have more than 50,000 members, and hardly any of them is capable of forming an effective government.

Critics are correct in stating that when the reforms began a sharp depoliticization followed, due to a massive "privatization of personal lives" as individuals began to focus on pursuing personal happiness.[96] However, this retreat from politics does not necessarily presage political instability.

Russian political parties have been formed around prominent personalities, and on the basis of gender, professional affiliation, common background, and ideological affinity. But none of these can provide a firm foundation for an enduring political party, particularly in a time of rapid social and economic change. Hence the parties have continued to fragment, disappear, and reappear under different names and leaders. Initially, Yeltsin refused to be formally affiliated with a particular party: "No, we do not need a presidential party. Let them naturally develop, twenty of them."[97] Then he came close to accepting the formation of a presidential party, if a powerful centrist opposition party could also be created.[98] In the spring of 1995 he advised Chernomyrdin and Rybkin to form two centrist parties, hoping that Chernomyrdin's party "Russia is Our Home" would become the de facto presidential party. His hope was not, however, fulfilled; the number of parties has continued to multiply. Yeltsin eventually came to the conclusion that for years to come he could not throw his support behind a specific party, because "the president is the guarantor of the Constitution, and the Constitution gives equal rights to all parties."[99]

In a democratic polity, civil society is the ultimate reservoir of political power. The primary power of various groups and movements is translated into political power through the mechanism of political parties. Thus civil society balances the power of governmental institutions. The multiparty system aids in the selection and maturation of the political elites, and it also serves as an instrument of change responding to new realities and priorities.

However, a modern society dominated by professionals tends to fragment into dozens of distinct social groups that cannot easily be lumped together into a few parties. Professionals tend to build long-lasting affiliations with their peers, who have similar aspirations and share a common mentality. They generally have strong feelings about a few specific issues:

religion, abortion, foreign policy, the proper role of government, gender relations, crime, and the environment. These issues usually reflect their perceptions of what threatens social safety and stability; the particular combination of concerns varies greatly from one social group to another. Thus professionals are concerned with many issues, in contrast to the less educated part of the electorate, which tends to care about only one or two. For this reason, professionals are reluctant to be firmly attached to a broadly-based political party and to accept its leadership's proposed solutions for a multitude of social problems. In short, in a society dominated by professionals, the two-party system is almost obsolete. In addition, some traditional functions of the multiparty system, like the selection of political elites, have been assumed by the media and various interest groups.

If the existence of several strong parties is crucial for a democratic system, then Russia's democracy will be in peril for many years to come. However, if our depiction of trends in Russia is correct, and she is on the way toward becoming a technocratic society of professionals, the current fragmentation of the political spectrum should not be surprising. A "virtual multiparty" system is likely to remain; it will evolve into what will arguably be a superior form of democracy, characterized by transient parties and instantaneous electronic voting.

In any case, it may take a long time for Russia to develop a viable political system based on either traditional multiparty mechanisms or a new form of electronic democracy. Meanwhile, Russia has to solve several pressing issues that would entail radically changing its constitution.

These pressing issues provide yet another argument in favor of a strong presidency in Russia, at least for the time being. However, in the longer run it will be essential to shift power from the president to parliament. Is it possible that a powerful and heroic personality like Yeltsin, who now commands the tremendous institutional power of the presidency, will share this power with such notoriously slow and inefficient institutions as parliament and the ministries of the government?

Most political analysts would flatly dismiss this possibility. They argue that for Yeltsin "the rhetoric of liberal democracy is little more than a useful cover for his ambition,"[100] that he "has fallen victim to his own insatiable drive for power,"[101] and that he has built an authoritarian regime to rule over.[102] Even his formerly close "comrade in arms," Mikhail Poltoranin, speculated that Yeltsin may have "bit off more power than he could chew."[103] Some observers go so far as to ascribe monarchic ambitions to Yeltsin:[104] they note that he revived the Czarist imperial heraldry[105] instead of embracing a more egalitarian version promoted by the democrats,[106] that he ordered a grandiose restoration of the Kremlin to its imperial glory, and that he supported the very expensive renovation of the Cathedral of Christ the Savior.

Is Yeltsin an Autocrat?

In late 1994 Yeltsin was subjected to an unprecedented wave of criticism. The media portrayed him as "a president who is isolated in the Kremlin, who is becoming ever more despotic, suspicious, and irrational";[107] they claimed that he had lost his political base and become "a hindrance to the democratic process."[108] However, in September 1995 Yeltsin surprised both his critics and supporters with new vigor and energy, prompting some skeptics to admit that they were again seeing the "Yeltsin of 1991."[109] One Western diplomat remarked: "Yeltsin looks presidential and like a man who wants to remain in power."[110]

In my view, Yeltsin's critics often confuse his operational style with his core motivations and ambitions. Most of all, they systematically underestimate his capability for learning, rejuvenation and change.

The *blitzkrieg* operational style with which Yeltsin attacks a problem prompts analysts to regard him as unpredictable. His single-mindedness, tendency to focus on a given problem, and fanatical determination to see it solved at any cost frighten many observers.[111]

They see him issuing decrees, dismissing and appointing new ministers and deputy prime ministers, sometimes without consulting the prime minister or his deputies,[112] lecturing the prime minister,[113] or scolding the press for its partiality. They point out that he has placed the army's general staff under his direct control without bothering to inform its chief in a timely fashion;[114] they not that he launched a massive military campaign without consulting the parliament, to say nothing of attempting to win public support. They accuse him of "turning the Security Council into his Politburo"[115] and "ignoring the parliamentary process, public opinion, and the law."[116]

Much of this criticism is well founded; the problem to which it points is directly related to Yeltsin's operational style. Once he has made up his mind, he does not want to waste time and lose momentum by trying to persuade intellectuals and the society at large that his decision is correct. With regard to Chechnia, he came to the conclusion that Dudayev understands and respects only force; he also knew that no one wanted to wage war, and that his political advisers would do everything to talk him out of using force. He made up his mind; he thought that he had a job to do, and he did not see why he had to play democratic games. Yeltsin does not care about being loved;

he cares about being respected. He does not pretend; he believes that he has nothing to prove to anyone, he simply wants to accomplish things quickly, because life is so short.

Thus Yeltsin's operational style is that of a hero and an activist. Throughout his life, it has changed little because it has been effective. After all, he has eventually won all the significant battles in his life.

But those who think that Yeltsin is motivated by a perpetual crusade for personal power are wrong. He vehemently denies this, and he is correct to do so. He is not driven by an insatiable appetite for power. For him, power is a means to the end of building; deep in his heart he is a builder. He picks his fights and fights with gusto; not because he thrives on confrontation, but because he has no patience for senseless, artificial obstacles preventing him from doing the building that he really enjoys.

As a teenager, Yeltsin built a sauna for his grandfather. He did it by himself, from scratch, carrying logs from the woods on his back in order to earn his grandfather's support for his decision to become a construction engineer. Such early experiences tend to leave a deep imprint on one's psyche, much deeper than the imprint left by later pragmatic compromises with the system.

Referring to the many social roles that Yeltsin has played in his life, one interviewer asked him how he would describe his calling. "I am a builder," responded Yeltsin. In 1990 he stated his mission clearly: to undo the damage done by communism and build a new democratic Russia. He had to demolish the totalitarian structure and clear away the resulting debris. When that was accomplished, in October 1993, Yeltsin said: "Half my headache has now gone, since all this fighting for power has ended. Now I can concentrate on building a state."[117]

He then plunged headlong into laying the foundation for the democratic system in Russia. He urged the political elite to finalize the constitution and pressured society to adopt it. For about four months, he ruled totally unchecked by the parliament, the government, or the constitutional court. Yet he did not take advantage of this situation to augment his personal power. He continued to press the Duma to appoint members of the constitutional court, offering one candidate after another. Why would a potential dictator want an independent institution that could overrule him?

The claim that he converted the Security Council into his Politburo also does not withstand close scrutiny. Its creation was initiated by Yuri Skokov, who envisioned the Security Council as "an effective instrument . . . to run the state." But as Skokov bitterly admitted, he failed to convince Yeltsin that the Security Council should become a ruling organ.[118] According to

Article 83 of the Yeltsin Constitution, "the president forms and heads the Security Council," and it plays an advisory role. It was appropriate for the president to consult it and ask it to approve military action in Chechnia. He invited both speakers of parliament, Shumeiko and Rybkin, to council meetings,[119] later making them voting members.[120] But as soon as the crisis in Chechnia ended, the Security Council no longer played a crucial role.

Yeltsin's Place In History

Hegel wrote that ordinary people should not be allowed to judge a great man because they lack the appropriate gauges and scales. Democracy, however, is about the *vox populi*, the voice of ordinary people.

Unfortunately, the *vox populi* manifests itself only periodically, in terms of the number of votes cast in elections; only later does folklore enshrine a leader's image in legends and myths. The public perception of a current leader comes to us mediated by experts' judgments, a study of which can be fascinating. The criticisms of Yeltsin made by the media, politicians, and political scientists during different stages of his career shed illuminating light on his potential place in history.

Yeltsin has been accused of being a ruthless neo-Bolshevik, a fanatic who can totally ignore public opinion in the name of an idea or ideal.[121] He has also been called a demagogue and a populist who tries "to please everyone,"[122] who "lies and promises impossible things to the people."[123]

He has been labeled a reckless adventurer, a gambler[124] who thrives on confrontation.[125] He has also been described as a weak leader who is manipulated by an *"eminence grise,"* by a "collective Rasputin,"[126] or by Washington.[127] Observers have claimed that he "has become a merely decorative figure"[128] and a captive of the "party of war."[129]

He is said to be an autocrat clinging to his personal power by all means,[130] who is capable of starting a war to distract public attention from his failures.[131] He allegedly can be so petty and vengeful as to send his bodyguards to intimidate a banker who supports his potential rival. But his critics also charge that he is wobbly, that his policy is highly inconsistent, and that he lacks a coherent strategy.[132] He is "old, in pain, desperately tired, and increasingly given to drink."[133]

Can he be both "a populist and neo-Bolshevik, a weak decorative figure and a reckless adventurer"? Hardly any acting world leader has elicited such diametrically opposed judgments.

In my view, there are two reasons why Russians react so emotionally toward Yeltsin and are so reluctant to show gratitude toward him while he is still at the helm. First of all, in this century they twice experienced the undiluted adoration and worship of two leaders, Lenin and Stalin, only to discover later that they had bloody tyrants. So their refusal to adore and worship Yeltsin is a sure sign of political maturity.

Secondly, it is difficult for most people to understand Yeltsin because he possesses a rare combination of qualities that are usually incompatible. His varied qualities have allowed him to move from one stage to another and to succeed in totally different social roles.

The second Russian revolution left the ground littered with debris left over from the political failures of both mediocre and talented people. Hundreds of political personalities surfaced meteorically to sudden fame and then left the scene as soon as political events took a new turn. First they experienced brief euphoria and then long-lasting bitterness; they nurtured great plans and subsequently suffered from crashing disillusionment. They could not cope with the dangers, uncertainty, and confusion of the complex and fast-changing political battlefield. They were able to play one role but could not adapt quickly to the changed situation. As a result, a new wave of politicians replaced them, who in turn were supplanted by others. Only a handful of politicians managed to survive more than two or three years.[134]

Yeltsin, on the other hand, has managed not only to survive ten years of extraordinarily turbulent politics but also to play a leading role in all stages of the second Russian revolution. It would be difficult to explain this extraordinary achievement by luck or coincidence. How did he manage to move from one stage of events to another, from one role to the next?

Yeltsin's books reveal with almost clinical accuracy the burdens of his doubts, despondency, anguish, and frustrations. He described his migraine headaches, sleepless nights, and depressions, and he has discussed how he managed to cope with them. He has evidently used alcohol periodically; psychologists would understand his drinking as a way "to alleviate anxiety, fear, and sorrow."[135] However, more important and productive has been his self-therapy, which he has also described in detail. He would subject himself and his predicaments to merciless analysis, sometimes in the solitude of night and sometimes in several days of seclusion. He keeps a diary and argues with himself, playing his own devil's advocate, until a clear picture emerges. He uses this technique to arrive at all major strategic decisions. When he reemerges from seclusion, rejuvenated and full of new energy and vigor, he often surprised his comrades in arms, colleagues and even enemies, who had written him off.[136]

Yeltsin keeps his doubts and agonies to himself, cultivating the image of someone who always knows what to do because he is lucky, possessing almost superhuman intuition and even the protection of heaven.

My more down-to-earth analysis is that he possesses a rare combination of qualities that have allowed him to move from one stage to another, from one social role to the next. He was a first rate athlete, a brilliant engineer, an extremely efficient manager, and an unorthodox party *apparatchik*. He then became a dissenter and popular hero, a leader of an opposition movement, and a skillful political infighter. He dismantled the totalitarian system and then returned to his original profession of builder, this time by constructing Russia's new statehood.

To succeed in such a multitude of different capacities, a leader must be extraordinarily talented: he must be both cautious and bold; he must be principled yet flexible, resolute yet patient, perceptive yet persistent, trusting and yet not gullible. In short, a successful leader must be both idealistic and cynical at the same time. He must be a good strategist and yet a skillful tactician; that is, he must have a taste for details yet keep the big picture in sight. He must be loyal to friends yet not allow his personal attachments to cloud his judgment. He must be enormously ambitious yet indifferent toward the trappings of power, able to disregard losses and make sacrifices at the altar of a greater goal. He must care about public approval yet be capable of unpopular measures. Finally, in Dean Simonton's words, only "motivation of the highest possible magnitude, . . . a monomaniacal preoccupation, the inherent passion for what he does "can turn this combination of conflicting qualities into greatness.[137]

Modern democratic societies with their high degree of specialization and dependence on the *vox populi* do not generally permit the development of heroic or great statesmen in politics; by definition, heroes are people who defy the system and "have the courage and the vision to challenge the beliefs and routines of their society."[138] Great statesmen, "event-making men who leave the positive imprint of their personalities upon history,"[139] are also out of place in a democracy, because they set their own agenda, instead of following the *vox populi*. Most great men in history, using Sidney Hook's words, "have carved out their paths of greatness by wars, conquests, revolutions, and holy crusades."[140] In addition, many of them became dictators and tyrants. Thus stable democracies have no need for heroes. Moreover, as Sidney Hook remarked, "a democratic community must be eternally on guard against a hero."[141] The culture of professionalism accordingly confines great men and heroes to their narrow professional pursuits.

The anticommunist revolution in Europe created a number of heroes, but only one of them has a good chance to be seen by history as both a hero and a great man. Yeltsin enjoyed great success in one culture; then he challenged it and helped bring about its collapse. He then led the construction of a new culture. If the vitality of the new structure proves strong and solid long after his departure, he will enter the annals of history as the last great statesman of the century. However, if Lord Acton was right, and absolute power corrupts absolutely, he may be judged more harshly.

Yeltsin has made no secret of his ambition to leave a mark on history[142] as one who stopped a pernicious experiment on the body of his beloved Mother Russia. He has accomplished a great deal but his job is not yet finished. He cannot afford to risk that the vanity and petty ambition of others will ruin the fruit of his gargantuan labor. He has said that he would gladly leave his post if a successor appears.[143] What he has not specified is that such a successor should be able to handle responsibly the enormous burdens and powers of the presidency. None of the known presidential contenders seems able to fulfill this requirement.

In 1996 Yeltsin will be 65 years old. To use Viacheslav Kostikov's words, "His age is such when a politician acquires an optimal combination of experience and temperament, political schooling and intuition. Of course, during the past decade, he has worked to the point of wear and tear, but he has a great reserve of generic durability."[144] However, his health may be a major source of concern. He must adopt more moderate habits and stop harming himself by working too hard, playing tennis too strenuously, and drinking too much. But as a heroic personality, he cannot spare himself, he has to burn himself out.[145]

Berthold Brecht remarked that "unhappy is the country that needs heroes." Russia is not yet a happy country and she needs a few heroic efforts before she can become a stable democracy. Russia should be on guard against heroic personalities and ensure that its next president is impeccably democratic and immune to the temptations and corruptions of power. I think that Yeltsin has proved to be such a man. In addition, it is in his interest to make the institution of the presidency less powerful before his successor takes office. If Yeltsin can limit the power of the presidency he will crown the edifice of democracy, ensure his place in history, and guarantee his personal safety.

An Evolving Culture

Throughout this book we have focused on personalities and elites and their conscious transformation of political, economic, and social institutions. We have described changes in the living and social conditions of the population. However, the main question remains: How deep are these changes and how do they relate to Russia's thousand-year-old culture? Can a group of outstanding personalities representing one segment of the intelligentsia impose a totally new set of values on a society in opposition to long-standing traditions and national character?

Will the Russian national character tolerate such inevitable ills of capitalism as social inequality, "political anarchy," unemployment, and professional crime? Or will Russians revolt by electing someone like General Lebed, and let his nationalist party, the Congress of Russian Communities, sweep away this alien democratic culture and restore authoritarian order and the Russian Empire?

How much do Russians really suffer from wounded national pride and lost national identity? How powerful is their imperial instinct, their longing for law and order, their alleged love for the iron fist? Are they still unruly, wild, unpredictable, and dangerous?

Theories of Social Change

The concept of national character has reigned in historical thinking for centuries. It assumes that climate, geography, religion, and collective experience yield characteristics that are shared by enough members of a given people to compose their "national character." The more a nation has been isolated from outside influences, the more likely it is to develop a distinct national character. This character then defines a nation's sociopolitical culture and its relationships with other nations. This theory does not, however, explain cultural change.

In the nineteenth century the concept of national character was seriously challenged by the emphasis on class struggle. According to this view each nation is made up of classes with differing social positions, and more or less political and economic power. The struggle for power among these classes defines both their behavior and sociopolitical change in the society at large.

Obviously, each of these theories is inadequate. Perhaps for this reason, they have always been supplemented by a theory that assigns an important role to great men and heroes. Even the social determinism of communism allowed room for outstanding personalities who better than the rest of the society understood the objective laws of history and thus were entitled to lead the masses.

A culture-based approach attempts to bridge all these theories by introducing the concepts of culture and subcultures. Climate and geography shape temperament (what used to be known as national character) and the basic mentality. The social environment shapes the sociopolitical mentality. Literature, folk lore, religion, arts, music, and traditions perpetuate a system of beliefs, which constitutes certain pattern of perceiving and thinking that distinguishes one culture from another.

Within a culture, however, there are subcultures defined by varying sociopolitical mentalities and access to different forms of power. The interaction of subcultures and the competition of social groups for power determines the political process. Outstanding personalities who represent social groups and yet are capable of transcending the limitations of their subcultures bring about sociopolitical and cultural change.

If one looks at twentieth-century Russian history from this perspective, one is struck by the tremendous environmental change that has occurred, which must have had a dramatic impact on the national culture. The relationships between man and the natural environment, among social groups, and between man and society have all changed significantly. Accordingly, Russians' overall picture of the universe and their society, and even their national character, must have changed to a corresponding degree.

Traditional Russian Culture

A huge literature exists about the Russian mind, the Russian heart, and the "mysterious Slavic soul," yet no consensus exists about the Russian national character.

If anything, experts agree on its contradictory features. This view was depicted in one of the newest tourist guides to Russia: "Russians have the ability to arouse directly contradictory opinions among those who encounter them. Some people find them open, helpful, hospitable, and generous; others find them sullen, suspicious, underhanded, and servile. The truth, for once, is not somewhere between these two extremes, but rather that they both represent aspects of the Russian stereotype, for both kinds of behavior are met with in different contexts."[146] After centuries of Western struggle to understand the Russian puzzle, Ronald Hingley found an ingenious solution to the "riddle wrapped in a mystery inside an enigma." He declared this unity of contradictions to be the very essence of Russian national character.[147]

The Russians, paraphrasing Nikolai Berdiaev's words, fell victims to the vast expanses of a monotonous and open plain. The absence of natural protective boundaries, such as mountains and seas, evoked both fear of invading hordes and an exploratory instinct. Perhaps if the Ural mountains had been higher and connected to the Caspian Sea, Russians would have been different. Instead, open, sparsely populated spaces and a lack of resistance from neighbors lured Russians to new territories. Rather than focusing on the betterment and perfection of their land, they crossed on foot thousands of miles of extremely inhospitable terrain in Siberia, reached the Pacific Ocean, continued another two thousand miles north to the Bering Strait, crossed it, and constructed forts and churches in Alaska and northern California. Hardly any economic, military, or religious motivation could explain such behavior. It is clear, however, that the boundless expanses of Russia promoted insatiable curiosity, a restless exploratory instinct, and a tendency toward extensive rather than intensive development of the environment.

Russia's climate had its own distinct impact on the national psyche. Its depressing autumn and cruel winter confined the Russians for two-thirds of the year. They tended to fall into the famous Russian *toska,* which is not just a melancholy mood or depression. It is a manifestation of helplessness and what the Romans called *taedium vitae* - disgust, aversion to life. At the same time, lengthy confinement dictated by the weather makes man introspective, teaches him patience, and induces long-term planning. When spring comes and the prison walls of ice and snow collapse, Russians explode with energy. Their *toska* turns into a burst of activity. This is not a time to conserve and evenly distribute efforts, because so much must be done during the four-month-long respite.[148] This attitude is epitomized in the famous Russian *udal* and *molodechestvo*—a complete, unrestrained expression of strength, bravery, generosity, or violence. It demonstrates that man can defy the forces of nature and triumph over the hostile environment and social confinement.

Such a natural environment seems to shape a Hobbesian world view: the physical environment is hostile, and life is seen as an incessant struggle for survival. It also cultivates a strong and resilient character, as well as an impulsive and unrestrained temperament. A typical Russian knows no moderation: like Yeltsin, as his press secretary described him, "he is impulsive and impatient, he wants to see the world rebuilt quickly."[149] "No other people in Europe can generate such spasms of energy as the Russians. Nor can we find anywhere in Europe such lack of steady, disciplined, evenly deployed work," wrote the nineteenth-century Russian historian Kliuchevski.[150] The Russian experiences a periodic urge to escape the constraints of the environment or the routine and monotony of life. To control such an impulsive and unruly people, scattered throughout enormous distances, the regime had little choice but resort to despotic methods. Hence the institution of serfdom—an attempt to keep the Russians on the land. These coercive means, in turn, only promoted the need to resist, revolt, and escape.[151] As a result, a typical Russian is suspicious of the authorities and has little respect for the law, because in his mind it is designed to enslave him.[152]

In sum, the climate and geography that for thousands of years were the principal shapers of the Russian national character bred a psychological type distinguished by lack of methodical constancy, lack of patience for measured and long-lasting efforts, aversion toward perfectionism and thrift, and contempt for materialism and regimentation of all kinds. Such qualities are ill suited to an industrialized and democratic way of life.

However, industrialization was inescapable if only because Russia's European neighbors periodically taught her bitter lessons about the superior power of technology. Peter the Great was the most talented student in the class on "Technology and National Might," but Russians at large have eventually come to love technology.

The Industrial Subculture

In the second half of the nineteenth century, after yet another bitter lesson about the importance of technology was taught by advanced Western countries (Britain and France) during the Crimean War, Russia began to industrialize in earnest and the physical environment began to change. By the end of the century Russians had managed to connect their land with railroads and develop several highly industrialized and urbanized regions. Not coincidentally, the regime's grip on society significantly relaxed, tremendous efforts were made to eliminate illiteracy. The remaking of the environment through industrialization and urbanization continued under the communist regime, particularly during the period following World War II.

By the 1980s Russia had reached the level of urbanization of developed countries and had attained almost universal literacy. The victory over space promoted the sense of personal independence from physical confinement. Heavy industry and machinery influenced the perception of the power of man vis-a-vis the environment. Literacy and electrification greatly extended the ability to process information.

At the turn of the century, with the liberalization of controls over internal migration, people began to exercise one of the most basic freedoms: the choice of habitat. Later, after the liberalization of emigration policy led to the massive emigration of Jews in the 1970s, the idea of the of emigration made inroads among Russians. An entire generation of Russians grew up accepting the right to emigrate. This belief represented a staggering change in their mentality. During Stalin's regime citizens were not permitted to enter a railroad station without a ticket, and they could not buy a ticket without an internal passport, which peasants were not allowed to have. For the three-quarters of the population who live in urbanized areas, life is not so much a struggle against the elements anymore as it is a struggle in the social environment, which requires different methods, qualities, and skills.

The social environment has also undergone monumental changes during the twentieth century. First, Russia was plunged into a half-century of social turmoil. Three generations of Russians lived through the life-wrenching traumatic experiences of three wars, three famines, purges, collectivization, and a totalitarian regime that deprived individuals of any form of power. By the end of this period, as many social scientists have argued, traditional Russian culture was shattered. The stark features of socialist culture—communal living, obligatory service in the army, and ubiquitous labor camps—were imposed by the totalitarian regime on society, leading to the creation of *Homo Sovieticus*.[153] Analysts have found few positive traits in the social portrait of *Homo Sovieticus*. He was considered to be obedient and aggressive; immoral and envious;[154] and prone to conspiratorial theories, authoritarianism and subserviency, laziness and greed.[155] Some observers even suggested that the communist experiment had lowered the average Soviet citizen's IQ.[156]

It seems, however, that many of the qualities of *Homo Sovieticus* were understandable temporary behavioral responses to the demeaning pressures of a totalitarian system, rather than permanent features of a new national character. Some of them, such as obedience, envy, subservience, and laziness, disappeared as quickly as the communist system itself. As Aleksandr Yakovlev has noted, property and political freedom induce man to be kinder and more constructive.[157]

More important and lasting was the impact that socialist culture had on the mentality of people. It promoted and reinforced, contrary to the official doctrine of brotherhood and social justice, "the perception of the supposedly evil nature of man, which requires constant guarding against."[158] The double life and dual thinking imposed on society by the totalitarian regime undermined belief in absolute values and universal morality, which is the basis of the cognitive consistency vital for confidence and mental stability. The powerlessness of an individual vis-a-vis the totalitarian system generated insecurity and paranoia. These features of a Hobbesian basic mentality can be clearly seen in the views of many "patriotic," chauvinistic, and fascist leaders of Russia; for example, in Lebed's manifesto, which was quoted above.

Still, after the death of Stalin, as Yeltsin perceptively noted, two generations of Soviet people "lived a rather peaceful, stable life. The basic principles of world civilization began to take hold. These were: the well-being of the family, culture, education, the upbringing of children, responsibility toward society and oneself."[159] With the disappearance of communal living, an appreciation for privacy and respect for individuality began to take root.[160] The boom in the construction of private houses in the 1990s clearly demonstrated the powerful appeal of private living to the urban population; it proved wrong the theory that there is an inherent communal streak in the Russian national character.

Although the Communist Party used them for indoctrination, the mass media have nevertheless tremendously expanded popular horizons and promoted universal values. Finally, following the advent of nuclear weapons, the threat of foreign invasions has faded away. Few Russians are genuinely worried about foreign occupation. So, when the "patriots," such as Lebed, try to appeal to the traditional Russian fear of invasion, the threat that they envision is spiritual, industrial, financial, or cultural, rather than military.

In short, industrialization, urbanization, mass education, and the development of mass communications have palpably changed both the mentality and temperament of the Russian people. General education and professional training, institutional affiliations and the demands of the technological environment, at some point began to overshadow such agents of the traditional culture as the natural environment, the church, and family. This trend has become more pronounced as Russia has entered the post-industrial era.

The Emerging Technocratic Subculture

During the 1960s, driven by the competition with the United States, the Soviet Union began to adopt a technocratic culture, although in a strange and twisted way. While the bulk of the society continued to live in a backward and primitive world, the Soviet Union developed a gigantic military-industrial complex, which, by the late 1980s totally dominated the economic life of the nation and even out produced its America counterpart in terms of gross output. By the 1990s approximately twelve million people were directly involved in high technology industries such as electronics, nuclear energy, aviation, and ship-building. In other words, they lived in a technocratic environment.

Such an environment exerts a significant influence on a person's orientation and behavior, and it changes a person's world view. Allegorically speaking, the climate becomes warmer, distances shorter, daytime longer, life more comfortable and predictable. The huge amount of specialized information that one must internalize, the complex technological processes that one must master, the production standards to which one must adhere, all foster certain habits and attitudes: diligence, attention to detail, perfectionism, measured efforts, punctuality, and cooperation.[161]

In sum, even though modernization was driven by military imperatives, it ensured that a large segment of Soviet society was well prepared mentally for modern technocratic society. Nevertheless, the simultaneous transition to a technocratic culture, democracy, and a free-market system required a painful adaptation on the part of members of society. At the end, no segment of society, not even the *narod*, remained unaffected.

Cultural Shifts

Russia today is characterized the coexistence and competition of three subcultures: the traditional one, which to a large extent still dominates the rural areas and some peripheral regions; the industrial subculture concentrated around two dozen large cities; and the technocratic subculture, which is rapidly developing mostly in and around the two capitals of Russia, Moscow and St. Petersburg. In a way, social groups are migrating from one subculture to another, and the general direction seems to be from the traditional toward the technocratic subculture. For example, when hundreds of thousands of urbanites settle in rural areas, they bring with them the industrial subculture. When Moscow banks open branches in the provinces, they bring with them the electronic age. When a modern supermarket is built in a Siberian town, it introduces the culture of consumerism. No one can escape the invasion of new technologies and the market.

Totalitarian power dictated its own rules. Pretense, cheating, hypocrisy, and stealing were effective tactics of survival vis-a-vis an omnipotent state. But when the state withdrew from many areas of human activity and abandoned them to the market, the strategy and tactics of survival changed. One had to compete in a job market that cared little about one's past, political views, social background, or general education. Instead, markets value specific personal qualities and professional skills. A former *apparatchik* might become a much more effective marketing director than a former dissident, while a former scholar might become a much more successful commercial banker than a former Soviet bank official.

To survive and prosper in an environment of multiple markets, a person must first choose a particular form of power and a corresponding profession. Then, one has to focus his or her entire attention and energy on achieving excellence in the chosen profession. In other words, one has to learn how to acquire and use a particular type of personal power and thus carve out one's place in society.

For some, the choice was obvious and natural; for others, it was agonizing. This process generated millions of personal dramas, although the outcomes were not necessarily tragic. One can only imagine, for example, what it took for an army officer to become an independent farmer. The transition was unique in every individual case. So many factors were involved in each case that few generalizations can be made. Basically, youth was an advantage. However, because some elites transformed themselves much more successfully than others, one's as well as proximity to a form of power that lent itself to privatization seemed to be crucial factors.

Red directors and industrialists were often eager to acquire the power to make decisions that they were forbidden to make during the era of central planning.[162] For them, power meant "freedom to do what [they knew] should be done," as one industrialist said.[163] Many of them became company managers, entrepreneurs, and bankers, and rather quickly "became completely different people."[164] According to Russian and Western observers, they have "proved more knowledgeable, more enthusiastic, and more capable of learning than might have been expected by some in the West."[165] In April 1994, 89 percent of directors of large and mid-sized enterprises supported the free-market system.[166] "They work very hard to pull their companies out of crisis,"[167] and "have shown a great deal of ingenuity in overcoming" all kinds of difficulties.[168]

Those *apparatchiks* who chose the security of administrative positions have become ordinary bureaucrats. There is a significant difference, however, between a party *apparatchik* and a bureaucrat. The *apparatchik* was an operative of the totalitarian machine of power, while a bureaucrat is a functionary of an administrative apparatus that has no jurisdiction over many areas of human activity. True, bureaucrats exercise their power through granting licenses and adjudicating property rights, particularly during the process of privatization. However, their power will inevitably diminish when many spheres of activity are privately controlled.

The competition for political power in an open parliamentary context also modifies behavior and sociopolitical mentality. In this regard, the case of Gennadi Ziuganov is very instructive. He was and remains a sworn communist. But as Adam Michnik the famous Polish human right champion, remarked with regard to Poland: "They say   the communists are in power. But communism does not exist anymore."[169] Indeed, a parliamentary communist party is totally different from its totalitarian predecessor. Ziuganov has to market his party's political platform and compete with other parties, and he does this much more successfully than many democrats. But in the process, as Shumeiko noted, "Ziuganov became a social democrat."[170] Indeed, he speaks in favor of mixed forms of property and ownership of land, favors a multiparty parliamentary republic,[171] rejects class struggle, denounces revolutionary means of achieving political goals,[172] and emphasizes the importance of Russian history[173] and Christianity.[174] In short, fifteen million Russians who cast their votes for Ziuganov's Communist party, voted for his socio-democratic program, not for communism, Stalin or Soviet empire.

Currently, Russia is in the hands of former *apparatchiks*, industrialists, red directors and scientists. Because the overwhelming majority of them have an extensive technical education,[175] Russia may be the only major developed society in the world that is governed entirely by technocrats. The government, the presidential structures and the parliament, banking, and large industrial conglomerates[176] are all dominated by technocrats in their forties and fifties. They are *derzhavniks*, as we described their philosophy in Chapter Two. They are workaholics, "pragmatic and self-reliant people with a distinctly middle-class value system focused on the family."[177] They "believe in Russia's future and put their money in the land."[178] According to their own words, they "represent the force on which this nation will be able to develop into a mighty and prosperous country."[179]

While technocrats are growing more self-confident and assertive, many literati have become disillusioned and apocalyptic.[180] Some have even joined ranks with their former bitter enemies[181] and thus have returned to their "customary place, in opposition to power."[182] Characteristically, one former anticommunist admitted: "The most terrible thing is that my old enemies tell the truth."[183]

The literati, naturally, tend to continue to rely on their natural talent, the power of their art and their knowledge, which, in market conditions, is not that effective. Although a few literati thought that the discipline of the market might benefit them,[184] the majority were convinced that it would harm high culture. They continue to predict the "inevitable death of the intelligentsia."[185]

Of course, high culture will survive and so will the literati, which create it. However, their sphere of influence will be drastically reduced. "Popular culture" will dominate. The church will replace the intelligentsia as "moral upholder of the nation," as writer Daniil Granin suggested.[186] Their influence will be confined to campuses, a few elitist magazines, art galleries, and cultural centers.

The Emerging Class of Professionals

While present-day Russia belongs to middle-aged technocrats, the future of Russia belongs to the class of professionals.

In many parts of the world, the culture of professionalism is supplanting traditional cultures based on religions, ideologies, and rigid social stratification. This is a worldwide phenomenon that affects Russia. As *Business Week* keenly observed, "the culture of professionalism is definitely taking hold" in the nation.[187]

Foreign observers note that the generation of Russians who are now in their twenties "has grown up free of the dollop of degradation swallowed by every slightly ambitious citizen," so that they resemble their Western professional counterparts.[188] "They are emerging as the key to the country's competitiveness in the next century... Well-educated and multilingual, they are fast developing a work ethic aggressive enough to rival that of any American yuppie."[189]

The Mentality and Social Vision of Professionals

The basic mentality of professionals worldwide corresponds with that of the middle class of North America in the mid-1960s:

1. Man cherishes nature, but he is its master;
2. Man lives in the present, but he lives for the near future;
3. Man is capable of conquering both time and space;
4. Human nature is a mixture of good and evil, which can be readily modified in the direction of the greater good;
5. Man's paradise is a material and moral heaven on earth.[190]

The sociopolitical mentality of Russia's professionals closely approximates that of the yuppies of the West.

Someone who has mastered his profession acquires power over society, usually expressed in terms of monetary rewards. This power gives him the freedom to build his own personal paradise. Thus professionals oppose stringent controls over individual forms of power, as well as any attempts to equalize its distribution in society. However, professionals are suspicious about the "unfair play" that can result when power is used illegitimately to enhance one's position in society. For this reason, they readily agree on restraining mechanisms that prevent the merger of different forms of power into one. They believe that the boundaries between different forms of power should be well demarcated, in order to exclude unfair competition. For them, political power is just another form of power based on professional skills, and elections are only a market mechanism. In other words, they perceive the sociopolitical environment as a market in which all forms of power compete for customers.

They are driven by challenge and a quest for self-realization.[191] They strive for perfection and are capable of intense, single-minded effort. They have a bent for practical rather than wishful thinking; they have a penchant for data, facts, categories, and technical details; they "are ruled not by emotions but by their heads."[192] In the words of one movie producer, they are distinguished by "energy, entrepreneurship, self-reliance and inner freedom"; they are aggressive, and they lack the warmth and sentimentality of generalists.[193] They are careerists characterized by hedonistic attitudes; they reject ideology and they frequently exhibit political disengagement.

In their attitude toward government and the state, professionals are libertarians. They resent coercive forms of power, and they want them to be subordinated to political institutions. They oppose government intervention and regulations, and they oppose redistribution of income and confiscatory taxation.[194] They reject any use of coercive power by the state, because they believe in the supremacy of individual human rights over the rights of the state.

The *etatist* philosophy, on the other hand, holds to the principle that in order "to preserve its sovereignty and integrity, the state can and must use force,"[195] because the state is the ultimate "life-taker."

The continued progress of the culture of professionalism in Russia (and its victory over the *etatist* philosophy) should lead to a further decline of imperialism and militarism in society, and a corresponding decrease in the power of the government.

Changing Values and Attitudes

In Russian society at large, political analysts have noted a change of values and attitudes only a few years after the collapse of the totalitarian regime. Despite the pains and anxiety accompanying the transition, as presidential adviser Mark Urnov has noted, militant nationalism has drastically declined and the attitude toward coercive methods has become more negative; while respect for law, freedom of the press, and the sanctity of individual rights has grown significantly.[196]

Private ownership of the means of production has been embraced with surprising speed.[197] One survey showed that while in 1989 only 20 percent of the population supported private ownership, in 1991 at least 60 percent did.[198] However, unlimited private ownership of land is not fully accepted by society. About 25 percent of the population rejects completely unrestricted ownership of land by individuals.[199]

The concept of the separation and balance of powers seems to have been fully internalized. In the view of many observers, "the Duma has become an integral part of the political system of the new Russia."[200] Indeed, the fact that there were about forty aspirants for each seat in the Duma in the December 1995 elections[201] seems to indicate that parliamentary culture is taking root in the Russian sociopolitical mentality.[202] Although the December 1995 parliamentary elections demonstrated serious flaws in the electoral system, they nevertheless proved the fact of a paramount importance: the universal acceptance of the democratic rules of political life in the society. Sixty-five percent of eligible voters, defying severe weather conditions chose to exercise their right of political choice. Even the militant opposition chose, in Gavriil Popov's words, to come "from the streets to the open political forum"[203] and "to play by parliamentary rules."[204]

There are early signs of a softening of the most notorious feature of *Homo Sovieticus*—his intolerance toward others and differing views.[205] Not only have Russians displayed little desire to vent their hatred and frustration through cruelty and atrocities,[206] they are now showing more tolerance toward homosexuals, prostitutes, drug addicts, vagrants, and so on.[207]

Finally, Russians' messianic zeal (never strong in the *narod* anyway), which drove them to defend and unite their Slavic brethren, or wage ideological war against the capitalist world, has largely been supplanted by a "healthy pragmatism,"[208] which is directed inwards.

In sum, the democratic, free-market system in Russia seems to have a fairly firm cultural foundation; it has a reasonably good chance to withstand pressures from nationalist, fascist, and communist forces.

Conclusion

Where does Russia stand in the world? What does she want to be? How should the world treat her?

The Question of Russian Neo-imperialism

Western political experts believe that Russians were humiliated by their defeat in the Cold War, in which they lost their empire, their status as a superpower, and their identity. They are said to be disillusioned by the sluggish financial support from the West and to be bitter and angry at being dominated by the West. This resentment makes the crippled giant dangerous and unpredictable, like the Weimar Republic. Some political experts warn that Russia is likely eventually to regain its strength and "try to retake the empire,"[209] and not just "the former Soviet Union."[210] Russia's European neighbors feel particularly insecure and actively seek the protection of the West.[211]

Although such revanchist sentiments do exist among certain segments of the Russian population, they do not characterize the psychological state of the nation as a whole.

All major European nations pursued empire building at some point, with varying degrees of success. Even the United States experienced an imperial phase. The desire, indeed, the need to extend one's power is a manifestation of vitality in a nation. Only after World War II, and then reluctantly, did Europeans begin to abandon their colonial empires and redirect their energy solely into cultural and economic development. The reasons were purely pragmatic: in a technological age, coercive power is simply not cost effective. Thus it is extremely risky to suggest that imperialism is imprinted in the genetic code of any particular nation, Russia included.

Russia is an industrialized culture entering the modern technological age, and the new Russian political elite realizes that it cannot afford "to carry its imperial past into the new international environment."[212] Russians by and large have matured, and they are ready for the post-industrial epoch. This is why they so easily "gave up all the conquests of Peter the Great, Catherine, Alexander I, and Alexander II combined (in Martin Malia's words)."[213]

Russia was forced to subsidize the Soviet empire to support the Communist Party's struggle for world domination. In the 1980s Russians came to realize that they benefited little from their "empire," that many "colonies" enjoyed much higher living standards than they did. Four years after separation, the subsidizing role of Russia in the Soviet empire has become apparent. The Russian economy is doing much better than those of practically all her former "colonies," thus confirming Gaidar's original argument that the former "colonies" were a major burden and liability rather than a source of power and pride.[214]

Better than any other consideration, this national consensus seems to explain Russia's withdrawal of its forces from former Soviet colonies, its liquidation of its bases and infrastructure, and the dramatic reduction of its armed forces and defense industry. Indeed, the Russian armed forces were cut by 1.1 million men[215] to less than 1.5 million troops.[216] The Russian Air Force was cut almost in half, from 11,000 aircraft to 6,000 aircraft.[217] One hundred twenty-seven nuclear-powered submarines were decommissioned, and 150 more submarines will be decommissioned by the year 2000.[218]

Strategic nuclear forces are being reduced by two-thirds, and all tactical nuclear weapons are now within Russia's borders. Stockpiles of chemical weapons are being destroyed.[219] The Russian defense budget has been reduced to less than 4 percent of GNP. These measures have led to a reduction of the combined military expenditures of two former blocs by at least $165 billion a year.[220]

While Russia's steps toward unilateral disarmament have made large-scale offensive operations impossible for decades, many foreign policy experts nevertheless argue that Russia's military and economic meddling in the affairs of the "near abroad" still betrays her imperial intentions.[221]

Stephen Sestanovich has given a simple and convincing response to this allegation: Russia is vitally interested in the political stability and economic prosperity of its neighbors.[222] Indeed, even before the formal separation from the former republics in December 1991, a number of tribal, religious or territorial disputes erupted on the Russia's periphery. Ethnic Russians were crying out for protection, and hundreds of thousands of refugees flooded Russia, which was in the grip of a severe economic crisis itself. Russia accordingly had little choice but to play an interventionist peacekeeping role. By intervention and mediation, Russia helped stop fighting in Moldova, Ossetia, Abkhazia, and Nagorno-Karabakh; it also brought a halt to two bloody civil wars, in Tajikistan and Georgia. At the same time, Russia refused to support separatists in the Crimea, despite its strong ethnic, cultural, military, and sentimental bonds with the peninsula's inhabitants. By protecting borders with Iran and Afghanistan, Russian forces have curtailed the flow of narcotics and arms and have helped keep Muslim fundamentalism at bay. Thus Russia has protected not only itself but the entire former Soviet Union from external destabilization.

But doesn't Russia use economic pressure to keep other former republics under its domination? Indeed, Russia has subsidized members of the Commonwealth of Independent States by providing them with cheap credits, energy, and raw materials.[223] However, this policy was dictated not by neo-imperialism but rather by Russia's dependence on the survival of her traditional trading partners. Due to the ongoing structural revolution in the Russian economy, this dependency is rapidly diminishing; Russian subsidies to the former republics have now almost completely stopped. In addition, Russia's trade with the West is expanding by about 25 percent annually, while it is stagnating with neighboring states.

In short, it is Russia's growing self-sufficiency, wealth, and economic progress that drive many former republics to seek closer integration with her[224]—not plots and trickery on the part of Russian neo-imperialists.[225]

As Herbert Ellison noted, "neither the motives nor the form and scope of [Russian] policy to date can justify . . . fears" of Russian neo-imperialism:[226] an "imperialist state would act differently."[227]

Russia's Identity Crisis

How much do Russians suffer from an identity crisis? To answer this question we should distinguish between the imperial and cultural components of national identity.

Russian cultural identity is hardly in question. Its literature, music, movies, religion, and architecture are clearly identifiable and distinguishable as Russian in character. For a relatively short period of time, Russia's cultural identity was indeed suppressed and obscured by communist internationalism. But as early as 1942 Russians were fighting against Hitler's armies in defense of Mother Russia rather than communism. That is, Russians fought for survival as a national and cultural entity. Since then, Russian culture and identity have inexorably strengthened.

Russians who felt humiliated by defeat in the Cold War and suffered from wounded imperial pride belonged to the part of the *nomenklatura* for which the Soviet empire was a source of power, pride, prestige and livelihood. They admittedly exert pressure on the Russian government to take a more assertive stance in international affairs.

The traditional Russian intelligentsia has also suffered from an identity crisis. Popular culture, as well as the mass consumer and technocratic cultures, threaten traditional Russian culture and its bearers. This threat creates a genuine identity crisis, which most developing countries are also experiencing. Traditional cultural values are being pushed from the foreground; as a result, an Indian computer programmer or doctor may feel more in common with a Brazilian counterpart than with most of his compatriots.

Most Russians were not humiliated by the defeat in the Cold war, because Russia was not beaten by the Western alliance; the totalitarian system was. Russia was not humiliated by occupying foreign powers or by the revolt of its "colonies." Russians did not lose their cultural identity as a result of de-communization and de-colonization. On the contrary, they are now rediscovering their songs, forgotten writers, traditions, and values.

Traditional Russian imperialism and its Soviet counterpart are dead. Their replacement, if any, will take political, economic, and cultural (but no military) forms. Post imperial Russia will be led by new elites, who are quickly growing stronger and more confident.[228] The new elites can see that

Russia's integrity has been preserved; they sense that the economic slump is over, and they know that the ruble has stabilized, foreign trade is exploding, and the democratic regime has shown its first signs of viability. Indeed, neither the bad harvest, Chechen separatism, nor even the illness of the president have destabilized the political situation or derailed economic recovery.[229] Accordingly the new elites believe that the country is on the right track.

In sum, Russia's new assertiveness comes not from weakness, desperation, or wounded pride.[230] On the contrary, it stems from a sense of recovery and regained strength. But should this not be a source of even greater anxiety for the international community?

Russia and the World

Russia bears full responsibility for the most grandiose, radical, painful, and disastrous sociopolitical experiment in modern history. The Communists set themselves no less a goal than remaking human nature itself. By depriving individuals of any personal power,[231] the communist regime hoped to eradicate evil. Instead, it created a much greater evil that threatened the very existence of humanity. We should remind ourselves that at one point communist parties directly controlled he lives of one and a half billion people and affected the lives of another billion. The CPSU-KGB apparatus conducted a decades-long systematic war of subversion, disinformation, terrorism, and corruption throughout the world. Crack Soviet divisions were stationed only 400 miles from Paris; the world was held hostage to the threat of nuclear annihilation and forced to spend trillions of dollars on armaments.

Nevertheless, the main victim of the CPSU was the Russians themselves. They endured long-lasting, systematic, and comprehensive violence, both physical and mental. I am greatly surprised that they survived this traumatic experiment and found the strength to end it. They liberated themselves and hundreds of millions of other people from totalitarianism. In addition, they contributed the lion's share to the defeat of the other totalitarian plague of this century, Nazism.

One political writer argued that "Russia did not acquire new friends and has lost its old ones."[232] He is wrong: the Soviet Union had no genuine friends but many implacable enemies. Perhaps the new Russia does not yet have genuine friends, but neither does she have unrelenting enemies. She will have to work hard to earn the trust of her neighbors. They, in turn, would be well advised to give her the benefit of the doubt.

The twentieth century has proven that Russians are "one of the most talented and intriguing peoples of the world."[233] They are responsible for more than totalitarianism and good airplanes, rockets, and tanks. They have been rightfully credited for giving the world superb composers, writers, philosophers, dancers, musicians, chess players, scientists, artists, poets, and athletes. Russia also deserves credit for its superb architecture, its daring feats of space exploration, and its accomplishments in engineering.[234]

Russian's minds have been as open as the steppes; Russians have never placed themselves at the center of the universe. On the contrary, they have always looked beyond the horizon, eagerly assimilating others' ideas and striving to perfect them. They were such zealous Christians that they called their peasants *krestiane* (christened people) and pledged to preserve the Christian faith in its original purity. Many nations merely flirted with the ideals of communism, but the Russians tried to implement them.

Now the Russians they have embarked on building a modern technocratic democracy with comparable zeal. Their mission has prompted Peter Ustinov to remark: "The West should be concerned not with the Russian Army . . . but with the tremendous speed with which Russians are learning Western ways."[235] Indeed, Russian business and political elites dream of making Russia "one of the most powerful and prosperous countries in the world."[236] They claim that "Russia is doomed to be a great power," because of her spirituality and rich culture,[237] "immense territory, huge population, vast resources, and universal literacy."[238] In a typically Russian manner, they envision the future Russia as "the most democratic and richest country in the world."[239] They intend "to solve the problems facing other democratic countries and start the construction of a model society."[240] Whether they achieve such ambitious goals or not, their intentions are noble.

Russian democracy is still fragile; the economy has yet to demonstrate sustained growth; the federal structure needs a major overhaul; organized crime ,must be defeated; and the public sector has yet to recover sufficiently to support science and high culture and to assist the needy. Nevertheless, what had been fish soup is in the process of becoming an aquarium. Russia is vital, as some foreigners believe, it "will rise up much faster than we assume and become a democratic European country."[241]

Yeltsin once stated that "the main nerve of world changes lies in Russia."[242] This may be an exaggeration, but the world will greatly benefit from the presence of a democratic and prosperous Russia. The prodigal son of European civilization deserves a warm welcome, encouragement, and assistance from the community of civilized nations.

NOTES

Introduction

[1] Alexis de Tocqueville, *Democracy in America* (New York: Doubleday & Co., 1969), pp. 412-413.

[2] The quotation is from one of the best books about post-revolutionary Russia: Maurice Hindus, *Humanity Uprooted* (New York: J. Cape & H. Smith, 1931), p. X.

[3] I cannot agree with Zbigniew Brzezinski who characterized this conflict as a struggle for world domination between Russia and the United States. See *Game Plan* (Boston: The Atlantic Monthly Press, 1986), p. 26.

[4] Karen Dawisha and Bruce Parrot, *Russia and the New States of Eurasia* (England: Cambridge University Press, 1994), p. 297.

[5] John Gray, *Post-Communist Societies in Transition: A Social Market Perspective* (London: The Social Market Foundation, 1994), p. 39.

[6] The title of a book by David Pryce-Jones (New York: Henry Holt & Co., 1995).

[7] Martin Malia, *The Soviet Tragedy* (New York: The Free Press, 1994), p. x.

[8] Hedrick Smith wrote: In the West, there has always been a tendency to "see things [in Russia] in either utopian or apocalyptic terms: success or failure, stability or collapse, dictatorship or chaos, black or white." *The New Russians* (New York: Random House, 1990), p. xxx.

[9] Jerry Hough, Severyn Bialer, Stephen Cohen, and Marshall Shulman were champions of this method.

[10] Helene Carrere d'Encausse, *Confiscated Power: How Soviet Russia Really Works* (New York: Harper & Row, 1982). She and Martin Malia came closer others to grasping the significance of totalitarian power for all aspects of life. See also Malia, p. 33.

[11] John Thornhill, "Russians find capitalism is in the genes," *Financial Times*, Nov. 3, 1995, p. 3.

Chapter 1

[1] I borrow this term from C. Wright Mills and believe that it is very pertinent to Russia. See *The Power Elite* (New York: Oxford University Press, 1959).

[2] Robert Presthus wrote: "Organizations are a major disciplinary force in our society. Their influence spills over the boundaries of economic interest or activity into spiritual and intellectual sectors; the accepted values of the organization shape the individual's personality and influence his or her behavior in extravocational affairs." *The Organizational Society* (New York: St. Martin's Press, 1977), p. 11.

[3] Brian Lancaster, *Mind, Brain and Human Potential: The Quest for Understanding of Self* (Rockport, MA: Element, Inc., 1991), pp. 125-6. See also Robert R. McCrae and Paul T. Costa, Jr., *Personality in Adulthood* (New York: The Guilford Press, 1990), p. 176.

[4] These are the words of Bruce Parrot and Karen Dawisha, in *Russia and the New States of Eurasia* (England: Cambridge University Press, 1994), p. 2.

[5] Richard W. Wilson, *Compliance Ideologies: Rethinking Political Culture* (England: Cambridge University Press, 1992), p. 3.

[6] Bertrand Russell, *Power: A New Social Analysis* (New York: W. W. Norton, 1938), p. 11.

[7]Hans J. Morgenthau, *Politics Among Nations: The Struggle for Power and Peace* (New York: Alfred Knopf, 1973), p. 28.

[8]Richard Chackerian and Gilbert Abcarian, *Bureaucratic Power in Society* (Chicago: Nelson-Hall, 1984), p. 143. See also Edgar Z. Friedenberg, *Coming of Age in America* (New York: Random House, 1965), pp. 47-48.

[9]This definition is close to Rollo May's statement that "power is the ability to cause or prevent change." See *Power and Innocence* (New York: W. W. Norton, 1972), p. 99.

[10]May, ibid., p. 25. See also John O. Beahrs, *Limits of Scientific Psychiatry: The Role of Uncertainty in Mental Health* (New York: Brunner/Mazel, 1986), p. 66.

[11]Harold D. Lasswell and A. Kaplan, *Power and Society* (New Haven, Conn.: Yale University Press, 1950), p. 87. See also J. R. P. French, Jr., and B. Raven, "The Basis of Social Power," in D. Cartwright (ed.), *Studies in Social Power* (Ann Arbor, Mich.: University of Michigan Press, 1959), pp. 150-167.

[12]Karl A. Wittfogel called it "total power." I prefer "totalitarian." See *Oriental Despotism: A Comparative Study of Total Power* (New Haven: Yale University Press, 1957).

[13]"This is a glorious time to be involved in research on the mind," according to Daniel Dennett. See *Consciousness Explained* (Boston: Little, Brown & Co., 1991), p. 257.

[14]R. P. Abelson, E. Aronson, W. J. McGuire, T. M. Newcomb, M. J. Rosenberg, & P. H. Tattenbaum (eds.), *Theories of Cognitive Consistency: A Sourcebook* (Chicago: Rand McNally, 1968).

[15]Robert Ornstein wrote: "While there is much more to emotions than a simple positive/negative, stop/start, approach/avoid program, more of our life is determined by these primitive appraisals than we... might believe." *Evolution of Consciousness: The Origins of the Way We Think* (New York: Touchstone Books, 1991), p. 153.

[16]Raymond Smith: "This system of values may be unconscious and non-verbalized, but it is a system." *Negotiating with the Soviets* (Bloomington: Indiana University Press 1989), p. 67.

[17]"Personal beliefs are what we are all about. . . . The presence of beliefs in our species results from the way the human brain is constructed. Without a belief in some kind of order there is a sensation of capriciousness, of instability, of lack of control." Michael S. Gazzaniga, *The Social Brain: Discovering the Networks of the Mind* (New York: Basic Books, 1985), pp. ix, 99, 180.

[18]Elliot Aronson, "The Theory of Cognitive Dissonance: A Current Perspective," in Leonard Berkowitz (ed.), *Cognitive Theories in Social Psychology* (New York: Academic Press, 1978).

[19]Ornstein, *Evolution of Consciousness*, p. 153.

[20]Ole Holsti, "Foreign Policy Formation Viewed Cognitively," in Robert Axelrod (ed.), *The Structure of Decision*, (Princeton: Princeton University Press, 1976), p. 19.

[21]Milton Rokeach, *Beliefs, Attitudes, and Values*, (San Francisco: Jossey-Bass, 1969), p. 6.

[22]Thomas Sowell has shown that social and political conflicts stem from "a conflict of visions." *A Conflict of Visions* (New York: William Morrow, 1987).

[23]Erich Fromm, *Man for Himself* (New York: Fawcett, 1947), Ch. 4.

[24]Clyde Kluckhohn, introduction to Florence Rockwood Kluckhohn's "Dominant and Variant Value Orientations," in Clyde Kluckhohn and Henry A. Murray (eds.), *Personality in Nature, Society, and Culture* (New York: Alfred Knopf, 1964), p. 342.

[25]James Glass, *Delusion: Internal Dimensions of Political Life* (Chicago: University of Chicago Press, 1985).

[26]Edward Hall, *The Hidden Dimension* (Garden City, N.Y.: Doubleday, 1969) p. x.

[27]See Carl R. Rogers, "Rollo May: Man and Philosopher," *The Humanist*, Vol. 2, No. 1, Summer 1981.

[28]Abraham H. Maslow, in I. David Welch, George A. Tate, and Fred Richards (eds.), *Humanistic Psychology* (Buffalo: Prometheus Books, 1978), p. 11.

[29]Carl R. Rogers, "Toward a Science of the Person" in I. David Welch, George A. Tate, and Fred Richards (eds.), *Humanistic Psychology* (Buffalo, NY: Prometheus Books, 1978), p. 330.

[30]Edward C. Stewart, *American Cultural Patterns: A Cross-Cultural Perspective* (Chicago: Intercultural Press, 1981).

[31]Brian Lancaster, *Mind, Brain and Human Potential: The Quest for Understanding of Self* (Rockport, MA: Element, Inc., 1991), p. 35.

[32]Michael Gazzaniga suggested that monotheism and polytheism are connected to one's assumptions about harmony and chaos. See *The Social Brain: Discovering the Networks of the Mind* (New York: Basic Books, 1985), p. 172. James Glass argued that the idea of life after death is crucial to one's cognitive structure, that the perception that "there is no life after death" should increase one's level of anxiety and preoccupation with power. See *Delusion: Internal Dimensions of Political Life* (Chicago: University of Chicago Press, 1985), pp. 12, 18.

[33]Ornstein, *Evolution of Consciousness*, p. 153.

[34]Christopher, p. 52.

[35]Margaret Mead, *Cultural Patterns and Technical Change* (UNESCO, 1953), p. 197.

[36]Edward C. Stewart, *American Cultural Patterns: A Cross-Cultural Perspective* (Chicago: Intercultural Press, 1981), p. 66.

[37]Thomas Hobbes, *Leviathan* (New York: Macmillan, 1977), p. 100.

[38]Confucius said: "I believe that people are born good, and that learning and knowledge will keep them good." Erich Fromm said that the inherent goodness of man gives him the right and duty to "assert his own life, happiness, growth, freedom." *Man for Himself: An Inquiry into Psychology of Ethics* (New York: Rinehart, 1958), p. 130.

[39]Hadley Cantril, "The Human Design" in Neil J. Kressel (ed.), *Political Psychology* (New York: Paragon, 1993), pp. 75-82. Abraham H. Maslow: "As far as I know we just don't have any intrinsic instincts for evil. If you think in terms of the basic needs; instincts, at least at the outset, are all 'good'." See I. David Welch, George A. Tate, and Fred Richards (eds.), *Humanistic Psychology* (Buffalo: Prometheus Books, 1978), p. 11.

[40]Charles Reich expressed it this way: "There are no enemies... There is nothing on the other side... Nobody wants war except the machine... And even businessmen, once liberated, would like to roll in the grass and lie in the sun. There is no need, then, to fight any group of people in America." *The Greening of America: The Coming of a New Consciousness and the Rebirth of a Future* (New York: Random House, 1970), p. 348.

[41]Lloyd S. Etheredge, "The Hardball Practitioner," in Neil J. Kressel (ed.), *Political Psychology* (New York: Paragon, 1993), p. 114-123.

[42]James Glass, "The Paranoid Factor in Political Philosophy," *Political Psychology*, Vol. 9, No. 2, 1988, pp. 220-223.

[43]Thomas Sowell, *A Conflict of Visions* (New York: William Morrow, 1987), pp. 36-39; Edward C. Stewart, *American Cultural Patterns: A Cross-Cultural Perspective* (Chicago, Intercultural Press, 1981).

[44]Paul Tornier, *Escape From Loneliness* (Philadelphia: Westminster Press, 1961), p. 53.

[45]Erik Erikson argued that "sense of basic mistrust" leads to a preference for totalitarianism and excessive reliance on institutional support and a delusion of wholeness. *Identity: Youth and Crisis* (New York: W. W. Norton, 1968), pp. 83-85.

[46]Very few Western analysts have fully recognized this. Among those who have, Michael McFaul, "Why Russia's Politics Matter," *Foreign Affairs*, Vol. 74, No.1, 1995, p. 88.

Chapter 2

[1]Boris Fedorov accused the "red directors" led by Chernomyrdin of carrying out an "economic coup." See Lee Hockstader, "Yeltsin Rules Out Policy Retreat," *The New York Times International*, Jan. 28, 1994, p. 1.

[2]Yuri Afanasiev, "Revanche," *New Times*, No. 6, Febr. 1994, pp. 20-22.

[3]Julia Wishnevsky, "Democratic opposition in Russia: An alternative to Yeltsin?," *The Washington Quarterly*, Spring 1995, p. 25. She also wrote that Yeltsin fulfilled and "restored the pre-1985 system." See "Restoration," *Nezavisimaia Gazeta*, Aug. 18, 1992.

[4]Leonid Radzikhovsky, "The Monomakh Crown," *Stolitsa*, No. 13, 1994, pp. 6-14.

[5]*Scientific Communism* (Moscow: Progress Publishers, 1986), p. 207.

[6]George Fischer, *The Soviet System and Modern Society* (New York: Atherton Press, 1968), pp. 4-12.

[7]Leonid Rybakovski (ed.), *Naselenie SSSR Za 70 Let* (Moskva: Nauka, 1988), p. 168.

[8]*Narodnoe Khoziaistvo SSSR Za 70 Let* (Moskva: Statistika, 1988).

[9]The term technocrat was promoted by Alexandr Shtromas. See "How the End of the Soviet System May Come About," in Alexander Shtromas and Morton A. Kaplan (eds.), *The Soviet Union and the Challenge of the Future* (New York: Paragon House, 1988), vol. 1, p. 215.

[10]Similar ideas were expressed by A. Efimov. See "Elitist groups, their formation and evolution," *Znanie-sila*, No. 1, 1988.

[11]This figure is calculated on the basis of the statistics in *Narodnoe Khoziaistvo SSSR Za 70 Let* (Moskva: Statistika, 1988).

[12]Nicholas Lampert, *The Technical Intelligentsia and the Soviet State* (London: Holmes and Meier Publications, 1979). See also Jeffry Klugman, *The New Soviet Elite: How They Think and What They Want* (New York: Praeger, 1989).

[13]Milovan Djilas, *The Imperfect Society* (London: Unwin Books, 1972), pp. 146-147.

[14]Boris Shragin, *The Challenge of the Spirit* (New York: Alfred Knopf, 1978), p. 157.

[15]Nicholas Berdyaev, *The Origin of Russian Communism* (Ann Arbor: University of Michigan Press, 1966), p. 148.

[16]See the suicide letter of Aleksandr Fadeyev, in *Izvestia*, Sept. 20, 1990, p. 3.

[17]Alexandr Sevastianov gave a picture of the highly contrasting position and power of the American intelligentsia in *Literaturnaia Gazeta*, Sept. 21, 1988, p. 10.

[18]The average salaries of the intelligentsia were 30-40 percent lower than those of blue-color workers in the construction and industrial sectors. See L. Chizhova, *Sobesednik*, No. 5, 1988.

[19]Viacheslav Kostikov, "About 'The Phenomena of Lokhankin' and the Russian Intelligentsia," *Ogoniok*, No. 48, 1988, p. 6.

[20]Leon Festinger, *A Theory of Cognitive Dissonance* (Stanford, CA: Stanford University Press, 1957).

[21]Richard Crossman (ed.), *The God That Failed* (New York: Bantam Books, 1949), p. 7.

[22]Hedrick Smith, *The Russians* (New York: Times Books, 1976); David K. Shipler, *Russia: Broken Idols, Solemn Dreams* (New York: Times Books, 1983); Robert G. Kaiser, *Russia: People and Power* (New York: Atheneum, 1976).

[23]Robert Tucker, *The Soviet Political Mind* (New York: Frederick Praeger, 1963), pp. 86-7.

[24]Vladimir Shliapentokh, *Soviet Public Opinion and Ideology: Mythology and Pragmatism in Interaction* (New York: Praeger, 1986), p. 113.

[25]R. V. Burkes, "The Coming Crisis in the Soviet Union," in Shtromas and Kaplan, *The Soviet Union*, vol. 1, p. 150.

[26]Vladimir Kormer, "Dual Consciousness and Pseudoculture," *Voprosy Filosofii*, No. 9, 1989, p. 68.

[27]James M. Glass, *Delusion: Internal Dimensions of Political Life* (Chicago: The University of Chicago Press, 1985).

[28]Boris Shragin, *The Challenge of the Spirit* (New York: Alfred Knopf, 1978), p. 153.

[29]In fact, some thought that they did not even belong to the intelligentsia. See Alexandr Zhelenin, "I look with sadness at the life and death of the Russian intelligentsia," *Nezavisimaia Gazeta*, Aug. 20, 1993, p. 8.

[30]See the somewhat caricature-like description of the young reformers' background in Alexandr Kantor, "Mystery of Democrats," *Segodnia*, March 4, 1994, p. 9.

[31]Gavriil Popov, *Nauka i Zhyzn*, Oct. 1988, p. 22. See also *Ogoniok*, No. 48, 1988, pp. 6-7.

[32]Among several sources about the political elites of the Soviet Union, I can recommend *Narodnye Deputaty SSSR (People's Deputies of the USSR)*, (Moskva: Vneshtorgizdat, 1990); *Who is Who in Russia* (Moskva: Novoye Vremia, 1993), and the list of candidates in the State Duma, *Rossiiskaia Gazeta*, Nov. 12-Dec.6, 1993 *FBIS-SOV-93-234*.

[33]Robert G. Kaiser, *Russia: People and Power* (New York: Atheneum, 1976), p. 393.

[34]Yuri Afanasiev, "Russian Reform Is Dead," *Foreign Affairs*, March/April, 1994, p. 22.

[35]Max Weber referred to bureaucracy's "purely technical superiority over any other organizations. . . . Precision, speed, unambiguity, knowledge of files, continuity, discretion, strict subordination, reduction of friction and of material and personal costs." See "Bureaucracy," in Hans Gerth and C. Wright Mills (eds.), *From Max Weber* (New York: Oxford University Press, 1946), p. 214.

[36]Anthony Downs, *Inside Bureaucracy* (Boston: Little, Brown and Co., 1967), p. 26.

[37]Robert Vance Presthus, *The Organizational Society* (New York: St. Martin's Press, 1977), p. 12.

[38]Karl Marx, *The Eighteenth Brumaire of Louis Bonaparte* (New York: International Publishers, 1963), p. 121.

[39]Jeffry Klugman, *The New Soviet Elite: How They Think and What They Want* (New York: Praeger, 1989).

[40]As Richard Pipes noted, "Even the most dedicated Communists retained a sphere of personal autonomy." "Breakdown," Review of David Remnick's *Lenin's Tomb, Commentary*, December 1993, p. 54.

[41]Vladimir Voinovich, "Not Even The Rulers Have Rights," *RL/RFE* 339/85.

[42]Anatoly Fedoseyev, "The Passage to New Russia and Some Thoughts on Its Alternative Constitutional Order," in Shtromas and Kaplan, *The Soviet Union*, vol. 1, p. 450.

[43]See, for example, Janos Kornai, *The Socialist System* (Princeton, N.J.: Princeton University Press, 1992), p. 41.

[44]Mikhail Voslensky, *Nomeklatura* (Garden City, N.Y.: Doubleday, 1984), pp. 182-187.

[45]A manager of a large industrial enterprise (with more than 10,000 workers) had a monthly salary of about 700 rubles, equivalent of about $1,050. Richard Dobson, "Socialism and Social Stratification," in *Contemporary Soviet Society*, Jerry G. Pankhurst and Michael Paul Sacks (eds.) (N.Y.: Praeger, 1980), p. 100. The price of one kilo of decent sausage was fifteen rubles; a dinner for two, forty rubles, a pair of good shoes, eighty rubles. *Wall Street Journal*, Feb. 14, 1989.

[46]Michael Voslensky, *Nomeklatura* (Garden City, N.Y.: Doubleday, 1984), p. 187.

[47]Voslensky, *Nomeklatura*, p. 188.

[48]For example, Yuri Skokov, Yeltsin's close associate, complained that his "father, a KGB officer, risked his life many times, but when he died he didn't leave enough money to bury himself." Interview with Steven Erlanger, *The New York Times*, Aug. 2, 1993.

[49]New General Secretaries liked to punish such activities to drive fear into the hearts of *apparatchiks* and subdue the party establishment.

[50]Roy A. Medvedev, *On Socialist Democracy* (New York: Alfred Knopf, 1975), p. 293.

[51]Gavriil Popov, *Nauka i Zhyzn*, Oct. 1988, pp. 22-29.

[52]A. M. Rekunkov, the USSR Procurator General, in *Pravda*, March 25, 1987, p. 3.

[53]*The New York Times*, Sept. 13, 1988.

[54]Maurice Hindus, *Humanity Uprooted* (New York: J. Cape & H. Smith, 1931), p. 238.

[55]Giorgio Galli, "A Bureaucracy Under Fire," in *Dilemmas of Change in Soviet Politics*, Zbigniew Brzezinski (ed.), (New York: Columbia University Press, 1969), p. 59.

[56]Shumeiko, interview, *Vek*, Nov. 6-13, 1992, p. 3.

[57]By the 1990s this social group's higher-education rate was close to 92 percent. See *Narodnoe Khoziaistvo SSSR Za 70 Let* (Moskva: Statistika, 1988), p. 421.

[58]Shumeiko, interview, *Vek*, Nov. 6-13, 1992, p. 3.

[59]Regarding the red directors' motivations, their inner conflicts, and their resolutions, see Janos Kornai, *The Socialist System* (Princeton, N.J.: Princeton University Press, 1992), pp. 118-124.

[60]Shumeiko, interview, *Vek*, Nov. 6-13, 1992, p. 3.

[61]R. V. Burkes wrote that the red directors had to cope "with a constant trade-off between career advancement and professional standards." See "The Coming Crisis in the Soviet Union," in Shtromas and Kaplan, *The Soviet Union*, vol. 1, p. 150.

[62]Shumeiko, interview, *Vek*, Nov. 6-13, 1992, p. 3.

[63]These are the words of Joseph Walls, the former president of Galleon, a division of Dresser Industries, who spent many months with Russian factory managers. See "Defense Conversion in Russia: An American's view from inside the Enterprise," *Geonomics*, Vol. V, No. 5, Sept.Oct. 1993, p. 12.

[64]Yuri Skokov, interview, *The New York Times*, Aug. 2, 1993.

[65]Igor Yefimov-Moskovit, "The Intelligentsia and Soviet Power," in Shtromas and Kaplan, *The Soviet Union*, Vol. 2, p. 507.

[66]Quoted in Igor Yefimov-Moskovit, *op. cit.*, p. 507.

[67]Anatoli Sobchak, interview, *Obshchaia Gazeta*, No. 16, Nov. 1993, p. 4.

[68]Boris Shragin, *The Challenge of the Spirit* (New York: Alfred Knopf, 1978), p. 173.

[69]Gyorgy Konrad and Ivan Szelenyi, *The Intellectuals on the Road to Class Power* (New York: Harcourt Brace Jovanovich, Inc., 1979), p. 28.

[70]Gabriel Almond and Sidney Verba, *The Civic Culture* (Princeton: Princeton University Press, 1963), p. 15.

[71]In 1992, only 21.5 percent of Russians said they believed in God. Just over 50 percent of Russians, and more than 90 percent of those with higher education, said that they did not believe in life after death. See *Argumenty i Fakty*, No. 45, Nov. 1992.

[72]Boris Vasiliev, "Lubi Rossiiu v nepogodu" (Love Russia in bad weather too), *Izvestia*, Jan. 17, 1989.

[73]Vladimir Chernov, *Ogoniok*, No. 37, 1989, p. 18. See also, Elena Novikova, a Moscow University psychologist, *Literaturnaia Gazeta*, No. 9, March 1989, p. 10.

[74]Alexander Zinoviev, *The Reality of Communism* (London: Victor Gollancz Ltd., 1984) p. 58.

[75]Nathan Leites, *Psychopolitical Analysis* (New York: John Wiley & Sons, 1977), p. 313.

[76]See, for example, Gaidar: "Our *narod* is rational and full of common sense, and it will be triumphant. They want a normal, calm life." Interview, Ostankino Television, *FBIS-SOV*-94-018, Jan. 27, 1994; See also Boris Fedorov: "there are many more good people that bad ones." *Izvestia*, March 28, 1995, p. 2; see also *Argumenty i Fakty*, No. 32, August, 1993, p. 2. A young entrepreneur said: "I believe deeply that Russians are very talented people. I don't think Russians are lazy and passive." He is quoted in Daniel Yergin and Thane Gustafson, *Russia 2010* (New York: Random House, 1993), p. 275.

[77]Burbulis, interview, *Radical*, No. 25, July 2, 1991.

[78]M. Buianov, president of the Moscow Psychotherapeutic Academy, wrote: "Gaidar behaved as if all Russia consisted of scientists. He assumed that what was obvious to superintellectuals would be clear to the same degree to millions of voters." See "Elections Through the Eyes of a Psychiatrist," *Rossiiskie Vesti*, Dec. 16, 1993, p. 2.

[79]Burbulis called Mamardashvili's book the source of his spiritual roots. See his interview in Andrei Karaulov, *Vokrug Kremlia* (Around the Kremlin), (Moskva: Slovo, 1993), V. 2, p. 302.

[80]Merab Mamardashvili, interview, in Andrei Karaulov, *Vokrug Kremlia* (Around the Kremlin), (Moskva: Slovo, 1993), V. 1, pp. 298-312.

[81]A survey of the Russian population's religious sentiments in 1990-1991 revealed that only 15 percent of young technocrats with advanced scientific degrees believed in God, with another 27 percent vacillating between belief and nonbelief. See S. B. Filatov and D. E. Furman, "Religion and Politics in Mass Consciousness," *Russian Social Science Review*, Sept./Oct. 1993, p. 27.

[82]Stanley Budner, "Intolerance of Ambiguity as a Personality Variable," *Journal of Personality*, XXX, issue 1, March 1962, p. 30.

[83]Aleksandr Nevzorov gave a most explicit and clear expression of this chain of thought. See his interview in *Argumenty i Fakty*, No. 8, Feb. 1995, p. 3.

[84]Paul Hollander, *Soviet and American Society* (New York: Oxford University Press, 1973) p. 47.

[85]Hedrick Smith, *The New Russians* (New York: Random House, 1990), p. 428.

[86]*Materialy XXII S'ezda KPSS* (Moscow: Politizdat, 1961).

[87]*KPSS, O Formirovanii Novogo Cheloveka* (Moskva: Politizdat, 1976).

[88]David Shipler made this point adroitly in *Russia: Broken Idols, Solemn Dreams* (New York: Times Books, 1983), p. 325.

[89]Jeffry Klugman, *The New Soviet Elite: How They Think and What They Want* (New York: Praeger, 1989), p. 117.

[90]*Khrushchev Remembers*, p. 512.

[91]Hedrick Smith, *The Russians* (New York: The Times Book, 1976), p. 17.

[92]MP Sergei Yushenkov said that "there is nothing higher than the life of a human being." *Literaturnaia Gazeta*, Dec. 21, 1994, p. 11.

[93]The antagonism toward the army of students in an elite school in Moscow shocked officers of the prestigious Frunze military academy. See Karem Rash, "Where are we going?" *Molodaia Gvardia*, No. 10, 1989, p. 208.

[94]Richard Chackerian and Gilbert Abcarian, *Bureaucratic Power in Society* (Chicago: Nelson-Hall, 1984), pp. 144-146.

[95]Gaidar, interview, *Ogoniok*, Feb. No. 4, 1994, p. 34.

[96]Gaidar said: "A person must be certain that the state protects his property." See "We are not building paradise. We are trying to build a normal life," *Trud*, June 28, 1994, pp. 1,2.

[97]Gaidar, "We are not building paradise. We are trying to build a normal life," *Trud*, June 28, 1994, pp. 1,2.

[98]Burbulis, interview, *Nezavisimaia Gazeta*, Sept. 5, 1991.

[99]Petr Aven, a minister in the Gaidar cabinet. Interview, *Kommersant*, Oct. 11, 1994, p. 17.

[100]Walter B. Cannon, *The Wisdom of the Body* (New York: W. W. Norton & Co., 1932).

[101]Andrei Kozyrev, "Reborn Russia in the New World," *Izvestia*, Jan. 2, 1992.

[102]Jeremy Bentham, *An Introduction to the Principles of Morals and Legislation* (1789), in Edwin A. Burtt (ed.), *The English Philosophers from Bacon to Mill* (New York: The Modern Library, 1939), p. 843.

[103]Nikolai Berdyaev argued that Lenin "did not believe in man. . . . He did not believe in spirit and the freedom of the spirit, but he had a boundless faith in the social regimentation of man." See *The Origin of Russian Communism*, p. 127.

[104]Gorbachev: "If the leader of a *kolkhoz* does not force the farmers to work, they would probably not work at all." *Vanity Fair*, February 1990, p. 123.

[105]Yu. A. Sherkovin et al. (eds.), *Social Psychology and Propaganda* (Moscow: Progress Publishers, 1985), p. 40.

[106]Yuri Boldyrev, *Nezavisimaia Gazeta*, Apr. 10, 1992, p. 8.

[107]Gaidar, interview, *FBIS-SOV-93-185-S*, p. 15.

[108]We will see how this attitude explained Yeltsin's handling of the army during the critical hours in October 1993.

[109]In Rollo May's words, *Power and Innocence*, p. 102.

[110]Peter Nettl, "Power and Intellectuals," in Conor Cruise O'Brien and William Dean Vanech (eds.), *Power and Consciousness* (New York: New York University Press, 1969), p. 16.

[111]See the remarks of Grigori Revzin. Round table, *Segodnia*, Feb. 18, 1995, p. 10.

[112]Aleksandr Panchenko, interview, *Moscow News*, No. 50, Dec. 15-22, 1991, p. 16.

[113]Hedrick Smith, *The New Russians* (New York: Random House, 1990), pp. 191-4.

[114]See the interview of academician Vladimir Tikhonov, in *Yunost*, No. 10, 1989. See L. Nikiforov "Socialist property: problems of research, restructuring, and development," *Voprosy Ekonomiki* No. 3, 1988, p. 22; See also A. Liubinin, "Contradictory character of the public form of property," *Voprosy Ekonomiki* No. 9, 1988, pp. 31-51.

[115]Nikolai Ryzhkov, "Detour On Power," in *Perestroika: History of Betrayals* (Moscow: Novosti, 1992), pp. 345-370.

[116]In Gorbachev's speeches *derzhava* is referred to as a human body, with a brain, heart, skeleton, muscles, and circulatory and nervous systems. An explicit expression of this model can be found in Gorbachev's speech to the Belorussian intelligentsia. See *Pravda*, Mar. 1, 1991. Gorbachev has also likened secession of republics to the amputation of the limbs. See *Pravda*, June 20, 1990, p. 2.

[117]In 1995, after the totalitarian structure was dismantled, the Russian communist party leader Gennadi Ziuganov could still refer to Russia as a "united and integral organism."

[118]Alexandr Yakovlev urged Gorbachev to legalize the split of the CPSU into two parties, thus creating an orderly and controlled transition to a multiparty system, but Gorbachev could not accept the idea. See Yakovlev, *Delovoi Mir*, Dec. 5, 1993.

[119]Psychologist Boris Kochubey, *Literaturnaia Gazeta*, no. 51, 1990.

[120]Jeffry Klugman has advanced a similar notion of the Soviet elite's perception of the world. See *The New Soviet Elite*, p. 14.

[121]Lieutenant General Leonid Ivashov, "Russia can regain the status of a superpower," *Nezavisimaia Gazeta*, March 7, 1995, p. 3.

[122]*Behind the High Kremlin Walls*, p. 203.

[123]Vladimir Soloviov, *Russia and the Universal Church* (London: 1948).

[124]Nikolai Berdyaev, *Sud'ba Rossii* (Russia's Destiny) (Moscow: Leman and Sakharov, 1918).

[125]Sergei Stankevich, *Nezavisimaia Gazeta*, March 28, 1992.

[126]Shumeiko, interview, *Vek*, no. 13, Nov. 6-13, 1992, p. 3.

[127]Kozyrev, interview, *Izvestia*, Oct. 20, 1991.

[128]Anatoly Streliany, "Improvers of Socialism: the notes of an economics literature reader," *Izvestia*, April 29, 1994, p. 4.

[129]*Literaturnaia Gazeta*, Oct. 5, 1988, p. 13.

[130]A similar "marriage of planned economy and market economy" was propounded by Deng Xiaoping. See *The Washington Post*, June 21, 1989.

[131]Friedrich A. Hayek, *Individualism and Economic Order* (Chicago: University of Chicago Press, 1948).

[132]Leonid Abalkin, interview, "Our Difficulties come from Fuzzy Thinking," *Ekonomicheskie Novosti*, No. 13, July 1993, p. 4. See "Dominating Factor: The Economic Crisis and Ways of Overcoming It," *Delovoi Mir*, July 24, 1993, pp. 11-12. See also "To Pause and To Look Around," *Trud*, Aug. 28, 1993, p. 2.

[133]Alexei Novikov, "June Theses of Academician Bogomolov" *Novaia Ezhednevnaia Gazeta*, June 11, 1993, p. 3.

[134]Former Russian Ambassador to the United States Vladimir Lukin, "Russia: in Far and Near Circles," *Segodnia*, Sept. 3, 1993, p. 10.

[135]Yuri Skokov complained that "the government doesn't have a program, none." See interview, *The New York Times*, Aug. 2, 1993.

[136]Oleg Soskovets stated: "It is a myth that Western economies are free from the government. They are regulated and much more firmly than by Gosplan. Only the mechanisms are different — economic ones." See interview, *Trud*, Dec. 16, 29, 1993, p. 1. See also interview, *FBIS-SOV*-93-156, p. 33.

[137]Nikolai Klimontovich, "Intelligentsia's Down?" *Nezavisimaia Gazeta*, Feb. 1, 1992.

[138]Mikhail Ulianov, interview, *Modus Vivendi*, no. 2, March 1993.

[139]C. Wright Mills, *The Power Elite* (New York: Oxford University Press, 1959).

Chapter 3

[1]These are the words of the chief editor of Yeltsin's second book, Lev Gushchin. See *Rossiiskie Vesti*, April 16, 1994, p. 3.

[2]Yeltsin said: "Sometimes I think that I have lived three lives—that of a normal person, a political pariah, and a people's deputy." Boris Yeltsin, *Ispoved Na Zadannuiu Temu* (Moskva: Ogoniok, 1990), p. 94. That was in 1990; since then, he has lived three more lives.

[3]Alexei Kiva, "Why I am going to vote for Yeltsin," *Delovoi Mir*, April 17, 1993, p. 1.

[4]Leonid Radzikhovsky, "The Monomakh Crown," *Stolitsa*, no. 13, 1994, pp. 6-14.

[5]*Ispoved*, p. 16.

[6]Boris Yeltsin, *Zapiski Prezidenta* (Moskva: Ogoniok, 1994), p. 155.

[7]*Ispoved*, p. 36.

[8]In 1994, out of the 4.7 million people of Sverdlovsk oblast, 87 percent lived in cities, compared to 73 percent for the USSR as a whole. *Uralski Rabochi*, Feb. 3, 1995, p. 2.

[9]Nikolai Khotimsky, "What You Don't Know About President Yeltsin," *Vechernia Moskva*, March 3, 1994, p. 2.

[10]Robert Conquest, *Collectivization and Terror-Famine* (New York: Oxford University Press, 1986), p. 276.

[11]M. Maksudov, *Population Losses in the USSR: 1918-1958* (New York: Samizdat Register, 1981), p. 276.

[12]See Gorbachev's recollection of his family's plight in *Pravda*, Dec. 1, 1990.

[13]Fritz Redl and David Wineman wrote about "the hatred-producing power of poverty, social inequality, social disorganization, crowding, and neighborhood tensions." *The Aggressive Child* (Glencoe, IL.: The Free Press, 1957), p. 21.

[14]*Ispoved*, pp. 14, 15.

[15]William C. White gave a good description of the effects that such an environment can have on one's psyche. See *These Russians* (New York: Charles Scribners's Sons, 1931), pp. 4-5.

[16]For a more detailed description see Dmitry Mikheyev, *The Rise and Fall of Gorbachev* (Indianapolis, Hudson Institute, 1992).

[17]Yeltsin said: "My enemies always assumed that people are envious, treacherous, and vicious (*zlye*), but such people are only a tiny minority." *Ispoved*, p. 28.

[18]Yeltsin, interview, Moscow Ostankino TV, Nov. 16, 1993, *FBIS-SOV*-93-220, Nov. 17, 1993.

[19]Yeltsin said: "I am not deeply religious. No, I can't say that. But I have great respect for religion. Perhaps, gradually, this will grow into religiousness. Possibly." Interview, Moscow Ostankino TV, Nov. 16, 1993, *FBIS-SOV*-93-220, Nov. 17, 1993.

[20]*Zapiski*, pp. 284, 292, 296, 311.

[21]*Zapiski*, p. 342.

[22]*Zapiski*, p. 239.

[23]Yeltsin, interview, *Argumenty i Fakty* no. 42, 1992, p. 2. Moscow Ostankino TV, Nov. 16, 1993, *FBIS-SOV*-93-220, Nov. 17, 1993.

[24]*Zapiski*, pp. 46, 292.

[25]Gorbachev entered the Law Department of Moscow State University in Stalin's time, thus joining the repressive institutions of totalitarian power at an early age. He was an *apparatchik* by training and career.

[26]David Remnick, "Comrade Personality," *Esquire*, Feb. 1990, p. 78.

[27]See Roman Redlikh, *Stalinshchina, kak Dukhovny Fenomen* (Stalinism as Spiritual Phenomenon) (Frankfurt/Main: Posev-Verlag, 1971), pp. 122-140.

[28]For a social portrait of a "red director" and his responsibilities, see Vladimir Skripov, *Eko* no. 10, 1991, p. 126.

[29]John Morris, *Boris Yeltsin: From Bolshevik to Democrat* (New York: Dutton, 1991).

[30]*Pravda*, Nov. 3, 1987.

[31]For a more detailed analysis of the mentality of professionals pursuing a party *apparatchik*'s career, see Jerry Klugman, *The New Soviet Elite: How They Think And What They Want* (New York: Praeger, 1989), pp. 19-33.

[32]*Ispoved*, p. 25.

[33]*Zapiski*, pp. 46, 292.

[34]This was confirmed by many of Yeltsin's former associates interviewed by Vladimir Soloviov and Yelena Klepikova. See *Boris Yeltsin* (Moskva: Vagrius, 1992).

[35]Vladimir Sanarin, "By then B[oris] N[ikolayevich] Moved to Moscow," *Komsomolskaia Pravda*, March 26, 1994, pp. 1-2.

[36]See *Izvestia*, No. 268, 278, 289, 293, Nov.-Dec., 1991.

[37]This anecdote derives from recollections by Sverdlovsk residents.

[38]Former inhabitants of Sverdlovsk have told me that thanks to Yeltsin poultry became consistently available.

[39]The people of Sverdlovsk kept saying that: he treated them like human beings. T. D. Allman, "The man who saved the future," *Vanity Fair*, October 1991, p. 265.

[40]Liudmila Pertsevaya, "Do not Worship Blindly," *Moscow News*, no. 11, March 1992, p. 7.

[41]*Ispoved*, p. 47.

[42]Dimitri Simes, "The Return of Russian History," *Foreign Affairs*, Jan./Feb. 1994, p. 71.

[43]Sergei Maniakin, remarks at the October 1987 plenum of the Central Committee, "Yeltsin," *Vremia i My* no. 105, 1989, pp. 242-43.

[44]Some stunning confessions by former *apparatchiks* have recently become available. See, for example, the story of the Brezhnevite *apparatchik "Staia"* (Pack) in *Ogoniok* no. 49, 1990, p. 136.

[45]*Ispoved*, p. 40.

[46]Erich Fromm, *Man For Himself,* p. 247. See also E. H. Schein, *Coercive Persuasion* (New York: Norton, 1961).

[47]See the symposium of Soviet practicing psychiatrists, *Literaturnaia Gazeta* no. 9, March 1989, p. 10.

[48]Morton A. Kaplan, *Alienation and Identification* (New York: The Free Press, 1976), p. 134.

[49]*Ispoved*, p. 32.

[50]See Yeltsin's interview in Andrei Karaulov, *Vokrug Kremlia* (Around the Kremlin), (Moskva: Slovo, 1993), vol. 1, p. 78.

[51]Liudmila Pertsevaya, "Do not Worship Blindly," *Moscow News*, no. 11, March 1992, p. 7.

[52]Anthony Downs, *Inside Bureaucracy* (Boston: Little, Brown & Co., 1967), p. 110.

[53]*Ispoved,* p. 77.

[54]Yeltsin, interview, Moscow Ostankino TV, Nov. 16, 1993, FBIS-SOV-93-220, Nov. 17, 1993.

[55]*Zapiski*, p. 31.

[56]*Ispoved,* p. 80.

[57]*Ispoved,* p. 92.

[58]Yeltsin, interview, *Izvestia,* Nov. 16, 1993, pp. 1, 4.

[59]*Ispoved,* p. 93.

[60]By receiving 535 votes for and 502 votes against, Yeltsin had four votes more than was necessary. See *Moskovskie Novosti,* no. 22, 1990, p. 6.

[61]Richard Pipes, "The last Gasp of Russian Communists," *The New York Times International,* Oct. 5, 1993, p. A17.

[62]Steven Erlanger of *The New York Times,* "Russia Seeks to Keep Reformer in Cabinet" *The New York Times International,* Jan. 25, 1994, p. 2.

[63]This is how Yeltsin explained his September vacation of 1991. *Izvestia,* Nov. 20, 1991.

[64]*Ispoved,* p. 25.

[65]*Ispoved,* pp. 60-7.

[66]*Ispoved,* p. 65.

[67]Yeltsin, interview, Moscow Ostankino TV, Nov. 16, 1993, *FBIS-SOV*-93-220, Nov. 17, 1993.

[68]His thoughts about the *narod* could cause him almost physical pain: he felt "desperation and bitterness from the sight of dirty, impoverished Moscow and other Russian cities. . ." *Zapiski,* p. 239.

[69]*Ispoved,* p. 6.

[70]As James Barber pointed out, whether one perceives others as lovable or repulsive defines "one's style of behavior in dealing with the human environment." See "The Interplay of Presidential Character and Style: A Paradigm and Five Illustrations," in Fred I. Greenstein and Michael Lerner (eds.), *A Source Book of the Study of Personality and Politics* (Chicago: Markham, 1971), p. 386.

[71]See Yeltsin's, speech, "What is Russia to Be?" *Sovetskaia Rossia,* Dec. 16, 1990, p. 1.

[72]In the words of Sukhanov, *Tri Goda,* pp. 148, 153.

[73]*Zapiski,* p. 177.

[74]Paul Hendrickson, "Boris's Borscht Belting," *Washington Post,* Sept. 13, 1989, p. D8.

[75]Yeltsin's remarks at Columbia University, *Novoe Russkoe Slovo,* Sept. 12, 1989, p. 5.

[76]An Army Colonel described a very similar change of views after only a four-day trip to West Germany. See Mikhail Zakharchuk, "Give the Order of Hero to Zorin," *Nezavisimaia Gazeta,* Aug. 13, 1994, p. 4. Similarly, after a trip to Sweden, Nikolai Travkin, the founder of Democratic Russia, said that he was furious to discover the extent of his deception by Soviet propaganda. See his interview in Andrei Karaulov, *Vokrug Kremlia* (Around the Kremlin), (Moskva: Slovo, 1993), vol. 2, p. 163-4.

[77]Viktoria Chalikova, *Ogoniok,* no. 30, 1991.

[78]He has repeated many times: "Russia is first." See, for example, his interview Moscow Ostankino TV, Nov. 16, 1993, *FBIS-SOV*-93-220, Nov. 17, 1993.

[79]*Zapiski,* pp. 15, 396.

[80]Aleksei Yablokov, a Yeltsin adviser on ecological matters, said: "Neither Yeltsin nor anybody else around him, except Burbulis, possessed a vision of the future Russia." *Nezavisimaia Gazeta,* March 24, 1995, p. 3.

[81]*Rossiiskaia Gazeta,* June 13, 1991.

[82]Sergei Vasiliev, interview, *Moskovskie Novosti,* Nov. 17, 1992.

[83]Robert R. McCrae and Paul T. Costa, Jr., *Personality in Adulthood* (New York: The Guilford Press, 1990), p. 176.

[84]Mark Johnson, *The Body in the Mind: The Bodily Basis of Meaning, Imagination, and Reason* (Chicago: University of Chicago Press, 1987), p. 87.

[85]Hugh Gregory Gallager, *F.D.R.'s Splendid Deception* (Arlington, VA: Vandamere, 1994), pp. 183-91, 213-16.

[86]Sukhanov, *Tri Goda s Yeltsinym (Three years with Yeltsin)* (Riga: Vaga, 1992), pp. 306-7. See also T. D. Allman, "The man who saved the future," *Vanity Fair*, October 1991, p. 200.

[87]According to his wife Naina, *Trud*, March 26, 1994, p. 1, and his aide Georgi Satarov, *Argumenty i Fakty*, no. 13, 1994, p. 2.

[88]*Zapiski*, p. 155.

[89]Yeltsin, interview on French Radio, May 2, 1994, *FBIS-SOV-94-085*.

[90]Shamil Tarpishchev, interview, *Komsomolskaia Pravda*, April 18, 1995, p. 1.

[91]Yeltsin, interviews, *Argumenty i Fakty*, no. 22, 1991, no. 42, 1992, Moscow Ostankino TV, Nov. 16, 1993, *FBIS-SOV-93-220*, Nov. 17, 1993.

[92]*Zapiski*, p. 155.

[93]*Ispoved*, p. 17.

[94]Yeltsin, interview, Moscow Ostankino TV, Nov 16, 1993, *FBIS-SOV-93-220*, Nov. 17, 1993. See also *Zapiski*, pp. 269, 311.

[95]Alexandr Gorbunov, "He plays tennis regularly, twice a week... He plays well for his age...[and] has a quick reaction... None of the ministers can equal the Yeltsin-Tarpishchev pair." See also "The Russian President's favorite game," *Moscow News*, Dec. 17, 1993, p. 16. Shamil Tarpishchev said that Yeltsin can serve with the speed of 115 miles per hour. *Argumenty i Fakty*, no. 51, Dec. 1994, p. 12.

[96]Shamil Tarpishchev, interview, *Argumenty i Fakty*, no. 51, Dec. 1994, p. 12.

[97]Shamil Tarpishchev, interview, *Komsomolskaia Pravda*, April 18, 1995, p. 1.

[98]See, for example, Vera Tolz's mentioning of "his health problems," *RFE/RL Research Report,* Vol. 3, no. 24, June 17, 1994, p. 4.

[99]Vladimir Nadein, "The President's health should not be a secret," *Izvestia*, Jan. 30, 1992, p. 2.

[100]Richard Nixon, *Beyond Peace* (New York: Random House, 1994), p. 48.

[101]Yeltsin, interview, Radio Rossii, *FBIS-SOV-94-070*, April 12, 1994.

[102]Lev Sukhanov, Yeltsin's assistant. *Tri Goda*, pp. 285, 299.

[103]*Zapiski*, pp. 155-8.

[104]Boris Yeltsin, *The Struggle For Russia* (Random House, 1994), p. 117.

[105]Yeltsin, *Struggle*, p. 118.

[106]Yeltsin, *Struggle*, p. 117.

[107]Yeltsin, *Struggle*, p. 117.

[108]*Nezavisimaia Gazeta*, Sept. 11, 1993, p. 1. According to his doctor, Anatoli Grigoriev, Yeltsin's pulse rate is 55-60 per minute, and his blood pressure is 120 over 80. *ITAR-TASS*, April 2, 1995. See also *ITAR-TASS*, April 21, 1995.

[109]Yeltsin explained: "The truth is that I simply overslept. I had been flying for 18 hours and prior to that I had missed so much sleep." Interview, Russian Television, *FBIS-SOV-94-191*, Oct. 3, 1994. See also Yeltsin Protocol Chief Vladimir Shevchenko's remarks, in *Komsomolskaia Pravda*, Sept. 22, 1995.

[110]Yeltsin Protocol Chief Vladimir Shevchenko's remarks, in *Komsomolskaia Pravda*, Sept. 22, 1995.

[111]He has written about numerous accidents that he has survived, involving cars, trucks, planes, helicopters, trains and horses. *Zapiski*, p. 295.

[112]Quoted in Peter Gumbel, "Reformed Maverick: Boris Yeltsin Alters Tone in Russian Campaign," *The Wall Street Journal*, June 7, 1991, pp. 1,6.

[113]*Zapiski*, p. 155.

[114]Lev Sukhanov described episodes indicating Yeltsin's reckless attitude toward his body and health. *Tri Goda*, pp. 297-308.

[115]"It was always in my character to strive to be first." *Zapiski*, p. 269.

[116]Viacheslav Kostikov, interview, *Rossiiskie Vesti*, Jan. 30, 1993, p. 2. Serge Schmemann wrote: "He demonstrates robust energy for a man of 60, maintaining a grueling schedule of travel and public appearances." See "The ambiguities of a Russian leader," *The New York Times*, Feb. 28, 1992.

[117]Valentin Yumashev, quoted by T. D. Allman, "The man who saved the future," *Vanity Fair*, October 1991, p. 267.

[118]Iliushin, interview, *Argumenty i Fakty*, no. 19, 1994, p. 3. In November 1993, the top President's aide Viktor Iliushin allowed foreign journalists to see a two-week working schedule of his boss which was filled to the last minute. *La Republica*, FBIS-SOV-93-216, Nov. 10, 1993.

[119]He has recently shown the signs of willingness to moderate his work habits: "I should not wear myself out the way I did before." See interview, *ITAR-TASS*, Dec. 29, 1995.

[120]*Ispoved*, pp. 17-19.

[121]According to Dr. Griazin and Leonid Volkov, former members of the Interregional Group, Dr. Griazin and Leonid Volkov, during its meetings Yeltsin was one of the least talkative participants.

[122]Sukhanov, *Tri Goda*, pp. 108-20.

[123]On the subject of Gorbachev's delusions about the true state of affairs in the Soviet Union, see Dmitry Mikheyev, *The Rise and Fall of Gorbachev* (Indianapolis: Hudson Institute, 1992), p. 134.

[124]Yeltsin, interview, *Argumenty i Fakty* no. 42, July 1992, p. 2. Viacheslav Kostikov, interview, *Rossiiskie Vesti*, Jan. 30, 1993, p. 2.

[125]Minister of the Interior Viktor Yerin stated: "I give the president all the facts, including the most unpleasant facts, which can hurt me." Interview, *Argumenty i Fakty*, no. 6, 1994, pp. 1-3.

[126]Yeltsin, interview, *Argumenty i Fakty* no. 42, 1992, p. 2.

[127]Viktor Iliushin, *Moscow News*, no. 28, July 15-21, 1994, p. 6. Former press secretary Pavel Voshchnov confirmed: "He looks through practically all the newspapers. He reads some during the day and takes the rest home." See interview, *Moscow News*, no. 47, Nov. 1991.

[128]Sukhanov said that "Yeltsin has a phenomenal memory." *Tri Goda*, p. 225. Shamil Tarpishchev said that the amount of information Yeltsin processes in one day would require three days for him. See his interview in *Argumenty i Fakty*, no. 51, Dec. 1994, p. 12. "He reads very fast," said former presidential press secretary Viacheslav Kostikov, a professional journalist. "I read very quickly, but I cannot read as fast as Boris Nikolaevich — he literally swallows up pages." Interview, *Rossiiskie Vesti*, Jan. 30, 1993, p. 2. See also, Viktor Iliushin, *Argumenty i Fakty*, no. 19, 1994, p. 3.

[129]Yeltsin, interview, Moscow Ostankino TV, Nov. 16, 1993, FBIS-SOV-93-220, Nov. 17, 1993.

[130]In *Zapiski*, Yeltsin makes the following comments. Korzhakov is "*poriadochny* (honest), *umny* (intelligent), strong, and *muzhestvenny* (courageous)," (p. 199); his son-

in-law Valeri has "all the best qualities: [he is] straightforward, independent, strong," (p. 20); Skokov "strong man [who] is first of all an intelligent man," (p. 262); Yerin is "deep, intelligent, very conscientious, and absolutely reliable;" (p. 350); Kozyrev is "absolutely reliable" (p. 351); and Fedorov is "tough, strong, almost aggressive;" (p. 366).

[131]*Zapiski*, pp. 46, 292.

[132]See his discussion of Mstislav Rostropovich: "He charges me with his optimism, energy, and his light and pure openness." *Zapiski*, p. 374.

[133]In *Zapiski* Skokov is said to be "surrounded by enemies," (p. 263) and Rutskoi is characterized by "inner hatred" (p. 49).

[134]Michnik said that "Yeltsin is a very genuine man," interview, *Izvestia*, April 13, 1994, p. 7.

[135]Solzhenitsyn said that "Yeltsin is too Russian to engage in lying, cunning, guile, to indulge in hypocrisy, to practice demagoguery and mythology." He is quoted in Alexei Kiva, "Why I am going to vote for Yeltsin," *Delovoi Mir*, April 17, 1993, p. 1.

[136]Nixon, *Beyond Peace*, p. 45.

[137]T. D. Allman, "The man who saved the future," *Vanity Fair*, October 1991.

[138] Anatoly Lysenko, *Rossiiskaia Gazeta*, Dec. 23, 1993, p. 7.

[139]Burbulis, interview, *Delovoi Mir*, March 28, 1992.

[140]Burbulis admitted that he tried to change Yeltsin's public image but failed. See his interview, *Moscow Magazine*, Apr./May 1992, p. 19.

[141]Yeltsin, interview, Moscow Ostankino TV, Nov. 16, 1993, *FBIS-SOV*-93-220, Nov. 17, 1993.

[142]*Zapiski*, pp. 37, 270

[143]Georgi Satarov, interview, *Argumenty i Fakty*, no. 33, 1994, p. 3.

[144]As one political analyst explained Yeltsin's attitude, "Russians don't like talkative leaders; the gregarious Khrushchev and Gorbachev have been imprinted in the popular memory as windbags." See Anatoli Kostikov, "Rutskoi is Yeltsin yesterday, only shorter and with a mustache," *Megapolis-Express*, Sept. 8, 1993, p. 19.

[145]Anatoly Lysenko, interview, *Rossiiskaia Gazeta*, Dec. 23, 1993, p. 7.

[146]Josef Dzialoshynski, interview, *Argumenty i Fakty*, no. 23, 1994, p. 3.

[147]Josef Dzialoshynski, interview, *Argumenty i Fakty*, no. 21, 1994, p. 3.

[148]*Zapiski*, p. 342.

[149]*Zapiski*, p. 173.

[150]*Zapiski*, p. 162.

[151]*Tri Goda*, pp. 121, 179.

[152]Vladimir Nadein, *Izvestia*, Sept. 30, 1994, p. 1.

[153]Sukhanov described how Yeltsin took away the notes of Steven Muller (the president of Johns Hopkins University), so that "both of them could speak without paper." *Tri Goda*, p. 121.

[154]At the National Press Club in Washington in June 1991, he openly indicated his desire to dispense with ceremony and turn to substance. In Germany in 1994, during the celebration of the withdrawal of Russian troops, he took the baton from the conductor of the orchestra and started to do his own impromptu conducting and singing.

[155]Yeltsin, interview, Moscow Ostankino TV, Nov. 16, 1993, *FBIS-SOV*-93-220, Nov. 17, 1993.

[156]John M. Oldham and Lois B. Morris, *The Personality Self-Portrait: Why we think, work, love, and act the way we do* (New York: Bantam, 1990).

[157]Liudmila Pertsevaya, "Do not Worship Blindly," *Moscow News*, no. 11, March 1992, p. 7. Burbulis also noted that Yeltsin is "more spontaneous, emotional, and intuitive than other politicians." Interview, *Literaturnaia Gazeta*, Nov. 13, 1991.

[158]See "Aggressive Style," Oldham and Morris, *The Personality Self-Portrait*, p. 336.

[159]Nikolai Fedorov, a former minister of justice in Yeltsin's government, said: "He feels comfortable only in an extreme situation. So the president will constantly create confrontational situations because this is for him a form of existence—both as a man and politically." *Literaturnaia Gazeta*, Feb. 22, 1995, p. 10.

[160]*Zapiski*, p. 155.

[161]*Zapiski*, pp. 292, 343.

[162]*Zapiski*, p. 44.

[163]Leonid Radzikhovsky, "The Monomakh Crown," *Stolitsa*, no. 13, 1994, pp. 6-14.

[164]Yeltsin, *Ispoved*, p. 79.

[165]*Zapiski*, p. 239.

[166]Ernest Hartmann, *Boundaries in The Mind* (New York: Basic Books, 1991), pp. 9-17.

[167]Oldham and Morris, *The Personality Self-Portrait*, p. 80.

[168]*Zapiski*, pp. 44, 173, 250.

[169]*Zapiski*, p. 305.

[170]Oleg Lobov, interview, *Moscow News*, no. 29, July 1994, p. 6. See also the remarks of Yeltsin's national security adviser Yuri Baturin, quoted in Alexandr Shalnev, "More Powerful Than Generals," *Izvestia*, June 8, 1994, p. 4.

[171]Aleksandr Livshits said: "He can be persuaded. This is an absolutely priceless quality for a leader. A rare quality." See his interview in *Literaturnaia Gazeta*, July 13, 1994, p. 10.

[172]Mikhail Poltoranin, interview, *Delovoi Mir*, June 11, 1994, p. 4. Yeltsin's wife Naina said exactly the same thing. See her interview, *We/My*, August 1992, p. 9.

[173]Oleg Lobov, interview, *Moscow News*, no. 29, July 1994, p. 6.

[174]Maxim Meyer, "Struggles in Yeltsin's entourage gain momentum," *New Times*, No. 8, Feb. 1994, p. 12.

[175]Viktor Gerashchenko spoke in favor of allowing foreign banks access to the Russian market. See *Nezavisimaia Gazeta*, June 21, 1994, p. 1.

[176]*Nezavisimaia Gazeta*, June 16, 1994, p. 1; See also *Financial Izvestia*, May 4, 1995, p. I.

[177]This was confirmed by representatives from opposite ends of the political spectrum. See Lobov, *Moscow News*, July 22-28, 1994, p. 6; Gaidar, *Moscow News*, no. 2, 1992, p. 9; and Aleksei Yablokov, *Nezavisimaia Gazeta*, March 24, 1995, p. 3.

[178]Serge Schmemann, "The ambiguities of the Russian leader," *The New York Times*, Feb. 28, 1992.

[179]Anders Aslund wrote: "Yeltsin does the opposite of what a populist would, by definition, have done. He has staked out a hard and difficult course." See his interview in *Aftenposten*, Jan. 18, 1992, *FBIS-SOV*-92-015.

[180]His first aide Viktor Iliushin has emphasized that particularly strongly. *Argumenty i Fakty*, no. 19, 1994, p. 3.

[181]Leonid Radzikhovsky, "The Monomakh Crown," *Stolitsa*, no. 13, 1994, pp. 6-14.

[182]Gennadi Osipov, director of the Institute of Sociopolitical Research, wrote: "The implementation of any reform requires calculating its consequences with mathematical precision." *Delovoi Mir*, Feb. 27-March 5, 1995, p. 15.

[183]Fedor Burlatsky, "Yeltsin: A Turning Point," *Transition* (Jamestown's publication), March 15, 1995, p. 9.

[184]Former Minister of Justice, Nikolai Fedorov, interview, *Literaturnaia Gazeta*, Feb. 22, 1995, p. 10.

[185]His former press secretary turned critic, Pavel Voshchnov, interview, *Sobesednik*, no. 18, 1992, p. 10.

[186]Yeltsin, speech, Nov. 3, 1993, ITAR-TASS, *FBIS-SOV*-93-212, Nov. 4, 1993.

[187]Anders Aslund said: "With him it is a very short distance from thought to action." Interview, *Aftenposten*, Jan. 18, 1992, *FBIS-SOV*-92-015.

[188]Valeri Semionchenko, head of the president's organizational department, interview, *Rossiiskie Vesti*, April 2, 1993, p. 2.

[189]Viacheslav Kostikov, interview, *Rossiiskie Vesti*, Jan. 30, 1993, p. 2.

[190]This description of Yeltsin's work habits was not included in the English-language version of his book *see Zapiski*, pp. 193-9.

[191]*Zapiski*, p. 347.

[192]*Zapiski*, p. 12.

[193]Vladimir Soloviov and Yelena Klepikova interviewed a number of former close associates of Yeltsin and found a consensus regarding his operational style. See *Boris Yeltsin* (Moskva: Vagrius, 1992), p. 169.

[194]Dimitri Simes, "The Return of Russian History," *Foreign Affairs*, Jan./Feb. 1994, p. 70.

[195]Georgi Satarov, interview, *Profil* (Austria), *FBIS-SOV*-93-195, Oct. 12, 1993. See also Yeltsin's remark: "I am going on a short vacation in the next few days. I hope I will be able to work out a number of fundamental decisions with regard to future strategic matters." Interview, Radio Mayk, *FBIS-SOV*-95-174, Sept. 8, 1995.

[196]Robert Endleman, *Psyche and Society: Exploration in Psychoanalytic Sociology* (New York: Columbia University Press, 1981), p. 399.

[197]Gorbachev, interview, *Time*, Dec. 23, 1991, p. 24.

[198]Press conference, *Pravda*, March 17, 1990.

[199]Nixon, *Beyond Peace*, p. 43-4.

Chapter 4

[1]Many analysts have mistakenly viewed the 1989 elections as free; for example, Jonathan Steele, *Eternal Russia* (Cambridge, MA: Harvard University Press, 1994). In fact, competition was allowed for only 15 percent of the seats. The rest were reserved for such organizations as the CPSU, Komsomol, trade unions and so on. Ironically, Steele insisted that the December 1993 elections to the Federal Assembly were not free. See pp. xvi, 390.

[2]Dawn Mann, "The Congress of People's Deputies: The Election Marathon Ends," *Report on the USSR*, June 2, 1989, pp. 3-5.

[3]Yeltsin, interview, *Izvestia*, July 15, 1989.

[4]*Komsomolskaia Pravda*, Oct. 30, 1990. See also *Poisk*, March 22-28, 1991, pp. 4-5.

[5]Yuri Manaenkov, CPSU Central Committee secretary, interview, *Nezavisimaia Gazeta*, July 2, 1991, p. 5.

[6]Dawn Mann, "The RSFSR elections: The Congress of People's Deputies," *Report on the USSR*, Vol. 2, No. 15, April 13, 1991, pp. 11-17.

[7]*TASS*, Sept. 19, 1990.

[8]*Sovetskaia Rossia*, Nov. 1, 1990.

[9]*Washington Times*, May 6, 1991.

[10]For more details on the creation of the council, see Alexander Rahr, "Yeltsin Sets Up System for Governing Russia," *Report on the USSR*, Vol. 3, No. 34, 1991.

[11]See Alexander Rahr, "Are Yeltsin and Gorbachev now allies?" *Report on the USSR*, Vol. 3, No. 27, July 5, 1991.

[12]David Remnick, *Lenin's Tomb: The Last Days of the Soviet Empire* (New York: Random House, 1993), p. 482.

[13]In an off-hand remark, seen on CNN, he clearly indicated that he thought that Gorbachev was a co-conspirator.

[14]*Zapiski*, p. 7.

[15]*Zapiski*, pp. 162-3.

[16]Maxim Sokolov, "Power-hungry president," *Kommersant*, Sept. 16, 1991, p. 3.

[17]*Kuranty*, Aug. 31, 1991, p. 2.

[18]Burbulis, interview, Aug. 23, 1991, *Vokrug Kremlia*, vol. 2, pp. 300-304, and *Literaturnaia Gazeta*, Nov. 13, 1991.

[19]*Rossiiskaia Gazeta*, Sept. 19, 1991, p. 1.

[20]*Washington Post*, Aug. 27, 1991.

[21]*Kommersant*, Sept. 2, 1991, p. 3.

[22]Trud, Sept. 11,1991. See also Boris Bogdanov in *Nezavisimaia Gazeta*, Nov. 1, 1991.

[23]*Zapiski*, p. 163.

[24]Emil Pain, "After the Chechen War," *Izvestia*, Jan. 13, 1995, p. 4.

[25]A Canadian journalist, Maks Rois, *Chuzhak v Kremle* (Stranger in the Kremlin), (Moskva: Biznes-Press, 1993), pp. 56-8.

[26]Yeltsin, *Ispoved,* p. 81.

[27]Anotoli Sobchak, *Khozhdenie vo Vlast*, pp. 39, 155.

[28]This was the view of Andranik Migranian, future member of Yeltsin's Presidential Council. See "Dolgii Put' v Evropeiski Dom" (A Long Way to the European Home), *Novy Mir*, No. 7, 1989.

[29]Sobchak, interview, *Vokrug Kremlia*, vol. 1, pp. 160-164.

[30]See, for example, Aleksandr Yakovlev, interview, *Rabochaia Tribuna*, May 16, 1991, pp. 2-3.

[31]Lev Anninski, interview, *Nedelia*, No. 38, 1991, p. 4.

[32]Gavriil Popov, "Economic Reform in the Country and the Capital," *Russian Social Science Review*, May/June 1993, p. 39. See also academician Vladimir Tikhonov, interview, *Yunost*, No. 10, 1989.

[33]See Alexander Rahr and William Pomeranz, "Russian democrats yesterday and today," *Report on the USSR*, Vol. 3, No. 19, May 10, 1991, p. 17.

[34]*Zapiski*, p. 241.

[35]Pavel Voshchanov, at the time Yeltsin's press secretary, said: "If you want to know who Yeltsin listens to, it is certainly Burbulis. He is closer to Yeltsin than anyone else." interview, *Sobesednik*, No. 18, 1992, p. 10.

[36]Burbulis, interview, *Moscow Magazine*, April/May 1992, p. 22.

[37]Burbulis, interview, *Radical*, No. 25, July 2, 1991.

[38]Burbulis, interview, *Radical*, No. 25, July 2, 1991.

[39]Burbulis, interview, *Nezavisimaia Gazeta*, Sept. 5, 1991, p. 2.

[40]Joseph Waisburd, who now lives in Indianapolis, was a member of the Discussion Tribune board.

[41]*Rossia: Partii, Assotsiatsii, Soiuzy, Kluby* (Russia: Parties, Associations, Unions, Clubs), (Moscow: RAU-Press, 1991), vol. 1, p. 92.

[42]Burbulis, interview, Aug. 23, 1991, in *Vokrug Kremlia*, vol. 2, p. 297. Aslo see *Zapiski*, p. 241.

[43]Burbulis, interview, *Radical*, No. 25, July 2, 1991.

[44]Burbulis, interview, *Komsomolskaia Pravda*, May 18, 1991, p. 6.

[45]As former residents of Sverdlovsk told me, the family of a director of a huge local meat-processing plant had to stand in line to buy meat in the store.

[46]Burbulis lifted weights, boxed, and played soccer in a local professional league. See interview, *Moscow Magazine*, April/May 1992, p. 22. According to Aleksandr Gorbunov, Burbulis was one of the best tennis players among all the top officials of Russia. *Moscow News*, Dec. 17, 1993, p. 16.

[47]"Enigmatic Explosion: Burbulis Targeted?" *Moscow News*, July 2, 1993.

[48]As one observer wrote: Burbulis "discerned in the disgraced Communist functionary a figure capable of becoming the first president of Russia and played a key role in making his vision [of Russia] came true." *Moskovskie Novosti*, Dec. 20, 1992, p. 4.

[49]Aleksei Yablokov, *Nezavisimaia Gazeta*, March 24, 1995, p. 3.

[50]Burbulis, interview, *Komsomolskaia Pravda*, May 18, 1991, p. 6.

[51]Gennadi Burbulis, *Moscow News*, No. 36, Sept. 8-15, 1991, p. 4.

[52]Burbulis, interview, *Nezavisimaia Gazeta*, Sept. 5, 1991, pp. 1, 2.

[53]Igor Sichka wrote: "At the earliest moments, when something starts happening or may happen, Burbulis' hand is suspected right away." See *Novaia Yezhednevnaia Gazeta*, Apr. 16, 1993.

[54]Voldemar Koreshkov, "The President and His Team take up Starting Positions," *Rossiiskaia Gazeta*, Feb. 26, 1993, p. 2.

[55]Nikolai Troitski, "Two fighters on the eve of a decisive battle," *Megapolis Express*, March 2, 1994, p. 18.

[56]Aleksandr Peresvetov, "Gennadi Eduardovich Burbulis," *Ogoniok*, No. 14, 1994, p. 2.

[57]These are the words of the young democratic leader Oleg Rumiantsev. See Michael McFaul and Sergei Markov, *The Troubled Birth of Russian Democracy: Parties, Personalities, and Programs* (Stanford, CA: Hoover Institution Press, 1993), p. 92.

[58]*Zapiski*, p. 103. Voldemar Koreshkov, *Rossiiskaia Gazeta*, April 14, 1993.

[59]*Moskovskie Novosti*, Dec. 20, 1992, p. 4.

[60]*Zapiski*, p. 163.

[61]*Financial Times*, Nov. 5, 1991.

[62]Liudmila Telen, "Russia's White House: in disrepair?" *Moscow News*, No. 42, Oct. 20-27, 1991, p. 4.

[63]Vladimir Soloviov and Yelena Klepikova, *Boris Yeltsin* (Moskva: Vagrius, 1992), p. 372.

[64]At the time, the council included the following academicians and professors: Yuri Ryzhov (born 1930), rector of Moscow Aviation Institute; Dmitry Volkogonov, (born 1929) colonel-general, military historian; and Georgi Arbatov (born 1923), former Andropov aide; The council also included the following economists: Oleg Bogomolov (born 1927), Pavel Bunich (born 1929), Gavriil Popov, (born 1936), Anatoli Rakitov (born 1928), Tatiana Zaslavskaia (born 1927), Nikolai Shmelev (born 1937), and Valentin Fedorov, (born 1939). Sviatoslav Fedorov, (born 1929).

[65]Alexei Golovkov, interview, *Nezavisimaia Gazeta*, Jan. 16, 1992, p. 2.

[66]Yuri Rhyzhov, *Radikal*, No. 13, April 1991.

[67]Grigori Yavljnski favored the preservation of the USSR, albeit in a modified form: "The breakdown of the Soviet Union was a poorly thought through matter. For me, it is not even clear if the empire had existed at all. After all, nobody can accuse Russians of living better than others." *Delovoi Mir*, April 15, 1993, p. 11.

[68]For example, he published a brilliant article on privatization. In it he demonstrated knowledge of all the major competing schools and concepts and offered a mixed model. See Yevgeni Yasin, "Destatization and Privatization," *Kommunist*, No. 5, 1991, pp. 99-111.

[69]Yeltsin asked Yasin to prepare an expert analysis of what would happen after the liberalization of prices. He predicted 8-15 percent monthly inflation and recovery in 1993. Yasin, interview, *Moscow News*, No. 6, 1992, p. 11.

[70]John Tedstrom, "Russia's radical reform program," *Report on the USSR*, vol. 3, no. 20, May 17, 1991, p. 17.

[71]Nikolai Testin, *August of 1991: Russia according to Participants* (Moscow: Limbus Press, 1993), p. 218. According to Dmitry Balakin of the Institute of History, 55 percent of the defenders of the White House were members of the intelligentsia and professionals. "Defenders of the White House," *Nezavisimaia Gazeta*, Sept. 5, 1991.

[72]See the remarks of Aleksandr Rutskoi: "Burbulis selects ministers and deputy ministers, he defines the functions of the vice-president and controls access to Yeltsin." See his interview on Dec. 20, 1991, *Vokrug Kremlia*, vol. 2, p. 441.

[73]For an analysis of their platforms, See Anders Aslund, "The Soviet Economy After the Coup," *Problems of Communism*, Nov.-Dec. 1991, pp. 49-51.

[74]Yegor Gaidar, in *August of 1991: Russia according to Participants* (Moscow: Limbus Press, 1993), p. 230.

[75]Golovkov, interview, *Megapolis Express*, April 22, 1992.

[76]Vitaly Melik-Karamov, "Tale of a Boy" (Skaz o Mal'chishe), *Ogoniok*, Feb. No. 4, 1994, pp. 35-37.

[77]See Anders Aslund, in *Changing the Economic System in Russia* (New York: St. Martin's Press, 1993), p. xiv.

[78]He said: "I take risks with my health because I rely on my body's resilience." *Zapiski*, p. 156.

[79]*Zapiski*, p. 236.

[80]Petr Aven, former Minister of Foreign Trade, interview, *Kommersant*, Oct. 11, 1994, p. 17.

[81]Yeltsin, interview, *Izvestia*, Nov. 20, 1991, p. 3.

[82]See interviews with Stankevich, Starovoitova, and others. *Moscow News*, Oct. 20-27, 1991, p. 6.

[83]Quoted in Anders Aslund, "The Soviet Economy After the Coup," *Problems of Communism*, Nov.-Dec. 1991, p. 51.

[84]See the article by Gadar *Nezavisimaia Gazeta*, Sept. 26, 1992.

[85]Gleb Yakunin, USSR People's Deputy, *Sovietski Patriot*, No. 38, Sept. 1991, p. 4. *FBIS-SOV*-91-043.

[86]See the program-manifesto by Gaidar and his team, *Nezavisimaia Gazeta*, Sept. 26, 1991.

[87]Yeltsin's speech, *Sovetskaia Rossia*, Oct. 29, 1991.

[88]Anders Aslund and Richard Layard (eds.), *Changing the Economic System in Russia*, (New York: St. Martin's Press, 1993), p. xii.

[89]*Zapiski*, pp. 164-5.

[90]*Zapiski*, pp. 164-5.

[91]Gaidar, interview, *Stolitsa*, No. 6, Feb. 1994, p. 1.

[92]*Zapiski*, p. 164.

[93]Alexei Golovkov said: "They like each other." See his interview in *Nezavisimaia Gazeta*, Jan. 22, 1992. "We are all close friends," confirmed Petr Aven. See his interview *Nezavisimaia Gazeta*, Feb. 27, 1992.

[94]Burbulis: "We needed a congruent 'team' that could rely on the political will of the head of the government and its own professionalism." *Argumenty i Fakty*, No. 31, 1992.

[95]Burbulis, interview, *Nezavisimaia Gazeta*, Jan. 29, 1992.

[96]Lev Zakharov, "I have a plan," *Kommersant*, Nov. 4, 1991, p. 1. See also the commentary of Maxim Sokolov on p. 7.

[97]*Kommersant*, Nov. 11, 1991, p. 15.

[98]*Kommersant*, Nov. 11, 1991, p. 15.

[99]Yuri Petrov, "There is no organized opposition in the Yeltsin *apparat*." *Izvestia*, Oct. 9, 1991.

[100]Gaidar said: "Yeltsin supports and absolutely trusts us in our solution of professional issues. He doesn't make the amendments a politician concerned about his popularity would logically make." See interview, *Moscow News*, No. 2, 1992, p. 9.

[101]Rutskoi, interview, Dec. 20, 1991, in *Vokrug Kremlia*, vol. 2, p. 442.

[102]Malei, interview, *Komsomolskaia Pravda*, Sept. 17, 1993, pp. 1,3.

[103]Yasin, interview, *Moscow News*, No. 6, 1992, p. 11.

[104]Anatoli Sobchak, interview, *Obshchaia Gazeta*, No. 16, Nov. 1993, p. 4.

[105]Alexei Novikov, "June Theses of Academician Bogomolov," *Novaia Ezhednevnaia Gazeta*, June 11, 1993, p. 3.

[106]Alexei Novikov, "June Theses of Academician Bogomolov," *Novaia Ezhednevnaia Gazeta*, June 11, 1993, p. 3. See also Stanislav Shatalin, "The crisis of power: Is there a way out? The Federation has to be re-created from the bottom up." *Nezavisimaia Gazeta*, April 8, 1993, pp. 1-2, and "The market needs to be governed" *Economika i Zhyzn*, No. 5, Feb. 1994, p. 1.

[107]See the roundtable discussion, *Rabochaia Tribuna*, Nov. 7, 1991, p. 2. See also Eduard Shevardnadze, interview, *Mezhdunarodnaia Zhyzn*, No. 10, Oct. 1991, pp. 5-14.

[108]Gavriil Popov, "What next? Notes on the present moment," *Izvestia*, Oct. 18, 1991, p. 1.

[109]Yeltsin's address, *Ostankino TV*, Jan. 17, 1992, *FBIS-SOV*-92-013.

[110]Yeltsin, *TASS*, Jan. 9, 1992.

[111]*Zapiski*, p. 151.

[112]Vladimir Bukovsky, "Boris Yeltsin's Hollow Victory," *Commentary*, June 1993, p. 31. A similar view was expressed by Vladimir Soloviov and Yelena Klepikova, *Boris Yeltsin* (Moskva: Vagrius, 1992), p. 379.

[113]In November 1991, immediately after Yeltsin appointed Nikolai Podgornov head of administration of Vologda Oblast, the latter abolished price controls in the province. See *Izvestia*, July 31, 1992.

[114]Valeri Kachurin, "While we are dividing power, a power vacuum reigns," *Rabochaia Tribuna*, Nov. 12, 1991, pp. 1,2.

[115]Sergei Vasiliev, "Economic Reform in Russia: Social, Political, and Institutional Aspects," in Anders Aslund and Richard Layard (eds.), *Changing the Economic System in Russia* (New York: St. Martin's Press, 1993), p. 75.

[116]Stanislav Shatalin, interview, *Izvestia*, Feb. 5, 1992, p. 2.

[117]Gaidar's interview, *Komsomolskaia Pravda*, Jan. 10, 1993.

[118]Sergei Vasiliev, "Economic Reform in Russia: Social, Political, and Institutional Aspects" in Anders Aslund and Richard Layard (eds.), *Changing the Economic System in Russia* (New York: St. Martin's Press, 1993), p. 75.

[119]Ronald Grigor Suny, *The Revenge of the Past: Nationalism, Revolution, and the Collapse of the Soviet Union* (Stanford: Stanford University Press, 1993), p. 129.

[120]As Richard Pipes astutely remarked, "I cannot think of any parallel of this kind of collapse. Great empires usually wear down or are defeated in war, but this kind of implosion is unprecedented." *The International Herald Tribune*, Nov. 29, 1993, p. 1.

[121]Zbigniew Brzezinski, *Out of Control: Global Turmoil on the Eve of the 21st Century* (New York: Robert Stewart Books, 1993), p. 167.

[122]Former political prisoners and human rights champions Sergei Kovaliov and Kronid Liubarski took this view. See Moskovskie Novosti, No. 8, 1993. See also Max Rois, *Chuzhak v Kremle* (Stranger in the Kremlin) (Moskva: Biznes-Press, 1993), p. 251.

[123]*Zapiski*, p. 166.

[124]Popov, "What next? Notes on the present moment," *Izvestia*, Oct. 18, 1991, p. 1.

[125]Yeltsin, speech to 5th People's Deputies Congress, *Sovetskaia Rossia*, Oct. 29, 1991, p. 3.

[126]*Sovetskaia Rossia*, March 28, 1990.

[127]Kronid Liubarsky, "Falsification Two," *Novoe Vremia*, No. 9, 1994, pp. 10-13.

[128]Yeltsin, interview on the *BBC*, Jan. 29, 1992, *FBIS-SOV*-92-020.

[129]Burbulis, interview, *Izvestia*, Oct. 15, 1992, p. 5.

[130]Yeltsin, interview, *Izvestia*, July 15, 1992, pp. 1, 3.

[131]Yeltsin, interview, *Izvestia*, June 11, 1992.

[132]Yeltsin said that the strategy should be charted by "different people with a different mentality." See interview, *Izvestia*, June 11, 1992.

[133]Burbulis, interview, *Izvestia*, Oct. 15, 1992, p. 5.

[134]Yeltsin, television address, *Rossiiskie Vesti*, Aug. 22, 1993.

[135]Richard Pipes, "The Last Gasp of Russian Communists," *The New York Times*, Oct. 5, 1993, p. A17.

[136]Vladimir Bukovsky, "Boris Yeltsin's Hollow Victory," *Commentary*, June 1993, p. 33. See also Alexandr Solzhenitsyn, *Izvestia*, Sept. 21, 1993.

[137]*Zapiski*, p. 168.

[138]Meeting of President Yeltsin with journalists, *Izvestia*, July 15, 1992, pp. 1,3.

[139]Sergei Tsypliaev, plenipontentiary of Petersburg and Leningrad Oblast, *Segodnia*, March 16, 1993.

[140]In November 1992 the alliance of heads of administrations of 53 regions of Russia supported the president and advocated the prolongation of his emergency powers. *Rossiiskie Vesti*, Nov. 19, 1992.

[141]*Stolitsa*, No. 32, 1992.

[142]Viacheslav Volkov, interview, *Izvestia*, Feb. 18, 1993.

[143]Vladimir Shumeiko, at the time vice-premier in charge of personnel policy, admitted that many positions in the government were "tailored to suit certain individuals and certain situations, or as a safe haven for ex-dignitaries." *Moscow News*, Oct. 18-25, 1992.

[144]As Viktor Iliushin noted, "While the President's entourage keeps changing with time, the composition of the service of assistants remains immutable." *Moscow News*, Sept. 24, 1993.

[145]Fred Hiatt, *The Washington Post*, Sept. 12, 1993.

[146]Alexandr Pochinok, interview, *Economika i Zhyzn*, No. 48, Nov. 1993, p. 2.

[147]Magomet Bekov, the administrative head of the education of cadres for state service, *RFE/RL Daily Report*, May 18, 1992.

[148]Yuri Petrov: "Why should there be two managers where one is enough?" *Moscow News*, No. 31, Aug. 1992.

[149]Burbulis, interview, *Russkaia Mysl*, April 9-15, 1993, p. 8.

[150]Fred Hiatt wrote: "The churning within Mr. Yeltsin's administration is remarkable: of eight men serving as deputy prime ministers last September, one is now prime minister, five have been dropped and two remain in their posts." See *The Washington Post*, Sept. 12, 1993.

[151]According to Shakhrai, Yeltsin intentionally introduces into his team people of different persuasions, so that "they can neutralize each other, thus creating stability for the President." See interview, *Literaturnaia Gazeta*, No. 35, 1992, p. 11.

[152]Burbulis, interview, *Moscow News*, No. 14, 1992, p. 6.

[153]In the words of Yeltsin aide Aleksandr Sokolov. Quoted in David Remnick, *Lenin's Tomb: The Last Days of the Soviet Empire* (New York: Random House, 1993), p. 505.

[154]Yeltsin characterized Golovkov's shortcomings in these words. *Zapiski*, p. 247.

[155]*Zapiski*, p. 164-5.

[156]Yeltsin, "Russia is Strong in Intellect, Resources, and Culture. This Potential will Enable it to Achieve a Breakthrough in the Future." *Rossiiskie Vesti*, April 21, 1993, pp. 1,2.

[157]On this point, see Anatoly Fedoseyev, a former leading Soviet scientist who defected to England, "The Passage to New Russia and Some Thoughts on Its Alternative Constitutional Order," in Alexander Shtromas and Morton A. Kaplan (eds.), *The Soviet Union and the Challenge of the Future* (New York: Paragon House, 1988), vol. 1, p. 450.

[158]These figures were provided by the Institute of Social Studies of Russia's Academy of Science. See, G. Kostin, "What kind of elite is in power now?" *Argumenty i Fakty*, No. 35, 1994, p. 3. See also, Vladimir Kvasov, chief of staff of Chernomyrdin's government, interview, *Trud*, June 22, 1993, p. 2.

[159]*Zapiski*, p. 249.

[160]Alexei Kirpichikov, "Yeltsin strengthens executive branch," *Kommersant* No. 19, 1992.

[161]*Moscow News*, No. 31, Aug. 1992.

[162]*Moscow News*, Jan. 21, 1993.

[163]Regarding Oleg Soskovets, see *Izvestia*, Jan. 19, 1995, p. 5; regarding Chernomyrdin, see Stanislav Turchonok, "The Man and His Career," *Moskva*, No. 3, March 1994, pp. 4, 5, 11. His rise in business was characterized as a "typical dream-come-true for the post-communist generation of entrepreneurs." *Kommersant*, Dec. 22, 1992. Regarding Shumeiko, see interview, *Rossiiskie Vesti*, July 21, 1992, p. 3. Regarding Skokov, see *Novoe Vremia*, No. 32, 1992.

[164]Yeltsin, interview, *Izvestia*, June 11, 1992.

[165]*Zapiski,* pp. 268-269.

[166]Stephen Sestanovich, "Russia Turns the Corner," *Foreign Affairs*, Jan/Feb. 1994, p. 89.

[167]Vladimir Orlov, "Yeltsin and his team of six," *Moscow News*, No. 12, 1992, p. 2.

[168]Anatoli Chubais recommended Georgi Khizha; Gaidar nominated Vladimir Shumeiko. *Izvestia*, June 6, 1992.

[169]*Literaturnaia Gazeta*, No. 22, 1992, p. 2.

[170]Yeltsin, *The Struggle For Russia*, p. 237.

[171]The best examples are Viktor Chernomyrdin and Vladimir Shumeiko.

[172]The best example of such a turnaround has been that of Sergei Glaziev, one of the original Gaidarians, and former Minister of Foreign Economic Relations. See his articles: "Not just the market," *Delovoi Mir*, Sept. 20-26, 1993; "The fight against inflation," *Ekonomika i Zhyzn*, No. 47, 1993, pp. 1,2; "The lessons of the latest reforms," *Nezavisimaia Gazeta*, Nov. 9, 1993, pp. 1,4.

[173]*Zapiski,* p. 169.

[174]Yeltsin, interview, *Izvestia*, June 11, 1992.

[175]Dubinin and Gerashchenko, for example, were both known as "top-notch professionals." *Kommersant*, Nov. 22, 1994, p. 21.

[176]Oleg Lobov, interview, *Moscow News*, No. 29, July 1994, p. 6.

[177]Emil Pain, Georgi Satarov, and Leonid Smirniagin complained that after October 1994 Yeltsin stopped listening to them and they were removed from the decision making process. See Sergei Parkhomenko, "Conflict with reality," *Segodnia*, Oct. 20, 1994, p. 3.

[178]The leading democrat Sergei Stankevich confirmed this shift. See interview, *Literaturnaia Gazeta*, March 11, 1992, p. 11. Foreign Minister Kozyrev said: "We are looking for intelligent people, not political comissars." See interview, *Espress* (Lisbon), *ITAR-TASS*, March 31, 1992.

[179]A good example is Yuri Boldyrev, former chief inspector, who, as Yeltsin complained, caused "too many conflicts" with local authorities. *Financial Times*, April 27, 1993. Another example is Ella Pamfilova, former Minister of Social Protection of the Population. See *The Washington Post*, Dec. 22, 1992.

[180]During 1993 and 1994, many gifted and intelligent personalities left Yeltsin's administration. Among them were Burbulis, Gaidar, Nechayev, Fedorov, Shokhin, Dubinin, Kostikov, Filippov, Gerashchenko, and Khlystun.

[181]*Pravda*, March 28, 1990.

[182]*Constitution (Fundamental Law) of the Soviet Socialist Republics* (Moscow: Novosti, 1977).

[183]Gavriil Popov, "The October Events Were Programmed," *Nezavisimaia Gazeta*, Dec. 10, 1993, p. 5.

[184]*Nezavisimaia Gazeta*, July 13, 1993; *Izvestia*, July 15, 1993.

[185]Vladimir Barabanov was appointed Head of Administration of Brianskaia *oblast* by Yeltsin in January 1992 and began to eliminate the soviets. *Rabochaia Tribuna*, April 14, 1992. Yeltsin had to dismiss the overzealous reformer. See *Rossiiskaia Gazeta*, May 14, 1993.

[186]Georgi Vladimov, "There are no victors in this battle," *Moscow News*, No. 41, Oct. 8, 1993, p. 4.

[187]Petr Filippov, interview, Ostankino television, "Public Opinion," Feb. 24, 1993.

[188]Yeltsin, "Russia is Strong in Intellect, Resources, and Culture. This Potential Will Enable Her to Achieve a Breakthrough in the Future." *Rossiiskie Vesti*, April 21, 1993, pp. 1,2.

[189]The following statement was characteristic: "The time has come to apply forceful means (*primenit' vlast*) to get out of the intolerable power impasse." See interview, *Argumenty i Fakty*, No. 42, July 1992, p. 1.

[190]As a leading political observer wrote, Yeltsin rejected "the option of managing the country by exceptionally strong authoritarian methods." See Vitali Tretiakov's editorial, *Nezavisimaia Gazeta*, vol. iv, no. 4-5, August 1993, p. 4.

[191]Konstantin Katanian, "Who Will Be Left With Khasbulatov?" *Kuranty*, Jan. 10, 1993.

[192]Grigori Yavlinsky, interview, *Komsomolskaia Pravda*, Nov. 9, 1993, p. 3.

[193]Lilia Shevtsova, "The Two Sides of the New Russia," *Journal of Democracy*, July 1995, Vol. 6, No. 3, p. 62.

[194]Shumeiko, interview, *Izvestia*, Sept. 30, 1993, p. 2.

[195]Editorial, *Financial Times*, Sept. 22, 1993.

[196]*Zapiski*, p. 348.

[197]Shumeiko, interview, Moscow Ostankino TV, *FBIS-SOV*-93-185, Sept. 27, 1993.

[198]Yeltsin, interview, Moscow Radio Mayak, *FBIS-SOV*-93-168, Sept. 1, 1993.

[199]William Safire reported that "General Grachev traveled to the U.S. and talked with President Clinton in the office of the national security adviser, Anthony Lake." *The New York Times,* Sept. 23, 1993.

[200]121 civilians, 18 police and six army personnel died. *Izvestia*, Dec. 28, 1993, p. 1.

[201]Burbulis, interview, *Il Giornale*, in Italian, Oct. 21, 1993, *FBIS-SOV*-93-204, Oct. 25, 1993.

[202]Yeltsin, interview, Ostankino TV Channel, *FBIS-SOV*-93-189-S, Oct. 1, 1993.

[203]Ostankino TV Channel, Sept. 30, 1993, *FBIS-SOV*-93-189.

[204]Vladimir Shumeiko, *Delovoi Mir*, Sept. 30, 1993, p. 1.

[205]Moscow Mayor Luzhkov, a participant in the negotiations, said: "We came to agreement on all issues. It was a great relief because we lived under the threat of bloodshed. The meeting of experts had to start in a few hours to discuss the details of surrender of weapons." *Moscow News*, No. 41, Oct. 8, 1993, p. 4.

[206]*Nezavisimaia Gazeta*, Oct. 2, 1993, p. 1.

[207]Luzhkov, interview, *Moscow News*, No. 41, Oct. 8, 1993, p. 4.

[208]*Komsomolskaia Pravda*, Oct. 15, 1993, p. 3.

[209]Yevgeni Sevastianov, *Moscow News*, Oct. 29, 1993, p. 2.

[210]Yeltsin, address to the nation, *Izvestia*, Oct. 5, 1993.

[211]Alexei Kiva, remarks during a roundtable discussion, *Rossiiskaia Gazeta*, March 31, 1994, p. 3.

Chapter 5

[1]*Newsweek*, Feb. 20, 1978, p. 18, and *Science*, Vol. 201, Sept./ 15, 1978, pp. 994-998.

[2]For example, Russian mass transportation systems account for more than 85 percent of all motorized urban trips, compared to 3 percent in the United States.

[3]From the manifesto of a large group of economists, including S. Shatalin, N. Petrakov, G. Yavlinsky, B. Fedorov, Ye. Yasin, S. Aleksashenko, A. Vavilov, L. Grigoriev, M. Adornov, V. Martynov, V. Mashchits, A. Mikhailov, and T. Yarygina, *Argumenty i Fakty*, No. 36, Sept. 1990, pp. 1, 2.

[4]See the remarks of Leonid Abalkin, Vladimir Tikhonov, Nikolai Shmeliev, Viktor Belkin and Gennadi Lisichkin. *The New York Times,* June 18, 1989.

[5]Vasili Leontiev, "To the market under the control of the government," in *Trudny Povorot k Rynku* (Moskva: Ekonomika, 1990), pp. 261-8, and *Ekonomika i Zhyzn*, No. 16, 1990.

[6]Marshall I. Goldman, *Lost Opportunity: Why Economic Reforms Have Not Worked in Russia* (New York: Norton, 1994), p. 256.

[7]Among Western proponents was Marshall I. Goldman. See *Lost Opportunity*, p. 244.

[8]Marshall I. Goldman, "Soviet and Chinese economic reform," *Foreign Affairs*, vol. 66, Winter 1988.

[9]Gorbachev said: "We must keep key consumer goods, including food, under [state] control." *Pravda*, Apr. 28, 1990. For a more detailed discussion of the issue, see Dmitry Mikheyev, *The Rise and Fall of Gorbachev* (Indianapolis, Hudson Institute, 1992).

[10]Valeri Kachurin, "While we are dividing power, a power vacuum reigns," *Rabochaia Tribuna*, Nov. 12, 1991, pp. 1, 2.

[11]V. Gerasimov, Director of the Humanitarian Center for Social Policy, wrote that "the domestic experts saw the results of the liberalization of prices in a rosier light than their foreign colleagues." See also "What happens when price restrictions are removed?" *Pravda*, Nov. 26, 1991, pp. 1, 3.

[12]The overall cost for western Germany was estimated to be (by 1996) $430 billion. See *Der Spiegel*, as quoted in Michael Lindermann, "Row over East Germany's lost DM 65 bil.," *Financial Times*, Feb. 14, 1995, p. 3. See also Karen Miller, "The Worst is Finally Over in Eastern Germany," *Business Week*, June 19, 1995, p. 54.

[13]*The World Factbook, 1994* (Washington, D.C.: Central Intelligence Agency), p. 149.

[14]Gaidar, interview, *Russian TV*, Jan. 23, 1992. *FBIS-SOV-92-016*.

[15]Robert Tucker, *The Soviet Political Mind* (New York: Frederick Praeger, 1963), pp. 86-87.

[16]Janos Kornai, *The Socialist System: The Political Economy of Communism* (Princeton, N.J.: Princeton University Press, 1992), pp. 85-88.

[17]Andrei Shleifer and Robert W. Vishny, "Privatization in Russia: First Steps," in Oliver J. Blanchard, Kenneth A. Froot, and Jeffrey D. Sachs, *The Transition in Eastern Europe* (University of Chicago Press, 1994), pp. 146-148.

[18]*Ekonomika i Zhyzn*, No. 7, Feb. 1995, p. 1.

[19]Vladimir Shumeiko provided a very insightful picture of this process. See *Vecherniaa Moskva*, May 6, 1994, p. 2.

[20]As a technology engineer in the 1970s at a 400 employee electrical equipment factory in Kiev, I was once able to keep a production line working for twelve days by unearthing spare parts from a forgotten corner of the factory. One Soviet era survey estimated that $18 billion worth of imported equipment was idling unpacked around the country because of the unfinished construction of thousands of industrial buildings.

[21]The estimate is by Leonid Pleshakov. See his interview with Leonid Abalkin, *Ogoniok*, No. 13, March 1989, pp. 8-19.

[22]This is estimated on the basis of the data for the Soviet Union with Russia's share assumed to be 60 percent. The estimate is by Viktor Gubarev, chairman of the Committee for Budget and Finance of the USSR Supreme Soviet. *Moscow Radio-1*, Nov. 12, 1991, *FBIS-SOV-91-219*, According to USSR Ministry of Finance, individuals' savings in October 1991 were R861 billion. *Ekonomika i Zhyzn*, No. 47, Nov. 1991, p. 5. Vladimir Shumeiko said that enterprises had R616 billion in their bank accounts. *Vechernia Moskva*, May 6, 1994, p. 2.

[23]Ruslan Aprelikov, deputy chairman of the RSFSR State Supply Committee, *Rossiiskaia Gazeta*, Sep. 19, 1991, p. 1.

[24]*Kommersant*, Nov. 18, 1991, p. 15.

[25]*Rossiiskaia Gazeta,* July 13, 1993.

[26]$13 billion in 1950 is equivalent to $78 billion in 1987 dollars. See Michael J. Hogan, *The Marshall Plan* (New York: Cambridge University Press, 1987), According

to the World Bank, the amount would be 105 billion in 1994 dollars. *Transition*, The World Bank Newsletter, Vol. 5, No. 5, May/June, 1994, p. 8.

[27]Sergei Glaziev, "Is it really Russia'a Choice?" *Nezavisimaia Gazeta*, Nov. 11, 1994, p. 1.

[28]Dmitry Mikheyev, "How Privatization Can Unleash the Russian Economy," *Hudson Briefing Paper*, No. 141, June 1992.

[29]Seventy-one percent of all enterprise managers comprised the largest group of supporters of the liberalization of prices. See "What happens when price restrictions are removed?" *Pravda*, Nov. 26, 1991, pp. 1, 3.

[30]*The Economist*, April 22, 1995, p. 69.

[31]Thus in November 1991 the dollar was worth 100 rubles on the black market but only 67 kopeks at the commercial rate for companies.

[32]Gregory Yavlinski spoke about $150 billion, while Nikolai Shmeliov and Abel Aganbegian estimated $200 billion, *Dialog*, No. 4, 1990.

[33]Aslund, *How Russia Became a Market Economy*, p. 134.

[34]Marshall Goldman, "To Russia, with Cash," *Business Month*, Nov. 1988, pp. 44-51.

[35]Goldman, *Lost Opportunity*, p. 115.

[36]Burbulis' remarks in Stockholm, *TASS*, Jan. 20, 1992.

[37]Burbulis, interview, *Swenska Dagbladet*, Jan. 19, 1992, p. 6. *FBIS-SOV*-92-015.

[38]*Financial Izvestia*, Jan. 19, 1995, p. 1.

[39]Opinions differ as to how much it increased. Vladimir Yurovski and Alexandr Mironychev, "Good-bye the almighty dollar," *Delovye Lyudi*, No. 45, May, 1994, p. 31. See also *PlanEcon Report*, Vol. IX, No. 44-45, 1993, p. 38. Mikhail Deliagin of the President's Analytical Center estimated that from January 1992 through October 1994 the buying power of the dollar in Russia fell about sixteen times. *Delovye Lyudi*, Oct. 3-9, 1994, p. 6. The economists of *Kommersant* believe that since 1993 the dollar "has become five times cheaper." *Kommersant*, Oct. 11, 1994 p. 5. In 1994, the dollar lost 14 percent of its purchasing power. *Kommersant-Daily*, Feb. 17, 1995, p. 2.

[40]Peter Maber, "Banking the Bear: Financing Marketization in Russia," *The Columbia Journal of World Business*, Winter 1994.

[41]Scott Gerber, "The Financial Revolution," U.S. Department of Commerce, *BISNIS BULLETIN*, Jan./Feb. 1995, p. 1.

[42]Aslund, *How Russia Became a Market Economy*, pp. 3, 11.

[43]Aslund, *How Russia Became a Market Economy*, p. 140.

[44]According to Yevgeni Yasin, 1.3 percent of all enterprises produced 25.7 percent of the nation's output. See "Destatization and Privatization," *Kommunist*, No. 5, 1991, p. 101.

[45]Malcolm Warner, Elena Denezhkina and Adrian Campbell, *How Russian Managers Learn* (Judge Institute of Management Studies, Cambridge University, 1993).

[46]S. Shatalin, N. Petrakov, G. Yavlinsky, B. Fedorov, Ye. Yasin, S. Aleksashenko, A. Vavilov, L. Grigoriev, M. Zadornov, V. Martynov, V. Mashchits, A. Mikhailov, and T. Yarygina, *Argumenty i Fakty*, No. 36, Sept. 1990, pp. 1, 2.

[47]See Larisa Piasheva *et al.*, "Give it away for free," *Izvestia*, Feb. 14, 1992; Vasili Seliunin, "In spite of everything, it will be done our way," *Izvestia*, March 23, 1992; L. Piasheva, A. Isaev, V. Seliunin, G. Lisichkin, L. Ivanovski, B. Pinsker, "Nevertheless it must be returned," *Rossiiskaia Gazeta*, April 7, 1992.

[48]Yeltsin, interview, *Argumenty i Fakty*, No. 22, June 1991, p. 2.

[49]Yeltsin, speech at the Fifth Congress of People's Deputies, *Sovetskaia Rossia*, Oct. 29, 1991, p. 3.

[50]Burbulis' remarks in Stockholm, *TASS*, Jan. 20, 1992.

[51]One reporter wrote: "Well-informed sources revealed that Yeltsin is more open to Filippov's arguments than those of Oleg Bogomolov." *Segodnia*, Oct. 22, 1993, p. 1. See also *Kommersant-Daily*, March 3, 1993.

[52]Petr Filippov, interview, *Rabochaia Tribuna*, Nov. 27, 1991.

[53]Filippov, interview, *Rossiiskaia Gazeta*, March 10, 1992.

[54]Aslund, *How Russia Became a Market Economy*, p. 315.

[55]See Petr Aven, interview, *Delovoi Mir*, June 24, 1995, p. 6.

[56]Chubais, interview, *Obshchaia Gazeta*, Sept. 10, 1993, p. 8.

[57]Chubais, interview, *Izvestia*, Feb. 26, 1992, p. 3.

[58]Chubais, interview, *Komsomolskaia Pravda*, March 29, 1994, p. 3.

[59]Chubais, interview, *Komsomolskaia Pravda*, March 29, 1994, p. 3.

[60]Gaidar, interview, *Ekonomika i Zhyzn*, No. 49, Dec. 9, 1993, p. 1.

[61]These figures are according to the Ministry of Economics. *Torgovaia Gazeta*, Dec. 28, 1994, p. 2. Goskomstat, cited in *Rossiiskaia Gazeta*, March 31, 1995, p. 3.

[62]Goskomstat, cited in *Rossiiskaia Gazeta*, Mar. 31, 1995, p. 3.

[63]Goskomstat, cited in *Delovoi Mir*, Jan. 18, 1995, p. 4.

[64]Chubais, interview, *INTERFAX*, June 30, 1994.

[65]Chubais, interview, *INTERFAX*, June 30, 1994.

[66]*Financial Times*, Aug. 5, 1993, p. 4.

[67]In Moscow, St. Petersburg and Vladivostok. See *Kommersant*, Sept. 1, 1993, p. 14.

[68]Energia, a firm that makes rockets, was among the privatized firms. Moscow Radiostation *Ekho*, May 6, 1994, *FBIS-SOV*-94-088, p. 27.

[69]For example, in metallurgy 82 percent of enterprises were privatized. *Kommersant-Daily*, Jan. 19, 1995, p. 3.

[70]Alfred Kokh, acting director of the GKI, *Izvestia*, Oct. 14, 1995, p. 4.

[71]Petr Mostovoi, deputy chairman of the Committee of State Property, *Argumenty i Fakty*, No. 33, 1994, p. 5.

[72]Alfred Kokh, first deputy of the GKI, *Delovoi Mir*, June 12-18, 1995, p. 33.

[73]In 1994 102 state controlled enterprises were certified as bankrupt, and 1,200 were classified as insolvent. *Segodnia*, Nov. 24, 1994, p. 2.

[74]In comparison, there are only a few dozen investment privatization funds in the Czech republic. See Alec Kinnear, *Business Central Europe*, April 1995, pp. 55-56.

[75]Roman Sheinin, "Russia for sale: Phase II," *Crossroads*, Oct. 15, 1994, p. 12.

[76]Lynn Nelson and Irina Kuzes, "Coordinating the Russian privatization program," *RFE/RL Research Report*, Vol. 3, No. 20, May 1994, p. 27.

[77]Aslund, *How Russia Became a Market Economy*, *passim*.

[78]For my view and that of Alan Reynolds (Director of Economic Research of the Hudson Institute) on privatization, see *The International Economy*, March/April 1992.

[79]Burbulis, interview, *Komsomolskaia Pravda*, Jan. 21, 1992, pp. 1, 2.

[80]Oleg Vite, "Privatization as Effected by the Nomenklatura," *Moscow News*, Dec. 1-8, 1991, p. 9.

[81]Yelena Rubliova, "The reemergence of the command economy is hindered by privatization," *Financial Izvestia*, Feb. 3-9, 1994, p. I.

[82]Yeltsin's address, ITAR-TASS, Nov. 2, 1993.

[83]Matthew Wyman, Stephen White, Bill Miller and Paul Heywood, "Public Opinion and Voters in the December 1993 Russian Elections," *Europe-Asia Studies*, Vol. 47, No. 4. 1995, p. 599.

[84]According to a simple formula we suggested, an experienced mechanic would have received twenty times more shares than a young unskilled worker. See Dmitry Mikheyev, "How Privatization Can Unleash the Russian Economy," *Hudson Briefing Paper*, No. 141, June 1992, p. 10.

[85]Bozidar Djelic, "Mass privatization in Russia: The role of vouchers," *RFE/RL Research Report*, Vol. 1, No. 41, Oct. 16, 1992, pp. 40-44.

[86]Joseph Blasi of Rutgers University, who for 18 months thoroughly studied the Russian economy, wrote that the endemic Western pessimism was not justified because "Russia has made a far more promising start than its critics seem willing to admit." See "Privatizing Russia — A Success Story," *The New York Times*, June 30, 1994, p. 13.

[87]Quoted by John Lloyd, *Financial Times*, Dec. 9, 1993, p. 2.

[88]Jan Vanous, "Russia has Led the CIS in Privatization and Market Development," *PlanEcon Report*, Dec. 19, 1993.

[89]See Anthony Robinson, "Polish Privatization Gets Under Way," *Financial Times*, July 14, 1995, p. 2, and the special supplement on the Polish economy, *Financial Times*, March 28, 1995, pp. I-XII.

[90]See Nathaniel Nash, "Privatization in Hungary: Once More, With Feeling," *The New York Times*, Oct. 17, 1995, pp. C1, C3.

[91]Vincent Boland, "Slovakia prepares its sale of the century," *Financial Times*, Aug. 25, 1994, p. 2.

[92]For a summary of Yeltsin's fight for privatization against the Supreme Soviet, see Domenic Gualtieri, "Russia's New 'War of Laws,'" *RFE/RL Research Report*, Vol. 2, No. 35, Sept. 3, 1993, pp. 10-13.

[93]*Rossiiskaia Gazeta, Delovoi Mir,* July 23, 1994.

[94]Quoted in Leonid Bershidsky, "Post-Voucher Investment Fall Predicted," *The Moscow Times*, July 31, 1994, p. 41.

[95]Dmitry Vasiliev, interview, *Izvestia*, June 29, 1994, p. 9.

[96]*A Study of the Soviet Economy*, vol. 2 (Paris, Feb. 1991), p. 37. Quoted in Aslund, *How Russia Became a Market Economy*, p. 152.

[97]*Ekonomika i Zhyzn*, No. 7, February 1995, p. 1.

[98]6.5 percent of which were owned by federal or municipal authorities. Anatoli Kulikov, Minister of Internal Affairs, interview, *Business in Russia*, No. 59, 1995, p. 9.

[99]Andrei Zverev, head of the Department of Finance of the government, *Delovoi Mir*, Oct. 24, 1994, p. 4.

[100]Ziuganov, interview, *Kommersant-Daily*, July 6, 1995, p. 4.

[101]Eighty-two percent of the population was lived in the countryside. *Narodnoe Khoziastvo SSSR Za 70 Let* (Moskva: Statistika, 1988), p. 373.

[102]Hugh Seton-Watson, *The Russian Empire: 1801-1917* (Oxford University Press, 1967), pp. 649-657.

[103]Edmond Thery, *La transformation de la Russie* (Paris: 1914), quoted in Mikhail Heller and Alexandr Nekrich, *Utopia u Vlasti* (Frankfurt: Polyglot-Druck GmbH, 1982), vol. I, pp. 10-11.

[104]Lazar Volin, U.S. Department of Agriculture, "Agricultural Policy of the Soviet Union," in *Readings on the Soviet Economy*, Franklin Holzman (ed.) (Chicago: Rand McNally, 1963), pp. 516-519.

[105]Lazar Volin, op. cit., p. 518.

[106]Harry Schwartz, *Russia's Soviet Economy* (New York: Prentice-Hall, 1954), p. 294.

[107]Interview with Leonid Voronin, Chairman of *Gossnab*, *Pravda*, Sept. 23, 1987.

[108]Gale Johnson and Karen McConnell Brooks, *Prospects for Soviet Agriculture in the 1980s* (Bloomington: Indiana University Press, 1983), pp. 4, 56.

[109]According to a study by Nikolai Radugin, Soviet farmers used 274 kg. of fuel for 1 hectare, while the typical American farmer used 115 kg. *Kommersant*, No. 1, 1995, p. 63.

[110]Prof. A. Belozertsev, "Russia's Grain," *Zemlia i Liudi*, No. 21, May, 1995, p. 3.

[111]Lester Brown, *State of the World* (New York: W.W. Norton, 1990), p. 74.

[112]Nikolai Radugin, "On the way to the market," *Selskaia Zhyzn*, June 19, 1993, p. 2.

[113]Marshall Goldman, *Lost Opportunity*, p. 37; *Sovetskaia Rossia*, Oct. 14, 1986; *Izvestia*, June 25, 1990.

[114]*Pravda*, Aug. 12, 1990.

[115]Prof. A. Belozertsev, "Russia's Grain," *Zemlia i Liudi*, No. 21, May 1995, p. 3.

[116]*Rabochaia Tribuna*, Oct. 19, 1990.

[117]See Rimma Godai, *Sovetskaia Rossia*, Dec. 10, 1989.

[118]*Moscow News*, Aug. 12, 1990; *Pravda*, Aug. 16, 1990.

[119]*Izvestia*, March 14, 1991.

[120]*Pravda*, Dec. 20, 1991.

[121]These are the words of a radical reformer in the Russian Parliament, Valeri Riumin, Mayor of Riazan. Russian Central Television, Aug. 8, 1990.

[122]*INTERFAX*, Oct. 31, 1991.

[123]*Rossiiskaia Gazeta*, Dec. 31, 1991.

[124]*Izvestia*, Dec. 28, 1991, p. 1.

[125]"Decree of the Government of Russia on the Order of reorganization of Kolkhozy and Sovkhozy," *Ekonomicheskaia Gazeta*, No. 3, January 1992, p. 1.

[126]Director of the department of agricultural statistics of Goskomstat, Viktor Nefedov, *Delovoi Mir*, No. 39, Feb. 27, 1992.

[127]"Radicals Criticize Draft Edict on Land," *Segodnia*, Oct. 22, 1993, p. 1. He was later forced to resign because of his radicalism. *Segodnia*, April 26, 1994, p. 2.

[128]Minister of Agriculture of Russia Viktor Khlystun, *Izvestia*, Feb. 17, 1992.

[129]The Chairman of the Land Committee, Roskomzem, Nikolai Komov, *Segodnia*, Nov. 26, 1994, p. 2.

[130]Regarding the social origins of farmers, see *Sovetskaia Rossia*, March 24, 1992 and *Nezavisimaia Gazeta*, April 29, 1992.

[131]Corresponding member of the Russian Academy of Science, Alan Soskiev, interview, *Ekonomicheskaia Gazeta*, No. 34, Aug. 1995, p. 4.

[132]John Crystal, president of the International Development Fund of Iowa, *Selskaia Zhyzn*, Nov. 6, 1991, p. 3.

[133]Yeltsin: "I keep on saying that the reorganization of collective and state farms does not mean they are going to be disbanded." *Ostankino Television*, Jan. 23, 1992. *FBIS-SOV*-92-016.

[134]Lapshin, interview, *Izvestia*, Nov. 27, 1993, p. 4.

[135]Viktor Khlystun, Chairman of Committee for Land Reform," *INTERFAX*, Nov. 6, 1991.

[136]"Decree of the President of Russia on the Regulation of Land Relations and the Development of Agrarian Reform in Russia," *Izvestia*, Oct. 29, 1993, p. 1.

[137]V. Zakharov, deputy chairman of the Committee of Agriculture and Food of the Parliament, *Ekonomika i Zhyzn*, No. 35, August 1993, p. 7.

[138]This figure derives from government data. *Delovoi Mir*, Sept. 14, 1995, p. 2.

[139]Stephen K. Wegren, "Rural Migration and Agrarian reform in Russia," *Europe-Asia Studies,* Vol. 47, No. 5, 1995, p. 881.

[140]Leonid Cheshinski, chairman of the Committee of Bread Products of the Ministry of Trade and Material Resources. *Rossiiskie Vesti,* Aug. 11, 1992.

[141]*Financial Izvestia*, Nov. 16, 1995, p. I.

[142]In 1993 the on-the-ground harvest was estimated to be 120 million tons. Only 99 million tons were threshed and stored. That is, about 18 percent of the grain was lost. See First Deputy Prime Minister Oleg Soskovets' interview, *INTERFAX,* June 20, 1994. In 1994 losses were about 17 percent. Yelena Yakovleva, "Russia managed to stop grain imports, not for long," *Izvestia,* Jan. 12, 1995, p. 2.

[143]Alexandr Belozertsev, "Production and Consumption of Grain in Russia," *Financial Izvestia*, April 21-27, 1994, p. VIII.

[144]Viktor Khlystun, Chairman of the Committee for Land Reform, *INTERFAX,* Nov. 6, 1991.

[145]I. Kalashnikov, "A Reliable Roof for the Grain," *Zemlia i Liudi,* No. 22, June 1993, pp. 1, 2.

[146]On these activities in the Kaluga *oblast*, for example, see Vladimir Sudakov, "The Formula of Happiness," *Delovoi Mir*, July 15, 1995, p. 5.

[147]Viktor Nefedov, *Delovoi Mir*, No. 39, Feb. 27, 1992.

[148]A. Malyi, "The comeback of MTS (machine-tractor stations)," *Ekonomika i Zhyzn*, No. 3, Jan. 1995, p. 20.

[149]Leonid Polezhayev, head of administration of Omsk *oblast*, interview, *Argumenty i Fakty*, No. 16, 1994, p. 12.

[150]*Kommunist* No. 8, 1985.

[151]Goskomstat, *Sotsialno-economicheskoe Polozhenie Rossii 1993 g.* (Moscow, 1994), pp. 44-45.

[152]*Argumenty i Fakty*, No. 26, June 1995, pp. 1, 2.

[153]Valery Konovalov, "There is more meat on the shelves," *Izvestia,* July 13, 1994, pp. 1-2.

[154]Aleksandr Belozertsev, "Production and Consumption of grain in Russia," *Financial Izvestia*, Apr. 21-27, 1994, p. VIII.

[155]Goskomstat, *Segodnia,* Oct. 15, 1994, p. 2.

[156]Zaveriukha, *ITAR-TASS,* Dec. 28, 1994.

[157]Deputy Prime Minister Alexandr Zaveriukha, *Rossiiskaia Gazeta*, Dec. 3, 1993, p. 1.

[158]Goskomstat, *Segodnia*, Jan. 17, 1995, p. 11.

[159]Leonid Cheshinsky, president of Roskhlebproduct, *INTERFAX,* Feb. 16, 1995.

[160]Andrei Sizov, "Russia's grain production is falling, while its exports are rapidly growing," *Financial Izvestia*, May 16, 1995, p. II.

[161]Vice-Premier Aleksandr Zaveriukha, interview, *ITAR-TASS*, June 28, 1995.

[162]Zaveriukha, interview, *Komsomolskaia Pravda,* Jan. 31, 1995. See also Andrei Sizov, "Russia's grain production," ibid.

[163]Goskomstat, *Segodnia*, Jan. 17, 1995, p. 11.

[164]Edwina Moreton, "Comrade Colossus: The Soviet Military Industry," in Curtis Keeble (ed.), *The Soviet State* (Boulder, CO: Westview, 1985), p. 88.

[165]From 1984 to 1988 the Soviet Union's hard-currency income from arms sales was about $64 billion. U.S. arms sales were about $50 billion. *SIPRI Yearbook* (Oxford: Oxford University Press, 1989).

[166]Dmitry Mikheyev, *The Rise and Fall of Gorbachev* (Indianapolis, Hudson Institute, 1992).

[167]British Defense Minister Tom King's speech in the House of Commons. C-SPAN, January 1990.

[168]Alan P. Pollard (ed.), *USSR: Facts and Figures*, Vol. 15 (New York: Academic International Press, 1991), p. 69. See also *Soviet Military Power 1990* (Washington, DC: U.S. Government Printing Office, 1991), and *Understanding Soviet Naval Developments* (Washington, DC: U.S. Government Printing Office, 1991), p. 63.

[169]This comparison was made by the respected military analyst Pavel Felgengauer. See "New tanks for Russia?" *Segodnia*, July 9, 1993, p. 1.

[170]*Krasnaia Zvezda*, Aug. 4, 1994, p. 2.

[171]*Russian Defense Business Directory* (U.S. Department of Commerce, 1993). See also, Julian Cooper *The Soviet Defense Industry and Economic Reform* (New York: Council on Foreign Relations Press, 1991), p. 12.

[172]*Delovoi Mir*, Dec. 5-11, 1994, p. 7.

[173]Chubais, interview, *Literaturnaia Gazeta*, May 23, 1995, p. 9.

[174]Yaroslav Golovanov, "The Sword and the Hammer," *Vek*, No. 12, No. 15, 1993.

[175]G. Kuznetsova, V. Yermakov and Yu. Volkov, researchers at the "Conversion" center, *Ekonomicheskaia Gazeta*, No. 3, Jan. 22, 1993, p. 18.

[176]Mikhail Malei, *Komsomolskaia Pravda*, Sept. 17, 1993, pp. 1, 2.

[177]Gaidar, "We are not building paradise. We are trying to build a normal life," *Trud*, June 28, 1994, pp. 1, 2.

[178]Gaidar, interview, *Argumenty i Fakty*, No. 25, June 1994, p. 2.

[179]Gaidar, "The race with the crisis," *Novoe Vremia*, No. 48, November 1991, p. 7.

[180]Gaidar, interview, *Trud*, Jan. 28, 1992, p. 2.

[181]Gaidar, interview, *Argumenty i Fakty*, No. 25, 1994, p. 2.

[182]Viktor Glukhikh, Chairman of the Committee for the Defense Industry, *Delovye Liudi*, April 1993, p. 22. See also Yakov Urinson, First Deputy Minister of the Economy, *ITAR-TASS*, June 28, 1994, and Gaidar, interview, *Argumenty i Fakty*, No. 25, 1994, p. 2.

[183]This figure is provided by Alexei Shalunov, President of the League of Defense Enterprises, *Nezavisimaia Gazeta*, June 8, 1994, p. 1.

[184]This figure is provided by V. Katkov, Deputy Prime Minister of Udmurdia, *Delovoi Mir*, Nov. 9, 1994, p. 6.

[185]Anders Aslund, "Russia's Success Story," *Foreign Affairs*, September/October, 1994, p. 63.

[186]Viktor Glukhikh, *Delovye Liudi*, April 1993, p. 22.

[187]Insiders said that the number of MIC factories should have been cut by 60 percent. See Leonid Kosals and Rozalina Ryvkina, *Segodnia*, Oct. 18, 1994, p. 9.

[188]Glukhikh, interview, *Nezavisimaia Gazeta*, Aug. 18, 1994, pp. 1, 2.

[189]Liudmila Pertsevaia, "Privatization, Defense Conversion work hand in hand," *Moscow News*, June 9-15, 1995, p. 8.

[190]*Financial Izvestia*, Aug. 18-24, 1994, p. IV.

[191]Glukhikh, *Delovye Liudi*, April 1993, p. 22.

[192]Lyalya Arslanova, "Privatizing the defence industry: with or without the intellect," *Delovye Liudi*, September 1994, p. 34.

[193]See "Swords and Ploughshares," *The Economist*, Jan. 16, 1993, p. 52.

[194]Viktor Glukhikh, *Delovye Liudi*, April 1993, p. 22.

[195]These figures are provided by A. Shalunov, president of the League for Support of Defense Enterprises, *Ekonomika i Zhyzn*, No. 15, April 1994, p. 1.

[196]These figures are provided by Viktor Glukhikh, *Delovye Liudi*, April 1993, p. 22. See also *Trud*, Dec. 1, 1992.

[197]This information is provided by Alexei Shalunov, President of the League of Defense Enterprises, *Nezavisimaia Gazeta*, June 8, 1994, p. 1.

[198]Glukhikh, *Izvestia*, Dec. 30, 1993, p. 4.

[199]Mikhail Malei, Russian television, Jan. 26, 1995, *FBIS-SOV-95-019*.

[200]Oleg Lobov, "The VPK Displays Goods to Good Effect." *Rossiiskie Vesti*, June 30, 1993, p. 5.

[201]These figures are provided by Alexandr Livshits, deputy director of the Analytical Center of the President's Administration, *Nezavisimaia Gazeta*, Dec. 23, 1993, p. 4.

[202]Goskomstat, *Delovoi Mir*, Jan. 30 - Feb. 5, 1995, pp. 12-13. See also Yakov Urinson, First Deputy Minister of the Economy, interview, *ITAR-TASS*, June 28, 1994.

[203]See, for example, the article about Saratov's SAPO, *Delovoi Mir*, No. 171, 1994.

[204]*Delovoi Mir*, No. 289, Dec. 26, 1994.

[205]*Rossiiskie Vesti*, April 9, 1994, p. 2.

[206]*Izvestia*, July 21, 1994, p. 2.

[207]*Izvestia*, March 17, 1995, p. 2.

[208]Yuri Ponomariov, "The Russian bus in the year 2000," *Moscow News*, No. 16, April 16, 1994, p. 8.

[209]Yelena Yakovleva, "Russia has managed to stop grain imports, not for long," *Izvestia*, Jan. 12, 1995, p. 2.

[210]*Izvestia*, Oct. 26, 1994, p. 2.

[211]Academician Valentin Pashin, "Will Russia remain a great maritime power?" *Segodnia*, Oct. 13, 1994, p. 6.

[212]A. Sharshunov, "The road into the future," *Ekonomika i Zhyzn*, No. 26, 1994, p. 24.

[213]V. Yurasov, *Gudok*, Oct. 27, 1994, p. 1.

[214]*Delovoi Mir*, Aug. 22-28, 1994, p. 24.

[215]Russian television Jan. 26, 1995, *FBIS-SOV-95-019*.

[216]*Segodnia*, Feb. 25, 1995, p. 3.

[217]Vladimir Radchuk, chief designer of KBKhA, *Delovoi Mir*, June 8, 1995, p. 4.

[218]General director Yevgeni Maizlakh, interview, *Delovoi Mir*, Nov. 1, 1994, p. 5.

[219]Julian Cooper, *The Soviet Defense Industry and Economic Reform* (New York: Council on Foreign Relations Press, 1991), p. 22.

[220]See the interview with Stepan Sulakshin, "Nobody's Cities," *Delovoi Mir*, July 19, 1994, p. 1.

[221]Viktor Mikhailov, Minister of Atomic Energy, interview, *Delovoi Mir*, Feb. 9, 1994, pp. 2-3.

[222]Shumeiko, interview, *INTERFAX*, July 21, 1994.

[223]Yuri Afanasiev is an example. See his "Seems Like Old Times? Russia's Place in the World," *Current History*, Oct. 1994, Vol. 93, No. 585, p. 305.

[224]Economic analyst Leonid Lopatin, *Delovoi Mir*, Dec. 15, 1994, p. 1. The military budget for 1995 FY was 48.7 trillion rubles. This figure is taken from Duma hearings. See *Segodnia*, March 16, 1995, p. 1.

[225]1995 Russian GNP is projected to reach 2,100 trillion rubles, while defense expenditures will be 76 trillion rubles. Vladimir Panskov, Minister of Finance, interview, *INTERFAX*, July 5, 1995.

[226]Moisei Gelman, *Delovoi Mir*, Dec. 27, 1995, p. 1.

[227]Glukhikh, interview, *Nezavisimaia Gazeta*, Aug. 18, 1994, pp. 1, 2; Anders Aslund, "Russia's Success Story," *Foreign Affairs*, September/October, 1994, p. 66.

[228]*Segodnia,* Dec. 14, 1994, p. 11.

[229]Leonid Kosals and Rozalina Ryvkina, *Segodnia,* Oct. 18, 1994, p. 9.

[230]Leonid Kosals and Rozalina Ryvkina, *Segodnia,* Oct. 18, 1994, p. 9.

[231]As one analyst noted, a disproportionate large number of "scientists became businessmen." See the unattributed article "In 1992, the loss to science through emigration was insignificant." *Izvestia*, April 30, 1993, p. 15.

[232]Andrei Sveshnikov, *Financial Izvestia*, April 26, 1994, p. I.

[233]This information is provided by the State Department. See Seymour M. Hersh, "The Wild East," *Atlantic Monthly*, June 1994, p. 68. See also the interview of General Vitaly Yakovlev, an official of the Russian Ministry of Defense, *Literaturnaia Gazeta*, June 1, 1994.

[234]Scott Gerber, "The Financial Revolution," U.S. Department of Commerce, *BISNIS BULLETIN*, Jan./Feb. 1995, p. 1.

[235]*Financial Izvestia*, July 4, 1995, p. I.

[236]The number increased 19 percent in one year. *Financial Izvestia*, May 25, 1994, p. XIII.

[237]Goskomstat, *Rossiiskaia Gazeta*, March 31, 1995, p. 3.

[238]The number was cited in hearings in the Duma, See *Segodnia,* Nov. 29, 1994, p. 12.

[239]*Financial Izvestia*, Sept. 14, 1995, p. I.

[240]Regarding the creation of the office enforcing the tax code, see the article by the chief tax inspector of Moscow, Dmitry Chernik in *Delovoi Mir*, Dec. 12-18, 1994, p. 25.

[241]*Moscow News*, Feb. 4-10, 1994, p. 7.

[242]*Financial Izvestia*, Dec. 15, 1994, p. I.

[243]*Rossiiskaia Gazeta*, Dec. 8, 1994, pp. 4-15.

[244]These are the words of Lane Blumenfeld, director of the U.S.-based Center for Institutional Reform, quoted in David Filipov, "Civil Code Promises to Untie Red Tape," *The Moscow Times,* July 31, 1994, p. 21.

[245]*The Economist*, Feb. 18, 1995, p. 51.

[246]Frederick Berliner, senior adviser to KPMG/Barents Group, *The New York Times*, Sept. 7, 1995, p. A14.

[247]Aleksandr Livshits, interview, *Delovoi Mir*, July 29, 1994, p. 1.

[248]A managing director of KPMG, Jonathan Buckley, made this claim: "In three to four years, Russia's securities market will look like New York or Hong Kong," *The Moscow Times*, July 31, 1994, p. 48.

[249]Thousands of automated bank machines were installed in the country. Most Bank alone installed 600 of them. *Delovoi Mir*, Sept. 30, 1994, p. 5.

[250]Veronika Novikova, "Moscow Banks," *Delovoi Mir*, No. 289, Dec. 26, 1994, p. 5. Six Russian banks were on the list of the thousand leading banks of the world. *Financial Izvestia*, July 18, 1995, p. I. Eighteen Russian banks were certified by the European Bank for Reconstruction and Development. *Financial Izvestia*, July 20, 1995, p. I.

[251]Central Bank official Andrei Kozlov, *Kommersant*, No. 49, Dec. 1994, p. 49.

[252]These are VISA's estimates. *Segodnia*, Sept. 29, 1995 p. 4. In 1995, Moscow's Stolichny bank and VISA electronics planned to issue 1 million credit cards. *Delovye Liudi*, May 1995, p. 12. See also, Sergei Mitin, *Financial Izvestia*, June 29, 1995, p. III.

[253]*Delovoi Mir*, July 14, 1995, p. 4.

²⁵⁴Chrystia Freedland, "Russia's Credit Craving Moves to Regions," *Financial Times*, July 11, 1995, p. 3.

²⁵⁵*The Economist*, Jan. 7, 1995, p. 60.

²⁵⁶Alec Kinnear, "Boom and Bust," *Business Central Europe*, April 1994, pp. 55-56.

²⁵⁷Liudmila Pertsevaia, "Privatization, Defense Conversion Work Hand in Hand," *Moscow News*, June 9-15, 1995.

²⁵⁸In 1994 foreign investors bought an estimated 10 percent of the shares of Russian joint stock companies. *Ekonomika i Zhyzn*, No. 26, June 1995, p. 8.

²⁵⁹Chalva Chigrinski, President of S+T company, *Delovye Liudi*, May 1995, p. XV.

²⁶⁰In April 1995, 30 percent of the shares of the ailing automobile giant ZIL were purchased by the financial giant Mikrodin. See *Kommersant*, May 2, 1995. In July Koloss, a food giant, launched a public tender to buy a controlling interest in Red October, a well-known chocolate factory. See *Financial Times*, July 12, 1995. See also the interview of Petr Aven, president, AlfaBank, *Delovoi Mir*, June 24, 1995, p. 6.

²⁶¹John Thornhill, "Debt market offers rewards for the brave," *Financial Times*, Sept. 14, 1995, p. 3.

²⁶²See the report of the Analytical Agency Inter-Rate, *Delovoi Mir*, July 19, 1995, p. 2.

²⁶³Chrystia Freeland, "Heart Illness Puts Role of Yeltsin in Doubt," *Financial Times*, July 12, 1995, pp. 1, 12.

²⁶⁴Gaidar, interview, *Ekonomika i Zhyzn*, Dec. 9, 1993, p. 1.

²⁶⁵The production of *Kirovets* heavy tractors, for example, fell from 28,000 in 1988 to about 1,000 in 1994. *Gudok*, Oct. 27, 1994, p. 1.

²⁶⁶Valeri Saikin, general director of AMO ZIL, interview, *Kommercheski Vestnik*, July 11-12, 1995, p. 8.

²⁶⁷The production of the 1.5 ton *Gazel* truck increased from 13,000 in 1993 to 60,000 in 1995. See *Segodnia*, Jan. 18, 1995, p. 11. For information about new models of the *Gazel,* see *Financial Izvestia*, Oct. 19, 1995, p. II.

²⁶⁸Production of Volgas grew almost twofold to 106,000 in 1993 and 118,000 in 1994. *Kommersant*, May 2, 1995, p. 17.

²⁶⁹In 1993, production of spare parts for automobiles was up 23 percent, and production of tires 10 percent. *Nezavisimaia Gazeta*, Dec. 23, 1993, p. 4. See also A. Sharshunov, "The road into the future," *Ekonomika i Zhyzn*, No. 26, 1994, p. 24. The remarks of an automobile expert were characteristic: "Now we know what kind of cars and trucks are in demand and can concentrate on them." Aleksandr Solntsev, *Delovoi Mir*, Dec. 3, 1994, p. 5.

²⁷⁰*Kommersant*, Aug 11, 1993, p. 18.

²⁷¹In 1995 the Russian company West, for example, plans to produce 100,000 personal computers. Sergei Borodin, "Russian computers?" *Segodnia*, Jan. 19, 1995, p. 9.

²⁷²*Ekonomika i Zhyzn*, No. 7, February 1995, p. 1.

²⁷³Dozens of them can arrange for international travel. Nikolai Novichkov, *Financial Izvestia*, Nov. 17, 1994, p. IV.

²⁷⁴The estimate appears in, *Izvestia*, Dec. 14, 1994, p. 13. See also *Argumenty i Fakty*, No. 12, 1995, p. 9.

²⁷⁵*Moscow News*, Jan. 13-19, 1995, p. 8. See also *Financial Izvestia*, Oct. 25, 1994, p. IV; and Anastasia Naryshkina, "Effectiveness of domestic advertising is much higher than that of the West," *Segodnia,* Nov. 1, 1994, p. 13. One minute of advertising on Russian television costs $8,000, the third most expensive in eastern Europe, after Hungary and Poland. See *Argumenty i Fakty*, No. 47, 1994, p. 12. The volume of advertising

in newspapers increased in two years from R3 billion in 1993 to R150 billion in 1995, or seven times in real terms. See *Financial Izvestia*, Feb. 9, 1995, p. VIII.

[276]See Goskomstat, *Rossiiskaia Gazeta*, March 31, 1995, p. 3. and *Torgovaia Gazeta*, Dec. 28, 1994, p. 2.

[277]Briansk's automobile repair factory, for example, expanded its volume of work five times. *Delovoi Mir*, July 7, 1995, p. 2.

[278]Yuri Yurkov, chairman of Goskomstat, "Statistical mirror of the market," *Ekonomika i Zhyzn*, No. 35, August 1994, p. 1. See also Mikhail Berger, *Izvestia*, Sept. 7, 1994, p. 2, and Yevgeni Vasilchuk, "Reforms from the structural point of view," *Financial Izvestia*, July 28 - Aug. 3, 1994, p. II. According to Goskomstat, the increase was 50 percent. See *Financial Izvestia*, Jan. 19, 1995, p. I. See also Leonid Rybakovski (ed.), *Naselenie SSSR Za 70 Let*, (Moskva: Nauka, 1988), p. 207.

[279]Goskomstat, *Delovoi Mir*, Jan. 18, 1995, p. 4. In 1995 communications services tripled in volume and reached R21 trillion. This claim is made by Vladimir Bulgak, Minister of Communications, , *Delovoi Mir*, July 29, 1995, p. 1.

[280]Goskomstat, *Financial Izvestia*, Jan. 19, 1995, p. II.

[281]According to Goskomstat in 1994, it was R356 trillion. See *Financial Izvestia*, Jan. 19, 1995, p. II.

[282]Aslund, *How Russia Became a Market Economy*, p. 44.

[283]Urinson, interview, *Kommersant*, Nov. 22, 1994, p. 21.

[284]*Rossiiskaia Gazeta*, Nov. 29, 1994, p. 3.

[285]Oleg Soskovets, *Delovoi Mir*, Oct. 22, 1994, p. 1.

[286]In Gaidar's words: "Now we know what is likely to happen if this or that monetary lever is pulled." *Segodnia*, Dec. 30, 1994, p. 2.

[287]Aslund, *How Russia Became a Market Economy*, p. 275. See also Andrei Illarionov and also "Financial Stabilization in Russia," *Delovoi Mir*, July 10-16, 1995, pp. 27-28.

[288]Jonathan Steele, *Eternal Russia: Yeltsin, Gorbachev, and the Mirage of Democracy* (Cambridge, MA: Harvard University Press, 1994), Chapter 12.

[289]John Ross, economic adviser of a Labor Party faction in the British Parliament, "The Price of Catastrophe," *Delovoi Mir*, Dec. 5-11, 1994, p. 22.

[290]Sergei Glaziev, *Krasnaia Zvezda*, Nov. 29, 1993, p. 1.

[291]Goskomstat, *INTERFAX*, Jan 17, 1995.

[292]Yuri Yurkov, chairman of Goskomstat, *Trud*, Oct. 12, 1994, p. 2.

[293]Istvan Dobozi, *Transition*, Vol. 6, No. 9-10, September-October 1995, p. 20.

[294]Istvan Dobozi and Gerhard Pohl, the World Bank, "Real Output in Transition Economies — Forget GDP, Try Power Consumption Data!" *Transition*, Vol. 6, No. 1-2, Jan.-Feb. 1995, p. 17. Indeed, the output of the energy sectors fell only 20 percent between 1990 and 1995. Deputy Minister of Energy and Fuel Vitali Bushuyev, *Financial Izvestia*, July 20, 1995, p. IV. Since 1991, the consumption of electrical power fell by 20 percent. See *Delovoi Mir*, July 2, 1995, p. 11.

[295]There is no consensus on how much industrial production fell. According to *Kommersant* analysts, in three years it fell by 54.3 percent. See *Kommersant*, No. 31, Aug. 23, 1994, p. 46. According to other analysts, by August 1994 industrial production had fallen by about 55.6 percent compared to January 1990. See *Financial Izvestia*, Sept. 8-14, 1994, p. II. In 1994 GNP fell 15 percent. Goskomstat, *INTERFAX*, Jan. 17, 1995. In the first three months of 1995 it fell a further 6 percent. Goskomstat, *INTERFAX*, Apr. 22, 1995.

[296]Yuri Ivanov, deputy chairman of the Statistical Committee of the CIS, *Financial Izvestia*, July 14-20, 1994, p. VIII.

[297]See the interesting discussion in D. Valovoi, "Piramida" (Pyramid), *Pravda*, Sept. 19, 1988.

[298]Nikolai Ryzhkov, Prime Minister under Gorbachev, once confessed that he did not have an accurate account of defense expenditures.

[299]Philip Hanson observed: "The [economic] statistics have become very dicey... We have seen so much fudging and distortions." *Wall Street Journal*, March 10, 1987. "It's never happened that the Soviets would publish such blatantly inconsistent numbers," remarked Jan Vanous, president of the Washington-based firm PlanEcon, Inc. See *The Washington Post*, Oct. 17, 1989. Vitali Golovachev called Soviet statistics a "distorting mirror." See *Trud*, Oct. 12, 1994, p. 1.

[300]At least it was accepted by the "revisionists," as Walter Laqueur called them. *The Dream That Failed*, pp. 91-109. Marshall Goldman, for example, wrote: "The only example of rapid and impressive economic growth in the twentieth century that Western economists had to draw upon was the Soviet Union." See "China and the Soviet Model," *International Security*, Vol. 5, No. 2, Fall 1980, p. 55.

[301]Martin Malia, "From Under the Rubble - What?" *Problems of Communism*, April 1992.

[302]See Robert Conquest, *The Washington Post*, April 2, 1990.

[303]John W. Wright and Lincoln Paine (eds.), *The Universal Almanac: 1990* (New York: Universal Press, 1990), pp. 481, 496. See also *The World Fact Book* (Washington, D. C.), 1989.

[304]*The Universal Almanac* (New York: 1990).

[305]As the German ambassador to the United States once said at the Hudson Institute.

[306]As Daniel Yergin and Thane Gustafson wrote, entrepreneurs are forced to "minimize figures to avoid the taxman (whether from the government or the mafia) and to evade regulations." "Let's get down to business, comrade," *Financial Times*, July 9/10, 1994, pp. I, X.

[307]Viktor Chernomyrdin made this point. See *Delovoi Mir*, July 16, 1994, p. 1.

[308]Despite the obvious "rapid growth of the private economy," wrote Yergin and Gustafson, "No one has any idea how big this market economy is." Daniel Yergin and Thane Gustafson, "Let's get down to business, comrade," *Financial Times*, July 9/10, 1994, pp. I, X.

[309]Yuri Yurkov, chairman of Goskomstat, the Russian Federation State Committee for Statistics. Interview, *Trud*, Oct. 12, 1994, pp. 1-2.

[310]Forty-six percent of retail trade is in unregistered consumer goods, according to V. Salganov, head of the economic crimes department of the Ministry of Interior. His claim appears in *Ekonomika i Zhyzn*, No. 37, Sept. 1994, p. 1. According to Andrei Neshchadin of the Expert Institute of the Union of Industrialists and Entrepreneurs, the figure is 42 percent. See *Izvestia*, Sept. 21, 994, p. 9. The figure is about 50 percent according to the Ministry of Economics. See *Torgovaia Gazeta*, Dec. 28, 1994, p. 2.

[311]*PlanEcon Report*, Vol. IX, No. 44-45, 1993, p. 41.

[312]The Ministry of Foreign Trade estimated that imports worth aproximately $ 7.5 billion are being smuggled into Russia by about three million private shoppers in their luggage. These imports, of course, are omitted in official statistics. See Artiom Shadrin, *Delovoi Mir*, July 30, 1994, pp. 4-5. See also Stephanie Capparell, "Turks' 'Luggage Trade' with CIS Countries Benefits Both Sides," *Wall Street Journal*, May 31, 1995, pp. 1, 4.

[313]Yuri Yurkov, chairman of Goskomstat, "Statistical mirror of the market," *Ekonomika i Zhyzn*, No. 35, August 1994, p. 1.

[314]Yuri Yurkov, chairman of Goskomstat, *Trud*, Oct. 12, 1994, p. 2.

[315]Elizabeth Hebert, "Markets Emerge from Chaos," *The Moscow Times,* July 31, 1994, p. 49.

[316]Polish economist Marek Dombrovsky made the same point about the Polish economy. See "Economic slump leads to healthier economy," *Financial Izvestia*, Nov. 22, 1994, p. II.

[317]Aslund, *How Russia Became a Market Economy*, p. 279. See also Istvan Dobozi and Gerhard Pohl, the World Bank, "Real Output in Transition Economies — Forget GDP, Try Power Consumption Data!" *Transition*, Vol. 6, No. 1-2, Jan.-Feb. 1995, p. 17. Six months after this chapter was written, Goskomstat revised the figure for the decline of Russia's GNP in 1991 to 1994 from 47.3 percent to 35.2 percent. See Yelena Fedorova, "Asseassment of GNP became more reliable." *Financial Izvestia*, Sept. 29, 1995, p. II.

[318]*Financial Izvestia*, Dec. 21, 1995, p. I.

[319]Marshall I. Goldman, "Losing Ground," *World Monitor*, March 1991, p. 42.

[320]In January 1992 Russia's gold reserves were 160 tons. Yevgeni Bychkov, interview, *Pravitelstvenny Vestnik*, No. 48, Nov. 1991. See also Petr Aven, interview, *Kommersant*, Oct. 11, 1994, p. 17, and Andrei Illarionov, *Rossiiskie Vesti*, Nov. 27, 1993, p. 1.

[321]Goskomstat, *Segodnia*, Jan. 17, 1995, p. 11.

[322]Tatiana Paramonova, interview, *Delovoi Mir*, Aug. 26, 1995, p. 1.

[323]Deputy Prime Minister Oleg Davydov, *Rossiiskie Vesti,* Feb. 9, 1995, p. 1. See also John Thornhill, "Russia seeks more time to repay its debt," *Financial Times,* Aug. 27-28, 1994, p. 24.

[324]Burbulis, interview, Russian television, Jan. 10, 1992. *FBIS-SOV-92-008.*

[325]Friedrich Hayek, *Individualism and Economic Order* (Chicago: University of Chicago Press, 1948), p. 189.

[326]Aslund, *How Russia Became a Market Economy*, p. 11.

[327]Walter Laqueur, *The Dream That Failed*, p. 192.

[328]See Marshall I. Goldman's book, op. cit. See also Alexandr Dalin, "Where Have All the Flowers Gone?" in Gail W. Lapidus (ed.), *The New Russia: Troubled Transformation* (Boulder, CO: Westview Press, 1995), p. 251.

[329]Quoted in Richard Stevenson, "An American in Moscow," *The New York Times,* Sept. 20, 1995, p. C4.

[330]Michael McFaul, "Why Russia's Politics Matter," *Foreign Affairs*, Vol. 74, No. 1, 1995, p. 88.

[331]Aslund, *How Russia Became a Market Economy*, p. 312.

Chapter 6

[1]Feodor Burlatski, "The late Yeltsin: Where to lead Russia?" *Nezavisimaia Gazeta*, Feb. 17, 1995, p. 3. See also G. Vodolazov and Yu. Burtin, "Russian *Nomenklatura* Democracy Was Built," *Izvestia*, June 1, 1994, p. 1.

[2]Eduard Limonov, former exiled writer, chairman of the National-Bolshevik Party, interview, *Argumenty i Fakty*, No. 32, 1993, p. 6.

[3]Yuri Vlasov, "We are drowning while the orchestra is playing on the top deck." *Sovetskaia Rossia*, Nov. 14, 1992, p. 6.

[4]The Russian Communist Party leader Gennadi Ziuganov declared: "Mighty industry was ruined, great science destroyed, the majority of the social gains destroyed," while the effect on the population corresponded to "the universally accepted definition of geno-

cide." See the political report at the Third Congress of the CPRF, *Sovetskaia Rossia*, Jan. 24, 1995, p. 3.

[5]David E. Powell, Harvard University, "Free from Communism, Russia rushes toward catastrophe," *Insight*, July 25, 1994, p. 37.

[6]Seymour M. Hersh, "The Wild East," *Atlantic Monthly*, June 1994, p. 86.

[7]Natalia Gevorkian, "How to Survive in Russia," *Moscow News*, Sept. 15-24, 1996, p. 21.

[8]According to Mikhail Berger, there are seventy casinos in Moscow. See "Russian Roulette doesn't Recognize the Ruble," *Izvestia*, July 29, 1995, p. 5.

[9]Alessandra Stanley, "In Moscow Again, Clubs Cater to 'Members Only,'" *The New York Times*, Aug. 4, 1995, p. A1.

[10]Alexandr Kharitonov and Gergi Rozon, "The Amazing Reality of Construction Technology," *Delovye Liudi*, May 1995, p. XXII.

[11]Andrew Borowiec, *The Washington Times*, Jan. 22, 1995, p. A7.

[12]According to the Institute for Sociopolitical Research, three years after the reforms began, 42 percent of people said that they have yielded nothing positive, and 39 percent—that results were negative. Only 8 percent believed that results were positive. See *Pravda*, Dec. 7, 1994, p. 4 and Walter Laqueur, *The Dream That Failed* (New York: Oxford University Press, 1994), p. VIII. David Powell, referring to "leading specialists," claimed that about 90 percent of the Russian population live below the poverty level. See "Free from Communism," op. cit.

[13]These claims were made in presentations by Radio Free Europe analysts Vera Tolz, Alexander Rahr, and Elizabeth Teague. See *RFE/RL Research Report* Vol. 3, no. 24, June 17, 1994, p. 4. The Chairman of the Duma Committee for Economic Policy, Sergei Glaziev, claimed that "everything is falling apart." See *Segodnia*, Oct. 27, 1994, p. 2.

[14]Powell, "Free from Communism, p. 37.

[15]This question is taken from a private letter of an American farmer who has traveled to Russia.

[16]Anders Aslund, *Dagens Nyheter*, Apr. 3 1994, p. A4. *FBIS-SOV-94-067*.

[17]The statement is by Bernard Cohen, correspondent of *Liberation*, quoted in *Moscow News*, Nov. 4-10, 1994, p. 7.

[18]Mikhail Sologub, a French economist, quoted in *Delovoi Mir*, June 11-17, 1994. p. 30.

[19]Anders Aslund, "Russia's success story," *Foreign Affairs*, September/October, 1994.

[20]Robert Kaiser revealed the list of topics that were subjected to censorship. It is too long to be quoted here but it included all aspects of life which, if presented honestly, could have cast a shadow of a doubt on the official picture of the Soviet system. See *Russia: People and Power* (New York: Atheneum, 1976), pp. 243-244.

[21]Regarding the corruption of the top party *nomenklatura*, see V. Sokolov, "Bandito-Crats," *Literaturnaia Gazeta*, No. 33, 1988, and Pavel Nikitin, "A Pack," *Ogoniok*, No. 49, 1990.

[22]Regarding the army see Sergei Kaledin, "Stroibat," *Novy Mir*, No. 4, 1989 and Yuri Poliakov, "Sto Dnei Do Prikaza," *Yunost*, No. 11, 1987. Regarding life among juvenile delinquents, see Leonid Gabyshev, "Odlian," *Novy Mir*, No. 6, 1989.

[23]One study even concluded that the terrible social conditions led to profound genetic changes in the population. See *Smena*, No. 12, 1989.

[24]Svetlana Alekseyeva, *Sovetskaia Rossia*, Nov. 12, 1994, p. 2.

[25]According to the Sociological service of *Rossiiskaia Gazeta*, 70 percent called inflation the main concern. See *Rossiiskaia Gazeta*, March 31, 1995, p. 2.

[26]Marshall I. Goldman, "Losing Ground," *World Monitor*, March 1991, p. 42.

[27]Goskomstat, *Rossiiskaia Gazeta*, Dec. 26, 1991, p. 3.

[28]Goskomstat, *INTERFAX*, Jan. 17, 1995.

[29]Mikhail Berger, "Chernomyrdin promises market not bazaar," *Izvestia*, Dec. 15, 1992, p. 1.

[30]The calculations were made on the basis of both official and market prices. See Keith Bush, "Retail Prices in Moscow and Four Western Cities in March 1982", *Radio Liberty Research Supplement*, June 4, 1982, p. 7.

[31]Aslund, *How Russia Became a Market Economy*, p. 275. See also Andrei Illarionov et al., "Financial Stabilization in Russia," *Delovoi Mir*, July 10-16, 1995, pp. 27-28.

[32]David Lipton and Jeffrey D. Sachs, "Prospects for Russia's Economic Reforms," *Brookings Papers on Economic Activity*, No. 2. 1992, p. 237.

[33]See excerpts from the book by G. Vachnadze, *The Military Mafia of the Kremlin* in *Moskovskaia Pravda*, Aug. 16, 1994, p. 8.

[34]The quotation is from Ariel Cohen, a Heritage Foundation analyst. See "Crime and corruption in Eurasia: A threat to democracy and international security," *Backgrounder*, No. 1025, March 17, 1995.

[35]The quotation is from Nikolai Zlobin, who even suggested that "this network of [mafia bureaucracy] could eventually stabilize society." See "The mafiacracy takes over," *The New York Times*, July 26, 1994, p. A15.

[36]Consider the following newspaper headline: "The state is losing the war with economic criminality. Russia is being destroyed not by arms but by financial adventurers." See *Nezavisimaia Gazeta*, Sept. 10, 1994, p. 1.

[37]Claire Sterling, quoted by Michael Ledeen, *Insight*, Sept. 26, 1994, p. 21. This statement almost exactly replicates Gennadi Ziuganov's assertion: "We have slid toward the despotism of the criminal-political mafia." See *Rossia*, Dec. 14, 1994, p. 1.

[38]In November 1994, 74 percent of Russian respondents expressed more concern with crime than with preserving human rights. Public Opinion Foundation, *INTERFAX*, Nov. 17, 1994; According to the sociological service of *Rossiiskaia Gazeta*. Fifty six percent of respondents named crime as their major concern. *Rossiiskaia Gazeta*, Mar. 31, 1995, p. 2.

[39]The Soviet Union claimed to have had crime rates five to seven times lower than those of West European nations. See *Izvestia*, Oct. 18, 1994, p. 5.

[40]Kaiser, *Russia: People and Power*, p. 243.

[41]Aleksei Iliushenko, Acting Procurator General, *Rossiiskaia Gazeta*, March 4, 1995, p. 7.

[42]*Izvestia*, Oct. 18, 1994, p. 1.

[43]*Report on the USSR*, vol. 1, No. 37, Sept. 15, 1989, p. 9.

[44]See *Izvestia*, Nov. 1, 1988, and Nov. 16 and 19, 1989, and *Pravda*, Sept. 17, 1989. The chairman of the Supreme Soviet Commission on Transport and Communications, V. Tetenov, spoke of acts of sabotage and terrorism on the railroad. See *Literaturnaia Gazeta*, Oct. 11, 1989.

[45]A. Katusev, the deputy general prosecutor of the USSR. See *Pravda*, March 23, 1989. See also Lieutenant Colonel of the MVD Dr. Alexandr Gurov, *Literaturnaia Gazeta*, No. 29, July 19, 1989.

[46]Kriuchkov, *Izvestia*, Oct. 26, 1989.

[47]Anatoli Golovkov, "The Phantom of Civil War," *Ogoniok*, No. 14, 1991, p. 4.

[48]The most influential liberal magazines and newspapers wrote about the merger of the organized criminal world with the party-state apparatus. See *Ogoniok*, No. 48, 1988.

[49]Vladimir Sokolov, *Literaturnaia Gazeta*, Aug. 17, 1988.

[50]*Ogoniok* No. 48, 1988, p 25.

[51]Yevgeni Dodolev, *Nedelia*, No. 29, 1988. Among western discussions of this subject see Jeffry Klugman, "The Psychology of Soviet Corruption, Indiscipline, and Resistance to Reform," *Political Psychology*, Vol. 7, No. 1, 1986. See also Klugman's *The New Soviet Elite* (New York: Praeger, 1989).

[52]Shakhrai, "There is no such party," *Izvestia*, Dec. 4, 1991.

[53]Konstantin Simis, *USSR: The Corrupt Society: The secret world of Soviet capitalism* (New York: Simon and Schuster, 1982).

[54]For more on the subject, see Georgi Rozhnov, "Extra Prison Cells," *Ogoniok*, No. 20, May 1989, pp. 11-15.

[55]A. Illesh, "Who and why serves time?" *Izvestia*, Mar. 13, 1989. See also Liudmila Salnikova, "Kids' Games," *Ogoniok*, No. 32, 1990, pp. 21-24.

[56]This figure is cited by Petr Filippov. See *Crossroads*, Oct. 15, 1994, p. 7.

[57]A. Kunitsyn, head of the information-analytical department of the Ministry of Justice. *Izvestia*, Mar. 13, 1989. See also *Literaturnaia Gazeta*, No. 9, 1989, p. 10.

[58]Studies of the Italian mafia show that "the mafioso-entrepreneur is indeed an innovator, introducing 'new productive combinations' that give him competitive advantages over other entrepreneurs." See Pino Arlacchi, *Mafia Business: The mafia ethic and the spirit of capitalism* (New York: Verso, 1987), p. xv.

[59]Artiom Vetrov, "Russian mafiosi change priorities," *Segodnia*, Aug. 9, 1995, p. 7.

[60]The figure appears in a study by the highly respected sociologist Olga Kryshtanovskaia. See "Portrait of the contemporary business elite," *Delovoi Mir*, Dec. 28, 1994, p. 9.

[61]Boris Sinelnikov, "Russian Mafia: You'll get to know it!" *Novoe Russkoe Slovo*, *Delovoi Mir*, Nov. 18, 1994, p. 24.

[62]Public opinion polls reveal that 73 percent of the population were convinced that criminal structures and the state bureaucracy implement state power. An additional 24 percent thought that the president does so. Nugzar Betaneli, director of the Institute of Sociology of Parliamentarianism, *Obshchaia Gazeta*, Dec. 2, 1994, p. 9.

[63]Jim Leitzel, Clifford Gaddy, and Michael Alexeev, "Mafiosi and Matrioshki," *The Brookings Review*, Vol. 13, No. 1, Winter 1995, p. 27. See also Carol S. Carson, "The underground economy: An introduction," *Survey of Current Business*, No. 7, 64, July 1984, pp. 106-119.

[64]Leonid Paidiev, "The mafia experiences a crisis," *Nezavisimaia Gazeta*, Dec. 24, 1994, p. 1.

[65]Vladimir Gurevich, *Moscow News*, March 17-23, 1995, p. 2.

[66]Rustam Narzikulov, "The Liberation From Superliberalism; the Decommercialization of the Russian State," *Segodnia*, Jan. 4, 1994, p. 8.

[67]Artem Vetrov, "The New Drug Lords," *Segodnia*, April 11, 1995, p. 7.

[68]Andrei Nechayev, "Statistics Know Everything," *Delovoi Mir*, Sept. 2, 1995, p. 5.

[69]Iliushenko, *Rossiiskaia Gazeta*, March 4, 1995, p. 7.

[70]The figures are cited in a report by the MVD, *Segodnia*, Feb. 23, 1995, p. 7. Still, by Western standards incidents of drug-related crimes remain extremely low. See the interview of drug enforcement agents, *Delovoi Mir*, June 20, 1995, p. 8.

[71]*Izvestia*, Aug. 5, 1995, p. 1.

[72]The figure in appears in the report by the MVD, *Segodnia*, Feb. 23, 1995, p. 7.

[73]Valeri Velichko, *Rossiiskie Vesti*, Aug. 16, 1995, p. 2.

[74]V. Salganov, head of the economic crimes department of the MVD, *Ekonomika i Zhyzn*, No. 37, Sept. 1994, p. 1. See also John Lloyd, "Violence turns Moscow into gun city," *Financial Times*, Sep. 2/3, 1995, p. 3.

[75]Rustam Narzikulov, "The Liberation From Superliberalism; the Decommercialization of the Russian State," *Segodnia*, Jan. 4, 1994, p. 8.

[76]Viktor Pokhmelkin, head of the Duma working group on preparation of the criminal code, interview, *Segodnia*, Aug. 2, 1995, p. 5.

[77]*INTERFAX*, July 19, 1995.

[78]In 1995 the number of students enrolled in police academies tripled relative to the previous year. In addition, 170 MVD officers were trained in the USA, Britain, and Austria. *INTERFAX*, Aug. 29, 1995.

[79]As Duma speaker Ivan Rybkin said, the Russian security forces have never been so well equipped. See *Delovoi Mir*, Aug. 11, 1995, p. 1.

[80]*Kommersant-Daily*, July 28, 1995, p. 14.

[81]Claire Sterling, "The Growing Power of Russia's Mob," *The New Republic*, April 11, 1994, pp. 19-20.

[82]*Rossiiskaia Gazeta*, Aug. 10, 1995, p. 2; *Pravda,* Nov. 30, 1994, p. 3; *Trud*, Nov. 10, 1994, p. 2; and *Izvestia*, Oct. 21, 1994, p. 5. Yevgeni Fedorov, chairman of the Duma subcommittee for economic security, estimated that 41,000 businesses are controlled by organized crime. See *Delovye Liudi*, May, 1995, p. 7.

[83]Deputy chief of the MVD Main Directorate, Major General Aleksandr Dementiev, *Kuranty*, Mar. 26, 1995, p. 9. In 1994 1,868 gangs with, on average, thirty members were operating in Russia. See A. Pyro, *Rossiiskaia Gazeta*, July 22, 1994, p. 15.

[84]Edmund Andrews, "The Mob's Truly Sorry: Killing Upsets the Police," *The New York Times*, Sept. 6, 1995, p. A4.

[85]Dementiev, *Kuranty*, March 26, 1995, *op. cit.* In September 1994 the MVD estimated that 1500 permanent criminal groups were operating in Russia. See *Izvestia*, Sept. 7, 1994, p. 4.

[86]Dementiev, *Kuranty*, Mar. 26, 1995, *op. cit.* Yevgeni Fedorov, the chairman of the Duma subcommittee for economic security, said that in 1994 the net income of organized crime was 1.5 trillion rubles. See *Delovye Liudi*, May 1995, p. 7.

[87]According to the Federal Council's data, organized crime controls finances equal to 0.2 percent of GNP. See *Pravda,* Nov. 30, 1994, p. 3.

[88]*Kommersant-Daily*, July 28, 1995, p. 14.

[89]Even major general Aleksandr Gurov, an outspoken champion of the fight against organized crime, has agreed that such a threat does not currently exist. See *Doverie*, No. 8, Sept. 1994, p. 5.

[90]These percentages are calculated on the basis of data gathered by the analytical center of *Izvestia*. See *Izvestia*, Oct. 18, 1994, p. 1. The 6 percent decline to 2,632,708 crimes in 1994 is taken into account. Aleksei Iliushenko, acting procurator general, *Rossiiskaia Gazeta*, March 4, 1995, p. 7. See also Vadim Bakatin, *Moskovskaia Pravda*, April 19, 1995, p. 10.

[91]The figure is provided by the MVD, *Segodnia*, Feb. 23, 1994, p. 7.

[92]*Ibid.*

[93]For nine-month data see *Izvestia*, Oct. 26, 1995, p. 1.

[94]Out of about 130 explosions reported in Moscow in seventeen months (February 1993-June 1994), during which 25 people were killed, almost all were economically, not politically, motivated. See Vladislav Pavliutkin, *Krasnaia Zvezda*, July 13, 1994, p. 2. Since the second putsch, the Federal Counterintelligence Services reported the existence of only one neofascist group: the "Werewolf Legion," which planned terrorist acts against political leaders. See *Segodnia*, July 6, 1994, p. 7. See also *Rossiiskaia Gazeta*, July 6, 1994, p. 8.

[95]*Izvestia*, Oct. 18-22, 1994.

[96]*Izvestia*, Jan. 14, 1994, p. 2.

[97]According to the MVD, *Segodnia*, Feb. 23, 1994, p. 7.

[98]Duma Human Rights Committee's report, *Doverie*, No. 8, Sept. 1994, p. 5.

[99]In Moscow 1,353 people were killed; *Izvestia*, Jan. 14, 1994, p. 2. In New York 2,345 were killed; *The New York Times*, Jan. 28, 1994.

[100]*Crime in the United States, 1992 Uniform Crime Reports* (Washington, D.C.: Federal Bureau of Investigation, 1993), p. 58.

[101]The German Minister of Internal Affairs, Manfred Kanter, as quoted in *Delovoi Mir*, Aug. 4, 1995, p. 7.

[102]Officials of the MVD estimate that about 70 percent of Russian crimes are not accounted for in crime statistics. See Valeri Velichko, *Rossiiskie Vesti*, Aug. 16, 1995, p. 2.

[103]Richard Lotspeich, "Crime in the Transition Economies," *Europe-Asia Studies*, Vol. 47, No. 4, 1995, p. 559.

[104]For example, in 1993 in Sweden, among foreigners detained for breaking laws there were 4,800 Yugoslavs, 3,800 Finns, 2,500 Poles, and only about 540 Russians. Fedor Lukianov, "Russian bandits in Sweden," *Segodnia*, Aug. 9, 1994, p. 4. The Baltic states were implicated for serving as a "drug window to Europe." See Artem Vetrov, "The New Drug Lords," *Segodnia*, April 11, 1995, p. 7.

[105]Claire Sterling, "The Growing Power of Russia's Mob," *The New Republic*, April 11, 1994, pp. 19-20.

[106]Artiom Vetrov, "Russian mafiosi change priorities," *Segodnia*, Aug. 9, 1995, p. 7.

[107]Aleksandr Shalnev, *Izvestia*, March 28, 1995, p. 3.

[108]Yuri Melnikov, interview, *Segodnia*, April 28, 1995, p. 7. Aleksandr Shalnev, *Izvestia*, March 28, 1995, p. 3.

[109]Chernomyrdis's remarks are cited by Chrystia Freeland, *Financial Times*, March 7, 1995, p. 4.

[110]Nugzar Betaneli, director of the Institute of Sociology of Parliamentarianism, *Obshchaia Gazeta*, Dec. 2, 1994, p. 9.

[111]Lotspeich, "Crime in the Transition Economies," op. cit. p. 566.

[112]David Remnick, "The Tycoon and the Kremlin," *The New Yorker*, Feb. 20, 1995, p. 136.

[113]Andrei Nechayev, deputy minister of economics, *Liberation*, Jan. 3, 1992, *FBIS-SOV-92-004*. See also Fedor Prokopov, director of the Federal Employment Service, *Trud*, Jan. 6, 1993, p. 2.

[114]*Delovoi Mir*, Dec. 27, 1995, p. 1.

[115]For a summary of these views, see Sheila Marnie, "Who and Where Are the Russian Unemployed?" *RFE/RL Research Report*, Vol. 2, No. 33, Aug. 20, 1993.

[116]Oleg Soskovets, First Deputy Prime Minister, *Delovoi Mir*, Sept. 21, 1994, pp. 1, 6.

[117]Aleksandr Livshits, interview, *Pravda*, June 4, 1994, p. 2.

[118]This paradox was brought to my attention by Martin Schrenk of the World Bank. See *Transition*, Vol. 6, No. 7-8, July-August 1995, p. 16.

[119]Anders Aslund estimated unemployment at about 4 percent. See "Gorbachev, Perestroika, and Economic Crisis," *Problems of Communism*, January-April, 1991, p. 18.

[120]Dr. Yevgeni Starikov estimated that there were 4 to 5 million people in these categories. The number of these people to be 4 to 5 million. See "Marginals," *Znamia*, No. 10, 1989, p. 149.

[121]Boris Beliakov, "Who needs the 'dead souls,'" *Sotsiologicheskie Issledovania*, No. 5, 1988.

[122]Starikov, "Marginals," *op. cit.*

[123]Elizabeth Teague, *RFE/RL*, Supplement, Feb. 1985, p. 23.

[124]Sergei Aukusionek and Rostislav Kapelyushnikov, "The Russian Labor Market in 1993," *RFE/RL Research Report*, Vol. 3, No. 29, July 1994, p. 30. See also *Delovoi Mir*, March 2, 1993, p. 1.

[125]Aleksandr Tkachenko, head of a department of the Ministry of Labor, *Delovoi Mir*, Jan. 12, 1994.

[126]Irina Milkhina of the Federal Employment Service, *Izvestia*, Aug. 8, 1995, p. 1.

[127]Tatiana Zaslavskaia, "Living Standards Are Falling," *Segodnia*, Aug. 2, 1995, p. 3.

[128]The number of job vacancies did, however, decline from 519,000 in July 1993 to 347,000 in June 1994. The Federal Employment Service, *Delovoi Mir*, Aug. 5, 1993, p. 9; *INTERFAX*, June 28, 1994.

[129]For example, in July 1993 in Moscow, there were 43,000 people seeking jobs, while the number of job vacancies was 86,600. *Financial Izvestia*, Aug. 13-19, 1993, p. VI.

[130]*Statistical Abstract of the United States: 1994* (Washington, D.C.: The National Data Book, 1994), pp. 391-395.

[131]Vladimir Shmyganovsky, "Gastarbeiters: Came to stay," *Izvestia*, June 18, 1994, p. 5. Russia is estimated to have 1.63 million illegal immigrants. The Department of Labor, *Delovoi Mir*, Dec. 19-25, 1994, p. 27. In 1994 Russia gave work to 129,000 *gastarbeiters* from Ukraine, China, Turkey, and other countries. See *Trud*, April 1, 1995, p. 2.

[132]The total number was derived from data provided by Chief of the General Stuff Mikhail Kolesnikov. See his interviews, *Izvestia*, June 17, 1994; Radio Maiak, Nov. 17, *FBIS-SOV*-94-222; *Nezavisimaia Gazeta*, Apr. 22, 1995, p. 1.

[133]Government Center for Economic Reforms. *Izvestia*, Sept. 7, 1994, p. 2.

[134]Goskomstat, *Delovoi Mir*, July 27, 1995, p. 5.

[135]Valeri Konovalov, "Neither work not jobless," *Izvestia*, July 21, 1995, p. 3. See also the interview of Deputy Minister of Labor Valeri Kolosov, *Delovoi Mir*, Feb. 5, 1994, p. 1.

[136]Ivan Gorbachev, Chairman of the Duma Committee on Trade, *Torgovaia Gazeta*, July 21, 1995, pp. 1, 2.

[137]Regarding the magnitude of this phenomenon, see Artiom Shadrin, *Delovoi Mir*, July 30, 1994, pp. 4, 5.

[138]For an example of such a business on the route between Moscow and Saratov, see Aleksandr Zilbert, "Saratov-Luzhniki and Back," *Izvestia*, July 25, 1995, p. 5.

[139]The figure is provided by Atomic Energy Minister Viktor Mikhailov. *INTERFAX*, Aug. 14, 1995.

[140]Fedor Prokopov, *Business World*, June 3, 1993, p. 7.

[141]Fedor Prokopov, *Trud*, Jan. 27, 1993, p. 2.

[142]The figure of one million is extrapolated; jobs were found for 762,300 people in the first nine months of 1994. See the Federal Employment Service report, *Delovoi Mir*, Nov. 7-13, 1994, p. 23.

[143]The Federal Employment Service, *Trud*, Jan. 27, 1993, p. 2. *INTERFAX*, June 28, 1994.

[144]*Rossiiskaia Gazeta* Sociological Service, "Do the Russians Want to return to the Past?" March 31, 1995, p. 2.

[145]Yuri Levada, "A comparative study of public attitudes in 1989 and 1994." *Segodnia*, Jan. 24, 1995, p. 10.

[146]In the Soviet Union, according to one estimate, up to 65 billion man-hours were lost annually waiting in lines. Aleksandr Radov, "Kill the Monster," *Ogoniok*, No. 46, 1989, pp. 4-7.

[147]All surveys consistently show this trend. See *Izvestia*, Sept. 11, 1993; *Ekonomika i Zhyzn*, No. 46, 1993; and *Segodnia*, Aug. 9, 1995, p. 3.

[148]See the Duma hearings reported in *Izvestia*, Dec. 21, 1994, p. 15.

[149]Aleksandr Nentsov, *Izvestia*, July 19, 1994, p. 4.

[150]This is according to an MVD report published in *Segodnia*, Feb. 23, 1995, p. 7.

[151]Boris Levin, *Argumenty i Fakty*, No. 8, 1995, p. 6.

[152]R. Lynn, *Personality and Character* (New York: Pegamon Press, 1971), pp. 53-56.

[153]Vladimir Rebrikov and Ekaterina Rybas, *Nezavisimaia Gazeta*, Dec. 6, 1994, p. 4. See also the Debates in the Duma reported in *Izvestia*, Dec. 21, 1994, p. 15.

[154]James R. Milam and Katherine Ketcham, *Under the Influence* (New York: Bantam Books, 1988), p. 8. About eighteen million Americans are thought to have problems with alcohol. See *Alcoholism and Drug Abuse Week 2*, No. 4, Jan. 24, 1990, p. 2.

[155]*Posev*, No. 3, 1985, p. 24.

[156]This statistic was provided by Viacheslav Titov, an MVD official, in *Selskaia Zhyzn*, April 25, 1991, p. 4.

[157]In 1993 home production was estimated to be 70 percent of state production. This estimate is taken from the report prepared for the Duma.

[158]Alan P. Pollard (ed.), *USSR: Facts and Figures* (Gulf Breeze, FL: Academic International Press, 1991), p. 124.

[159]According to Duma experts, relative to the average income vodka became 2.6 times cheaper. See *Delovoi Mir*, April 24-30, 1995. In 1990, according to the official ruble/dollar exchange rate, a half-liter bottle of imported vodka cost about $4, while in September 1994 it cost about $1.30. See *Delovoi Mir*, Sept. 15, 1994. Domestically made vodka cost about $0.80. See *Izvestia*, March 1, 1994 and Feb. 15, 1995.

[160]The average price of sugar in the country is about one dollar per kilo. See *Torgovaia Gazeta*, July 21, 1995, p. 2.

[161]For more information on this subject, see A. Yugov, *Posev*, No. 3, 1985, pp. 42-43.

[162]Mikhail Berger, "Vodka without borders," *Izvestia*, July 22, 1995. p. 4.

[163]Two taxi drivers told me that they could now afford a bottle of vodka every day and still have enough money to improve the living conditions of their families.

[164]Aleksandr Tolokonnikov et al., "We and alcohol," *Delovoi Mir*, June 12-18, 1995, p. 12.

[165]This was confirmed by my business contacts in Russia.

[166]Aleksandr Tiutiunik, "They drink champagne, no matter what their income," *Segodnia*, Aug. 24, 1995, p. 5. Regarding the growing consumption of good beer, see Aleksei Tarasov, *Izvestia*, Sept. 6, 1995, p. 5.

[167]From 1991 to 1994 the rate of suicide and death in the armed forces declined by 70 percent. See the interview of Minister of Defense Pavel Grachev and Chief of the General Staff Mikhail Kolesnikov in *Izvestia*, Sept. 19, 1993, June 17 and July 14, 1994, and *ITAR-TASS*, April 9, 1994. In 1994 the suicide rate among policemen declined by 12 percent Igor Astapkin, Lieutenant General of the Ministry of Interior see *Segodnia*, Sept. 9, 1994, p. 9. See also *Argumenty i Fakty*, No. 15, 1994, p. 1.

[168]*Statistical Abstract of the United States: 1994* (Washington, D.C.: The National Data Book, 1994), p. 859.

[169]Ernest Beck, "In gloomy Hungary, suicide takes on a life of its own," *The Wall Street Journal*, March 10, 1995, pp. 1, 10.

[170]"Lithuania's Suicide Rates are Highest in Europe," *The Baltic Observer*, Aug. 11-17, 1994, p. 1.

[171]Pollard, *USSR: Facts and Figures*, p. 93.

[172]Svetlana Tutorskaia, "Are we becoming a nation of sick people?" *Izvestia*, May 31, 1991, p. 7, and "Infectious diseases are spreading," *Izvestia*, July 8, 1994, p. 2.

[173]D. J. Peterson, "Understanding Soviet Infant mortality," *Report on the USSR*, Vol. 2, no. 14, April 6, 1990, p. 5.

[174]A. Vishnevsky et al., "Demographics of Russia," *Svobodnaia Mysl*, No. 2, 1993. The infant mortality rate in the U.S., by contrast, is 8 per thousand births. See *Statistical Abstract of the United States*, (U. S. Department of Commerce, 1994), No. 1353.

[175]Carl Haub, Population Reference Bureau, *Associated Press*, Jan. 10, 1995.

[176]Timon V. Riabushkin (ed.), *Sovetskaia Demografia Za 70 Let* (Soviet Demography in 70 Years), (Moskva: Nauka, 1987). See also Pollard, *USSR: Facts and Figures*, p. 92. See *Izvestia*, Dec. 21, 1994, p. 15.

[177]Professor Aleksandr Kiseliov, interview, *Literaturnaia Gazeta*, Aug. 10, 1994, p. 12.

[178]Vishnevsky, "Demographics of Russia," p. 98.

[179]Leonid L. Rybakovski (ed.), *Naselenie SSSR Za 70 Let* (Population of the USSR in 70 years), (Moskva: Nauka, 1988), p. 128.

[180]Vishnevsky, "Demographics of Russia." See also John L. Scheer (ed.), *USSR, Facts and Figures (life expectancy)* (Washington, DC: Central Intelligence Agency, 1989).

[181]Goskomstat, *Radio Rossii*, April 10, 1995, *FBIS-SOV-95-069*.

[182]*Argumenty i Fakty*, No. 52, 1994, p. 6.

[183]Goskomstat, *Izvestia*, Jan. 24, 1995, p. 1.

[184]Sergei Maksudov, "The Soviet System Under Demographic Challenge," in Alexander Shtromas and Morton A. Kaplan (eds.), *The Soviet Union and the Challenge of the Future* (New York: Paragon House, 1989), vol. 2, pp. 247-272.

[185]Murray Feshbach and Alfred Friendly, Jr., *Ecocide in the USSR: Health and Nature Under Siege* (New York: Basic Books, 1992), p. 4. See also *Argumenty i Fakty*, No. 45, 1989, p. 3.

[186]The quotation appears in presentations by Radio Free Europe analysts Vera Tolz, Elizabeth Teague, and Alexander Rahr, *RFE/RL Research Report* Vol. 3, no. 24, June 17, 1994, p. 4. Some observers came to these conclusions only three months after the beginning of reforms. See *Izvestia*, March 30, 1992.

[187]*Business Week*, Aug. 29, 1994, p. 20.

[188]Every year, one-fifth of Soviet women of child-bearing age were thought to have abortions. See A. Popov, "When there is no choice," *Ogoniok*, No. 33, April, 1988. See also David E. Powell, "Social Problems in Russia," *Current History*, October 1993, Vol. 92, No. 576, p. 327.

[189]Timothy Heleniak, *Transition*, Vol. 6, No. 9-10, September-October 1995, p. 5.

[190]Liudmila Biriukova, *Delovoi Mir*, Feb. 18, 1993.

[191]Gail W. Lapidus, "Social Trends," in Robert Byrnes (ed.), *After Brezhnev* (Bloomington, IN: Indiana University Press, 1983), pp. 192-200.

[192]Goskomstat, *Russian television*, Jan. 29, 1992, *FBIS-SOV-92-20*.

[193]On Dec. 31, 1991, the official rate was one dollar for 1.8 rubles. On Jan. 1, 1992, $1 became R110. See *Izvestia*, Dec. 31, 1991, p. 1. The average monthly salary was R530. See Goskomstat, *Russian television*, Jan. 29, 1992, *FBIS-SOV-92-20*.

[194]*Delovoi Mir*, Nov. 14, 1995, p. 1. Also see *Izvestia*, Jan. 10, 1996, p. 7.

[195]Kaiser, *Russia: People and Power*, p. 243.

[196]*The New York Times*, Dec. 5, 1990.

[197]For example, the *nomenklatura* of the Politburo enjoyed free food, housing, servants, cars, and so on. See the interview of Stepan Mikoyan, son of Politburo member Anastas Mikoyan. *Argumenty i Fakty*, No. 33, 1995, pp. 1, 5.

[198]D. Pyro, "Who lives on salary alone and how?" *Rossiiskaia Gazeta*, Sept. 2, 1995, p. 6.

[199]Gennadi Melikian, as quoted in Andrei Rumiantsev, "All taxpayers of Russia were given personal numbers," *Izvestia*, Aug. 30, 1995, p. 1.

[200]Feshbach and Friendly, *Ecocide in the USSR*, p. 93.

[201]Steven Erlanger, *The New York Times Magazine*, May 1, 1994, p. 51.

[202]Sergei Fateyev, head of the department of stategic studies of the international fund "Reform." *Delovoi Mir*, May 8-14, 1995, p. 44.

[203]Feshbach and Friendly, *Ecocide in the USSR*.

[204]The quotation is from a Russian student who returned to Russia after two years in the USA. See Julia Stepanian, "Back in the (former) USSR," *World Capitalism Review*, Vol. 2, No. 4, Fall 1994, p. 20.

[205]Some architects and artists complain that Western advertising has invaded Moscow and distorted its character. See Irina Medvedeva, "Moskva or Moscow?" *Delovoi Mir*, Nov. 10, 1994, p. 8.

[206]According to the Ministry of Economics, in three years their number grew sixfold. See *Torgovaia Gazeta*, Dec. 28, 1994, p. 2.

[207]According to the Department of Transportation of Moscow, 170 gas stations were built in 1994. See *Izvestia Financial*, Aug. 10, 1994, p. 11. Mobil proposed to open fifty more gas stations in Moscow and the surrounding vicinity in 1996. See *Izvestia*, Sept. 6, 1995, p. 3.

[208]In 1995 there were 4.4 times as many trade and industrial exhibits as in 1991. See Vladimir Petelin, *Delovoi Mir*, Aug. 9, 1995, p. 8, and "Fairs become a mass phenomenon," *Izvestia Financial*, July 25, 1995, p. VIII.

[209]According to *Goskomstat*, there were 14 percent fewer pollutants in the first half of 1994 than in the same period of 1993. See *Ekonomika i Zhyzn*, No. 38, 1994, p. 22.

[210]Franz-Olivier Giesbert, *Le Figaro*, May 2, 1994, *FBIS-SOV-94-085*.

[211]For information on a typical provincial town, Kostroma, see Vladimir Glotov, "Merchant, know thy place," *Business in Russia*, No. 58, 1995, pp. 47-55.

[212]I know only one notable exception. Anatoly Fedoseyev predicted: "The conversion [to democracy] will hardly be completely bloodless, but the bloodshed will not be on a scale which could be even remotely compared with that which followed the October revolution." See "The Passage to New Russia and Some Thoughts on its Alternative Constitutional Order," in Shtromas and Kaplan, *The Soviet Union and the Challenge*, Vol. 1, p. 414.

[213]Sergei Sedakov, "West promises food and medicine for the winter," *Kommersant*, Sept. 2, 1991, p. 3.

[214]Goskomstat, *INTERFAX*, April 23, 1992.

[215]Goskomstat, *Ekonomika i Zhyzn*, No. 6, Feb. 1994. See also Yuri Rykov, "The Cost of Strikes," *Rossiiskie Vesti*," May 18, 1994, p. 1.

[216]In the first half of 1995, 852,000 man-days were lost due to strikes. Out of 852 strikes, 575 were in the educational system. *Kommersant*, Aug. 8, 1995, p. 3.

[217]*Izvestia, Nezavisimaia Gazeta, Segodnia,* Nov. 8-9, 1994. See also Lev Gudkov, "Social tensions are subsiding," *Izvestia*, July 29, 1994, p. 1, and sociologist Oleg Saveliev, "Few people want to participate in demonstrations," *Argumenty i Fakty*, No. 26, 1994, p. 1.

[218]*Izvestia*, Dec. 24, 1994, p. 1.

[219]In 1993 in China there were "pitched battles during about 600 clan feuds, [which] resulted in more than 100 deaths and injuries to about 2,000 people." See "China Sounds Alarm Over Serious Rural Unrest," *International Herald Tribune*, May 4, 1994, pp. 1, 6.

[220]Gaidar himself said that he was surprised by the common sense of the Russian people. See interview, *FBIS-SOV-93-185-S*, p. 15.

[221]Mikhail S. Bernstam, "Trends and Economic Conditions of the Soviet Population and Labor Force Dynamics, 1959-2000," in Shtromas and Kaplan, *The Soviet Union and the Challenge*, Vol. 2, p. 307.

[222]Anatoli Vishnevski and Zhanna Zaiochkovskaia, "Waves of Migration," *Russian Social Science Review*, July-Aug. 1993, p. 45.

[223]Michael Mihalka, "German and Western Response to Immigration from the East," *RFE/RL Research Report*, Vol. 3, No. 23, June 10, 1994, p. 39.

[224]About 100,000 Russians emigrated and work (illegally) in the West. See *Delovoi Mir*, July 15, 1993, p. 9 See also, Vladimir Volokh, Deputy Head of the Federal Migration Service, *Delovoi Mir*, Oct. 22, 1993, p. 10.

[225]*Bristol Physics World Electronic News*, Aug. 17, 1995, *FBIS-SOV*-95-161.

[226]Russian Migration Service, *Kommersant-Daily*, Aug. 25, 1995, p. 3. By contrast, there were only 804,000 immigrants into the United States in 1994. See *The New York Times*, Sept. 25, 1995, p. A9.

[227]Even the more prosperous Baltic states lost population to Russia. See Nikolai Lashkevich, *Izvestia*, Aug. 12, 1994, p. 4. For example, 4 percent of the Estonian population emigrated to Russia. See *Delovoi Mir*, Feb. 17, 1995, p. 8.

[228]In 1994 the positive balance of migration was 366,000. Goskomstat, *Izvestia*, Jan. 24, 1995, p. 1. See also Dmitry Orlov, "Two million foreigners want to be Russians," *Rossiiskie Vesti*, Sept. 27, 1994, p. 2.

[229]Russian Migration Service, *Delovoi Mir*, June 11, 1994, p. 4, and April 5, 1995, p. 1. According to the presidential expert group, between 1992 and 1994 158,545 foreigners received Russian citizenship. See *Izvestia*, Oct. 12, 1994, p. 2.

[230]Yuri Arkhipov, head of Russia's immigration department, *International Herald Tribune*, July 7, 1994, p. 4.

[231]Anatoli Stepovoi, "Russia is ready to grant political asylum to foreigners," *Izvestia*, Aug. 2, 1994, p. 2.

[232]The Federal Migration Service, *Kommersant-Daily*, Aug. 25, 1995, p. 3.

[233]The Federal Migration Service is preparing for three million migrants. *ITAR-TASS*, Nov. 28, 1994; Goskomstat, *Delovoi Mir*, Nov. 1, 1994, p. 4. See also Dmitry Orlov, "Two million foreigners want to be Russians," *Rossiiskie Vesti*, Sept. 27, 1994, p. 2.

[234]These are the words of Federal Migration Service official Yevgeni Chernavtsev, *Delovoi Mir*, July 2, 1993.

[235]As one reporter wrote, "Russia compared to Belarus at the present time is something like Poland used to be compared to Russia, and Germany compared to Poland." See Yuri Kozlov, "Fifty-five customs agents on a transparent border," *Rossia*, No. 20, May 25-31, 1994, p. 3. The contrast is still more favorable with the Ukraine, where the average income is one-sixth that of Russia. See Vladimir Shmyganovsky, "Gastarbeiters: Came to stay," *Izvestia*, June 18, Dec. 22, 1994, p. 5.

[236]Chubais, "Signs of Recovery," *Business in Russia*, No. 56, 1995, p. 27.

[237]Goskomstat, *Segodnia*, Jan. 17, 1995, p. 11.

[238]The figure is a projection based on the results of the first seven months. See Goskomstat, *ITAR-TASS*, July 31, 1995, and *Izvestia Financial*, Aug. 17, 1995, p. I.

[239]Tatiana Paramonova, interview, *Delovoi Mir*, Aug. 26, 1995, p. 1.

[240]Chubais, interview, *Financial Izvestia*, Dec. 21, 1995, p. II. In comparison, the budget deficit of Japan is 4.1 percent; Britain's is 4.2 percent, France's is 5.0 percent, and Italy's is 7.8 percent. See *Business Week*, Oct. 9, 1995, p. 32.

[241]According to Goskomstat, the purchasing power of the dollar was equal 2,673 rubles. See *Delovoi Mir*, July 19, 1995, p. 2. According to estimates of the Expert Institute of the Union of Russian Enterpreneurs, in June 1995 the purchasing power of the dollar was equivalent to 1,300 rubles. See *Delovoi Mir*, June 20, 1995, p. 4.

[242]Yuri Melnikov, head of the Russian bureau of Interpol. See *Transition*, Vol. 6, No. 7-8, July-August 1995, p. 17.

[243]Yegor Gaidar estimated that in 1994 up to $16 billion returned. *Segodnia*, Dec. 8, 1994, p. 2.

[244]Viktor Gerashchenko noted this fact in passing. See his interview, *Nezavisimaia Gazeta*, June 21, 1994, p. 2. See also Ivan Zhagel, "Confidence in the ruble is growing," *Izvestia*, July 7, 1994, pp. 1, 2.

[245]Chernomyrdin, *Financial Times*, July 4, 1994, p. 3. See also Valeri Agronski, *Delovoi Mir*, Dec. 26, 1994, p. 1.

[246]Vladimir Panskov, *Delovoi Mir*, Dec. 2, 1994, p. 1.

[247]Viktor Chernomyrdin, *Rossiiskaia Gazeta*, July 20, 1995, p. 1.

[248]According to the Central Bank of Russia, savings in banks amounted to 45,441 trillion rubles. See *Izvestia Financial*, Sept. 7, 1995, p. III.

[249]*Izvestia*, Jan. 10, 1996, p. 11.

[250]Viktor Belikov, "Moscow has never built so much before," *Izvestia*, Feb. 10, 1995, p. 1. Nor is construction exclusively a Moscow phenomenon. For a view of the construction boom in the provinces see, for example, *Izvestia*, Nov. 28, 1995, p. 5. Overall, construction of private housing was growing at an annual rate of 16 percent in 1995. See *Izvestia Financial*, July 25, 1995, p. I.

[251]During 1995, 2,000,000 square meters of office space were restored in Moscow. *Izvestia Financial*, June 8, 1995, p. IV. In 1995 Moscow became the fifth costliest city of the world in terms of rents for prime office space. Moscow's annual rent per square foot was $89; comparable figures are $88 for London and $28 for New York. See *Business Week*, Oct. 9, 1995, p. 30.

[252]This figure is projected on the basis of the first ten months' results. See also Chernomyrdin, *Rossiiskaia Gazeta*, Nov. 29, 1994, p. 3.

[253]Mayor Yuri Luzhkov, *Delovoi Mir*, Aug. 10, 1995, p. 1.

[254]*Delovoi Mir*, Aug. 10, 1995, p. 1.

[255]In August, GNP grew by 3 percent. See *Izvestia Financial*, Sept. 21, 1995, p. I.

[256]The claim is made by Bob Clough, general director of Microsoft in Russia. According to Clough, Bill Gates believes that in the not-so-distant future Russia will become a major market for his company. See *Kommersant*, Nov. 29, 1994, p. 35. In 1995 software sales were estimated to approach 1 billion dollars. See *Izvestia*, Aug. 26, 1995, p. 3.

[257]This figure reflects the marketing research of Deitor Co. *Ekonomika i Zhyzn*, No. 35, Aug, 1994, p. 19.

[258]Tania Shuster, Department of Commerce, *Biznis Bulletin*, June-July 1995, p. 1.

[259]The figure is provided by Dataquest. See *Izvestia Financial*, Sept. 21, 1995, p. 1.

[260]The figure is a Microsoft projection. See *Segodnia*, Sept. 21, 1995, p. 3. In 1996 Intel projects that it will sell 1.6 million microprocessors and computers in Russia. See *Izvestia Financial*, Nov. 28, 1995, p. VI.

[261]Associated Press, quoted in *Izvestia Financial*, July 11, 1995, p. I.

[262]This is my estimate, made on the basis of annual sales and market research of computer companies. See the research report of Deitor Co., *Ekonomika i Zhyzn* No. 35, 1994, p. 19. See also Sergei Borodin, "Russian computers?" *Segodnia*, Jan. 19, 1995, p. 9.

[263]*Izvestia Financial*, Oct. 26, 1995, p. VI. See also *Delovoi Mir*, July 25-31, 1994, p. 10, and *Izvestia*, Dec. 7, 1994, p. 13.

[264]Several projects involving the participation of Russian financial groups and Western companies were launched in 1993. Motorola is participating in building a global system of information services, which will cost $ 3.37 billion and involve 66 communications satellites. The system should be finished by 1998; at the turn of the century it should serve about 2 million clients. See *Izvestia Financial*, July 2, 1993, p. II.

[265]The participants are: US West Co., Deutsche Bundespost, and France Telecom. *Kommersant*, No. 2, Jan. 25, 1994, p. 13. Another project aims at laying fiber-optic cable that will connect 50 Russian cities. *Kommersant*, Jan. 25, 1994, p. 13.

[266]Vladimir Bulgak, Minister of Communications, *Delovoi Mir*, Nov. 22, 1994, p. 4.

[267]*Izvestia*, Aug. 13, 1993, p. 5.

[268]More than 50,000 kilometers of fiber-optic cable is being laid by Russian and Western companies. *INTERFAX*, Oct. 6, 1994.

[269]*Izvestia*, May 14, 1993; *Business Contact*, No. 1, 1993, pp. 6-7.

[270]Michel Destresse, chief adviser to the International Monetary Fund, quoted in *Ekonomika i Zhyzn*, No. 39, 1995, p. 4.

[271]*Kommersant*, Sept. 8, 1993, p. 18.

[272]*Financial Izvestia*, April 20, 1995, p. I.

[273]*Financial Izvestia*, June 22, 1995, p. I.

[274]Jerry Schneider, president of APCUG, interview, *Delovoi Mir*, Oct. 3-9, 1994, p. 26.

[275]Regarding the competitive position of Russian producers of color television sets, see the remarks of Aleksandr Ladygin, deputy head of the department of electronic industry. See *Segodnia*, Sept. 19, 1995, p. 9.

[276]Dr. V. Belousov *et al.*, "Strategic Threat," *Business in Russia*, July/August 1995, p. 38.

[277]*Rossiiskaie Vesti*, Aug. 23, 1995, p. 1.

[278]The figure is provided by Roland Nash of the Russian Working Center for Economic Reform, who is quoted in Steven Erlanger, *The New York Times*, Aug. 8, 1995, p. A3. In February 1995, according to the Ministry of Social Protection the average pension was 145,000 rubles. *Izvestia*, Jan. 28, 1995, p. 9.

[279]Steven Erlanger, *The New York Times*, Aug. 8, 1995, p. A3.

[280]*Rossiiskaie Vesti*, Aug. 23, 1995, p. 1.

[281]*Delovoi Mir*, Sept. 2, 1995, p. 1.

[282]Yuri Yurkov, *Trud*, Oct. 12, 1994, p. 2, Goskomstat, *Argumenty i Fakty*, No. 24, 1994, p. 1.

[283]The Ministry of Labor estimated the number of "persons with average means" to be 27.4%. *Rossiiskaia Gazeta*, Sept. 12, 1994, p. 1.

[284]Liudmila Biriukova, *Rossiiskaie Vesti*, Aug. 23, 1995, p. 1. Considering that Russia has 2.5 million enterprises, the number of presidents and chief executive officers alone should amount at least 3 million. Anatoli Kulikov, Minister of Internal Affairs, interview, *Business in Russia*, No. 59, 1995, p. 9.

[285]The middle class spends only about 1 percent of its income on rent and utilities. See *Izvestia*, Sept. 29, 1995, p. 3.

[286]Zhanna Trofimova, "Anything you want," *Segodnia*, Aug. 23, 1995, p. 12.

[287]David Remnick, "The Tycoon and the Kremlin," *The New Yorker*, Feb. 20, 1995, p. 120. See also "What Russians Really Make," *Business Week*, Oct. 16, 1995, p. 34.

[288]V. Uzin, *Trud*, Oct. 10, 1995, p. 2.

[289]John Thornhill, "Rich Debate Rages Over Russian Poverty," *Financial Times*, April 19, 1995, p. 3.

[290]Marshall I. Goldman, "Moscow's Money Troubles," *World Monitor*, Vol. 3, Oct. 1990, p. 27.

[291]Anders Aslund, "Gorbachev, Perestroika, and Economic Crisis," *Problems of Communism*, January-April, 1991, p. 19.

[292]I. Gorbachev, chairman of the Duma Committee for Trade, interview, *Ekonomika i Zhyzn*, No. 50, 1994, p. 1. See also *Kommersant*, No. 2, Jan. 1995, p. 25, and Chrystia Freeland, *Financial Times*, July 3, 1995, p. 2.

[293]Raisa Firsova, *Delovoi Mir*, June 21, 1995, p. 8.

[294]Olga Tugina, *Krestianskaia Rossia*, June 19-25, 1995, p. 3. See also Albert Zilberg, "Welcome, Expensive Food," *Izvestia*, July 15, 1995, p. 1. Imported meat makes up only 13 percent of all meat sold. See *Financial Izvestia*, July 20, 1995, p. V.

[295]Yelena Yakovleva, *Izvestia*, Oct. 27, 1995, p. 1.

[296]Regarding the preference for Russian beer, sausages, chocolate, and dairy products, see Zhanna Trofimova, "Anything you want," *Segodnia*, Aug. 23, 1995, p. 12; Vadim Mikhnevich, *Delovoi Mir*, Aug. 23, 1995, p. 8; and Tatiana Korostikova, "Our sausages are better!" *Argumenty i Fakty*, No. 50, 1994.

[297]For examples of world-class Russian consumer goods, see *Delovoi Mir*, Nov. 9, and Dec. 26, 1994, and *Segodnia*, Nov. 22 and 24, 1994.

[298]Svetlana Alekseyeva, *Sovetskaia Rossia*, Nov. 12, 1994, p. 2.

[299]Goskomstat, in Leonid Lopatnikov, *Delovoi Mir*, June 20-26, 1994, p. 1.

[300]Forty-six percent of retail trade consists of unregistered consumer goods. See V. Salganov, head of the economic crimes department of the MVD, *Ekonomika i Zhyzn*, No. 37, 1994, p. 1. According to Andrei Neshchadin Expert Institute of Union of Industrialists and Entrepreneurs, the figure is 42 percent. See *Izvestia*, Sept. 21, 1994, p. 9. The figure is about 50 percent according to the Ministry of Economics. See *Torgovaia Gazeta*, Dec. 28, 1994, p. 2.

[301]*Kommersant*, No. 2, 1995, p. 25.

[302]Ivan Gorbachev, chairman of the Duma Committee on Trade, *Torgovaia Gazeta*, July 21, 1995, p. 1.

[303]Dozens of such supermarkets are being opened in Moscow. See *Izvestia*, Sept. 9, 1995, p. 1.

[304]Leonid Smirniagin, member of the presidential council, as quoted in Igor Duel, "Catastrophism is going out of style," *The Russian*, August 1995, p. 41.

[305] According to consultants of DRI/McGraw-Hill. *The Wall Street Journal*, Feb. 6, 1996, p. A7.

[306]Sergei Glaziev, *Moskovskaia Pravda*, July 26, 1995, p. 9.

[307]About 600 cases of cholera were reported in Daghestan in 1994. See *Segodnia*, *Izvestia* Aug. 22 and 25, 1994. However, the epidemic was localized and cannot even be compared to the outburst of cholera in 1970, which affected several regions. Ye. Beliaev, chairman of the State Epidemic Inspection Committee, *Argumenty i Fakty*, No. 33, 1994, p. 13. Less than two dozen people died. See *Izvestia*, Sept. 7, 1994, p. 1. Eight hundred seventy cases of AIDS were registered by 1995. See *Izvestia*, Feb. 3, 1995, p. 1.

[308]Characteristically, when he was asked to account for positive developments in Russia, Marshall Goldman responded that "good things were happening for the wrong reasons." Presentation at the Council for Foreign Relations, Indianapolis, Jan. 9, 1995.

[309]Duel, "Catastrophism," *ibid.* p. 40.

[310]*Moscow News,* No. 52, Dec. 30, 1994-Jan. 5, 1995, p. 10.

[311]Vladimir Resin estimated that there was $3 billion worth of construction in downtown Moscow alone in 1995. See *Delovye Liudi*, May, 1995, p. II; *Izvestia*, June 28, 1995, p. 9.

[312]According to Alexii II, the Patriarch of All Russia, the total number of functioning churches has reached 16,000. See *Literaturnaia Gazeta,* June 16, 1995, pp. 1, 11.

[313]About 300 such telephones were installed in 1995. See *Delovoi Mir*, June 22, 1995, p. 2.

[314]The system of residence permits was abolished in December 1995. *Izvestia*, Dec. 21, 1995, p. 1.

[315]There are 600 private schools in Russia. See *Izvestia*, Sept. 14, 1995, p. 5.

Chapter 7

[1]See the editorial "Will Russia reverse reform?" *The Economist*, Oct. 28, 1995, p. 15.

[2]Curiously, Anatoli Lukianov, former chairman of the Congress of People's Deputies of the Soviet Union, completely agrees with them. See his interview in David Pryce-Jones, *The Strange Death of the Soviet Empire* (New York: Henry Holt, 1995), p. 425.

[3]Burbulis, interview, *Izvestia*, Oct. 16, 1993, p. 5.

[4]Aleksei Kiva, "Will the supporters of democracy lose the parliamentary elections?" *Rossiiskaia Gazeta*, Aug. 12, 1995, p. 3. Irina Khakamada compared Russian democracy with an elephant walking on a tightrope, in *Segodnia*, Sept. 23, 1995, p. 6.

[5]Aleksandr Lebed, "Toward a Great Power," *Moskovskaia Pravda*, Aug. 15, 1995, p. 2.

[6]Only Bulgaria and Romania exceeded Russia in terms of the length of constitutional debate.

[7]It received 58.43 percent of the votes. See *Rossiiskaia Gazeta*, Dec. 21, 1993, p. 1.

[8]Andrei Kozyrev, interview, Moscow Ostankino TV, Dec. 15, 1993, *FBIS-SOV*-93-240.

[9]These are the words of Vasili Tarasenko, chairman of the Federation Council Committee on Federal Affairs. See *Segodnia*, Aug. 9, 1995, p. 5.

[10]These are the words of presidential adviser Aleksandr Livshyts, *Literaturnaia Gazeta*, July 13, 1994, p. 10.

[11]Ivan Rybkin (ed.), *Fifth Russian State Duma* (Moskva: Izvestia, 1994), p. VIII.

[12]Rybkin, *Obshchaia Gazeta*, Sept. 30, 1994, p. 8. See also Yelena Pestriukhina, "Duma finishes first term," *Moscow News*, July 29-Aug. 4, 1994, pp. 1, 2.

[13]Mikhail Mitiukov, deputy chairman of the Duma. See *Delovoi Mir*, Dec. 31, 1994, p. 1. On the inner workings of the Duma, see, for example, the coverage of the Duma's work in *Segodnia*, Oct. 27, 1994, p. 2.

[14]Mikhail Mitiukov, deputy chairman of the Duma. See *Delovoi Mir*, July 22, 1995, p. 1.

[15]Anna Ostapchuk, "First Case of Constitutional Court," *Nezavisimaia Gazeta*, March 16, 1995, p. 1.

[16]Yelena Tregubova, *Segodnia*, Feb. 8, 1995, p. 1.

[17]Professor Liudvig Karapetian, "The Constitutional Court, Born in Travail," *Segodnia*, Jan. 25, 1995, p. 9.

[18]Vladimir Tumanov, interview, *Moscow News*, March 19-23, 1995, p. 2.

[19]Vladimir Tumanov, interview, *Rossiiskaia Gazeta*, April 19, 1995, p. 2.

[20]Valeri Rudnev, *Izvestia*, June 8, 1995, p. 1.

[21]See the President's draft law on the judicial system of Russia. *Rossiiskie Vesti*, Feb. 2, 1995, p. 2.

[22]Yeltsin spoke about judicial reforms as one of his priorities for 1995. See his Federal Assembly address, Moscow Russian TV, Feb. 16, 1995, *FBIS-SOV-95-032*.

[23]In 1994, 173 trials by jury took place. *Izvestia*, March 16, 1995, p. 5.

[24]*Segodnia*, Sept. 28, 1995, p. 1. He appeared in court on October 25, 1995. *Izvestia*, Oct. 26, 1995, p. 1.

[25]Viacheslav Miliusin, director of Ostankino TV, interview, *Argumenty i Fakty*, No. 11, March 1995, p. 7.

[26]The statistics are provided by Mikhail Poltoranin. See his interview, *Delovoi Mir*, June 11, 1994, p. 4 See also Irina Zhuravskaia, *Ogoniok*, No. 27-28, 1994, p. 10.

[27]A critically-minded journalist like Yevgenia Albats, who has a basically pessimistic view of life in the new Russia, has written: "Right now Russia is the best place in the world for a reporter. You are a real fourth estate. The dirty guys in the government — they're afraid of you. They know you're watching them. My goodness, it's terrific." She is quoted by Jeff Goodell in *Elle*, October 1994, p. 152. "Russians Watch War on Uncensored TV," wrote Steven Erlanger, *The New York Times*, Dec. 20, 1994, p. 7.

[28]These are the words of analysts Aleksandr Golovkov and Teimuraz Malamadze, in *Izvestia*, Jan. 21, 1995, p. 2.

[29]Aleksandr Golovkov and Teimuraz Malamadze, "Forward to the past," *Izvestia*, Jan. 21, 1995, p. 2.

[30]Pavel Grachev's deputy was dismissed after the publicization of the corruption of army units then stationed in Germany. See *Moskovski Komsomolets* and *Nezavisimaia Gazeta*, Oct. 22, and Nov. 3, 1994.

[31]Steven Erlanger, "Russians Watch War on Uncensored TV." *The New York Times,* Dec. 20, 1994, p. A7.

[32]Pavel Yevdokimov wrote: "Many truly skilled specialists left to work in the private sector." "Intelligence and Politics," *Rossia*, Nov. 24-30, 1994, p. 3.

[33]*TASS*, Dec. 19, 1991.

[34]Burbulis, interview, Moscow TV, Dec. 29, 1991, *FBIS-SOV-92-001*.

[35]*Rossiiskaia Gazeta*, Jan. 30, 1992, p. 3.

[36]Yeltsin, interview, Moscow Ostankino TV, Dec. 22, 1993, FBIS-SOV-93-244, Dec. 22, 1993.

[37]*Delovoi Mir*, Jan. 12, 1994.

[38]*Novaia Ezhednevnaia Gazeta*, No. 9, 1993.

[39]Yevgenia Albats, *The State Within a State* (New York: Farrar, 1994), pp. 356-358.

[40]Peter Deriabin with T. H. Bagley, *KGB: Masters of the Soviet Union* (New York: Hippocrene Books, 1990), p. 165. See also *Nedelia*, No. 37, 1990.

[41]Sergei Stepashin, interview, *Argumenty i Fakty*, No. 40, Oct. 1994, p. 3.

[42]*Segodnia*, Nov. 24, 1994, p. 1.

[43]*Izvestia*, Aug. 12, 1995, p. 1.

[44]The development is moted by Vadim Yegorov, in *Nezavisimaia Gazeta*, Sept. 14, 1994, p. 1.

[45]Korzhakov wrote a letter to Chernomyrdin, proposing restrictions on foreign oil companies operating in Russia. See Irina Savateyeva, "Who is running the country?" *Izvestia*, Dec. 22, 1994, pp. 1, 2.

[46]Korzhakov, interview, *Argumenty i Fakty*, No. 3, Jan. 1995, p. 3.

[47]Chernomyrdin, interview, *Izvestia*, Sept. 13, 1995, p. 2.

[48]Shakhrai, interview, *Argumenty i Fakty*, No. 11, 1991.

[49]Shakhrai, "On Dual Power, Dictatorship, and the New Constitution," *Trud*, June 5, 1993, p. 2.

[50]Mikhail Sokolov, "All power to the Soviets of Security," *Segodnia,* Jan. 12, 1995, p. 3.

[51]*TASS*, Nov. 8, 1991.

[52]Aleksandr Snopov, "Chechen president declares 'holy war' against Russia," *Kommersant*, Nov. 11, 1991, p. 3.

[53]Dudayev, interview, *Moscow News*, No. 42, 1991, p. 10.

[54]The Congress of Democratic Russia recommended lifting the state of emergency. *All-Union Radio,* Nov. 9, 1991, *FBIS-SOV*-91-051. See also *Moscow Radio,* Nov. 10, 1991, *FBIS-SOV*-91-218.

[55]*TASS*, Nov. 11, 1991. See also *Izvestia*, Jan. 13, 1995, p. 1.

[56]In June 1992 the General Staff reported that in one location alone the Russian Army had to leave behind 42 tanks, 37 armored personnel carriers, 145 artillery pieces, 15 antiaircraft guns, and 40,000 small arms. *INTERFAX*, Feb. 25, 1995. See also Nikolai Astashkin, "Dzokhar Dudayev's Military Program," *Krasnaia Zvezda*, Nov. 28, 1991, p. 1. See also *Krasnaia Zvezda*, Jan. 15, 1992, p. 3, and Aleksandr Aleshkin, "Chechen Air Force," *Rossiiskaia Gazeta*, Feb. 17, 1992, p. 3.

[57]He represents two tribes from the southern, mountainous part of the province. See, for example, Igor Rotar, "Chechnia: Ancient trouble," *Izvestia*, Oct. 27, 1995, p. 5.

[58]Aleksei Iliushenko, *Rossiiskaia Gazeta*, March 4, 1995, p. 7.

[59]Moscow Petroleum Information Agency, *INTERFAX*, Aug. 31, 1995.

[60]Russian Defense Ministry, *ITAR-TASS*, Dec. 8, 1995.

[61]Kulikov, Russian 2x2 Television, *FBIS-SOV*-95-134, July 13, 1995.

[62]See the telegram to the president from leaders of the democratic factions. *ITAR-TASS*, Dec. 9, 1994.

[63]The liberals included Emil Pain, Georgi Satarov, Leonid Smirniagin, Mark Urnov, and Otto Latsis. See John Lloyd, "Yeltsin tries to quiet the chorus of criticism," *Financial Times*, Dec. 28, 1994, p. 2. See also Yuri Baturin, interview, *El Pais*, Feb. 27, 1995, *FBIS-SOV*-95-039.

[64]Minister of Justice Yuri Kalmykov was forced to resign after he protested the military action in Chechnia. See *Komsomolskaia Pravda*, Dec. 20, 1994, p. 3.

[65]*Segodnia*, Dec. 28, 1994, p. 1.

[66]*Segodnia*, Dec. 14, 1994, p. 3.

[67]*Izvestia*, Dec. 9, 17, 1994, p. 1.

[68]*Delovoi Mir*, Dec. 17, 1994, p. 1.

[69]Igor Korolkov, *Izvestia*, Dec. 22, 1994, p. 2.

[70]Aleksandr Kotenkov, deputy minister of the Ministry of Nationalities, accused Dudayev of spending $10 million to bribe the Russian media. See *Izvestia*, Dec. 22, 1994, p. 2.

[71]Valeri Yakov, *Izvestia*, Dec. 24, 1994, p. 4.

[72]*Segodnia*, Dec. 28, 1994, p. 1.

[73]Gennadi Burbulis said: "Yeltsin is risking becoming a president without the *narod*." He is quoted in Yevgeni Krasnikov, "The President managed to restore national unity," *Nezavisimaia Gazeta*, Dec. 14, 1994, p. 2. Similar views were voiced by Gavriil Popov. See "Boris Yeltsin and the authoritarian state," *Izvestia*, Dec. 24, 1994, p. 5.

[74]Chrystia Freeland called the assembly's action "a milestone for Russia's nascent democracy." See "Russia Vows to Pursue Tough Line on Economy," *Financial Times*, July 3, 1995, p. 1.

[75]*Izvestia*, Jan. 13, 1995, p. 1.

[76]Yeltsin, press conference, Russian Public Television, *FBIS-SOV*-95-175, Sept. 8, 1995.

[77]Yeltsin, press conference, Russian Public Television, *FBIS-SOV*-95-175, Sept. 8, 1995.

[78]*Sovetskaia Rossia*, Dec. 15, 1992.

[79]Emil Pain, "The disintegration of Russia: the problem has been removed," *Moscow News*, June 10-15, 1994, p. 2.

[80]John Lloyd, "Yeltsin Lays Down the Law to Leaders of Russia's Regions," *Financial Times*, Nov. 4, 1993.

[81]Yeltsin, interview, Ostankino Television, Nov. 4, 1993. *FBIS-SOV*-93-213, 1993.

[82]Leonid Polezhaev, governor of Omsk *oblast*, *Argumenty i Fakty*, No. 16, 1994, p. 12.

[83]On the relationship with Tatarstan, see Elizabeth Teague, "Russia and Tatarstan Sign Power-sharing Treaty," *RFE/RL Research Report*, Vol. 3, No. 14, Apr. 8, 1994.

[84]*Rossiiskaia Gazeta*, Feb. 17, 1994.

[85]Yeltsin, interview, *Izvestia*, July 21, 1994, p. 4.

[86]*Rossiiskaia Gazeta*, Aug. 30, 1995.

[87]*ITAR-TASS*, Oct. 6, 1995.

[88]Popov, "What next? Notes on the present moment," *Izvestia*, Oct. 18, 1991, p. 1.

[89]Daria Fane, "Soviet census data, union republics and ASSR, 1989," in Ian Bremmer and Ray Taras (eds.), *Nations and Politics in the Soviet Successor States* (New York: Cambridge University Press, 1993), pp. 550-560.

[90]Regarding Ossetian-Chechen conflicts in the Soviet period of Russian history, see the account of a former KGB officer in *Nezavisimaia Gazeta*, Dec. 3, 1992.

[91]Yeltsin, press conference, Russian Public Television, *FBIS-SOV*-95-175, Sept. 8, 1995.

[92]Eduard Rossel, Governor of Sverdlovsk *oblast*, interview, *Argumenty i Fakty*, No. 42, 1995, p. 3.

[93]*Nezavisimaia Gazeta*, June 11, 1993.

[94]*Sovetskaia Molodezh*, April 12, 1988.

[95]Sergei Filatov, interview, *Segodnia*, Sept. 8, 1995, p. 5. Fifty-four parties registered for the 1995 parliamentary elections by September 10. See *Segodnia*, Sept. 12, 1995.

[96]Leonid Zhukhovitski, "In search of social explosion," *Delovoi Mir*, Feb. 18, 1993, p. 2.

[97]*Izvestia*, June 11, 1992, pp. 1, 3. Sergei Shakhrai also has consistently insisted that "the president should not belong to any party." See his interview *Argumenty i Fakty*, No. 11, March, 1991. Burbulis held the opposite view. See his interview, *Moscow News*, Jan. 21, 1993.

[98]Yeltsin, interview, Ostankino Television, Dec. 22, 1993, *FBIS-SOV*-93-244.

[99]Yeltsin, address, Russian Television, *FBIS-SOV*-95-171, Sept. 5, 1995.

[100]Lilia Shevtsova, director of the Center for Political Studies in Moscow, "The Two Sides of the New Russia," *Journal of Democracy*, July 1995, Vol. 6, No. 3, p. 63.

[101]Vadim Bakatin, interview, *Rabochaia Tribuna*, Nov. 30, 1994, p. 3.

[102]Chrystia Freeland, "Chechnia's other loser," *Financial Times*, Feb. 10, 1995, p. 13.

[103]Poltoranin, interview, *Argumenty i Fakty*, No. 1-2, 1995, p. 6.

[104]Steven Erlanger, "Black Tie, Red Square, and Intrigue in Yeltsin's 'Court," *International Herald Tribune*, Oct. 20, 1994, p. 2.

[105]Anton Zhigulsky, "Yeltsin Revives use of Tsarist Heraldry," *The Moscow Times*, July 31, 1994, p. 29.

[106]Boris Krotkov, "State symbols of Russia," *Delovoi Mir*, Nov. 12, 1994, p. 1.

[107]Lilia Shevtsova, "The Two Sides of the New Russia," *Journal of Democracy*, July 1995, Vol. 6, No. 3, p. 66.

[108]Gavriil Popov, "Boris Yeltsin and the authoritarian state," *Izvestia*, Dec. 24, 1994, p. 5.

[109]*Kommersant*, No. 35, 1995.

[110]Quoted in John Thornhill, "Lively Yeltsin pounds on his ministers," *Financial Times*, Oct. 14/15, 1995, p. 2.

[111]One Russian businessman told me: "Yeltsin is dangerous because he is absolutely ruthless. He would do anything, sacrifice anything and anybody to assert his power."

[112]Alexandr Shokhin, Minister of Foreign Economic Relations, complained that he was not even informed that the minister of finance had been appointed. *INTERFAX*, Nov. 4, *ITAR-TASS*, Nov 6, 1994.

[113]In the words of Viacheslav Kostikov, "The President made serious remarks, offering tough criticism of the actions of the government," *ITAR-TASS*, May 19, 1994.

[114]The chief of the general staff disclosed that he learned about the change from the media. See *Izvestia*, Jan. 13, 1995, p. 1.

[115]Minister of Justice Yuri Kalmykov called this action "illegitimate," and resigned in protest against the forceful solution of the Chechnia problem. See *Komsomolskaia Pravda*, Dec. 20, 1994, p. 3.

[116]Yavlinsky, interview, *ITAR-TASS*, June 23, 1994.

[117]Yeltsin, speech in Yaroslavl, *The Economist*, Nov. 6, 1993.

[118]Yuri Skokov, interview, in *Pravda*, July 22, 1993, p. 2.

[119]*Kommersant-Daily*, April 2, 1994, p. 5.

[120]*Izvestia*, Jan. 17, 1995, p. 2.

[121]Mikhail Gorbachev, interview, *WPROST* in Polish, *FBIS-SOV-94-003*, Jan. 5, 1994.

[122]Steven Erlanger, *International Herald Tribune*, Dec. 24-25-26, 1993, p. 1.

[123]Aleksandr Tsypko, "About Gorbachev, 'traitors,' and the Russian Soul," *Nezavisimaia Gazeta*, April 6, 1995, p. 3.

[124]Editorial, *Financial Times*, Sept., 22, 1993.

[125]Nikolai Fedorov, a former Minister of Justice, said that Yeltsin "constantly creates confrontational situations because this is for him a form of existence." *Literaturnaia Gazeta*, Feb. 22, 1995, p. 10.

[126]Lev Ponomariov, Duma deputy and co-chairman of the Democratic Party. "The voluntary 'Foros' of president Yeltsin," *Segodnia*, Dec. 31, 1994, p. 11.

[127]Yuri Vlasov, "We are drawing while the orchestra is playing on the top deck." *Sovetskaia Rossia*, Nov. 14, 1992, p. 6.

[128]Yuri Afanasiev, "Russian Reform Is Dead," *Foreign Affairs*, March/April, 1994, p. 21.

[129]Gaidar, interview, *Il Messaggero, FBIS-SOV*-95-011, Jan. 18, 1995.

[130]Julia Wishnevsky, "Democratic opposition in Russia: An alternative to Yeltsin?," *The Washington Quarterly*, Spring 1995, p. 25.

[131]Nikolai Troitski, "The Technology of Power," *Obshchaia Gazeta,* Nov. 18, 1994, p. 7.

[132]John Lloyd wrote: "What Mr. Yeltsin believes is a real puzzle: time and again, he makes decisions based on what appears to be a genuinely liberal world view; time and again, his actions, either of commission or omission, contradict such a view." See "Rock solid against Yeltsin's reforms," *Financial Times*, Sept. 6, 1993, p. 11.

[133]Anatol Lievan, "Be ready for Yeltsin's demise," *The Times,* Dec. 29, 1994, p. 16.

[134]This rapid turnover is illustrated by comparing the monthly lists of the hundred most influential politicians composed by *Nezavisimaia Gazeta* in 1992, 1993, and 1995.

[135]J. R. Strange, *Abnormal Psychology* (New York: McGraw-Hill, 1965), p. 195.

[136]For example, in the middle of the military campaign in Chechnia, his political adviser Emil Pain said that there was only a slim chance that a "new Yeltsin, again committed to reform, could reappear." *Financial Times*, Jan. 16, 1995, p. 2.

[137]Dean Keith Simonton, *Greatness: Who Makes History and Why* (New York: The Guilford Press, 1994), pp. 138-141.

[138]Merton, R. K. "Anomie and Social Interaction: the Context of Deviant Behavior," in M. B. Clinard (ed.) *Anomie and Deviant Behavior* (New York: The Free Press, 1964), p. 20.

[139]Sidney Hook, *The Hero in History* (New York: John Day Co., 1943), p. 157.

[140]Hook, *The Hero*, p. 157.

[141]Hook, *The Hero*, p. 229.

[142]Boris Yeltsin, *Zapiski Prezidenta* (The President Notes), (Moskva: Ogoniok, 1994), p. 236.

[143]See Yeltsin's meeting with editors of leading newspapers. Viktor Loshak, *Moscow News*, Nov. 4-10, 1994, p. 2.

[144]Viacheslav Kostikov, *Moscow News*, Aug. 18-24, 1995, p. 10.

[145]His wife, Naina, said: "He is very careless about his health. He always has been." *INTERFAX*, Oct. 31, 1995.

[146]*Russia, the Republics and the Baltics* (New York: Fodor's Travel Publishing, 1991), p. 36.

[147]Ronald Hingley, *The Russian Mind* (New York: Scribner's Sons, 1977).

[148]A similar phenomenon was noted among Scandinavians. See Steve Lohn, "In the Long Days of Summer, Swedes Are Thinking Bright," *The New York Times*, June 23, 1989.

[149]Yeltsin's former press secretary Viacheslav Kostikov describing a "typical" Russian, interview, *Stolitsa*, No. 22, 1994, p. 14.

[150]Vasili Kliuchevski, *Collected Works* (Moskva: Mysl, 1967), p. 315.

[151]Hingley, *The Russian Mind*, p. 208.

[152]Consider the view of Wright Miller: "External authority to the Russians, it would seem, has always been an evil to be tolerated only because of overriding necessity." *Russians as People* (New York: Dutton, 1961), p. 115.

[153]Yevgenia Albats, *The State Within a State* (New York: Farrar, Straus, Giroux, 1994), p. 166.

[154]Andrei Amalrik, *Will the Soviet Union Survive Until 1984?* (New York: Harper & Row, 1970), p. 35.

[155]Hingley, *The Russian Mind*, pp. 43-44.

[156]A professor at American University, John Glad, has advanced a theory according to which IQ has decreased by as much as 21 points. See "Hypothetical Model of Soviet IQ Lowering Resulting From Political Murder and Selective Emigration" (unpublished work of the Washington D.C.-based Future Generations Institute, 1985).

[157]Alexandr N. Yakovlev, interview, *Moskovskie Novosti*, No. 5, Feb. 6, 1994, p. 11.

[158]Yulia Aleshina, *Literaturnaia Gazeta*, No. 9, March 1989, p. 10.

[159]*Zapiski Prezidenta*, p. 15.

[160]By 1995 only about 4 percent of Russians lived in communal apartments. *Argumenty i Fakty*, No. 26, 1995, p. 6.

[161]Peter F. Drucker, *Post-Capitalist Society* (New York: Harper, 1993), p. 45.

[162]Sheila M. Puffer, "Understanding the bear: a portrait of Russian business leaders," *Academy of Management Executive*, Vol. 8, No. 1, 1994, pp. 41-54.

[163]Aleksandr Volovik, President of Bi Gas Si, Inc., *The Russian*, August 1995, p. 34.

[164]Arkadi Volski, interview, *Trud*, March 10, 1993, p. 10.

[165]Malcolm Warner, Elena Denezhkina, and Adrian Campbell, *How Russian Managers Learn* (Judge Institute of Management Studies, Cambridge University, 1993), p. 27.

[166]Lann Nelson, Olga Klimashevskaia, and Igor Malikov, *Argumenty i Fakty*, No. 15, April, 1994, p. 5.

[167]Irina Khakamada, *Segodnia*, Sept. 23, 1995, p. 6.

[168]Simon Clarke, Peter Fairbrother, Vadim Borisov, and Petr Bizyukov, "The Privatization of Industrial Enterprises in Russia: Four Case Studies," *Europe-Asia Studies*, Vol. 46, No. 2, 1994, p. 179.

[169]Adam Michnic, interview, *Izvestia*, April 13, 1994, p. 7.

[170]Vladimir Shumeiko, interview, *Vechernia Moskva*, May 6, 1994, p. 2.

[171]Gennadi Ziuganov, *Pravda Severa*, June 9, 1994, p. 2.

[172]Gennadi Ziuganov, *Sovetskaia Rossia*, March 17, 1994, p. 1.

[173]Vladimir Sirotin, "National communism," *Moscow News*, Sept. 2-8, 1994, p. 6.

[174]Zivganov said: "A politician who does not understand the colossal and largely unique role played by the Orthodox faith in the establishment and development of our state and culture does not understand Russia." See *Pravda Rossia*, Oct. 5, 1995, p. 2.

[175]Thus, 46.6 percent [of the members of the Duma] were industrialists, 18.8 percent were scientific workers, 6.75 percent were [are?] students, and 3 percent were in the military. Ninety percent have advanced degrees, including 13.5 percent with scientific degrees and 63.9 percent with engineering degrees. Half of them speak English. See Brunislav Lisin, *Delovoi Mir*, April 1, 1994, p. 4.

[176]See, for example, Peter Galuszka, "The Conglomerate is Alive and Well in Russia," *Business Week,* Oct. 16, 1995, p. 58.

[177]According to one of the most respected researchers specializing in the new Russians, Olga Kryshtanovskaia, "The Elite Among New Russians Works Hard to Improve Itself," See *Izvestia,* Aug. 12, 1995, p. 5. See also Irina Khakamada, Duma Deputy, interview, *Novaia Yezhednevnaia Gazeta,* Dec. 28, 1994, pp. 1, 3.

[178]The quotation is from the head of the administration of Kemerov Oblast Mikhail Kisliuk, in *Argumenty i Fakty,* No. 50, 1994, p. 6.

[179]The quotation is from the closing statement of the First Congress of Russian Entrepreneurs in December 1994. See *Delovye Liudi,* January 1995, p. 74.

[180]Lev Gudkov, "Intelligentsia and Intellectuals," *Znamia,* Nos. 3-4, 1992, p. 203. Ovenes Meliakian wrote: "In music, literature, arts, and the movies, one can hear one and the same melody: hopelessness and apocalypse." See "Professor Trades in Luzhniki," *Nezavisimaia Gazeta,* Aug. 18, 1993, p. 8.

[181]According to Gennadi Ziuganov, such prominent figures cultural as Yuri Bondarev, Valentin Rasputin, Rasul Gamzatov, Aleksandra Pakhmutova, Irina Arkhipova, Yelena Obraztsova, and Boris Shtokolov have become members of the Russian Communist Party. See the political report at the Third Congress of CPRF, *Sovetskaia Rossia,* Jan. 24, 1995, p. 3.

[182]Alexei Kiva, "Futurological Studies in the Face of the Failure of Russian Liberalism," *Delovoi Mir,* July 1, 1995, p. 2.

[183]The quotation is from a former political prisoner, Andrei Siniavski. See "We Had It All Before," *Nezavisimaia Gazeta,* Oct. 13, 1993, p. 5.

[184]Daniil Granin, "Intelligentsia in the Absence of Apollo and Raikom," *Izvestia,* Sept. 14, 1993, p. 5. A similar view was expressed by the literary critic Benedict Sarnov in *Segodnia,* Nov. 19, 1994, p. 10.

[185]Liudmila Vorontsova and Sergei Filatov, "The Intelligentsia in Post-Soviet 'Capitalism,'" *Svobodnaia Mysl,* No. 5, 1994, p. 51. See also Svetlana Beliaeva-Konegen and Iosif Diskin, "The last temptation of Russia," *Literaturnaia Gazeta,* No. 5, Jan. 29, 1992.

[186]Daniil Granin, "Intelligentsia in the Absence of Apollo and Raikom," *Izvestia,* Sept. 14, 1993, p. 5.

[187]Peter Galuszka and Patricia Kranz, "Russia's New Capitalism," *Business Week,* Oct. 10, 1994, p. 80.

[188]Steven Erlanger, "To be Young, Russian and Middle Class," *The New York Times,* July 23, 1995, pp. 1, 7.

[189]Max Asgari, president of ABB Russia Ltd. said: "In five years, the young workers in Russia will have the same attitudes and work habits as those in the West." See Patricia Kranz, "The young and ambitious," special issue of *Business Week,* November 1994, p. 128.

[190]John Seeley, Alexander Sim and Elizabeth Loosley, *Crestwood Heights: A Study of the Culture of Suburban Life* (New York: John Wiley & Sons, 1967).

[191]Daniel J. McCarthy, Sheila M. Puffer and Stanislav V. Shekshina, "The Resurgence of an Entrepreneurial Class in Russia," *Journal of Management Inquiry,* Vol. 2, No. 2, June 1993, pp. 125-137. See also Sheila M. Puffer, "Understanding the bear: a portrait of Russian business leaders," *Academy of Management Executive,* Vol. 8, No. 1, 1994, pp. 41-54, and Igor Bunin, "Russian bears's new clothes," *Financial Times,* Sept. 27, 1994, p. 15.

[192]John M. Oldham and Lois B. Morris, *The Personality Self-Portrait: Why We Think, Work, Love, And Act The Way We Do* (New York: Bantam, 1990), pp. 56-78.

[193]Denis Yevstigneyev, interview, *Izvestia*, Oct. 19, 1995, p. 6. See also Natalia Rimashevskaia *et al*, "The Rich: Are there hopes for social peace?" *Delovoi Mir*, June 22, 1995, p. 5.

[194]Peter Ester and Henk Vinken, "Yuppies in Cross-National Perspective: Is There Evidence for a Yuppie Value Syndrome?" *Political Psychology*, Vol. 14, No. 4, 1993, pp. 667-696. See also P. Dekker and P. Ester, "The Political Distinctiveness of Young Urban Professionals: 'Yuppies' or 'New Class'?" *Political Psychology*, No. 11, 1990, pp. 309-330.

[195]See Yeltsin's annual address, in *The New York Times,* Feb. 17, 1995, p. 1.

[196]Mark Urnov, head of the Analytical Center of the President, interview, *Segodnia*, March 22, 1995, p. 9.

[197]John Thornhill, "Russians find capitalism is in the genes," *Financial Times*, Nov. 3, 1995, p. 3.

[198]Anatoly Sobchak, *Khozhdenie vo vlast* (In pursuit of power), (Moscow: Novosti, 1991), p. 222.

[199]See the discussion in *Novaia Yezhednevnaia Gazeta*, Nos. 34-36, 1995.

[200]Sergei Chugayev, "Duma fulfilled its historic role of transitional parliament," *Izvestia*, July 22, 1995, pp. 1, 2.

[201]Dmitry Yuriev, "The political landscape of Russia before the battle," *Segodnia*, Oct. 21, 1995, p. 3.

[202]Kronid Liubarski, "Life without Soviets," *Novoe Russkoe Slovo*, Oct. 2, 1994, p. 8.

[203]Gavriil Popov, "What October 1993 Gave Us," *Literaturnaia Gazeta*, Sept. 28, 1994, p. 2. Indeed, the leader of the Russian fascists, Aleksandr Barkashov, the former "hero" of the defense of the White House, has renounced "direct action" and has tried to become a "respectable politician." See Dmitry Pushkar, "Aleksandr Barkashov Revises His Methods," *Moscow News*, June 30-July 6, 1995, p. 2. See also Anatoli Stepovoi, "The Barkashovites are trying to get power legally," *Izvestia*, Oct. 26, 1994, p. 4. Another Russian fascist leader, Dmitry Vasiliev also ran for the Duma in December 1995.

[204]Aleksandr Yakovlev, interview, *Kuranty*, July 15, 1994, p. 6. See also Maxim Sokolov, *Kommersant*, Nov. 1, 1994, p. 5.

[205]This softening of attitudes is particularly pronounced among people in their twenties. See Olga Zdravomyslova, "New generation," *Vek*, No. 10, 1994, p. 12.

[206]Leonid Zhukhovitski, "In search of social explosion," *Delovoi Mir*, Feb. 18, 1993, p. 2.

[207]Yuri Levada, "Comparative study of public attitudes in 1989 and 1994," *Segodnia*, Jan. 24, 1995, p. 10.

[208]Burbulis, interview, *Argumenty i Fakty*, No. 28, July 1995, p. 3.

[209]Paul A. Goble of the Carnegie Endowment for International Peace, quoted by Peter Galuszka *et al*, "Inching back into mother Russia's arms," *Business Week*, Aug. 8, 1994, p. 42. See also Mark Helprin, "For a New Concept of Europe," *Commentary*, January 1996.

[210]George Melloan, "If Russia Wants Another Cold War, Fine," *The Wall Street Journal*, Sept. 18, 1995, p. A19.

[211]Lech Walesa is perhaps the most prominent representative of this view among East Europeans. See Paul Belard, "Walesa to Clinton: Russians Coming," *Washington Times*, July 7, 1994, p. A11.

[212]Burbulis, interview, *Nezavisimaia Gazeta*, Jan. 10, 1992.

[213]Martin Malia, "Tradition, Ideology, and Pragmatism in the Formation of Russian Foreign Policy," in Leon Aron and Kenneth M. Jensen (eds.), *The Emerging Priorities of Russian Foreign Policy* (Washington, DC: U.S. Institute of Peace Press, 1994), p. 47.

[214]I. Semenov, department head of the Ministry of the Economy, "Complexities of economic integration among the CIS countries." *Ekonomist*, No. 7, July 1995, *FBIS-SOV-95-164-S*, Aug. 24, 1995, pp. 18-23.

[215]The total number was derived from the data provided by Chief of the General Staff Mikhail Kolesnikov. See his interviews, *Izvestia*, June 17, 1994, p. 2, Radio Maiak, Nov. 17, 1994, *FBIS-SOV-94-222*, *Nezavisimaia Gazeta*, April 22, 1995, p. 1.

[216]By the end of 1995, according to the Duma, the armed forces were to consist of 1,469,000 troops. See *Segodnia*, March 16, 1995, p. 1.

[217]The number includes 2,500 combat planes, according to Colonel General Petr Deinekin, Commander-in-Chief of the Russian Air Force. *INTERFAX*, Aug 19, 1995.

[218]According to academician Valentin Pashin, "Will Russia remain a great maritime power?" *Segodnia*, Oct. 13, 1994, p. 6. See also *Moscow News*, April 14-20, 1995, p. 14. Some nuclear submarines are used for peaceful purposes, to deliver goods to the northern provinces of Russia. *ITAR-TASS*, Sept. 14, 1995.

[219]See Yeltsin's edict, *ITAR-TASS*, March 25, 1995.

[220]This number is supplied by the Institute of National Strategic Studies, *Strategic Assessment 1995*, p. 21. See the budgets of Russia and the United States for the 1995-96 fiscal year.

[221]See, for example, Ariel Cohen of the Heritage Foundation, who claims that "the fight for the reestablishment of the empire started in early 1992." See "The Empire that Would," *The World and I*, May 1995, p. 30.

[222]Stephen Sestanovich, *The New York Times*, Sept. 27, 1994, p. A15.

[223]Members of the Commonwealth owe Russia $9 billion. See *Financial Izvestia*, Oct. 20, 1995, p. I.

[224]Andrei Zagorsky, "CIS searches for unification without domination," *Moscow News*, Nov. 11-17, 1994, p. 3.

[225]The President of Kazakhstan, Nursultan Nazarbayev, promotes the idea of a Eurasian union with common armed forces and a common currency. See Anna Ostapchuk, "Ideas of Eurasian Union are back," *Nezavisimaia Gazeta*, Jan. 21, 1995, p. 1.

[226]Herbert J. Ellison, "Toward a New Realism," *The World and I*, May 1995, p. 38.

[227]Dmitry Riurikov, Yeltsin's foreign adviser, interview, *Lidove Noviny,* Dec. 15, 1993, *FBIS-SOV-93-242*.

[228]See Nikolai Bondaruk and Gennadi Bocharov, "Nobody can stop the new Russians," *Izvestia*, April 22, 1994, p. 4. See also Nikolai Makarov, vice-president of the Union of Russian Entrepreneurs, interview, *Delovoi Mir*, April 27, 1994.

[229]Karl Schlegel, a German East European expert, believes that due to Russia's vast and resilient national character, it has an extraordinary capacity to withstand social, economic, and political turbulences. See his interview in *Argumenty i Fakty*, No. 2, 1996, p. 2.

[230]Paul A. Goble is totally off the mark on this point. See "The Illusion of reform," *The World and I*, May 1995, pp. 24-29.

[231]Helene Carrere d'Encausse very poignantly called her book *The Confiscated Power*, op. cit.

[232]Andranik Migranian, member of the presidential council, in *Nezavisimaia Gazeta*, Dec. 10, 1993, p. 3.

[233]*Russia, the Republics and the Baltics* (New York: Fodor's Travel Publishing, 1991), p. 36.

[234]One American expert noted: "Few countries have produced more gifted and aggressive computer and electronic experts and engineers than Russia." See Michael Specter, "The latest films for just $2: Russia's video piracy booms," *The New York Times*, April 11, 1995, p. 7.

[235]Sir Peter Ustinov, interview, *Izvestia*, Sept. 8, 1995, p. 6.

[236]Anatoli Sobchak, interview, *Argumenty i Fakty*, No. 43, 1995, p. 3.

[237]Andrei Kozyrev, interview, *Izvestia*, Oct. 20, 1991.

[238]Vladimir Shumeiko, interview, *VEK*, Nov. 6-13, 1992, p. 3. A similar conviction was expressed by Ivan Rybkin. See *Obshchaia Gazeta*, Oct. 14, 1994, p. 5.

[239]Aleksandr Yakovlev, interview, *Nezavisimaia Gazeta*, Aug. 10, 1994, p. 5.

[240]Aleksei Yablokov, *Nezavisimaia Gazeta*, March 24, 1995, p. 3.

[241]The quotation is from Wolfgang Kartee, former head of the cartel department of the German government. He lived in Russia from 1992 to 1994. See *Delovoi Mir*, June 23, 1994, p. 1.

[242]Yeltsin, interview, *Izvestia*, July 21, 1994, p. 1.

Index

G

Gaidar, Yegor 32, 39, 73, 88, 91, 96, 97, 103, 107, 109, 111, 121, 122, 134, 135, 141, 145, 182, 217
glasnost 7, 28, 40, 43, 57-59, 61, 69, 76, 83, 110
Golovkov, Alexei 87, 88, 102, 103
Gorbachev, Mikhail 48
Gossnab 30, 82

I

Interregional Group of Deputies 83

K

Kalugin, Oleg 82
KGB 3, 22, 43, 50, 67, 76, 78, 80-82, 90, 110, 187-189, 193, 220
Khazbulatov, Ruslan 87, 91, 106, 190
Khrushchev, Nikita 36
kolkhozes 28
Komsomol 26, 53, 54
Kozyrev, Andrei 44, 184
Kriuchkov, Vladimir 82, 154
Kruglov, Anatoli 187

L

law on the press 78
Lebed, Aleksandr 3
Lenin 22, 28, 35, 54, 58, 93, 193, 202
Lobov, Oleg 104
lumpenproletariat 170

M

Malei, Mikhail 87, 91
Malia, Martin 143
Marx, Karl 26
military-industrial complex 55, 91, 210
miro-oshchushchenie 31
miro-vozzrenie 31, 38
Moral Code of the Builder of Communism 35

About the Author

Dmitry Mikheyev, a Senior Fellow of Hudson Institute, is a writer, political analyst, business consultant, and public speaker.

Born and raised in Russia, he completed his Ph.D. dissertation in laser research at Moscow University in 1970. Shortly thereafter, he was arrested, tried, and convicted for political dissent and attempted defection. While imprisoned in a KGB labor camp, he became an electrical mechanic. After his release in 1976, he worked as a technology engineer at a factory of nonstandard electrical equipment in Kiev. In 1979, he was forced to emigrate to the United States, and in 1985 he became a U.S. citizen. He worked for the U.S. government and various think tanks, and in 1988 he joined the Hudson Institute.

Mr. Mikheyev is the author of three books about the Soviet Union and Russia. *The Soviet Perspective on the Strategic Defense Initiative* (published in 1987), *The Rise and Fall of Gorbachev* (published in 1992), and *Russia Transformed* (published March 1996).

He played an instrumental role in the creation of the Indiana-Soviet Trade Consortium in 1991, and was one of the principal organizers of an international conference, Agrobusiness-93, in Moscow.

About Hudson Institute

Hudson Institute is a private, not-for-profit research organization found-ed in 1961 by the late Herman Kahn. Hudson analyzes and makes recom-mendations about public policy for business and government executives, as well as for the public at large. The institute does not advocate an express ideology or political position. However, more than thirty years of work on the most important issues of the day has forged a viewpoint that embodies skepticism about the conventional wisdom, optimism about solving prob-lems, a commitment to free institutions and individual responsibility, an appreciation of the crucial role of technology in achieving progress, and an abiding respect for the importance of values, culture, and religion in human affairs.

Since 1984, Hudson has been headquartered in Indianapolis, Indiana. It also maintains offices in Washington, D.C.; Madison, Wisconsin; and Brussels, Belgium.